PEACE

Veteran scholar and peace activist David Cortright offers a definitive history of the human striving for peace and an analysis of its religious and intellectual roots. This authoritative, balanced, and highly readable volume traces the rise of peace advocacy and internationalism from their origins in earlier centuries through the mass movements of recent decades: the pacifist campaigns of the 1930s, the Vietnam antiwar movement, and the waves of disarmament activism that peaked in the 1980s. Also explored are the underlying principles of peace – nonviolence, democracy, social justice, and human rights – all placed within a framework of "realistic pacifism." *Peace* brings the story up to date by examining opposition to the Iraq War and responses to the so-called "war on terror." This is history with a modern twist, set in the context of current debates about "the responsibility to protect," nuclear proliferation, Darfur, and conflict transformation.

DAVID CORTRIGHT is President of the Fourth Freedom Forum and Research Fellow at the Joan B. Kroc Institute for International Peace Studies, University of Notre Dame. He has served as consultant or adviser to various governments and agencies of the United Nations. A respected authority on economic sanctions, nuclear disarmament, counterterrorism, UN policy in Iraq, and nonviolent social change, he has authored or co-edited fifteen books, including *Uniting Against Terror: Cooperative Nonmilitary Solutions to the Global Terrorist Threat* (2007), *Gandhi and Beyond: Nonviolence for an Age of Terrorism* (2006), and *The Sanctions Decade: Assessing UN Strategies in the 1990s* (2000). The recipient of several awards, Cortright most recently was selected to receive the 2004 Gandhi Peace Award by Promoting Enduring Peace.

PEACE

A History of Movements and Ideas

DAVID CORTRIGHT

CAMBRIDGE
UNIVERSITY PRESS

CAMBRIDGE
UNIVERSITY PRESS

University Printing House, Cambridge CB2 8BS, United Kingdom

Cambridge University Press is part of the University of Cambridge.

It furthers the University s mission by disseminating knowledge in the pursuit of
education learning and research at the highest international levels of excellence

www.cambridge.org
Information on this title: www.cambridge.org/9780521670005

© David Cortright 2008

First published 2008
8 th printing 2014

A catalogue record for this publication is available from the British Library

ISBN 978-0-521-85402-3 hardback
ISBN 978-0-521-67000-5 paperback

Contents

Acknowledgments   *page* ix
List of abbreviations   xi

1 What is peace?   1
   Idealism and realism   2
   New wars   4
   Defining terms   6
   What's in a word?   8
   "Pacifist" Japan?   11
   Latin American and African traditions   12
   Pacifism and "just war"   14
   An outline of peace history   16
   An overview of peacemaking ideas   18

PART I MOVEMENTS   23

2 The first peace societies   25
   Stirrings   26
   Social origins and political agendas   29
   Elihu Burritt: the learned blacksmith   32
   The first peace congresses   34
   The right of self-determination   35
   Universalizing peace   38
   The Hague Peace Conference   40
   Not enough   43

3 Toward internationalism   45
   Concepts and trends   46
   The arbitration revolution   49
   A League of Nations   52
   Wilson's vision   54
   The challenge of supporting the League   58
   Outlawing war   62

4   Facing fascism   67
    Peace movement reborn   69
    Pledging war resistance   71
    Revolutionary antimilitarism   75
    The Peace Ballot   76
    Against appeasement   79
    Imperial failure   81
    The neutrality debate   84
    The emergency peace campaign   85
    Losing Spain   87
    The end of "pacifism"   88

5   Debating disarmament   93
    Early reluctance   95
    Disarmament to the fore   96
    Challenging the "merchants of death"   98
    The naval disarmament treaties   100
    World disarmament conference   103
    The collapse of disarmament   105
    Disarmament at fault?   106

6   Confronting the cold war   109
    Creating the United Nations   111
    The rise of world federalism   115
    Cold war collapse   117
    Militarization and resistance in Japan   120
    The leviathan   122
    Speaking truth to power   123

7   Banning the bomb   126
    The shock of discovery   126
    Scientists organize   128
    The Baruch plan   131
    For nuclear sanity   133
    The beginning of arms control   136
    Nuclear pacifism in Japan   138
    The rise of the nuclear freeze   139
    God against the bomb   142
    A prairie fire   145
    Ferment in Europe   146
    Who won?   149
    Lessons from the end of the cold war   151

8   Refusing war   155
    Vietnam: a triangular movement   157
    Challenging presidents, constraining escalation   159

Social disruption and political costs 162
Resistance in the military 164
The rise of conscientious objection 167
The movement against war in Iraq 170
Winning while losing 174
Countering the "war on terror" 176

PART II THEMES 181

9 Religion 183
Eastern traditions 185
Study war no more 188
Salaam and *jihad* 190
Christianity 193
Anabaptists and Quakers 195
Tolstoy's anarchist pacifism 197
Social Christianity 199
Catholic peacemaking 200
Niebuhr's challenge 203
Beyond perfectionism 206
The nonviolent alternative 208

10 A force more powerful 211
Religious roots 213
Action for change 216
Coercion and nonviolence 218
The power of love 220
Spirit and method 222
Two hands 224
A tool against tyranny 227
Courage and strength 229

11 Democracy 233
Early voices 234
Democracy against militarism 236
Cobden: peace through free trade 237
Kant: the philosopher of peace 240
Human nature 243
For democratic control 246
The Kantian triad 249
The insights of feminism 255
Empowering women 257

12 Social justice 260
Socialism and pacifism: early differences 262

Convergence   264
The Leninist critique   266
Scientific pacifism   269
Peace through economic justice   270
The development–peace nexus   273
Development for whom?   275

13 Responsibility to protect   279
    Bridging the cold war divide   280
    War for democracy?   283
    Opposing war, advancing freedom   286
    Human rights and security   287
    Debating Kosovo   289
    The responsibility to protect   292
    Peace operations   296
    The challenge in Darfur   299

14 A moral equivalent   302
    The belligerence of the masses   304
    Peace and its discontents: the Einstein–Freud dialogue   306
    Nonmilitary service   307
    Nonviolent warriors   310
    Transforming conflict   313
    Human security service   315
    Patriotic pacifism   317

15 Realizing disarmament   321
    From nonproliferation to disarmament   323
    The Canberra Commission   325
    Sparking the debate   328
    "Weapons of terror"   329
    What is zero?   331

16 Realistic pacifism   334
    Theory   335
    Practice   336
    Action   337

Bibliography   340
Index   355

Acknowledgments

Peace requires the collective effort of many people, and the same is true of a book about peace. In researching and writing this volume I benefited immensely from the assistance and advice of many colleagues and friends. I am grateful to everyone who supported and encouraged me along the way, although I alone take responsibility for any errors of judgment or fact here.

I am most indebted to Linda Gerber-Stellingwerf, Director of Programs at the Fourth Freedom Forum, who was senior researcher and editor throughout this project. Gerber-Stellingwerf researched literally hundreds of records and citations. She provided constant support by checking facts, preparing endnotes, compiling bibliographies, editing sections of the manuscript, maintaining liaison with researchers and editors, and managing the final production and preparation of the manuscript. This book would not have been possible without her skilled and enthusiastic assistance.

Many scholars commented upon portions of the manuscript. I received especially useful guidance from J. R. Burkholder of Goshen College, Lawrence Wittner of the State University of New York at Albany, Louis Kriesberg of Syracuse University, Ted Koontz of Associated Mennonite Biblical Seminaries, Sandi Cooper of the State University of New York at Staten Island, and Duane Shank of Sojourners. I also received research support from David Schrock-Shenk, Rachel Goosen, Shin Chiba, Seon Han Kim, Roger Chickering, Steve Sharra, and Dieter Brunn.

I benefited greatly from the critical comments and suggestions of colleagues at the Joan B. Kroc Institute for International Peace Studies at the University of Notre Dame, including George A. Lopez, Fred Dallmayr, John Paul Lederach, Patrick Mason, Gerald Powers, Rashid Omar, and Lt. Col. Kelly Jordan, then professor of military science at Notre Dame. Encouragement also came from Robert Johansen, Jackie Smith, Larissa Fast, and Hal Culbertson. Librarian Vonda Polega provided bibliographic assistance.

Especially valuable was the support of Scott Appleby, director of the Kroc Institute, who offered constant encouragement and critical commentary

on the manuscript as it emerged. I was aided immensely by Appleby –
intellectually through his important contributions to peace studies and
religious history, institutionally through the support of the Kroc Institute,
and personally through his enthusiasm for this project.

Many students assisted in this effort, providing research support, challenging me with questions, and critically reading the manuscript. I am especially grateful to Peter Quaranto, 2006 graduate of the University of Notre
Dame, who wrote several exceptionally useful research memos on a range
of topics and who read and critically commented on the entire manuscript.
Other Notre Dame students who provided research assistance were Julia
Fitzpatrick, Damon Lynch, Christine Braun, Ken Yamane, and Cora
Fernandez. My understanding of the peace traditions within Islam was
aided by Aurangzeb Haneef, a student in my class at Juame I University
in Castellon, Spain.

I gratefully acknowledge the administrative support of the staffs of the
Fourth Freedom Forum and the Kroc Institute, especially Ann Pedler,
Jennifer Glick, and Judy Gerhardstein. Natasha Sawatsky-Kingsley also
provided administrative help.

I am thankful to the editors and production staff at Cambridge
University Press who supported me in this effort and guided the book to
production, including Kate Brett, Gillian Dadd, and Elizabeth Davey.

This book, like all my research and writing over the past fifteen years, is
made possible by the generous support of the Fourth Freedom Forum and
its founder, Howard S. Brembeck. I hope that this work helps to elucidate a
path toward the more secure world that is Brembeck's vision.

My greatest debt, in this book as in all of life, is to my wife Karen Jacob.
Nurse, artist, peace activist, constant sounding board for new ideas – she
sustained and encouraged me throughout the long hours of writing and
research and inspired me to continue pursuing this inquiry into our shared
goal of a more peaceful future.

Abbreviations

AFSC	American Friends Service Committee
AMIS	Africa Mission in Sudan
APD	*Association de la paix par le droit*
APS	American Peace Society
AU	African Union
AUAM	American Union Against Militarism
CAIP	Catholic Association for International Peace
CCC	Civilian Conservation Corps
CFE	Conventional Forces in Europe
CGT	*Confédération générale du travail*
CIA	Central Intelligence Agency
CND	Campaign for Nuclear Disarmament
CNVA	Committee for Nonviolent Action
CPS	Civilian Public Service
CPT	Christian Peacemaker Teams
CTBT	Comprehensive Test Ban Treaty
CWC	Chemical Weapons Convention
DFG	*Deutsche Friedensgesellschaft*
ECCO	European Congress of Conscripts Organizations
ECOWAS	Economic Community of West African States
END	European Nuclear Disarmament
FAS	Federation of American Scientists
FOR	Fellowship of Reconciliation
GRIT	graduated reciprocation in tension-reduction
INF	intermediate-range nuclear forces
IPC	International Peace Campaign
ISM	International Solidarity Movement
KLA	Kosovo Liberation Army
LEP	League to Enforce Peace
LICP	*Ligue internationale des combatants de la paix*

LNU	League of Nations Union
LUB	League of Universal Brotherhood
NIEO	New International Economic Order
NPT	Nuclear Non-Proliferation Treaty
PBI	Peace Brigades International
PPU	Peace Pledge Union
R2P	Responsibility to Protect
RUP	*Rassemblement universel de la paix pour le droit*
SADC	South African Development Community
SALT	Strategic Arms Limitation Treaty
SANE	National Committee for a Sane Nuclear Policy
SDF	Self-Defense Forces
SDI	Strategic Defense Initiative
SDS	Students for a Democratic Society
SERPAJ	*Servicio Paz y Justicia en América Latina*
SORT	Strategic Offensive Reductions Treaty
START	Strategic Arms Reduction Treaties
SWP	Socialist Workers Party
UDC	Union of Democratic Control
UNCTAD	United Nations Conference on Trade and Development
UNDP	United Nations Development Programme
VVAW	Vietnam Veterans against the War
WCC	World Council of Churches
WILPF	Women's International League for Peace and Freedom
WPP	Woman's Peace Party
WRL	War Resisters League

What is peace?

Jesus said that peacemakers are to be blessed as children of God, but in the real world they are often dismissed as utopian dreamers or worse, quaking defeatists who live in denial of reality. Jane Addams was one of the most admired persons in the United States in the years before World War I, but when she opposed US entry into the war she was ridiculed and reviled.[1] Those who advocated peace during the 1930s were accused of helping Hitler and aiding appeasement. Disarmament activists during the cold war were sometimes considered dupes of the Soviet Union. Throughout history the cause of peace has been on trial, standing like a forlorn defendant before the court of established opinion, misunderstood and maligned on all sides. Peace is "naked, poor, and mangled," wrote Shakespeare.[2] To be called a pacifist is almost an insult, to be labeled cowardly or selfish, unwilling to fight for what is right. It is easy to arouse people to war, said Hermann Goering at the Nuremberg trials. "All you have to do is tell them they are being attacked and denounce the pacifists for lack of patriotism . . ."[3]

This book is a response to the charges against pacifism. It is an attempt to set the record straight by exploring the history of movements and ideas for peace – an opportunity for the cause of peace to have its day in court. This is not an apologia for or paean to pacifism, however – far from it. I am often critical of peace advocacy, especially absolute pacifism, and I try to present both the strengths and weaknesses of the various movements and theories for peace that have emerged over the centuries. I write as one who has been engaged with these issues for decades. I strive for rigorous scholarly standards and objective analysis, but I am hardly neutral in this debate. Questions of war and peace intruded into my life when I was drafted for

---

[1] Victoria Bissell Brown, "Addams, Jane," February 2000. Available online at American National Biography Online, www.anb.org/articles/15/15-00004.html (accessed 22 November 2006).
[2] *The Life of King Henry V*, act V, scene ii, line 34.
[3] G. M. Gilbert, *Nuremberg Diary* (New York: Farrar, Straus, and Co., 1947), 279.

the Vietnam War, and they have remained with me ever since. I spoke out against that war as an active duty soldier, was the director of the National Committee for a Sane Nuclear Policy (SANE) during the disarmament campaigns of the 1980s, and helped to found the Win Without War coalition to oppose the US invasion and occupation of Iraq. I have written about nuclear disarmament, economic sanctions, and nonviolent social change and have taught peace studies courses. I know only too well the many limitations of movements for peace and the inadequacy of theories on the causes and prevention of war. It is precisely because of my engagement with these issues that I feel qualified to offer this witness for the defense, to present the case of peace, and to examine its practices and principles.

IDEALISM AND REALISM

The book of Isaiah called believers to study war no more but offered little instruction about learning peace. The study of peace has been neglected over the ages and has emerged as a proper discipline only in recent decades.[4] The first academic programs and scholarly institutes dedicated to peace did not appear until after World War II, and refereed journals such as the *Journal of Conflict Resolution* and the *Journal of Peace Research* did not begin publication until 1957 and 1964 respectively. Pioneers in the field included Kenneth and Elise Boulding, who helped create the Center for Research on Conflict Resolution at the University of Michigan in the 1950s; Johan Galtung, who founded the International Peace Research Institute in Norway in 1959; and Adam Curle, the first chair of a peace studies program in Britain, at the University of Bradford in 1973. Major studies and books about peace appeared in earlier decades, of course, but the systematic application of rigorous scholarship and empirical analysis to the problems of peacemaking did not begin until quite recently.

This partly explains the inadequacies of many of the theories of peace. For much of history the cause of peace has predominantly been a religious concern. Moral reformers embraced the teachings of love and compassion in religious doctrine, but they often overlooked the challenges of political realism. Classical liberals extolled the virtues of democracy and free trade, but they underestimated the virulence of nationalism and the power of imperialism. Immanuel Kant probably came closest to crafting a comprehensive philosophy of peace, but his theory did not address questions of

---

[4] See George A. Lopez, special editor, "Peace Studies: Past and Future," *The Annals of the American Academy of Political and Social Science* 504 (July 1989).

social equality. Socialists and feminists brought these issues to the fore and broadened the peace agenda to include problems of economic injustice and patriarchy. In recent decades social scientists and political theorists have made progress in verifying and explaining the components of the so-called Kantian triad – mutual democracy, economic interdependence, and international cooperation – as predicates of peace. Links have been discovered between gender equality and a lessening of violence. Unresolved political grievances and a lack of economic development have been identified as factors that contribute to armed conflict. Many questions remain unanswered, but progress has been made in understanding the causes of and cures for war.

Peace societies emerged in the nineteenth century, but it was only in the twentieth century that peace movements as we presently understand them came into existence. Large-scale mobilizations against war took place in the years before and after World War I, during the 1930s, and especially in response to the Vietnam and Iraq wars. These movements challenged government policy, particularly that of the United States, and were generally anti-imperialist in outlook. Mobilizations for disarmament occurred during the interwar years and re-emerged in the cold war as a response to the threat of nuclear war. Disarmament activism reached a peak with the massive nuclear freeze and disarmament campaigns of the 1980s. Some of those organizing antiwar and disarmament campaigns were absolute pacifists, rejecting the use of force for any purpose, but most were more pragmatic and conditional in their rejection of war. They opposed dangerous weapons policies and unjust wars, but not all uses of force. Still the purist position often predominated, conveying an impression of implicit pacifism that limited the peace movement's public appeal.

Many opponents of war have emphasized the need for constructive alternatives. During the 1934–5 Peace Ballot in Britain the League of Nations Union (LNU) organized an informal vote on British security policy in which 11.6 million citizens participated. Among the options presented and endorsed was the use of multilateral sanctions, economic and even military, to counter aggression by one nation against another. The ballot results pressured the British government to propose League of Nations sanctions against Italy. During the nuclear freeze campaign of the 1980s US activists urged a bilateral halt to the testing, production, and deployment of nuclear weapons. European disarmament campaigners urged an end to both Soviet and US intermediate-range nuclear forces (INF) in Europe, which NATO officials effectively adopted as the "double zero" proposal, with zero INF weapons in Europe on both sides. During the Iraq antiwar debate many activists called for continued weapons inspections and targeted sanctions as alternatives to war and effective means of containing Saddam Hussein. In the debate over the so-called "war on terror" peace scholars and activists have insisted that terrorism as a tactic cannot be defeated by war. They have advocated alternative strategies for countering terrorism based on multilateral action, cooperative law enforcement, and the amelioration of political grievances.

The strategies and proposals of peace scholars and activists are often fully compatible with the requirements of sound security policy. Throughout the cold war disarmament advocates insisted that a nuclear war could never be won and must never be fought; this became Ronald Reagan's mantra during the 1980s. Those who opposed the Vietnam and Iraq wars did so not only on humanitarian grounds but on the basis of solid political reasoning. Hans Morgenthau spoke out against the Vietnam War because it was based on an erroneous theory of monolithic communism, was justified with false information, and ignored the history of southeast Asia.[5] John Mearsheimer and Stephen Walt opposed the war in Iraq for similar reasons: it misjudged the terrorist threat, was based on deceptive claims about Iraqi capabilities, and risked eroding US power and prestige in the world.[6] Peace advocates warned that the invasion and occupation of Iraq would play into the hands of Osama bin Laden and lead to an increase in terrorist violence. Warmakers are often wrong – disastrously so in the cases of Vietnam and Iraq. Peace advocates are sometimes right, especially when their ideas are not only morally sound but politically realistic.

NEW WARS

The nature of war has changed dramatically in recent decades. The old paradigm of industrial interstate war "no longer exists," declared General Rupert Smith in 2006.[7] Raimo Väyrynen, John Mueller, and other political scientists have written of the "waning of major war."[8] No instances of full-scale war have occurred between major industrialized states since the end of World War II. This is in part because of the extreme lethality of all forms of

[5] Hans J. Morgenthau, "We are Deluding Ourselves in Vietnam," *The New York Times Magazine*, 18 April 1965, SM25.

[6] John J. Mearsheimer and Stephen M. Walt, "An Unnecessary War," *Foreign Policy* no. 134 (January–February 2003): 50.

[7] Rupert Smith, *The Utility of Force: The Art of War in the Modern World* (London: Penguin Books, 2006), 1–2.

[8] Raimo Väyrynen, ed., *The Waning of Major War: Theories and Debates* (London: Routledge, 2006).

modern weaponry, nuclear and non-nuclear. It is also the result of the development of an integrated community of prosperous, secure, and interdependent nations in the heart of Europe where previous world wars originated. While interstate war has largely disappeared, intrastate conflicts have increased markedly. The new paradigm, wrote Smith, is "war amongst the people."[9] Of the thirty-one wars in the world in 2005 (as measured by the Uppsala Conflict Data Program), all were armed conflicts fought within nations between communities divided by ethnicity, language, religion, and/ or geography.[10] Nearly all military deployments, UN peacekeeping operations, and peace-building missions in recent decades have taken place in settings of intrastate conflict.

This change in the nature of war has not meant an end to the scourge of deadly violence. On the contrary the number of people dying in war in recent years has been extremely high. Since the 1990s millions have died in the Congo, Sudan, and other African countries, and hundreds of thousands in former Yugoslavia and Iraq. In today's "new wars," to use peace scholar Mary Kaldor's phrase, methods of terror, ethnic cleansing, and genocide are deliberate strategies to target civilians. The result is that more than 80 percent of the casualties are civilian, and the number of refugees and displaced persons has increased sharply. "Violations of humanitarian and human rights law are not a side effect" of armed violence, wrote Kaldor, "but the central methodology of new wars."[11] The strategy of violence in the new paradigm utilizes terror and destabilization to displace populations and gain control of territory and sources of income.[12]

In response to the rise of intrastate war international humanitarian action and peace-building efforts have increased. Those who seek to prevent war have recognized the need to act in the midst of violent conflict to ameliorate its consequences and prevent its recurrence. The responsibility to protect civilians has emerged as a new principle of global action, part of what Kaldor has termed "cosmopolitan politics." The urgency of stemming genocide, oppression, and terrorism has sparked a new wave of action and inquiry, and has led to an intensified search for ways to resolve and prevent deadly conflict.

---

[9] Smith, *The Utility of Force*, 3.

[10] Lotta Harbom, Stina Högbladh, and Peter Wallensteen, "Armed Conflict and Peace Agreements," *Journal of Peace Research* 43, no. 5 (2006): 617–31.

[11] Mary Kaldor, "Beyond Militarism, Arms Races and Arms Control" (essay prepared for the Nobel Peace Prize Centennial Symposium, 6–8 December 2001). Available online at the *Social Science Research Council*, www.ssrc.org/sept11/essays/kaldor.htm (accessed 22 November 2006).

[12] Mary Kaldor, *New and Old Wars: Organized Violence in a Global Era* (Stanford, CA: Stanford University Press, 2001), 115.

At the international level peacemaking programs have expanded and become institutionalized at the United Nations and in other multilateral and regional organizations. In the 1992 report *An Agenda for Peace* UN Secretary-General Boutros Boutros-Ghali identified four phases of international action to prevent and control armed violence: preventive diplomacy, which includes early warning, mediation, and confidence-building measures; peacemaking efforts such as arbitration and the negotiation of peace accords; peacekeeping, the deployment of impartial forces to monitor and implement peace settlements; and peace-building, which the UN defines as post-conflict efforts to rebuild war-torn societies and prevent the recurrence of violence.[13] These contemporary strategies correspond directly to peace principles and traditions in earlier periods of history.

DEFINING TERMS

At the outset we face definitional challenges and the need to differentiate among different terms and concepts. What exactly do we mean by peace? The term is highly emotive, historian Michael Howard wrote, and is often abused as a tool of political propaganda.[14] When peace is defined narrowly it can imply passivity and the acceptance of injustice.[15] During the cold war the word had subversive implications and was often associated with communism. Moscow sponsored ersatz "peace councils," which gave the word a negative connotation. Hesitancy about the meaning of peace existed long before the cold war. In the years before World War I Andrew Carnegie lavishly funded programs to prevent war and advance international cooperation, but he was uncomfortable with the word peace and wanted to leave it out of the title of the international endowment he left as his legacy.[16]

Peace is more than the absence of war. It is also "the maintenance of an orderly and just society," wrote Howard – orderly in being protected against the violence or extortion of aggressors, and just in being defended against exploitation and abuse by the more powerful.[17] Many writers distinguish between negative peace, which is simply the absence of war, and positive

---

[13] Boutros Boutros-Ghali, *An Agenda for Peace: Preventive Diplomacy, Peacemaking, and Peace-keeping*, Report of the Secretary-General Pursuant to the Statement Adopted by the Summit Meeting of the Security Council on 31 January 1992, A/47/277 – S/24111 (New York: United Nations, 1992).

[14] Michael Howard, "Problems of a Disarmed World," in *Studies in War and Peace* (New York: Viking Press, 1971), 225.

[15] David P. Barash, *Introduction to Peace Studies* (Belmont, CA: Wadsworth Publishing, 1991), 6.

[16] Charles Chatfield, *The American Peace Movement: Ideals and Activism* (New York: Twayne Publishers, 1992), 23.

[17] Howard, "Problems of a Disarmed World," 226.

peace, which is the presence of justice. "Peace can be slavery or it can be freedom; subjugation or liberation," wrote Norman Cousins. Genuine peace means progress toward a freer and more just world.[18] Johan Galtung developed the concept of "structural violence" to describe situations of negative peace that have violent and unjust consequences.[19] Violence in Galtung's expansive definition is any condition that prevents a human being from achieving her or his full potential. Leonardo Boff, the Brazilian priest and theologian, employed the term "originating violence," which he defined as an oppressive social condition that preserves the interests of the elite over the needs of dispossessed and marginalized populations.[20] Originating or structural violence can include impoverishment, deprivation, humiliation, political repression, a lack of human rights, and the denial of self-determination. Positive peace means transcending the conditions that limit human potential and assuring opportunities for self-realization.

Gandhi spoke of nonviolence rather than peace and emphasized the necessity of overcoming injustice. Gandhi's meaning was deftly summarized by Jonathan Schell: "Violence is a method by which the ruthless few can subdue the passive many. Nonviolence is a means by which the active many can overcome the ruthless few." Yet the word nonviolence is "highly imperfect," wrote Schell. It is a word of "negative construction," as if the most important thing that can be said about nonviolence is that it is *not* something else. It is a negation of the negative force of violence, a double negative which in mathematics would yield a positive result. Yet English has no positive word for it. Schell attempted to resolve this dilemma by defining nonviolence as "cooperative power" – collective action based on mutual consent, in contrast to coercive power, which compels action through the threat or use of force.[21]

Peace does not mean the absence of conflict, argued peace researcher and former Australian ambassador John W. Burton. Conflict is intrinsic in human relationships, although it does not have to be and usually is not violent. The challenge for peace practitioners is to find ways in which communities can resolve differences without physical violence. In this

---

[18] Norman Cousins, *Modern Man is Obsolete* (New York: Viking Press, 1946), 45–6.

[19] Johan Galtung, "Violence, Peace, and Peace Research," *Journal of Peace Research* 6, no. 3 (1969): 167–97.

[20] Leonardo Boff, "Active Nonviolence: The Political and Moral Power of the Poor," in *Relentless Persistence: Nonviolent Action in Latin America*, ed. Philip McManus and Gerald Schlabach (Philadelphia, PA: New Society Publishers, 1991), vii.

[21] Jonathan Schell, *The Unconquerable World: Power, Nonviolence, and the Will of the People* (New York: Metropolitan Books, 2003), 144, 227, 351.

context peace is understood as a dynamic process not an absolute end point. The goal of peacemakers is to develop more effective ways of resolving disputes without violent conflict, to identify and transform the conditions that cause war.

The term "pacifism" especially needs deconstruction. It entered the lexicon at the beginning of the twentieth century as a general term to describe the stance of those opposed to war. After World War I the term became synonymous with an earlier, more specific tradition of religiously based refusal to condone or participate in war in any form, also known as nonresistance. This purist position was distinct from the more widely accepted traditions of pragmatic or conditional pacifism, which opposed war in principle but accepted the possibility of using force for self-defense or the protection of the vulnerable. It also contrasted with internationalism, which along with political realism traced the causes of war to the condition of anarchy among nations, and which advocated transnational cooperation and the strengthening of international law and institutions as the means of preventing armed conflict. Absolute pacifism also differed from "just war" principles, developed by Augustine in the fifth century and accepted by official Christianity, which set limits on war but gave it justification.

Pacifism existed as a movement and set of ideas long before the actual word was coined in 1901. The term emerged during the tenth Universal Peace Congress in Glasgow, at a time when organizations seeking to prevent war were spreading throughout Europe and the United States. Proposals for arbitration and the development of international law were gaining support among political leaders on both sides of the Atlantic. Bertha von Suttner's book *Lay Down Your Weapons* was an international bestseller, published in thirty-seven editions and translated into more than a dozen languages. The ideology of the peace movement was maturing. The narrow religious base of the early Anglo-American peace societies was giving way to more secular, humanitarian perspectives, especially in continental Europe.

Prior to the Glasgow congress members of the various peace societies and international organizations generally referred to themselves as "peace workers," "peace advocates," or, most commonly, "friends of peace." These were awkward terms that satisfied no one. Activists sought to develop a better term that would more effectively convey the growing maturity and sophistication of the movement. It was Émile Arnaud of France, president of the *Ligue internationale de la paix et de la liberté*, who first introduced the word "pacifism." He and others used it in a generic sense to describe the broad international peace movement. It was meant to suggest a coherent body of thought and developed set of political beliefs and policies for preventing war and assuring peace. The term elevated the philosophy of peace into an official "ism." It had international appeal and could be integrated easily into different languages. The term was officially adopted at the Glasgow congress. Thereafter those who participated in the various peace organizations and societies around the world began to refer to themselves as "pacifists." It was a term of distinction and had a broad social connotation. It was meant to encompass all of those who worked to preserve peace and prevent war.

Pacifism also meant social action. It was not merely a philosophy but a political program and a commitment to social change. It was distinct from the quietist tradition of some religious sects, whose members tended to withdraw from public life and cede to the state the realm of practical politics. This was not what the early twentieth-century pacifists had in mind. Arnaud sought to distinguish pacifists from those who merely hope or pray for peace. "We are not passive types . . . we are pacifists."[22] Pacifism included a personal commitment to take action, to work for peace. It implied, historian Roger Chickering wrote, a "high degree of engagement in activity" to help reduce the level of violence in international relations.[23] The study of peace is thus a history of social action as well as of ideas, an examination of social movements and of intellectual development.

Soon after the term pacifism emerged debates developed over its exact meaning and application. Should it encompass the traditional peace societies, which were often quite conservative and in some cases supported military "preparedness?" Did it apply to internationalism, which tended to focus narrowly on promoting arbitration and international law and institutions? Internationalists could be either conservative or progressive, favoring the status quo (including the system of imperialism) or advocating greater equality of status among nations. Was the term pacifism appropriate for the socialist parties, which opposed imperialist war but were prepared to support the class war? What about the democratic nationalists who supported the use of force for the just cause of national liberation? Could all of these diverse approaches, each in its distinctive way claiming to embody the path to peace, fit within one broad pacifist movement? These differences

---

[22] Sandi E. Cooper, *Patriotic Pacifism: Waging War in Europe, 1815–1914* (New York: Oxford University Press, 1991), 60.
[23] Roger Chickering, *Imperial Germany and a World without War: The Peace Movement and German Society, 1892–1914* (Princeton, NJ: Princeton University Press, 1975), 16–17.

came to a head with the outbreak of war in 1914, when the peace movement collapsed and fractured. Most peace advocates, including internationalists and socialists, abandoned their commitment to transnational solidarity and marched off to war. Only a small remnant of the previously broad international movement stood apart from the nationalist frenzy and remained steadfast in opposing war.

In the years after World War I there was much recrimination and debate about the meaning of pacifism. The purists who had opposed the march to war claimed the term for themselves. They narrowed its definition to the unconditional rejection of war in all its forms. As revulsion at the horrific bloodletting of the war deepened, a growing number of people pledged never again to participate in or support war. These "pacifists" played a major role in the peace movement of the interwar era, which grew to unprecedented scale. Internationalists remained an important force, especially in Britain, where the LNU attracted widespread public support, but the influence of those who rejected war under all circumstances was substantial. The restrictive meaning of pacifism became the accepted standard and was adopted by A. C. F. Beales in his influential 1931 volume, *The History of Peace*.[24] Thereafter it became the standard in both scholarly and popular discourse.

This narrow definition of pacifism left most of the peace community out in the cold. Many of those who considered themselves pacifist were uncomfortable with the absolutist stand. As the menace of fascism mounted pacifism became increasingly marginalized and associated with isolationism. The term sank into disrepute and was largely abandoned, even by those who considered themselves advocates of peace. Many peace supporters, especially the internationalists, urged vigorous action to confront aggression. Some, such as Albert Einstein, tried to redefine pacifism to include rearmament and collective military resistance against Hitler. Others adopted a "peace with justice" perspective, arguing that the prevention of war depended on resolving political and economic grievances. The majority of peace advocates found themselves in a state of confusion and uncertainty. They were part of a broad social movement amorphously defined as for peace, but they lacked a coherent program for preventing the impending war and had no commonly accepted "ism" to describe the prevailing philosophy.

---

[24] A. C. F. Beales, *The History of Peace: A Short Account of the Organised Movements for International Peace* (London: G. Bell, 1931).

Scholars have attempted to remedy this frustrating imprecision by providing definitions for the various philosophies and political tendencies that exist within the peace community. The most elaborate and sophisticated attempt to parse the meaning of pacifism was provided by historian Martin Ceadel in his masterful volume, *Thinking about Peace and War*. Ceadel identified five distinct theories of war and peace, ranging from militarism to pacifism. He differentiated absolute pacifism from "pacificism." The latter term was coined by the historian A. J. P. Taylor to describe those who believe that war is always irrational and inhumane and should be prevented, but who accept that it may be necessary at times.[25] Ceadel defined pacificists as those who believe that war can be prevented and with sufficient commitment to justice can be abolished, or nearly so.[26] This is an apt description of the position of most peace advocates. The distinction that Ceadel and others make between absolute and pragmatic pacifism is vital, although often obfuscated. Few have adopted the "pacificist" label, however, which is awkward, confusing, and difficult to write or pronounce. It will not appear again in this volume. The general concept of pragmatic or conditional pacifism is nonetheless valuable, and will serve as the foundation for the definition employed here.

"PACIFIST" JAPAN?

In Japan absolute pacifism is official national policy, as enshrined in Article 9 of the postwar Constitution:

Aspiring sincerely to an international peace based on justice and order, the Japanese people forever renounce war as a sovereign right of the nation and the threat or use of force as means of settling international disputes.

In order to accomplish the aim of the preceding paragraph, land, sea, and air forces, as well as other war potential, will never be maintained. The right of belligerence of the state will not be recognized.

This extraordinary and unequivocal rejection of war has no precedent in history. Other countries have renounced war in their constitutions but never with such totality. Japan's Constitution was imposed by US occupation authorities, but many Japanese nonetheless supported its rejection of war, and a vigorous peace and disarmament movement developed over the

---

[25] Martin Ceadel, *Pacifism in Britain 1914–1945: The Defining of a Faith* (Oxford: Clarendon Press, 1980), 3.
[26] Martin Ceadel, *Thinking about Peace and War* (Oxford: Oxford University Press, 1987), 4–5.

decades – although the traditions of nationalism also retained their appeal among some conservatives.

Support for peace in Japan is understood as both a personal moral commitment and a social-political position that is linked to human rights, democracy, and economic well-being. The common term for peace advocacy is *heiwa shugi*, which is a combination of the Japanese words for "peace" and "ism." The ambiguity of the term makes it difficult to differentiate between absolute and conditional pacifism, and for many the meanings overlap and often coexist. The term *heiwa shugi* has no equivalent in English, although the original Glasgow definition of pacifism was intended precisely to convey the principled yet pragmatic commitment to peace conveyed by the Japanese term.[27]

Article 9 is absolute in its language, but the political and legal interpretation of the clause has been more pragmatic. In practice pacifism in Japan has meant a "presumption against the employment of force, rather than its absolute rejection," according to scholar Robert Kisala.[28] The common understanding is that force may be used in self-defense or in humanitarian or peacekeeping missions authorized by the United Nations, but that other uses of military force are unacceptable. The government has pursued its foreign policy objectives mostly through economic means, principally through overseas development assistance.[29]

LATIN AMERICAN AND AFRICAN TRADITIONS

In Latin America absolute pacifism is rare, but the use of nonviolent action as a method of social change is widespread. The commitment to nonviolence is often more pragmatic than principled, based on the calculation that violence leads to further oppression, and that *firmeza permanente* ("relentless persistence") can be a powerful means of achieving justice. The use of active nonviolence is rooted in the historical example of Latin America's indigenous communities, which struggled over the centuries to resist assimilation by Spanish conquerors and national governments, often through nonviolent methods of mass noncooperation. In recent decades numerous

[27] Mari Yamamoto, *Grassroots Pacifism in Post-war Japan: The Rebirth of a Nation* (London: RoutledgeCurzon, 2004), 10.
[28] Robert Kisala, *Prophets of Peace: Pacifism and Cultural Identity in Japan's New Religions* (Honolulu: University of Hawai'i Press, 1999), 8.
[29] Peter J. Katzenstein and Nobuo Okawara, *Japan's National Security: Structures, Norms, and Policy Responses in a Changing World* (Ithaca, NY: East Asia Program, Cornell University, 1993), 105–7.

Latin American social movements have utilized nonviolent action to overcome repression, end military dictatorship, and defend human rights. The commitment to nonviolent action gained momentum after the Second Vatican Council of 1962–5 and the Latin American bishops conference in Medellín, Colombia, in 1968, as liberation theology emerged to proclaim a "preferential option for the poor." Some appropriated the new theology to justify armed revolution, but most agreed with Leonardo Boff that liberation theology and active nonviolence were "two facets of a single reality." Both are rooted in the Gospel and seek to transform a society of violence and oppression into one of compassion and justice.[30]

In African traditions peace means order, harmony, and equilibrium, not merely preventing war.[31] Western concepts of absolute pacifism or nonresistance have little meaning in societies that place primary value on maintaining social harmony. Peace is a function of social justice. It depends on preserving the integrity of communities. This concept of shared humanity is embodied in the African phrase *ubuntu*, which literally means "I am because we are." The truth of *ubuntu*, wrote philosopher Augustine Shutte, is that we become ourselves by belonging to community.[32] Peace can only be realized in community with others, through the embrace of the other. Community elders are often called upon to preserve peace by adjudicating and resolving conflicts.

Africa remains deeply scarred by the brutal legacies of colonialism. In recent decades no continent has suffered more from war and pervasive economic deprivation. The presence of conflict and the absence of development are bound together in a downward spiral of violence and misery. In response African leaders have argued that peace is impossible without economic development and political freedom. Tanzanian president Julius Nyerere wrote: "for the sake of peace and justice, these economic inequalities in the world must be reduced and the mass of the people must be able to relieve themselves from the burden of poverty."[33] Bishop Desmond Tutu said in his Nobel Peace Prize speech in 1984: "There can be no real peace and security [in South Africa] until there be first justice enjoyed by all the

[30] Boff, "Active Nonviolence," ix–x.

[31] Godfrey Igwebuike Onah, "The Meaning of Peace in African Traditional Religion and Culture" (lecture, Pontifical Urban University, Rome, n.d.). Available online at Afrika World, www.afrikaworld.net/afrel/goddionah.htm (accessed 5 March 2007).

[32] Augustine Shutte, *Ubuntu: An Ethic for a New South Africa* (Pietermaritzburg, South Africa: Cluster Publications, 2001), 9.

[33] Julius K. Nyerere, *Freedom and Unity: Uhuru na umoja: A Selection from Writings and Speeches, 1952–65* (London: Oxford University Press, 1967), 235.

inhabitants of that beautiful land."[34] In Africa, as in Latin America and Asia, peace is inextricably linked to economic and social justice.

PACIFISM AND "JUST WAR"

Pacifism and the just war tradition are analytically distinct and are often considered opposites. The concept of pragmatic pacifism helps to bridge the gap and provides a more holistic framework for understanding peace advocacy. It reflects the dominant position of those who consider themselves peace supporters. Absolute pacifists have always been a minority, even within peace movements. The majority of those who work for peace seek to avoid war but are willing to accept some limited use of force for self-defense or to uphold justice and protect the innocent. Some uses of military force are more objectionable than others. This is evident from the fact that certain wars, such as those in Vietnam and Iraq, arouse vociferous movements of protest, while other uses of force, such as the multinational operation in Bosnia, are broadly accepted, even by many peace supporters. As the United States prepared to take military action in Afghanistan following the September 2001 terrorist attacks, Scott Simon of National Public Radio wrote "Even Pacifists Must Support This War."[35] Some peace advocates accepted the attack against Al Qaida as justified self-defense, but many cautioned against militarizing the struggle against terrorism. Because just war language is often abused by political leaders to justify military aggression there is concern that misuse of the framework can be a slippery slope toward the legitimation of indiscriminate violence. As Michael Walzer emphasized, just war reasoning is a challenge to political realism.[36] The just war doctrine establishes a rigorous set of moral conditions that must be met before armed conflict can be considered. If thoroughly and honestly applied these criteria would rule out most of the armed conflicts that political leaders claim to be just and would make war a rare occurrence.

Pragmatic pacifism can be understood as a continuum of perspectives, beginning on one end with the rejection of military violence and extending across a range of options that allow for some limited use of force under specific conditions. The presumption is always against the use of force and

---

[34] *The Nobel Peace Prize Lecture: Desmond M. Tutu* (New York: Anson Phelps Stokes Institute for African, Afro-American, and American Indian Affairs, 1986).

[35] Scott Simon, "Even Pacifists Must Support This War," *Wall Street Journal*, 11 October 2001.

[36] Michael Walzer, *Arguing about War* (New Haven, CT: Yale University Press, 2004), ix.

in favor of settling differences without violence, but reality dictates that some uses of force may be necessary at times to assure justice and prevent the greater violence that often results when exploitation and aggression are unconstrained. Even strict pacifists acknowledge that at times soldiers can play a role in preventing the spread of violence. I once asked a class of Mennonite students who described themselves as pacifist if they would support the continued deployment of NATO troops in Bosnia to keep the peace among the previously warring factions. All but one of the twenty students said yes. Pacifists may accept the use of force if it is constrained, narrowly targeted, and conducted by proper authority within the rule of law.[37] Mennonite theologian John Howard Yoder differentiated between war and the use of police power; the latter is subject to legal and moral constraints and is ethically superior to war.[38] Distinctions matter, and a vast difference exists between unilateral, unprovoked military aggression and multilateral peace operations to protect civilian populations. No one who considered herself pacifist would accept the former but a great many would accept the latter.

The just war position also contains a continuum of perspectives, extending from limited police action to all-out war, based on a set of moral criteria that can vary significantly in different settings. Views on whether a particular use of force is justified range from a restrictive interpretation that permits military action only under narrowly constrained circumstances, to more expansive claims that seek to justify large-scale military operations and even the unprovoked invasion of other countries. Analysts often differ on whether a particular use of force, such as the 1991 Gulf War, meets the classic moral criteria of a just war.[39] Most ethicists within the tradition agree, however, that the just war framework is based on a presumption against the use of military force. All share Walzer's insistence on addressing the moral reality of war.[40] The use of military force is not merely an extension of politics. It is a moral act of supreme importance that must be judged according to the strictest ethical standards.

The continuum of pacifism can be combined with that of just war to form a continuous range of options extending from absolute nonviolence at

---

[37] Gerald Schlabach, "Just Policing, Not War," *America* 189, no. 1 (7–14 July 2003): 19–21.

[38] John Howard Yoder, *The Politics of Jesus*, 2nd edn (Grand Rapids, MI: Eerdmans, 1994), 204.

[39] See Jean Bethke Elshtain and David E. DeCosse, eds., *But Was It Just? Reflections on the Morality of the Persian Gulf War* (New York: Doubleday, 1992).

[40] Michael Walzer, *Just and Unjust Wars: A Moral Argument with Historical Illustrations* (New York: Basic Books, 1992), 15.

the one end to the justification of war at the other. All the differing perspectives on war and peace thus can be considered in relation to one another. This is the approach employed by Ceadel in his classification of five major perspectives on peace and war.[41] John Howard Yoder also combined the two traditions in a standard lecture I had the privilege of hearing on several occasions. Yoder argued that a systematic and rigorous application of just war principles – just cause, right authority, last resort, probability of success, proportionality, discrimination – would make war extremely rare. Philosopher John Rawls wrote that justice demands a form of "contingent pacifism." The possibility of just war is conceded in principle, but the far greater likelihood is that war will be unjust, especially when waged by large and powerful states against weaker nations. Given the often predatory aims of state power the demands of justice may require resistance to war.[42]

An honest appraisal of war through the lens of just war criteria would forbid any consideration of nuclear strikes and would rule out virtually all forms of large-scale, unilateral military intervention. It would leave only self-defense and limited, legally constrained uses of multilateral force to protect civilians and restore conditions of justice. The "responsibility to protect" principles that have recently gained international endorsement embody this perspective. Walzer argued that the only morally justified reason for fighting is the defense of rights, most essentially the right of self-defense.[43] Rawls likewise acknowledged the principle of self-defense and the right of people to determine their own affairs without the intervention of foreign powers.[44] Combining the pacifist and just war traditions allows for a broader and richer examination of the peace tradition, one that more accurately reflects the thinking of those who consider themselves part of the peace movement. It takes into account the full range of peacemaking options and traditions that are part of the history of peace. It also conforms with the original definition and meaning of pacifism.

AN OUTLINE OF PEACE HISTORY

Peace societies first emerged in the United States and Britain in the early part of the nineteenth century and later spread across Europe and beyond.

---

[41] Ceadel, *Thinking about Peace and War*.
[42] John Rawls, *A Theory of Justice*, rev. edn (Cambridge, MA: The Belknap Press of Harvard University Press, 1999), 335.
[43] Walzer, *Just and Unjust Wars*, 72.   [44] Rawls, *A Theory of Justice*, 332.

In chapters 2 and 3 I draw from the work of Charles DeBenedetti, Sandi Cooper, Charles Chatfield, Roger Chickering, and others to review the social origins and political agenda of the early peace societies. Peace advocates focused on proposals for the arbitration of interstate disputes and the strengthening of international law. The internationalist agenda was partly realized in Woodrow Wilson's vision of the League of Nations. Although the League was flawed in design and fatally weakened by the lack of US participation, it established a precedent for the gradual strengthening of international institutions and laid the foundations for the United Nations.

Pacifism and internationalism attracted very broad public support during the interwar era. Peace advocates and internationalists were early opponents of fascist aggression in Manchuria and Abyssinia, and many urged the defense of the Spanish republic. They demanded League of Nations action to impose sanctions against Japan and Italy. The LNU organized the Peace Ballot as a way of demonstrating support for mutual disarmament and collective action against aggression. Chapters 4 and 5 help to refute the claim that peace advocates were responsible for appeasement. The decisions to betray Ethiopia and the Spanish republic and appease Hitler were taken by Western government leaders not peace advocates. Interwar pacifists can be faulted for many things – clinging too long to the failed promise of the League of Nations, supporting the illusion of neutrality, believing that diplomacy could stop the Nazi menace – but they were not culpable for war.

In the early years of the cold war, as described in chapter 6, peace advocacy fell to its lowest ebb of the century. Anticommunism and a suffocating atmosphere of political conformity combined with a backlash against pacifism to undermine the legitimacy of progressive internationalism. A significant movement for world federalism emerged in the late 1940s but rapidly declined with the onset of the Korean War. Peace scholars and activists addressed the problem of militarization and the growing tendency toward military interventionism. The development of atomic weapons and their terrifying spread created new dangers and sparked significant waves of disarmament activism, as examined in chapter 7. The first wave of antinuclear action was initiated by the atomic scientists who created the bomb. The second wave came in the late 1950s in response to atmospheric nuclear testing. Led by groups such as the Campaign for Nuclear Disarmament (CND) in Britain and SANE in the United States, the ban the bomb movement exerted significant pressure that led to the 1963 atmospheric test ban treaty. The arms race continued and intensified in the 1980s, prompting a third and even larger wave of disarmament activism. The nuclear freeze campaign in the United States and disarmament movements in Europe paved the way for significant nuclear reductions and the end of the cold war.

The movement against the Vietnam War was one of the largest and most intensive peace campaigns in history. Antiwar efforts influenced the Johnson and Nixon administrations and exerted sustained pressure for US military withdrawal. Antiwar activism developed even among active-duty soldiers and veterans, as I personally experienced. Conscientious objection reached an unprecedented scale and spread not only in the United States during the Vietnam era but in Europe and beyond in subsequent decades. Antiwar activism rose again in response to the US invasion and occupation of Iraq. In February 2003 an estimated 10 million people demonstrated against the Iraq war in hundreds of cities across the globe. This vast movement was unable to stop the US-led invasion, but it prevented the Bush administration from gaining UN endorsement and contributed to the political defeat of the administration's war policy. Chapter 8 concludes with a discussion of the so-called "war on terror," and efforts by peace advocates to craft an alternative strategy against terrorism based on principles of nonviolence and conflict prevention.

AN OVERVIEW OF PEACEMAKING IDEAS

The second half of the book examines substantive themes, beginning in chapter 9 with the role of religion in peacemaking. The religious traditions of Hinduism, Buddhism, Judaism, Islam, and Christianity all contain principles and practices to sustain peacemaking – although justifications for war can also be found in many sacred texts. The Gospel of Jesus is unequivocal in its commitment to love and nonretaliation for injury, as reflected in the absolute pacifism of the early Christian communities. Although the just war tradition replaced pacifism within official Christianity, the tradition of nonresistance continued and reemerged during and after the Reformation in the Anabaptist and Quaker movements. The Social Gospel of the late nineteenth and twentieth centuries brought peace and social justice issues into the mainstream of Christianity, but it also sparked renewed debate about the limitations of pacifism. The leading voice in this reappraisal was Reinhold Niebuhr, whose philosophy of Christian realism became a dominant influence in the twentieth century. John Howard Yoder's response to Niebuhr sought to preserve the integrity of pacifism through a more realistic, minimalist understanding of the possibilities for Christian perfectionism.

Niebuhr and Yoder were influenced by the achievements of Gandhi and the power of nonviolent action to achieve social justice. As noted in chapter 10, the Gandhian method inspired Martin Luther King, Jr. and the US civil rights movement. Nonviolent citizen movements have since become a "force more powerful," bringing democracy to the Philippines, a "velvet revolution" to eastern Europe, the end of apartheid in South Africa, and the overthrow of corrupt regimes in Serbia, Ukraine, and other former Soviet republics. Nonviolent action is the key to more realistic pacifism, a bridge between idealism and realism. Assertive nonviolence as developed by Gandhi provides an answer to the challenge of Niebuhr, transcending the passivity of nonresistance while offering a strategy for fighting effectively to resist social evil.

The rise of peace advocacy in recent centuries is directly tied to the spread and deepening of democracy. It is no accident that peace societies first emerged in democratic Britain and the United States, and that the largest peace mobilizations have occurred in democratic countries. Pacifism is by its very nature an activist commitment that depends for its expression on the right of people to assemble and speak freely. Chapter 11 explores the theoretical and empirical links between democracy and peace. The rise of socialism influenced pacifism by focusing attention on issues of equality and social justice, as examined in chapter 12. Relations between pacifism and socialism were decidedly cool at first, the result of different theories about the causes of war and the requirements for peace. Gradually the movements began to converge, as peace advocates broadened their agenda and socialists became less doctrinaire. In recent decades peace advocates and internationalists have supported more equitable economic development as an essential strategy for preventing war.

The advent of feminism and the growing involvement of women significantly influenced the agenda for peace. Women tended to give greater emphasis to the social dimensions of peace, and linked the concerns of family and community life with the larger realm of state and international affairs. In the late nineteenth and early twentieth centuries feminists noted the heavy burden of war on women, including impoverishment from the loss of male breadwinners. In the twentieth century they emphasized the rising death toll among women and children caused by the increased lethality of war and the spread of civil conflict. Feminists pointed to the connection between the institutionalized violence of war and violence against women. They sought to achieve greater equality for women as an essential requirement for creating a more just and peaceful world. They enlarged the definition of peace beyond narrow legalistic and institutional concerns to encompass a more holistic social, economic, cultural, and political strategy for preventing violence.[45]

Support for human rights has become an essential element of the strategy for peace and was a key factor in ending the cold war. The cause of political freedom is sometimes misused by governments, however, as when US and British leaders claimed a human rights argument for the invasion of Iraq. More legitimate human rights challenges were posed by genocide and the abuse of civilians in Bosnia, Kosovo, and Darfur – although in these instances the response from the major powers was initially timid. As examined in chapter 13 the moral and political imperative of responding to the slaughter of innocents has sparked an intense international debate about the responsibility to protect. Peace and human rights advocates are finding common ground in advocating more vigorous international action, including the use of force under specified conditions, as necessary means of ending oppression and securing peace with justice.

Patriotism is often pitted against pacifism. Throughout history the call to arms has trumped the appeal for peace. The phenomenon of mass belligerence was the subject of a famous 1932 correspondence between Einstein and Freud and motivated philosopher William James's search for "a moral equivalent of war" a generation earlier. Gandhi sought to harness the desire for patriotic service into a commitment to social justice through the idea of a nonviolent army. His concept echoes today in various citizen nonviolent peacemaking initiatives and conciliation programs in conflict zones around the world. Recent trends toward greater peacemaking duties for armed forces and proposals for a "human security response force" within the European Union suggest that the gap between traditional military service and peacemaking may be narrowing. Peace advocacy is itself a form of patriotic service, not only to nation but to the wider human community.

My goal in this book is to forge a synthesis among peacemaking traditions, giving the principles of nonviolence cardinal importance. This synthesis incorporates advances in the theory and practice of international peacebuilding, while also drawing from the contributions of democracy theory, feminism, socialism, and human rights. It addresses the rise of antiwar movements, the imperative of disarmament, and the contemporary challenges of countering terrorism and nuclear proliferation. Over the decades new possibilities have emerged for resolving conflict and achieving justice through nonviolent means. History's most violent era has also seen the

---

[45] Harriet Hyman Alonzo, *Peace as a Women's Issue: A History of the US Movement for World Peace and Women's Rights* (Syracuse, NY: Syracuse University Press, 1993), 8–14.

dawning of an age of nonviolence. While the dominant narrative has been and continues to be written in blood, a different, more hopeful story has emerged in the development of movements and ideas for peace. Gandhian principles of nonviolence have inspired new strategies and possibilities for achieving justice and overcoming social evil while remaining true to religious principles of peace. Growing numbers of people now recognize and act upon the realization that the peaceful resolution of conflict is both necessary and possible. In these pages I examine the history of that movement and the ideas that sustain it.

PART I

Movements

2

The first peace societies

The aspiration for peace, the desire to create a society in which war plays little or no part, has fired human imagination throughout history. It was only at the beginning of the nineteenth century, however, that people began to form voluntary societies to educate and advocate on behalf of peace. These were educated elites who not only believed in and prayed for peace but who also engaged in organized action to formulate proposals, raise awareness, and engage with public officials. Over the centuries peace organizations have ebbed and flowed, through waves of ideological ferment and popular mobilization, in response to changing threats of war and evolving prospects for peace. This chapter traces the early history of organized peace advocacy, from its origins among religious reformers in the United States and Britain, through its spread among democratic nationalists and cosmopolitan reformers in the latter half of the nineteenth century, to its growth in many countries and emergence as a significant international presence in the years before 1914. Peace advocacy emerged from multiple and sometimes conflicting sources. Pacifist religious sects, moral revivalism, free trade liberalism, social reform movements, democratic nationalism, internationalism, even industrial philanthropy and conservative monarchy – all contributed to an ever widening if not always consistent or coherent public discourse on peace.

The expanding networks of peace advocacy began to reach significant scale by the turn of the twentieth century, with strands of influence that included even Woodrow Wilson, a member of the American Peace Society (APS) whom Jane Addams considered a fellow pacifist (in the broad sense in which the term was understood at the time).[1] But the impression of power proved illusory, as so often in the history of peace movements. The presumed unity of the friends of peace cloaked diverse and sometimes

[1] Thomas J. Knock, *To End All Wars: Woodrow Wilson and the Quest for a New World Order* (New York: Oxford University Press, 1992), 12, 120.

contradictory impulses. Wide differences existed over fundamental issues – absolute versus conditional pacifism, whether and how to reach wider audiences, the relative importance of moral enlightenment versus political action, how to reconcile nationalism and internationalism, the viability of arbitration and international law. Peace societies had the ear of a president, the wealth of Andrew Carnegie, and the backing of many political leaders and diplomats around the world, but they did not have the political clout or conceptual coherence to stem the looming threat of world war.

STIRRINGS

The intellectual and social origins of the early peace societies were many. In Europe early peace advocacy tended to reflect the rationalist philosophy of Immanuel Kant. Writing during the Age of Reason, amid the ferment of the French Revolution, Kant envisioned peace based on the establishment of a federation of free republics governed by enlightened citizens. The American and French revolutions transformed political thinking, elevating the role of the individual citizen.[2] Peace was no longer a matter merely for kings and princes but was now claimed as a citizen's right.

In the United States and Britain organized pacifism emerged as part of a religiously inspired moral reform movement. The end of the eighteenth century witnessed an awakening of religious revivalism, which emphasized salvation and the moral regeneration of society. Personal piety combined with a strong social reform impulse to motivate campaigns against slavery and vice and on behalf of peace and foreign missionary work.[3] This revivalist impulse coexisted sometimes uneasily with the rise of Kantian liberalism, which emphasized reason over religious dogma, but the two movements shared a common belief in the irenic virtues of free trade. The religious awakening coincided with revulsion in Europe at the horrors of the Napoleonic wars and opposition in the United States to the war of 1812, which historian Samuel Eliot Morison described as "the most unpopular war that this country has ever waged."[4] These impulses inspired the creation

---

[2] Sandi E. Cooper, *Patriotic Pacifism: Waging War in Europe, 1815–1914* (New York: Oxford University Press, 1991), 5, 13.

[3] Charles DeBenedetti, *The Peace Reform in American History* (Bloomington, IN: Indiana University Press, 1980), 27.

[4] Samuel Eliot Morison, "Dissent in the War of 1812," in *Dissent in Three American Wars*, ed. Samuel Eliot Morison, Frederick Merk, and Frank Freidel (Cambridge, MA: Harvard University Press, 1970), 3.

of the world's first organizations specifically devoted to the promotion of peace.

The earliest known peace society appeared in the United States in August 1815 when the Connecticut born former teacher David Low Dodge joined with a small group of clergy and fellow merchants to form the New York Peace Society. The new society took inspiration from Dodge's booklet, *War Inconsistent with the Religion of Jesus Christ*, written in 1812 but released three years later.[5] Dodge and his colleagues believed that war was contrary to the spirit and example of Christ and that it led inevitably to intemperance and barbarism. Similar ideas and organizing efforts emerged independently that year in New England. In 1814 revolutionary war veteran Noah Worcester wrote *A Solemn Review of the Custom of War*, which blended reason and evangelical Christianity into an argument for organized social action against war, which he condemned as "a heathenish, savage, and barbarous custom." Worcester emphasized the importance of "human agency" to achieve divine purposes. "God can put an end to war," he wrote, through "the benevolent exertions of enlightened" humans.[6]

Simultaneous efforts were underway in London. A "friends of peace" movement had developed in Britain in the 1790s to oppose William Pitt the Younger's military intervention against the French Revolution. One of those who conveyed these antiwar sentiments to the prime minister was his close friend William Wilberforce, who later became a hero for his role in ending the slave trade.[7] It was not until after the Napoleonic wars, however, that a formal organization was created. As Martin Ceadel has observed, pacifism in Britain was deeply influenced by the Quaker renunciation of war.[8] Unlike religious sects that separated themselves from society, Quakers were often fully engaged in political action and in commerce and industry. In 1816 William Allen and other Quakers who were active in antislavery and social reform efforts founded the British Society for the Promotion of Permanent and Universal Peace.[9] The London society was open to all and

---

[5] Peter Brock, *Freedom from War: Nonsectarian Pacifism 1814–1914* (Toronto: University of Toronto Press, 1991), 19. See also A. C. F. Beales, *The History of Peace: A Short Account of the Organised Movements for International Peace* (London: G. Bell, 1931), 45.

[6] Noah Worcester, [Philo Pacificus], *A Solemn Review of the Custom of War; Showing That War is the Effect of Popular Delusion and Proposing a Remedy*, 5th edn (Cambridge, MA: Hilliard and Metcalf, 1816), 4–5.

[7] J. E. Cookson, *The Friends of Peace: Anti-War Liberalism in England, 1793–1815* (New York: Cambridge University Press, 1982), 127–9.

[8] Martin Ceadel, *The Origins of War Prevention: The British Peace Movement and International Relations 1730–1854* (Oxford: Oxford University Press, 1996).

[9] Brock, *Freedom from War*, 23.

quickly attracted Anglicans and other non-Quakers to its ranks. Like their US counterparts the British peace advocates believed that war was inconsistent with the spirit of Christianity and contrary to the interests of humankind. The early peace societies spread rapidly. By 1820, according to A. C. F. Beales, there were more than thirty in the United States, with about one-third that number in Britain.[10] The largest of these early groups was the Massachusetts Peace Society, which by 1823 reported some thousand members.[11]

Peace advocacy in the United States received a boost in 1828 when William Ladd, a retired sea captain from Maine, linked the fledgling peace groups into a national organization, the APS.[12] According to Charles DeBenedetti there were nearly fifty local peace societies in the USA in the early nineteenth century. Many of these affiliated with the APS. The new national organization was secular in orientation. Although Ladd and other organizers were absolute pacifists who opposed all war on religious grounds, they insisted that the APS adopt a broader, nonsectarian approach in order to appeal to a larger audience. Ladd and his colleagues preferred "organization above purification," DeBenedetti wrote.[13] The leaders of the APS combined a deep faith in Christian values with optimism about the possibility of resolving conflicts through reason and negotiation. The organization focused on promoting international dispute resolution through arbitration.

The first organized peace societies on the European continent appeared in Paris in 1821, the *Société de la morale chrétienne*, and in Geneva in 1830, the *Société de la paix de Génève*.[14] The early continental peace advocates, like their Anglo-American counterparts, were motivated by religious beliefs, but they were also inspired by the ideals of democracy and liberty.[15] They opposed the restored monarchies and repressive political order that followed in the wake of the Congress of Vienna. Among the first to speak out for peace on the continent were liberal economists and utopian socialists, including Jean-Baptiste Say, Charles Fourier, and Henri de Saint-Simon. They criticized the misuse of economic resources in war and excessive military spending. The unfolding forces of industry and technology, they

[10] Beales, *The History of Peace*, 52.
[11] Charles Chatfield, *The American Peace Movement: Ideals and Activism* (New York: Twayne Publishers, 1992), 5–6.
[12] Merle Eugene Curti, *The American Peace Crusade 1815–1860* (Durham, NC: Duke University Press, 1929), 34, 42–3.
[13] DeBenedetti, *The Peace Reform in American History*, 36, 38.   [14] Cooper, *Patriotic Pacifism*, 16.
[15] Roger Chickering, *Imperial Germany and a World without War: The Peace Movement and German Society, 1892–1914* (Princeton, NJ: Princeton University Press, 1975), 331.

believed, would create a new era of human prosperity and a world without war.[16] The growth of continental peace societies was aided by Anglo-American peace pioneers, who traveled to the Netherlands, Belgium, western Germany, and France in the first half of the nineteenth century, lecturing, arranging for the translation of documents, and inviting supporters to London.

Peace advocacy emerged in Japan in the late nineteenth century but did not reach mass scale until after World War II. As in Europe, Anglo-American influence was helpful in getting things started. A series of lectures in Japan by William Jones of the British Peace Society sparked the founding of the first peace society, *Nihon heiwa-kai*, in November 1889. The first issue of the newsletter, *Heiwa* (Peace), appeared in 1892.[17] The Christian writer Uchimura Kanzō is often considered Japan's most distinguished pre-World War II pacifist. Originally a supporter of the 1894–5 war against China, Uchimura changed his views in the wake of the brutalities of that conflict. He subsequently embraced a position of absolute pacifism and spoke out consistently against war and militarism until his death in 1930.[18]

Early Japanese peace reformers were influenced not only by Christianity but by neo-Confucianism and the "new religions" movement that began in the Meiji era. The new outlook stressed self-cultivation and inner moral development, a "philosophy of the heart," wrote historian Yasumaru Yoshio. Spiritual transformation was considered the key to social betterment. According to this view the concentric circles of peace begin with the individual and radiate outward to family, community, and the larger world.[19] It is not just policies and institutions that must change but also the human heart. "You better free your mind instead," sang John Lennon many decades later, well reflecting an Eastern philosophy of peace.

SOCIAL ORIGINS AND POLITICAL AGENDAS

The founders and members of the first European and American peace societies were middle-class liberals, persons of wealth and influence who

---

[16] Cooper, *Patriotic Pacifism*, 14–16.
[17] Nobuya Bamba, "Kitamura Tōkoku: His Pursuit of Freedom and World Peace," in *Pacifism in Japan: The Christian and Socialist Tradition*, ed. Nobuya Bamba and John F. Howes (Vancouver: University of British Columbia Press, 1978), 35, 56.
[18] John F. Howes, "Uchimura Kanzō: The Bible and War," in *Pacifism in Japan*, 91–2.
[19] Robert Kisala, *Prophets of Peace: Pacifism and Cultural Identity in Japan's New Religions* (Honolulu: University of Hawai'i Press, 1999), 3.

sought through public education to put an end to war.[20] They were generally not interested in creating mass membership organizations, and with the exception of the Massachusetts Peace Society and a few other groups, did not welcome women as members.[21] Peace society members in the USA were mostly "well educated members of the urban northeastern middle class," according to DeBenedetti, predominantly merchants, educators, and clergy.[22] They were personally conservative, mostly Congregationalist and Unitarian, with the active participation of Quakers. They were humanitarians and reformers who combined Christian millennialism with faith in human progress. In Europe as well peace advocates tended to be reform-minded members of the aristocracy and representatives or advocates of the rising bourgeoisie.

The early peace societies sought to avoid the controversial political issues of the day. The London Peace Society described peace as solely a humanitarian and religious concern, declaring in 1819, "with party politics, the friends of peace have nothing to do. The cause is a *religious*, not a *political* one."[23] Fearful of the revolutionary violence and social upheaval that had recently convulsed Europe, many peace advocates sought to preserve an emerging social and economic order from which they hoped to benefit. An official report of the APS proclaimed, "we aim at *conservative* reform."[24] In France peace leader Frédéric Passy echoed this plea for moderation. "We do not wish to . . . overthrow anything," he wrote in 1868.[25] Passy and Bertha von Suttner urged their contemporaries to eschew political controversies and to concentrate instead on building long-term support for peace. This conservative approach continued into the years before World War I. It helps to explain the peace passion of industrial barons like Andrew Carnegie and Henry Ford, who recognized that war is bad for business (except weapons makers) and that peace facilitates the preservation and accumulation of wealth. The conservative impulse helped to attract financial support and political acceptance among elites, but it clashed with the reformist zeal of many religiously motivated activists. It also impeded efforts to connect the cause of peace with broader social justice issues.

Throughout the nineteenth century peace reformers differed on two fundamental issues: whether to oppose war absolutely or conditionally; and whether to link peace with other social justice issues. The first

---

[20] Michael Howard, *War and the Liberal Conscience* (New Brunswick, NJ: Rutgers University Press, 1978), 36.
[21] Cooper, *Patriotic Pacifism*, 17.   [22] DeBenedetti, *The Peace Reform in American History*, 34, 37.
[23] Cooper, *Patriotic Pacifism*, 16–17.   [24] Emphasis in original. Brock, *Freedom from War*, 22, 50.
[25] Cooper, *Patriotic Pacifism*, 35.

discussion centered on what was called "defensive war." Many early peace advocates accepted that the use of force might be necessary at times to defend the nation or counter social evil. William Allen, president of Bowdoin College and an APS leader, thought that defensive war or armed police action could be consistent with the Christian gospel.[26] Noah Worcester and his Massachusetts colleagues were also in the pragmatist camp and were open to the possibility of defensive war as a last resort. They had practical political considerations in mind as well. To rally the required level of popular support for peace a more inclusive approach was necessary. The constitution of the APS condemned war among nation states as contrary to the spirit of the Gospel, but said nothing about and thus by silence condoned the use of force for defensive purposes.[27]

On the other side of the debate were absolute pacifists such as David Low Dodge of the New York Peace Society, who opposed war in any form. Dodge rejected the concept of defensive war and was concerned that the pragmatist position would shift the debate from a discussion of religious principles to matters of mere political expediency. Many religiously oriented pacifists in the United States and Britain clung to a position of Christian nonresistance. They opposed all forms of military violence as contrary to the teachings of Jesus and a scourge upon humanity.

Peace activism on the European continent tended to favor the pragmatic approach. European pacifists rejected the absolutist position prevalent among British and US Quakers and were more supportive of defensive war and the use of force for just cause. Self-described peace advocates in Italy, France, and other European countries considered war for national liberation a justifiable and sometimes necessary step toward global peace. The continental groups viewed peace more as a pragmatic requirement than as a moral imperative. They tended to believe that international law and political harmony would evolve from the progress of industry and technology. Some perceived a natural process of social evolution toward cooperation and ever larger spheres of political and economic interdependence. They were also more likely than their Anglo-American counterparts to link peace and justice concerns.[28]

By the 1840s some US peace activists were also making the connections to social justice issues. The growing involvement of women in movements against war and slavery broadened the agenda of the peace societies. Social harmony would not be possible, reformers insisted, as long as glaring injustices such as slavery persisted. Peace required the active promotion of

[26] Brock, *Freedom from War*, 47.   [27] *Ibid.*, 20, 50.   [28] Cooper, *Patriotic Pacifism*, 10, 20–1.

rights and equality for all, particularly the oppressed – negro slaves, workers, women, and national minorities. Leading the charge for this more radical and comprehensive peace vision was William Lloyd Garrison, and the New England Non-resistance Society, which was formed in 1838.[29] A Baptist with Quaker sympathies, Garrison and his small band of followers in the New England society combined a rejection of armed violence with a fierce opposition to slavery and social injustice. Later, as the crisis over slavery became increasingly bitter, Garrison abandoned his pacifist principles and reluctantly concluded that violence would be necessary to defeat the hated slave system.

Garrison and other peace advocates actively opposed the 1846–8 US war against Mexico. They linked their peace efforts to the antislavery cause, fearing that slavery would be extended to the territories conquered from Mexico. Antiwar sentiment was strongest in New England, where Ralph Waldo Emerson registered his opposition and his friend Henry David Thoreau went to jail rather than pay taxes for war and slavery. The antiwar movement had a significant impact on public opinion, according to DeBenedetti, creating a political climate that "frustrated [President] Polk in his attempt to conquer all of Mexico and ... helped to contain the violence and prevent further bloodletting."[30] This was the first time peace advocates engaged in political action to shape public opinion and influence government decision making. The struggle against the US invasion of Mexico marked the emergence of an organized anti-imperialist movement, which was later to become a major focus for peace advocates in the United States and many other countries.

ELIHU BURRITT: THE LEARNED BLACKSMITH

One of the most influential leaders in attempting to build a more holistic and inclusive peace movement was Elihu Burritt, described by Beales as "the greatest name in the history of American pacifism."[31] Unlike other early peace leaders Burritt was born into poverty. He learned the blacksmith's trade as a young man, but was also a voracious reader and student of languages. He tried to establish himself as an itinerant merchant but was unsuccessful and had to return to the forge. He continued to hone his literary and linguistic skills, however, and eventually found success as a lecturer and independent publisher. Billing himself "the learned

---

[29] Chatfield, *The American Peace Movement*, 8.
[30] DeBenedetti, *The Peace Reform in American History*, 51–2.   [31] Beales, *The History of Peace*, 71.

blacksmith" Burritt lectured far and wide on social reform issues and published his own weekly paper, *The Christian Citizen*. Burritt was an absolute pacifist who was deeply influenced by the Christian message of love and compassion. He was committed to many social reforms, but his greatest passion was for peace. He considered war the "sin of sins," and believed that genuine social reform would not be possible until Christianity ended its "unnatural, ungodly wedlock with ... the fiendish spirit of War."[32] Burritt was uncompromising in his rejection of war, but he was nonsectarian and inclusive in his organizing and public education efforts. He attempted to bridge class lines and reached out to the working class as well as the literate middle class.[33]

Burritt was indefatigable in his dedication to social reform and devoted most of his adult life to "superhuman labour" on behalf of peace.[34] He was uncomfortable with the conservativism of the APS and yearned for a more broadly based visionary movement to end war. He traveled to Europe and was especially popular among activists in France and Belgium.[35] During a visit to Britain in 1846 Burritt decided to create a new organization, the League of Universal Brotherhood (LUB). The LUB was opposed to war absolutely, but it also condemned slavery and other forms of social injustice that divide human communities and cause armed violence. The league promoted human solidarity among people of all colors and classes.[36]

Borrowing from the temperance movement, which organized support on the basis of a pledge to refrain from drinking, Burritt composed a peace pledge that committed signers to affirm human brotherhood and refrain from any form of support for war. Burritt promoted the LUB in Europe, while colleagues established a US branch. Within six months the LUB claimed the support of more than 30,000 people in Britain and 25,000 in the United States, including many signers from the working class and rural communities. The LUB lasted only about a dozen years, but it was the largest and most inclusive peace organization up to that time. It was also the first genuinely international peace organization, although mostly Anglo-American. The success of the LUB owed much to Burritt's irrepressible dedication and energy, but it also reflected the advantages of a nonsectarian, inclusive approach to pacifism.

---

[32] Quoted in DeBenedetti, *The Peace Reform in American History*, 48.
[33] Chatfield, *The American Peace Movement*, 10.   [34] Beales, *The History of Peace*, 71.
[35] Cooper, *Patriotic Pacifism*, 16.
[36] Peter Tolis, *Elihu Burritt: Crusader for Brotherhood* (Hamden, CT: Archon Books, 1968), 146–8.

THE FIRST PEACE CONGRESSES

As the fledgling peace societies matured and became aware of one another in different countries, the idea of an international peace congress developed. Drawing from the experience of the antislavery movement, which held an international assembly in 1840, peace leaders called for an international gathering to promote permanent and universal peace. The first congress, held at London's Freemasons' Hall in June 1843, attracted 324 delegates: 292 from Britain, 26 from the United States, and 6 from the European continent. The congress adopted two declarations, one in support of arbitration, the other favoring a congress of nations. It concluded with a public meeting in Exeter Hall attended by 2,000 people.[37]

Five years later British and US peace leaders joined with their European counterparts in convening a second international congress. The meeting was scheduled in August 1848 for Paris, but had to be relocated to Brussels because of the revolutionary violence that erupted in the French capital that summer. Most of the 300 participants who attended the Brussels congress in September were again British and American, with a few representatives from France, Belgium, and Spain. The delegates repeated the previous calls for arbitration and a congress of nations but added a new demand for disarmament, thus introducing for the first time a theme that was to become dominant among peace advocates in decades to come. The staid peace society representatives who met in Brussels remained aloof from the ferment of democratic revolt then sweeping France, Italy, Hungary, and other countries. A few delegates at the Brussels meeting urged support for national liberation struggles, but it would take another two decades before the causes were joined.

The most successful and impressive of the early international peace congresses was the August 1849 conference in Paris. Among the 840 official delegates in attendance were 670 from Great Britain, 100 from France, 12 from Belgium, 20 from the United States, and others from a range of European countries. The high point of the conference was a stirring inaugural address by Victor Hugo before an assembly of some 1,500 people. Emphasizing the need for a union of European nations, Hugo presciently declared:

A day will come when bullets and bomb-shells will be replaced by votes, by the universal suffrage of nations, by the venerable arbitration of a great Sovereign

---

[37] Beales, *The History of Peace*, 66–7.

Senate, which will be to Europe what the Parliament is to England, what the Diet is to Germany, what the Legislative Assembly is to France.[38]

The delegates at the Paris congress adopted practical resolutions encouraging steps toward common international standards for communications, postal reform, and a system of weights and measures. Subsequent peace congresses were held in Frankfurt in 1850 and London in 1851, smaller than the Paris gathering but significant in sustaining support for the now widely accepted peace agenda: arbitration, a congress of nations, and limits on armament. Notwithstanding the great effort that went into the early peace congresses, and the many earnest resolutions and statements that were adopted, these gatherings had little practical impact. The delegates may have been inspired and nurtured in their commitment to peace, but they lacked the political means to influence policy.

Ironically, as peace advocates became more active internationally they began to lose momentum and political coherence at home. By the 1850s the deepening divisions within US society over slavery split and eventually shattered the peace movement. Pacifism became increasingly untenable and many peace advocates joined Garrison in supporting the Union cause against slavery. For the APS and other groups the fight to preserve the Union and end slavery seemed the very definition of a just war. Organized peace advocacy in the United States disappeared and did not reappear until the guns fell silent.

In Europe the peace movement also experienced trauma and decline. The onset of political reaction in Europe following the failed revolutions of 1848 made reformist movements difficult to sustain. The Crimean War had an effect similar to that of the Civil War in the USA. When the British government joined the fight in the Crimea many liberals and reformers rallied to what they considered a just war against Russian imperialism. Also dampening the pacifist cause were the wars of national unification in Italy, Spain, and other European countries. Many liberal reformers supported democratic nationalism as a just cause and hoped it would be an antidote to autocracy and militarism.[39]

THE RIGHT OF SELF-DETERMINATION

After the chastening horrors of the US Civil War and the Crimean War, organized pacifist movements began to reappear in the United States and

---

[38] Inaugural address by Victor Hugo published in *Report of the Proceedings of the Second General Peace Congress, Held in Paris on the 22nd, 23rd and 24th of August, 1849* (London: Charles Gilpin, 1849), 11.
[39] Chickering, *Imperial Germany and a World without War*, 7–8.

Europe in the 1860s and 1870s. A few organizations, such as the APS, never ceased functioning, although they were mostly dormant during the fury of the war years. By the latter third of the century a new wave of peace advocacy emerged, and the scale of organized activity increased. Peace societies extended far and wide, attracting support from intellectuals, members of Parliament, and even leading industrialists. In the United States it was an era of optimism, of "cosmopolitan reform," as DeBenedetti phrased it.[40] In continental Europe peace societies multiplied in France and emerged in Scandinavia, the Latin countries, and even in imperial Germany and Austria–Hungary. The growth of the European peace societies brought new dynamism to the cause and introduced fresh political perspectives linking peace to national self-determination and social justice. In most of Europe peace groups overlapped with the rising socialist movement, as a new concept of "scientific" pacifism emerged under the influence of Darwin and positivism. Peace activism also emerged within the working class. In the 1870s W. Randal Cremer, the first British worker to be elected to the House of Commons and a winner of the Nobel Peace Prize in 1903, founded the Workman's Peace Association, which opposed excessive military spending and supported arbitration and the development of international law.[41]

Two distinct schools of thought and separate organizations emerged in the latter half of the nineteenth century. The *Ligue internationale et permanente de la paix*, formed in Paris in 1867, represented the more moderate wing of the movement. Its animating spirit was the French economist Frédéric Passy, later co-winner of the Nobel Peace Prize, a dominant figure among nineteenth-century European peace activists. The *Ligue* represented the "bourgeois, liberal, internationalist tradition within French pacifism," wrote historian Norman Ingram.[42] It considered peace the preeminent concern and necessary requirement for national liberation and all other social progress. Passy believed that political freedom and social justice would evolve naturally once the burdens of war and excessive military spending were lifted from society. Liberal economic policies would naturally lead to prosperity and would solve the problems of injustice and poverty. Passy disagreed with democratic revolutionaries who prioritized the struggle for social justice. He did not believe that democracy and greater social equality were prerequisites for peace. He advocated an incrementalist agenda that

[40] DeBenedetti, *The Peace Reform in American History*, 64–7.   [41] Cooper, *Patriotic Pacifism*, 48, 56–7.
[42] Norman Ingram, *The Politics of Dissent: Pacifism in France 1919–1939* (Oxford: Clarendon Press, 1991), 20.

sought to achieve international arbitration agreements rather than wholesale social change. Progress would come through lobbying for gradual reform, he argued, not through demands for revolution. He disdained radicalism as alienating to the middle-class constituencies that he believed had to be won over to the cause of peace.[43] The *Ligue* changed its name a couple of times over the decades and in 1922 merged into the *Association de la paix par le droit* (APD), which remained in existence until after World War II.[44]

An alternative perspective was articulated by the *Ligue internationale de la paix et de la liberté*, which was formed in Geneva in 1867 and continued until 1939. The *Ligue* was the largest and most influential continental peace organization of the nineteenth century. It was home to those who believed that peace required a commitment to social justice, national liberation, and democracy. The agenda of the *Ligue* prefigured the concern for social justice and human rights that was to become the hallmark of peace activism in the twentieth century. The *Ligue* was inspired by Giuseppe Garibaldi and Victor Hugo and was led by Edmond Potonié-Pierre and Charles Lemonnier. Wars would not end, Garibaldi famously argued, until oppressed nationalities won their freedom, through war if necessary. National liberation, democracy, and human rights were prerequisites for peace. Many socialists held similar views. Self-determination for oppressed nationalities and the extension of the franchise to women and previously excluded populations – these were the foundations for a more peaceful society.

The *Ligue internationale de la paix et de la liberté* sponsored the largest peace congress of the nineteenth century at its founding meeting in Geneva in September 1867. The crowd of 6,000 people in attendance included Europe's leading democrats and nationalist radicals.[45] Presiding over the congress was Garibaldi, who stirred controversy by calling for the overthrow of the Papal States in Italy. The League's journal was *Les États-Unis d'Europe*, which openly supported wars of national liberation. An article in 1868 read: "War is . . . legitimate and just against oppressors. Every armed struggle is a crime if it does not have the noble aim of attaining the eternal, immutable right of peoples and individuals for self-determination."[46] The *Ligue*'s Lausanne meeting in 1869 was also memorable because of the opening address of Victor Hugo, who came out of exile to preside at the assembly. His message in 1869 was more sober and less utopian than his famous oration at the Paris congress twenty years earlier. He spoke not of

[43] Cooper, *Patriotic Pacifism*, 45.   [44] Ingram, *The Politics of Dissent*, 21.
[45] Cooper, *Patriotic Pacifism*, 36.   [46] Quoted in *ibid.*, 39.

a United States of Europe but of a necessary struggle for national liberation and democracy:

The first condition of peace is liberation. For this liberation, a revolution is needed which shall be a great one, and perhaps, alas a war which shall be the last one. Then, all will be accomplished. Peace . . . will be eternal; no more armies, no more kings. The past will vanish.[47]

The people of Italy, Germany, and other European countries were successful in forging unified nations, but the peace of which the nationalists dreamed proved illusory, as the principle of justifiable war gave way to militarism, world war, and dictatorship.

UNIVERSALIZING PEACE

In the late nineteenth century peace societies began to appear throughout Europe. In Denmark Fredrik Bajer, a Member of Parliament and co-winner of the Nobel Peace Prize in 1908, helped to organize the Society for the Promotion of Danish Neutrality. By 1907 the organization claimed 6,000 members in sixty-nine chapters.[48] In Sweden Klas P. Arnoldson and other Members of Parliament launched a similar effort to build support for neutrality. The Swedish society also worked to resolve the emerging dispute between Sweden and Norway, which separated peacefully in 1905. The Scandinavian peace societies helped to steer their governments toward support for neutrality and away from involvement in the great power alliances of the major European states.

The French peace movement expanded significantly in the late nineteenth century. In Nîmes an energetic group of mainly Protestant students formed the *Association des jeunes amis de la paix*, which later became the APD. Peace societies emerged in many of the provinces. At the national level Émile Arnaud succeeded Charles Lemonnier as leader of the *Ligue internationale de la paix et de la liberté*. By 1910, according to historian Sandi Cooper, France had "the largest and most diversified peace movement on the Continent."[49] Thirty-six separate organizations were active at the time, some with many local branches. The French national council, the *Délégation permanente des sociétés françaises de la paix*, attracted broad support from many sectors of society, including labor unions, chambers of commerce, members of local municipal councils, educators, and eminent writers and intellectuals. One estimate placed the number of French men

---

[47] Victor Hugo, *Actes et Paroles. Pendant l'Exil 1852–1870* (Paris: Nelson, Éditeurs, 1912), 450–1.
[48] Cooper, *Patriotic Pacifism*, 56, 73.   [49] *Ibid.*, 65.

and women involved in peace societies at 300,000. The peace movement also developed in Italy, where the *Unione lombarda per la pace* was established in Milan in 1887 and a national network of peace activists was created at a congress in Rome in 1889. By 1904 there were twenty-five separate Italian peace societies, which came together in Turin to create a national coordinating committee.[50]

The first peace society emerged in the Netherlands in 1870. Within a year the nascent Dutch Peace League had twenty-six branches, although few of these lasted. It was not until the turn of the century that an enduring peace movement took root, when the Peace League merged with the Dutch section of the Women's League for International Disarmament to create a new organization, Peace through Justice (*Vrede door Recht*). The group organized public meetings, monitored textbooks, and actively participated in international peace congresses. It also produced a children's book on the life of the great Dutch pioneer of international law, Hugo Grotius. Peace through Justice grew slowly at first but expanded rapidly in the months before the war.[51]

Peace movement groups emerged in Germany and Austria as well. They were inspired by Bertha von Suttner, whose international success and popularity provided a launching pad for the Austrian Peace Society in 1891. The first peace society in Germany emerged in 1850, but it was hounded by the police in the counterrevolutionary atmosphere of that time and was soon disbanded. It was not until 1886 that the first enduring peace society appeared in Frankfurt. Germany was seen as a "citadel of militarism," to use Von Suttner's words,[52] and the emergence of peace groups there gave hope to peace advocates elsewhere. Most German peace groups were concentrated in the liberal southwest part of the country, but a few emerged even in authoritarian Prussia. By the 1890s dozens of peace societies were active, with thousands of members. Von Suttner's protégé Alfred H. Fried was the driving organizational and intellectual force in the German peace movement. In 1892 he helped to create the *Deutsche Friedensgesellschaft* (DFG), which developed into a substantial national organization in the years prior to the world war.[53]

---

[50] *Ibid.*, 64–6.

[51] Jonkheer B. De Jong Van Beek En Donk, "History of the Peace Movement in The Netherlands," first published in 1915, in Sandi E. Cooper, "Introduction," in *Peace Activities in Belgium and the Netherlands*, ed. Sandi E. Cooper (New York: Garland Publishing, 1972), 9, 18, 27.

[52] Quoted in Chickering, *Imperial Germany and a World without War*, 44.

[53] Guido Grünewald, "War Resisters in Weimar Germany," in *Challenge to Mars: Essays on Pacifism from 1918 to 1945*, ed. Peter Brock and Thomas P. Socknat (Toronto: University of Toronto Press, 1999), 68.

In 1889 peace groups from throughout the world gathered in Paris at the time of the international exposition celebrating the hundredth anniversary of the French Revolution. This was the first universal peace congress. Subsequent congresses were held nearly every year thereafter for the next twenty years. At the third universal peace congress, held in Rome, the participants agreed to set up a permanent headquarters in Berne. The resulting International Peace Bureau began operations in 1892. It won the Nobel Peace Prize in 1910 and is still active. The universal peace congresses were prestigious events that attracted the support of leading political figures. During the 1908 congress in London delegates were given a reception by the king at Buckingham Palace and a dinner with Prime Minister H. H. Asquith, who offered a toast to the international peace movement.[54]

The 1889 Paris exposition also featured a meeting of European parliamentarians, mostly British and French, who founded the Interparliamentary Conference, later renamed the Interparliamentary Union, which continues today. Over the following decades annual meetings of the Interparliamentary Conference attracted hundreds of participants, primarily Members of Parliament but also ministers, diplomats, and professors of international law. In 1904 the conference gathered in St. Louis. Afterwards a delegation of parliamentarians was invited to the White House for a meeting with President Theodore Roosevelt. In 1906 more than 600 parliamentarians attended the Interparliamentary Conference in London, which sat in the House of Lords. By 1910 the Interparliamentary Conference included delegations from twenty countries, and counted nearly 2,900 parliamentarians as members.[55]

THE HAGUE PEACE CONFERENCE

One of the most remarkable and strangest episodes in the history of peace was the 1899 Hague Peace Conference. It was sponsored by a most unlikely source, the imperial government of Tsar Nicholas II. Peace advocates and liberals had frequently condemned the militaristic and autocratic policies of Russia, but many were willing to suspend doubt and were pleasantly surprised when they learned of the tsar's invitation for world leaders to attend an international peace conference. The announcement came in the form of a "Rescript," which read like a tract from the peace movement. It

[54] Martin Ceadel, "A Legitimate Peace Movement: The Case of Interwar Britain, 1918–1945," in *Challenge to Mars*, 137.
[55] Cooper, *Patriotic Pacifism*, 85–6.

was a completely unexpected bolt out of the blue, a "thunderclap" in Cooper's words.[56] When von Suttner first saw the Rescript, she thought it was written by her colleague Frédéric Passy. "The intellectual and physical strength of the nations," the document read, "are for the major part diverted from their natural application and unproductively consumed." Massive systems of armament "are transforming the armed peace of our days into a crushing burden." If the incessant building of arms is allowed to continue, it will "inevitably lead to the very cataclysm which it is desired to avert." The goal of the conference, the document declared, was to "make the great idea of universal peace triumph over the elements of trouble and discord," to establish "the principles of justice and right" as the foundation for security and public well-being.[57] Von Suttner herself could not have said it better.

Peace advocates were elated by the announcement of the conference. They sent congratulatory messages to the tsar and lobbied their governments to participate. In Britain and Denmark hundreds of thousands of petition signatures were collected and local meetings were convened to support the conference. The crusading English editor William T. Stead launched a highly visible campaign to urge that the Hague conference adopt measures to halt the build-up of arms in Europe. Peace scholars sent proposals and technical papers on ways to resolve international conflict. Most governments were skeptical of Russia's motives, but they were swept up in the strong wave of public enthusiasm for the conference and agreed to send delegates. The broad support generated by peace organizations made it difficult for governments to ignore the proposed gathering. In all twenty-six nations sent representatives to the Hague.[58]

Diplomatic historians have dismissed the Hague conference as a "side show" of no importance to political relations among the major powers.[59] The press ridiculed the conference as a boring waste of time that produced meaningless and "illusory" agreements.[60] The diplomatic results of the conference were indeed meager, but its larger implications for legitimizing the demand for peace were significant. Peace advocates took the conference seriously and were present at the Hague, lobbying government delegates and providing information to governments and the press. The conference

---

[56] *Ibid.*, 97.
[57] "Rescript of Tsar Nicholas II, 24 August 1898, to Representatives of the Powers Accredited to Saint Petersburg," in Cooper, *Patriotic Pacifism*, 221–2.
[58] Cooper, *Patriotic Pacifism*, 108.
[59] William L. Langer, *The Diplomacy of Imperialism, 1890–1902*, vol. II (New York: A. A. Knopf, 1935), 591.
[60] Cooper, *Patriotic Pacifism*, 103.

gave greater credibility to the cause of peace and international conflict resolution. The hope for a more pacific world was "in the air," Passy observed, and the conference contributed to a "gradual growth of the spirit of peace."[61] The final declaration of the Hague conference proved to be deeply disappointing, however. It included promises by the assembled nations to resolve conflicts peacefully, but these were hedged with loopholes that preserved national sovereignty and the right to wage war. A Permanent Court of Arbitration was created, but it was entirely voluntary, consisting merely of a college of experienced arbitrators who would be available for countries in the event of disputes. Agreements were reached to strengthen the Geneva Conventions, which beginning in the 1860s set rules governing the treatment of prisoners and the protection of noncombatants during wartime. Otherwise the conference produced only pious platitudes: nothing about arms reduction, and no binding commitment to arbitration and the mediation of disputes. The delegates pledged to convene another international conference, but no date was set.

It was not until 1907 that the second Hague Peace Conference was held. Peace supporters again played an important role in building support for the conference and advancing their agenda. Their primary goal was to strengthen the arbitration tribunal established at the first Hague conference. The Interparliamentary Union that gathered in London in 1906 developed a detailed proposal for presentation at the second Hague conference. The plan took the form of a model treaty for mandatory arbitration. It identified an array of issues not touching on matters of vital national security that could be referred automatically to the Permanent Court of Arbitration without governmental review. The delegates hoped that this plan for obligatory referral of noncontroversial issues would make arbitration more palatable to governments and pave the way for eventual acceptance of more complete arbitration procedures.

Peace advocates initially had high hopes for the second Hague Peace Conference. The number of countries in attendance increased from twenty-six to forty-four. The diplomats stayed in session for four months, nearly twice as long as previously. Peace activists were again present, lobbying the delegates and members of the press to promote their agenda. The proposal for obligatory arbitration was indeed a major topic of consideration at the conference, but despite the pleadings of peace advocates the assembled governments balked. The diplomats agreed to restructure the Permanent Court, but they did not accept proposals for automatic referral. More

---

[61] Quoted in *ibid.*, 103.

sweeping proposals for a binding arbitration treaty were also rejected. The conference did not even agree on further steps toward reforming the rules of war. Once again peace supporters were disappointed in their hopes of winning governmental approval of binding arbitration procedures.

NOT ENOUGH

The international peace movement reached the apogee of its public influence and support in the years immediately preceding World War I. Pacifism broadly defined emerged as a significant international presence. Peace societies and internationalist organizations were multiplying, substantial funding was available through Andrew Carnegie and other philanthropists, and governments were beginning to adopt bilateral arbitration agreements and international courts to settle disputes without war. Peace movement congresses were being held annually, and an international parliamentary conference had been established. It was a golden age for peace, embodied in the construction of the Palace of Peace in the Hague in 1913. As Michael Howard wrote, in these years there was genuine hope that the abolition of war might be "almost within reach . . . [through] the civilized intercourse of rational [people] representing the aspirations of the broad, peace-loving masses."[62]

A survey of the international movement at the time counted 190 peace societies, some with thousands of members, in dozens of countries. Heads of state greeted meetings of the Interparliamentary Union and the Universal Peace Congress. Peace leaders could point to some significant achievements: the laws of war were crafted and refined, governments sponsored the Hague peace conferences, dozens of bilateral treaties and arbitration agreements were signed, and a Permanent Court of Arbitration was created. Peace reformers such as Jane Addams and Bertha von Suttner commanded wide respect. The understanding of what causes war and the requirements for peace advanced, as peace advocates gained a greater appreciation for the role of international law, arbitration, and institutionalized cooperation among nations. Democratic freedom, self-determination, and social justice were recognized as vital components of peace.

Yet for all the apparent strength of the peace movement, it was far too weak politically and ideologically to counter the vast historical forces that were propelling Europe toward disaster. Below the surface impression of peace and progress rumblings of the coming military catastrophe were

[62] Howard, *War and the Liberal Conscience*, 53.

already being felt. Military alliances divided the nations of Europe into armed camps, with the major powers lined up on opposite sides of the nationalist wars in the Balkans. A fierce competition was underway in the building of navies and the production of artillery and other military equipment. General staffs worked furiously on elaborate plans for rapid military mobilization in the event of crisis. Nationalist fervor was at high pitch. Europe had become a "very bellicose, very militarist society," wrote Michael Howard. It was infected with an "inflated spirit of patriotism and xenophobia which fuelled an alarmingly intensive arms race."[63] The peace movement was much too small to influence the tidal forces of nationalism, economic self-interest, and political rivalry. It could not prevent "the submerged warrior society," as John Keegan called it, from breaking through the surface of the peaceful landscape.[64] Europe and much of the world succumbed to what von Suttner termed the "ancient despotism" of deep-seated fear.

Von Suttner died in June 1914, just a few weeks before the conflagration she had spent her life attempting to avoid. The premonitions of disaster were plainly evident. Two years earlier she recognized that her optimistic hopes for peace were not likely to be realized in her lifetime:

We have been mistaken – not as to our principles but in our estimate of the level of civilization to which the world in general had attained. We thought there was a far more widespread desire for justice ... and a far deeper abhorrence of despotism than appears to be the case ... [This] does not prove the falsity of beliefs held by the peace party. It merely proves ... that the peace movement is not yet powerful enough.[65]

---

[63] *Ibid.*, 61.   [64] John Keegan, *A History of Warfare* (New York: Alfred A. Knopf, 1993), 22.
[65] Quoted in Cooper, *Patriotic Pacifism*, 184.

3

Toward internationalism

For centuries philosophers and reformers promoted the vision of a more lawful international order as an essential requirement for peace. Just as the development of law helped to create order and reduce violence within domestic societies, it was hoped that the emergence of international law would tame the anarchy of political relations among nations. The early peace societies in the United States and Europe were internationalist in outlook and experience, and many actively campaigned to establish agreements and institutions for the arbitration of international disputes. During the nineteenth century the first practical steps were taken to establish and codify principles of international law, as part of a movement to regulate and humanize the conduct of war and to establish mechanisms for preventing the outbreak of war. The decades that followed saw the creation of international law societies, agreements to regulate transnational commerce and communications, the beginnings of international arbitration, and the emergence of a wide array of legal agreements to regulate and prevent conflict among nations. Thus began a movement that has continued to this day toward ever expanding networks of international law and multilateral institutions.

Analyzing the movement for internationalism poses conceptual challenges, and reveals complex and sometimes contradictory impulses among those involved. The terminology available – internationalism, pacifism, peace advocacy – is too imprecise to capture the many differences in nuance and political perspective that exist. As described below, internationalism can be either conservative or liberal. It can emphasize the preservation of existing relations of power, or seek to create more equitable structures. Some see international institutions as guaranteeing the established order while others see them as mechanisms of social change. Some support international agreements as a means of bolstering the national interest while others support them in the hope of transcending nationalism and broadening global governance. Some focus narrowly on the security dimensions of peace while others emphasize the need for social and economic justice to prevent war. Pacifism (broadly understood) includes internationalism, usually of the liberal variety, but its agenda is wider and includes a range of other issues. Absolute and pragmatic pacifists agree in their support for internationalism, but absolutists place greater emphasis on the need for reform while pragmatists are more willing to work with existing mechanisms.

In this chapter I employ the term internationalism to describe groups that support the development of stronger legal and institutional mechanisms to ameliorate and prevent armed conflict. Internationalism embodies a narrower and more conservative political outlook than pacifism and thus is able to attract greater political support among ruling elites. It provides a gateway through which peace advocates can interact with decision makers and gain a wider hearing for parts of their agenda. In this narrative I examine the links between campaigns for internationalism and the broader peace movement and also the differences between the two. I review the conceptual origins of internationalism, the rise of organized movements for the arbitration of international conflict in the nineteenth century, the creation of the League of Nations, the movement to outlaw war, and the failure of collective security in the interwar era. Along the way I show how elements of the broader peace agenda have influenced the evolution of internationalism, and how essential principles of peace have yet to find transnational expression.

CONCEPTS AND TRENDS

The roots of international law in the West date from the early seventeenth century, when the great Dutch jurist Hugo Grotius wrote his treatise *On the Law of War and Peace*. Grotius' writings emerged at a time when the medieval order of ecclesiastical authority was giving way to the Reformation and the rise of the modern nation state in Europe. In the absence of the supranational moral guidance provided by the Church, emerging nations lacked common standards to regulate political relations with one another. Grotius developed a set of principles, based on religious teachings, which sought to place moral constraints on when and how military force could be used. His system was founded on the concept of natural law, the assumption that right reason can deduce laws to regulate the interaction of peoples in society. He developed a secular variant of the medieval doctrine of a law above nations.[1] He argued that the supreme law of states is to maintain

---

[1] Seyom Brown, *The Causes and Prevention of War*, 2nd edn (New York: St. Martin's Press, 1994), 165.

peace, and that this could be achieved by respecting and preserving the individual sovereignty of each nation.

Over the centuries the Grotian principle of state sovereignty faced many challenges. The growing interdependence of nations, the rise of global commerce, the development of international humanitarianism, global environmental concerns – all contributed to the development of a new concept of sovereignty, which political scientist Joseph Nye has termed the sovereignty of peoples not merely of states.[2] The narrow insistence on absolute state sovereignty became less relevant in an increasingly globalized world threatened by transnational dangers. The principle of protection against external aggression remained an important guarantee of peace, but it was no longer considered absolute. A movement emerged to assert the higher principle of international law. Multilateral institutions developed to enhance transnational cooperation and promote the common interest of nations.

As the movement for international law developed in the nineteenth and twentieth centuries two distinct tendencies emerged. Conservative internationalists recognized the need for greater cooperation among nations, but they insisted on preserving state sovereignty and were skeptical of proposals for binding arbitration and permanent international institutions. They favored ad hoc rather than institutionalized cooperation. Some believed that the spread of Western or democratic values could exert a "civilizing" influence on "backward" peoples. Andrew Carnegie envisioned a future in which the English-speaking nations would lead others toward a cooperative order based on Anglo-American political principles. Britain, the United States, Japan, and other major powers spoke of their global and regional "responsibilities," as internationalism shaded into imperialism and attempts at military and economic domination. Some internationalist groups, such as the LNU in Britain, were vigorously pro-imperial and denied any contradiction between the creation of an international organization and the maintenance of empire.[3]

Progressives developed a very different concept of internationalism. They advocated binding legal arrangements and permanent international institutions to resolve conflict and prevent war. They espoused principles of universal participation, equality of status, humanitarianism, and self-determination for all nations and colonized peoples. The progressive agenda

---

[2] Joseph S. Nye, Jr., *Understanding International Conflicts: An Introduction to Theory and History*, 4th edn (New York: Longman, 2003), 253–4.
[3] Donald S. Birn, *The League of Nations Union 1918–1945* (Oxford: Clarendon Press, 1981), 55, 24.

sought to place constraints on the right of states to wage war, while strengthening international organizations and multilateral mechanisms for resolving conflicts.[4] Progressives also favored greater international efforts to promote economic opportunity and reduce the conditions of poverty and exploitation that many believed were root causes of war. They opposed imperialism and rejected the presumed right of great powers to intervene militarily in the affairs of other nations. They were willing to support the use of sanctions and even military force to defend against aggression, but only if such action was authorized by a council of nations and/or international courts, as part of a collective security system designed to preserve peace and prevent major war.

As international law evolved it followed two parallel tracks: the development of rules constraining the use of violence once war was underway, and the creation of mechanisms to prevent war by adjudicating disputes among nations. The former corresponded to the just war principles of *jus in bello*, relating to conduct within war; the latter to *jus ad bellum*, the justification for going to war. Placing limits on violence through the Geneva Conventions and other rules of war proved easier than restricting the right of states to go to war. The first practical steps toward international law focused on developing codes of conduct for how to fight wars. Agreements to protect prisoners of war and noncombatant civilians emerged during and after the US Civil War and the Crimean War. In 1864 European governments met in Geneva to adopt the Convention for the Amelioration of the Conditions of the Wounded in Armies in the Field. A year earlier they had established a neutral organization with a distinctive red cross on white to care for wounded soldiers.[5] Over the following decades many additional agreements were reached and codified in law to distinguish between combatants and noncombatants, protect the rights of prisoners and wounded soldiers, regulate behavior during sieges and blockades, define proper standards of surrender, and more recently, provide for the punishment of leaders responsible for war crimes.[6]

Efforts to prevent war through arbitration and dispute resolution proceeded more slowly and were less successful. Arbitration agreements implied limits on a state's decision to wage war, which political leaders

---

[4] Cecelia Lynch, *Beyond Appeasement: Interpreting Interwar Peace Movements in World Politics* (Ithaca, NY: Cornell University Press, 1999), 129–30, 215.

[5] Charles DeBenedetti, *The Peace Reform in American History* (Bloomington, IN: Indiana University Press, 1980), 63.

[6] Michael Doyle, *Ways of War and Peace: Realism, Liberalism, and Socialism* (New York: Norton, 1997), 387.

were (and are) reluctant to accept. Governments clung tenaciously to what they considered to be their absolute right to use military force. The principle of sovereignty, which Grotius identified as the foundation of state security, proved to be an impediment to the development of the structures of international law that he believed were needed to enhance collective security. The clash between individual sovereignty and collective responsibility has been and remains a fundamental contradiction within the nation state system limiting the prospects for cooperative peace.

THE ARBITRATION REVOLUTION

For much of the nineteenth century arbitration was the primary objective of internationalist and peace societies. There were different variants of the arbitration concept, but all boiled down to the stipulation that nations agree to submit their differences to impartial adjudication before resorting to the use of armed force. As early as the 1840s the APS and its president William Jay championed the idea of requiring nations to incorporate arbitration procedures into international agreements. Jay and his colleagues focused on Anglo-American relations as the easiest and most likely place to begin a broader global effort to institutionalize arbitration. They argued that binding arbitration agreements would increase international security and diminish the likelihood of war.[7]

The arbitration issue catapulted to the top of the public agenda in 1871 when the famous *Alabama* case was successfully resolved through third-party mediation. This dispute over US demands for Civil War indemnity was settled by a five-member international tribunal, whose judgment was accepted by the US and British governments in the Treaty of Washington. The *Alabama* decision gave a major impetus to peace movement demands for the strengthening of international law.[8] The case touched off a flurry of political activity on behalf of arbitration. In 1873 British peace leaders W. Randal Cremer and Henry Richard secured passage of a resolution in the House of Commons calling for the arbitration of international disputes. In the United States Senator Charles Sumner introduced a similar measure endorsing the principle of third party arbitration that was approved by both houses of Congress.[9] In France Frédéric Passy gained 112 signatures from

---

[7] DeBenedetti, *The Peace Reform in American History*, 47.

[8] Sandi E. Cooper, *Patriotic Pacifism: Waging War in Europe, 1815–1914* (New York: Oxford University Press, 1991), 46.

[9] Charles Chatfield, *The American Peace Movement: Ideals and Activism* (New York: Twayne Publishers, 1992), 13.

members of the Chamber of Deputies in support of a Franco-American arbitration agreement. Similar campaigns on behalf of arbitration emerged in the Netherlands, Italy, Belgium, Austria, Switzerland, Sweden, Denmark, and Canada.[10]

In 1873 European supporters of arbitration founded the *Association pour la réforme et la codification du droit des gens*, which in 1897 became the International Law Association. Its members included lawyers, business executives, bankers, and government officials. In the United States, Frederick Stanton, the former governor of Kansas, formed the National Arbitration League.[11] In London pacifist and advocate of industrial cooperation Hodgson Pratt established the International Arbitration and Peace Association, which in 1881 attracted delegates from eighteen nations to an international arbitration assembly in Brussels.[12] In 1895 Belgian scholar Édouard Descamps developed an incremental strategy to win political support for arbitration, proposing the creation of voluntary tribunals to address noncontroversial issues. This was the basis upon which the Permanent Court of Arbitration was established at the 1899 Hague Peace Conference. Descamps and other progressives hoped that the beginning of arbitration, even if on a limited basis, would establish the habit of third party mediation among nations, and that the practice would become steadily more institutionalized and extend to matters of national security.[13]

At the turn of the century the campaign for arbitration and international law expanded further. The American Society of International Law was founded in 1906, and the American Society for the Judicial Settlement of International Disputes emerged in 1910. These efforts were supported by some of the nation's wealthiest and most influential industrialists, including John Hays Hammond, John D. Rockefeller, and Andrew Carnegie. In 1907 tens of thousands of Americans, including cabinet officers, senators, and Supreme Court justices, packed a four-day national arbitration and peace congress in New York, which DeBenedetti described as "the largest and most respectable peace rally in American history" up to that time.[14] Bilateral arbitration agreements between governments began to spread. In the 1890s sixty-three successful arbitration decisions were reached. More than a hundred bilateral treaties incorporating arbitration provisions were signed between 1903 and 1910.[15] Most of these arbitration agreements covered

---

[10] Cooper, *Patriotic Pacifism*, 48, 56.   [11] DeBenedetti, *The Peace Reform in American History*, 65.
[12] Cooper, *Patriotic Pacifism*, 47, 53–4.   [13] *Ibid.*, 93–5.
[14] DeBenedetti, *The Peace Reform in American History*, 82–3.   [15] Cooper, *Patriotic Pacifism*, 91, 115.

commercial matters rather than vital security issues, but they were none-theless indications of the spreading reach of international law.

As support for international law and arbitration mounted, conservative defenders of national self-interest began to circle the wagons. Many political leaders were in favor of arbitration as a general principle, but were unwilling to accept meaningful constraints on their authority to initiate military action or defend imperial interests. When Washington and London nego-tiated a treaty in 1897 that included provisions for the arbitration of disputes, the US Senate first emasculated the treaty and then refused to ratify it. Conservative senators objected to the requirement for arbitration as an infringement on US sovereignty and interference with the Senate's prerogative in foreign affairs.[16] A few years later a similar drama unfolded when the Taft administration submitted to the Senate two arbitration treaties, one each for Britain and France. The 1911 agreements followed a remarkably successful round of peacemaking diplomacy by Secretary of State Elihu Root that produced twenty-four bilateral arbitration conven-tions. Once again nationalist voices in the Senate, supported by former president Theodore Roosevelt, objected to any dilution of sovereign rights and attached reservations that gutted the treaties. A frustrated Taft admin-istration abandoned the effort, thus ending further attempts to institution-alize arbitration in the prewar years.[17] The political resistance that blocked these arbitration agreements was a harbinger of the opposition that pre-vented US entry into the League of Nations a few years later.

Although the vast international effort for arbitration failed to win support for the mediation of security disputes, the internationalist movement none-theless achieved some progress. The arbitration campaigns of the nine-teenth and early twentieth centuries laid the groundwork for the development of institutionalized conflict resolution mechanisms in subse-quent decades. The creation of the Permanent Court of International Justice at the Hague in 1922 was in many respects a fulfillment of the ideas and principles advocated by prewar peace leaders. The International Court of Justice created by the UN Charter was a further embodiment of these ideas. Ad hoc UN mediation efforts over the decades have prevented or resolved hundreds of conflicts. All of these developments are rooted in the principles of arbitration that arose in the nineteenth century.

DeBenedetti described the decades before World War I as a golden age for internationalism. The movement for international law enjoyed lavish

---

[16] Chatfield, *The American Peace Movement*, 14.
[17] DeBenedetti, *The Peace Reform in American History*, 88–9.

financial backing, thanks mainly to Andrew Carnegie, and had the support of key political decision makers. Presidents, prime ministers, Members of Parliament, and ministers from many countries supported or attended national and international conferences and advocated the creation of an international court to institutionalize the arbitration of disputes among nations. Never before or since have peace advocates enjoyed such high levels of legitimacy and financial backing. Yet these optimistic attempts to build the foundations of international law failed to prevent the horrors of World War I.

The experience of the arbitration movement revealed the limitations of internationalism, which was characterized by what DeBenedetti termed "narrow class vision, political conservatism, and optimistic nationalism."[18] The political elites who backed this movement assumed naïvely that the mere existence of arbitration mechanisms would convince nations to settle their disputes without bloodshed. Their support for the established political order meant accepting a system that was becoming increasingly militarized and linked to vast networks of imperialism. Internationalists did little to address the accelerating competition in armaments production and its destabilizing effects. When the administration of Theodore Roosevelt proposed building battleships for the US fleet, the APS took no stand on the issue.[19] When the war began, many internationalists closed ranks behind their national colors.

A LEAGUE OF NATIONS

For centuries peace advocates had proposed the creation of a congress of nations as an indispensable means of preventing war. The earliest political philosophers recognized that the anarchy of nation states created constant strife and competition for power. The absence of an accepted supreme authority to regulate the interactions among states leaves each nation alone, forced to resort to "self-help" (i.e. war) to defend its sovereign rights. Enlightenment thinkers argued that trends toward cooperation among nations were also evident, and that states could better protect their security and solve common problems by strengthening multilateral mechanisms. By subordinating some of their individual sovereignty for the sake of mutual benefit, states could mitigate the consequences of anarchy and reduce the threat of war.

[18] *Ibid.*, 105.   [19] Chatfield, *The American Peace Movement*, 25.

One of the earliest proposals for international organization came from the French monk, Émeric Crucé, in *Le Nouveau Cynée* in 1623. Similar proposals were offered by William Penn, *Essay Toward the Present and Future Peace of Europe*, 1693, and the Abbé de Saint-Pierre, *Project of Perpetual Peace*, 1712. Many of the early proposals for international organization focused on the states of Europe, but Crucé's proposal was universal. Crucé envisioned a federation not only of European states but of Turkey, Persia, India, China, and the kingdoms in Africa, along with the Vatican and representatives of the Jews. The early proposals for international organization had common features: (1) a central council of government representatives whose decisions would be binding on all members; (2) procedures for negotiation and the arbitration of disputes among member nations; and (3) an international court of adjudication to resolve differences. Many of the internationalist plans also included enforcement provisions based on the principle of collective security. The members of an international organization would pledge to use collective military force if necessary to compel aggressors or reluctant states to comply with common decisions. Even the Quaker William Penn proposed a plan for collective security. In the event of a nation resorting to arms unilaterally or refusing to accept arbitration, Penn wrote, "all other Sovereignties, united as one strength, shall compel the submission" of the recalcitrant state.[20]

In 1914 many peace advocates saw the lack of effective machinery for resolving interstate disputes as a major cause of the world war. In Britain the Union of Democratic Control, which formed immediately after the outbreak of hostilities, linked its demand for greater democratic control of foreign policy with a call for the creation of an international peace organization and an international council to settle disputes among nations.[21] In both Britain and the United States major campaigns developed to advocate the creation of an international organization that would keep the peace. In March 1915 a group of eminent British leaders formed the League of Nations Society, calling for a league with the authority and enforcement machinery to settle international disputes and impose sanctions against aggressors.

In the United States a similar prestigious group formed under the leadership of former president William Howard Taft. In June 1915 some 120 prominent leaders in business, education, law, and politics gathered at

---

[20] William Penn, *An Essay towards the Present and Future Peace of Europe: By the Establishment of an European Diet, Parliament, or Estates* (London: Peace Committee of the Society of Friends, 1936), 18.

[21] Michael Howard, *War and the Liberal Conscience* (New Brunswick, NJ: Rutgers University Press, 1989), 76.

Independence Hall in Philadelphia to found the League to Enforce Peace (LEP). The LEP platform called for a postwar assembly of nations in which disputes between countries would be submitted to an international tribunal that would arbitrate disputes and render binding decisions. A nation waging war without first submitting its grievances to the tribunal would be subject to economic and military sanctions. The LEP plan called for a world organization that could "prevent war by forcing its members to try peaceable settlement first."[22] The LEP had 4,000 branches in forty-seven states and exerted considerable influence on public opinion.[23] It benefited from substantial financial support and had a staff of twenty-three full-time workers, making it, in DeBenedetti's words, "the most powerful wartime pressure group on behalf of the ideal of a postwar league of nations." The LEP succeeded in building substantial political support for a postwar League of Nations prior to the US entry into the war. Once the USA entered the fray the LEP launched a major campaign to persuade the public that the war was being waged for the sake of an international organization that would preserve peace in the future.[24]

WILSON'S VISION

No one played a more significant role in creating the postwar League of Nations than Woodrow Wilson. As internationalist scholar Leland Goodrich observed, "[h]ad it not been for President Wilson's insistence that the League Covenant be made an integral part of the peace settlement ... it is quite unlikely that any League of Nations would have been established."[25] As a committed internationalist and peace supporter Wilson had long espoused arbitration and the strengthening of international law and multilateral cooperation. Wilson's deeply held beliefs and interactions with progressives and internationalists helped to shape his vision of a postwar League of Nations, which he began to advocate in 1916 and promoted during his reelection campaign that year.

In January 1917 Wilson gave his famous "Peace Without Victory" speech to the US Senate. The address was intended to outline the terms upon which a future peace agreement should be established. The creation of a League of Nations, Wilson declared, was the central goal of a future peace

[22] League to Enforce Peace, *Enforced Peace* (New York: The League to Enforce Peace, 1916), 13–15, 131.
[23] Thomas J. Knock, *To End All Wars: Woodrow Wilson and the Quest for a New World Order* (New York: Oxford University Press, 1992), 56.
[24] DeBenedetti, *The Peace Reform in American History*, 92–3, 98.
[25] Leland M. Goodrich, *The United Nations* (New York: Thomas Y. Crowell, 1959), 8–9.

settlement. The end of the war "must be followed by some definite concert of power which will make it virtually impossible that any such catastrophe should ever overwhelm us again." The United States must play a part in such organization, he insisted. "No covenant of cooperative peace that does not include the peoples of the New World can suffice to keep the future safe against war." He called for a collective security arrangement in which force would be used as a guarantee against any attempt to violate the peace. Wilson outlined four basic principles upon which the future peace must be built: equality of status among all nations, the right of self-government for all peoples, the assurance to every nation of access to the sea, and overcoming the problem of "great preponderating armaments."[26] Wilson thus committed the United States to a postwar organization that would not only provide collective security but guarantee equality of status, decolonization, open trade, and disarmament. Wilson's speech had an electrifying impact on progressive opinion within the United States and around the world.

Wilson's most famous address was his "Fourteen Points" speech delivered to a joint session of Congress in January 1918. It was hailed by the *New York Herald* as "one of the great documents in American history."[27] The first five points were a repetition of Wilson's earlier principles of progressive internationalism: (1) "open covenants openly arrived at" and the abolition of secret treaties; (2) freedom of the seas; (3) the removal of all economic trade barriers and support for equality of commerce; (4) the reduction of all national armaments to the lowest point consistent with domestic safety; and (5) the impartial settlement of colonial claims according to the principle of self-determination. Other points dealt with specific territorial adjustments. Wilson considered the fourteenth point most important: "A general association of nations must be formed under specific covenants for the purpose of affording mutual guarantees of political independence and territorial integrity to great and small states alike."[28]

The public response to Wilson's speech was overwhelmingly positive, but many political leaders in the United States and Europe were deeply skeptical of the proposed League of Nations. In the US Senate Republicans led by Henry Cabot Lodge and William Borah spoke out against the president's plan and mounted a campaign of opposition that would

---

[26] Woodrow Wilson, "Essential Terms for Peace in Europe" (speech, US Senate, 22 January 1919). Reprinted in Mario R. DiNunzio, ed., *Woodrow Wilson: Essential Writings and Speeches of the Scholar-President* (New York: New York University Press, 2006), 391–7.

[27] Quoted in Knock, *To End All Wars*, 144.

[28] Woodrow Wilson, "The Fourteen Points" (speech, US Congress (joint session), 18 January 1918). Reprinted in DiNunzio, *Woodrow Wilson*, 403–7.

ultimately doom the prospects for US participation. Prime Minister Lloyd George sent word from London that Wilson's ideas were "entirely in harmony" with his own, but he was not in favor of an association of nations that would limit Britain's freedom of action. A US Treasury official traveling in Europe at the time reported that Lloyd George "laughed at the proposed League in my presence, and [French leader] M. Clemenceau has sneered at it."[29] The prospects for support of Wilson's grandiose agenda were diminished further in Britain when the Conservatives won a major victory in the so-called khaki election of December 1918, and many of the strongest advocates of the League, including Arthur Ponsonby, H. N. Brailsford, and Arthur Henderson, were voted out of office. During the election campaign Lloyd George had pandered to public feelings of hatred and vindictiveness toward Germany.[30] Wilson's idealism and progressive internationalism thus clashed head on with conservative nationalism.

Wilson was convinced of his ability to persuade, however, and he went to the postwar peace conference determined to win support for a postwar League. On his way to the meeting with heads of state at Versailles he conducted a triumphant tour of European cities and was hailed as a hero for justice and peace. In Paris an unprecedented crowd of two million cheered "Wilson, the Just." In Rome vast throngs gathered behind banners reading "Welcome to the God of Peace." In Milan he was proclaimed "The Moses from Across the Atlantic."[31] It is hard to imagine today the extent to which Wilson came to embody the hopes of people throughout the world for an end to war and a more peaceful future. He strode across the stage of history as a savior to deliver humankind from the scourge of war. H. G. Wells wrote at the time,

For a brief interval Wilson stood alone for [humankind] . . . in that brief interval there was a very extraordinary and significant wave of response to him throughout the earth. So eager was the situation that all humanity leapt to accept and glorify Wilson . . . It seized upon him as its symbol. He was transfigured . . . He ceased to be a common statesman; he became a Messiah.[32]

The political leaders of Europe were unimpressed. They dug in their heels to resist Wilson's vision, especially on the question of self-determination for former colonies. According to historian Thomas Knock, "the quarrel

[29] Woodrow Wilson, 5 July 1918, in *Woodrow Wilson: Life and Letters*, vol. VIII, ed. Ray Stannard Baker (Garden City, NY: Doubleday, Page & Co., 1927–39), 253.
[30] Knock, *To End All Wars*, 198–9.
[31] *Ibid.*, 195.   [32] H. G. Wells, *The Shape of Things to Come* (New York: Macmillan, 1936), 82.

over colonies collided with the League of Nations with perhaps greater force than any other issue at the peace conference."[33] Wilson was horrified by the insistence of the major powers on maintaining their colonies and dividing the spoils of the former German possessions. His hopes for a trusteeship arrangement that would end the colonial era were disappointed. The scramble for additional territories, Wilson believed, reflected a "fundamental lack of faith in the League of Nations." If the process of annexation went on, "the League of Nations would be discredited from the beginning."[34] The hypocrisy of the major powers on the colonial question was a major factor in undermining the legitimacy of the Versailles Treaty and the entire peace conference.

Although the postwar system was constructed by the victors as a means of preserving their power and privileges, the Covenant of the League nonetheless contained some concessions to Wilsonian idealism and incorporated many of the proposals that had been advocated by internationalist groups and peace societies. States joining the League were obligated to respect the territorial integrity and political independence of each member nation. They were required to submit disputes to the League Council for arbitration and peaceful resolution. Member states accepted the need for arms reduction and agreed to develop plans for mutual disarmament. They created a mandate system for guiding the subjected nations and colonies of the defeated powers toward self-determination. (No such provision was provided for the colonies of the victorious powers, much to the chagrin of nationalist leaders who gathered at Versailles, including the young Ho Chi Minh.)

The dispute settlement and collective security architecture of the Covenant was especially ambitious, reflecting Wilson's desire to create a mechanism that would replace the balance of power system among nations. Articles 12 through 15 of the Covenant required members to bring any dispute to the League for arbitration by its Council or the Permanent Court of International Justice. States were required to refrain from military action for a three-month cooling off period and were prohibited from waging war in violation of League procedures and arbitration judgments. Article 16 of the Covenant, which was entitled "Sanctions of Pacific Settlement," was the heart of the collective security system. A member state going to war in violation of League procedures would "*ipso facto*, be deemed to have committed an act of war against all other Members." In response those members would be required to isolate and impose trade and financial

---

[33] Knock, *To End All Wars*, 213. [34] Quoted in *ibid.*, 211.

sanctions against the violating state. The Council would also be required to determine what military force would be used "to protect the covenants of the League."[35] The proposed system contained loopholes and did not outlaw war entirely, but it nonetheless represented a significant step toward international acceptance of the principles of collective security.

THE CHALLENGE OF SUPPORTING THE LEAGUE

The peacemaking provisions of the League were delivered as part of a vindictive and highly punitive Versailles peace agreement that was fatally flawed and that many feared would foster revanchism and renewed war. The British Labour Party described the Versailles Treaty as "a capitalist, militarist and imperialist imposition. It aggravates every evil which existed before 1914."[36] In the United States peace leader Oswald Garrison Villard excoriated the Paris agreement as a piece of "intrigue, selfish aggression, and naked imperialism." The terms of the treaty violated Wilson's principles, he wrote, and left the president "discredited and condemned."[37] The "Versailles diktat," as it was called, imposed extremely harsh conditions on Germany, preserved the imperial privileges of Britain and France, rejected the nationalist aspirations of colonized peoples, and exacerbated underlying economic and social tensions. In all these aspects it increased the likelihood of war.[38] Dutch pacifist Bart de Ligt rejected not only the treaty but the League of Nations as well. He considered the organization a "false . . . Messiah," a mechanism for preserving an imperialist system that was the fundamental cause of war.[39]

Peace advocates were placed in a difficult situation. They rightly condemned the provisions of the Versailles Treaty, but most actively supported the creation of the League of Nations. Pacifist groups described the treaty as a betrayal of peace ideals, but they portrayed the League as "a landmark on the road to world peace," hoping that multilateral decision making would tame great power politics.[40] They lobbied to democratize the League's structure and improve its peacemaking potential. They advocated a

---

[35] League of Nations, *The Covenant of the League of Nations* (Boston, World Peace Foundation, 1920), 49.

[36] Howard, *War and the Liberal Conscience*, 84.   [37] Quoted in Knock, *To End All Wars*, 253–4.

[38] John Maynard Keynes, *The Economic Consequences of the Peace* (London: Macmillan, 1920).

[39] Quoted in Herman Noordegraaf, "The Anarchopacifism of Bart de Ligt," in *Challenge to Mars: Essays on Pacifism from 1918 to 1945*, ed. Peter Brock and Thomas P. Socknat (Toronto: University of Toronto Press, 1999), 94–5.

[40] A. C. F. Beales, *The History of Peace: A Short Account of the Organised Movements for International Peace* (London: G. Bell, 1931), 318.

strengthening of the League's arbitration procedures and greater efforts toward disarmament. They urged the admission of the Soviet Union and Germany as League members. They campaigned for decolonization and the admission to the League of former colonies and smaller states. The desire to strengthen the League and fulfill the principles embodied in its Covenant dominated the agenda of peace and internationalist organizations throughout the next decade and into the 1930s.

The debate over the mission of the League of Nations and the shape of the postwar world reflected the continuing divide between progressive and conservative internationalism. In the United States the progressive camp included liberal leaders within the Democratic Party but also leftists and socialists outside the political mainstream, such as Jane Addams of the Woman's Peace Party (WPP) and Lillian Wald and Amos Pinchot of the American Union against Militarism (AUAM). The progressives supported the League but they did so in the hope of altering the existing state system to address the underlying causes of war – suppressed nationalism, inequality, and economic exploitation.[41] They wanted an organization that would work for justice and help to create a more equitable international political and economic order. The conservatives sought to preserve the status quo and protect the existing system of privilege. Led in the United States by Taft and the LEP they supported international law and arbitration as means of securing the established order. They believed in the "civilizing" mission of colonial rule. They were comfortable with political leadership by enlightened elites, in whose company they placed themselves.

Advocacy on behalf of the League was strongest in Britain and had a decidedly conservative character. In 1919 prominent British internationalists formed the LNU, which was led by Lord Robert (later Viscount) Cecil, a cabinet minister and Conservative Party member who played a significant role in the interwar years advocating on behalf of international cooperation and the League. Government officials participated in the LNU leadership structure, and the prime minister was usually listed as honorary president, with cabinet officers registered as LNU vice-presidents. (Ironically the only prime minister who declined to be so listed was Labour leader Ramsay MacDonald.) The LNU was founded and led by elites but enjoyed political support throughout British society. It had branches in every part of the country and among all social groups. It was enormously influential in organizing church, women's, and student groups. The LNU reflected

---

[41] Chatfield, *The American Peace Movement*, 48–50.

"a broad consensus of all parties and all classes," according to Michael Howard.[42] "Never before or since," wrote Martin Ceadel, "has a peace association enjoyed such support and status."[43] It was by far the largest peace membership group in Britain, peaking at approximately 400,000 dues-paying members in the early 1930s.[44] Its mission was to "secure the whole-hearted acceptance by the British people of the League of Nations as . . . the final arbiter in international differences, and the supreme instrument for removing injustices which may threaten the peace of the world." It also sought the "progressive limitation of armaments . . . in all countries."[45]

Support for the League of Nations was widespread throughout Europe and beyond. An International Federation of League of Nations Societies was created in Brussels in December 1919 with representation from sixteen countries.[46] In France religious groups and women's organizations joined with traditional peace and rights groups to form associations that worked to build political support for the League. The APD carried on the internationalist tradition of the prewar years into advocacy for the League. It cooperated closely with the *Union internationale des associations pour la Société des nations*, with the philosopher Théodore Ruyssen serving as leader of both groups.[47] French groups advocated a stronger and more democratic League and greater steps toward international cooperation. Some promoted the idea of a United States of Europe, which would operate as a separate entity but work in parallel with and help to strengthen the League of Nations. In Germany a reborn peace movement was sharply critical of the Versailles Treaty, for obvious reasons, but activists supported the League of Nations and campaigned for early German admission (which came in 1926). German peace groups were loosely federated within the German Peace Cartel, which in 1928 had twenty-two member groups representing some 100,000 members.[48] Like most of their compatriots German peace advocates considered French control of the Rhineland and the onerous impositions of Versailles completely unacceptable and contrary to the spirit of peace. They pleaded for an end to sanctions and other postwar punishments. In nearly every country in Europe League of Nations Associations emerged to build public support for the new organization.

---

[42] Howard, *War and the Liberal Conscience*, 86.
[43] Martin Ceadel, "A Legitimate Peace Movement: The Case of Interwar Britain, 1918–1945," in *Challenge to Mars*, 134–48, 139.
[44] Lynch, *Beyond Appeasement*, 99.　　[45] Quoted in *ibid.*, 31.
[46] Birn, *The League of Nations Union 1918–1945*, 13–14.
[47] Norman Ingram, *The Politics of Dissent: Pacifism in France 1919–1939* (Oxford: Clarendon Press, 1991), 21–2.
[48] Guido Grünewald, "War Resisters in Weimar Germany," in *Challenge to Mars*, 67–88, 69.

Ironically and tragically support for the League was weakest in the United States. This was in large part because of Wilson's inability to mobilize political support for his vision. Prior to the peace conference he had been unwilling to share his thinking about the League with the public or members of Congress, thus alienating both conservative and progressive camps. Senate Republicans were able to use Wilson's aloofness and political weakness (compounded by his failing health) to undermine support for a postwar League. Progressives and internationalists were repulsed by the provisions of the Versailles Treaty. Wilson lost support among progressives by acquiescing to rising racial violence in the United States and the suppression of civil liberties during the war and afterwards.[49] Wilson undercut his domestic political position at the very moment he most needed allies to counter Republican opponents in the Senate. Peace advocates watched helplessly and with a sense of foreboding as Republicans attached crippling reservations to the League Covenant and then sent the treaty down to defeat. The senators who rejected the League did not wish to see US sovereignty compromised by membership in an international organization. Underlying this concern was a desire to avoid US entanglement in the military affairs of Europe. Some in the peace community shared these isolationist sentiments. They felt that Americans had been deceived about the nature and purpose of the war. Soldiers had been sent to fight not for democracy but to preserve a corrupt system of imperial privilege and militarism. The fact that the League was embedded in an unjust peace agreement reinforced the skepticism of conservatives and progressives alike.

Despite the lack of US participation prominent internationalists campaigned to support the League. In 1923 members of the former LEP joined with other internationalists to form the League of Nations Non-Partisan Association, which later became simply the League of Nations Association. Unlike its British counterpart the League of Nations Association did not attract a mass following, peaking at approximately 19,000 members in 1930.[50] Its primary focus in the 1920s was campaigning for US membership in the League's Permanent Court of International Justice, also known as the World Court.[51] It was hoped that participation in the Court would be a first step toward eventual membership in the League itself, but US leaders refused to take even that initial step.

---

[49] DeBenedetti, *The Peace Reform in American History*, 102.   [50] Lynch, *Beyond Appeasement*, 32.
[51] DeBenedetti, *The Peace Reform in American History*, 113.

OUTLAWING WAR

As pacifist sentiment grew in the years after World War I a movement developed to outlaw war. The idea originated in the United States with Chicago attorney Samuel Levinson, who pointed out that war remained legal under international law. The League Covenant permitted states to take "such action as they shall consider necessary" if the Council did not reach unanimous agreement.[52] As long as war was still considered a legitimate act of statecraft, Levinson and others argued, national leaders would continue to use it as the expected means of settling differences. The answer was obvious: war must be outlawed. In support of that aim Levinson joined with philosopher John Dewey and others to form the American Committee for the Outlawry of War in 1921, which campaigned on behalf of a treaty prohibiting war.

The seemingly simple idea of outlawing war contained conceptual contradictions. What should be done if states signed the proposed treaty but then ignored its provisions and proceeded with military action against another country? Many argued that the prohibition against war had to include a commitment to apply sanctions against violators, perhaps including collective military action. This was the idea of collective security as embodied in the Covenant. On the other hand if the prohibition was merely a moral principle, with no enforcement mechanism, it would be a meaningless gesture with no practical effect. The logic of the proposal thus pointed toward the need for some form of enforcement mechanism, which meant membership in the League. Many of the members of the committee on outlawry had supported US participation in the League, but they knew that this was not possible politically after the bitter debates of 1919–20. They hoped that outlawry would be a way of achieving the goals of the League by other means.

The outlawry movement emerged at the time when the US government was considering membership in the World Court. Levinson recognized that US participation in the World Court was not realistic and wanted to keep the concept of outlawry separate from debates over US involvement in international institutions. Borah and other Senate isolationists had different ideas. They seized upon the outlawry concept as a way of derailing support for the World Court, favoring a treaty against war that would avoid any entanglements or collective commitments that might lead to war. Peace

---

[52] The Covenant of the League of Nations, Article 15(7), reprinted in Goodrich, *The United Nations*, 341.

advocates were caught in a political crossfire. Support for one of their goals, outlawry of war, was used to undermine another, US membership in the World Court. Pacifists and internationalists tried to find a formula that would allow support for both, drafting a "harmony plan" in 1924 for US entry into the World Court on the condition that the Court would outlaw war. Borah and his isolationist colleagues were unpersuaded. They were determined to keep the United States out of any international institution that might imply an obligation to become involved in the military disputes of other nations. Borah joined with other members of the Senate to attach a series of rigid reservations to the World Court proposal, thus effectively scuttling US participation. The only option left for pacifists and internationalists was outlawry, and a watered down and toothless version at that.

Outlawry jumped to the center of international political attention in 1927 when James T. Shotwell, a prominent internationalist who had been an adviser to the Wilson administration, suggested the idea of outlawing war to French Foreign Minister Aristide Briand. The French minister quickly embraced the concept and proposed a US-French treaty that would outlaw war and bind the two sides to the arbitration of disputes. Borah was suspicious of Briand's bilateral proposal and wanted to avoid an agreement that might obligate the United States to come to the defense of France or any other nation. He convinced Secretary of State Frank Kellogg to negotiate on the basis of the principle "renounce all war or no war at all."[53] Paris accepted Washington's demands, and the two sides quickly concluded negotiations for the Treaty on the Renunciation of War, known as the Kellogg–Briand Pact or the Pact of Paris. In August 1928 representatives of dozens of nations, including the United States and the other major powers, gathered for an elaborate ceremony in Paris at which they signed the treaty and solemnly pledged to renounce war as an instrument of national policy.[54]

Peace advocates were unimpressed by the grandstanding in Paris. Critics pointed out that the treaty had no mechanism for enforcing the pious pledges of its signers. It was merely a statement of intention, and not a very convincing one at that. The treaty was accompanied by a memorandum that exempted wars of self-defense. The British Foreign Office attempted to insert a reservation to protect the "special and vital interest" of the empire. Although Kellogg squelched that effort, few doubted that the United States, Britain, and other powers would reserve the right to use force

---

[53] Charles DeBenedetti, *Origins of the Modern American Peace Movement, 1915–1929* (Millwood, NY: KTO Press, 1978), 205.
[54] DeBenedetti, *The Peace Reform in American History*, 120.

in their respective spheres of influence. At the very moment that US diplomats were signing the Pact of Paris, US troops were maintaining their military occupation of Nicaragua and Congress was approving the largest naval appropriations Bill in peacetime history.[55]

A treaty outlawing war should have been the apotheosis of the peace movement, the goal pacifists had sought passionately for so many centuries: a formal commitment by nations to end war and settle disputes through peaceful means. The very fact that the treaty existed was a powerful tribute to the force of public opinion against war, and to the very considerable lobbying effort of peace organizations. Negotiation of the treaty "capped a decade of achievement for pacifists and internationalists," wrote Norman Ingram.[56] The revulsion against the slaughter of war was so intense, and public advocacy for international cooperation so widespread, that political leaders felt obligated to respond. Kellogg admitted as much in a message to Briand: "there is a tremendous demand in this country and probably in foreign countries for the so-called outlawry of war."[57] Yet the very activists who campaigned to end war were the most skeptical of the resulting agreement and understood only too well that it would do little or nothing to reduce the likelihood of armed conflict.

The debate over the Pact of Paris reflected an underlying contradiction that has plagued peace advocacy throughout history and remains unresolved to this day: how to balance the principle of noninterference with the challenge of collective security. The system of international law that Grotius developed and that was codified at Westphalia was based on the preservation of state sovereignty. States were not to intervene militarily in the affairs of others. The League of Nations, on the other hand, was an attempt to create a system of collective security, in which member states would be obligated to submit disputes to international arbitration, and would be required to take action, including the use of military force, in response to aggression and violations of international law. The debate over intervention and collective security continued and intensified into the 1930s. When critical challenges to international peace emerged in Manchuria, Ethiopia, Spain, and Czechoslovakia, political leaders were put to the test and failed to respond. The solemn vows of the Kellogg–Briand Pact and the Covenant of the League of Nations were ignored.

Many peace advocates were skeptical of the collective security concept and doubtful that a League dominated by the major imperial powers would

[55] *Ibid.*, 120.   [56] Ingram, *The Politics of Dissent*, 55.
[57] Quoted in Lynch, *Beyond Appeasement*, 146.

be able to act decisively against aggression. As philosopher Bertrand Russell wrote, it was unrealistic to expect that members of the League would use military force to block Japanese aggression in Manchuria. The British government had friendly relations with Japan, France was preoccupied closer to home, and both governments were busy policing their colonial possessions. Similar self-interested calculations prevented collective action during the crises in Ethiopia and Spain. To counter fascist aggression would have required a substantial military commitment and perhaps major combat, which could have spread into the general conflagration that political leaders were attempting to avoid. "Nations will only go to war," Russell observed, "when they believe their national interests to be involved; and the enforcement of international law is not yet recognized as in itself a national interest."[58] The desire to use the League's collective security machinery was based on peace sentiment, yet it depended upon the willingness to wage war. This inherent contradiction crippled the League and has plagued the United Nations as well.

The League of Nations was an obvious failure, but as Goodrich observed, to speak of the League failing is misleading, since responsibility for its effectiveness, or lack thereof, rested with specific government leaders in the leading states. The League did not have autonomy or separate authority apart from that of its leading members. It was like the United Nations today, a loose federation not a unitary organization, and had no powers over and above those of its member states. Individual nations did not find it in their interest to employ the machinery that was created at Versailles. There were many reasons for this, some having to do with the vindictive nature of the postwar settlement, others with the continuing imperial ambitions of the major powers, and in the United States with an isolationist impulse that rejected collective engagement with other nations. Some argued that the League was doomed from the outset because it was not sufficiently universal or comprehensive. Only a truly supranational authority, Einstein and other idealists believed, could prevent aggression. The halfhearted and contradictory provisions of the Covenant were inadequate to the task of preventing war.

Political realists argued that the failure of the League was proof that international peace and security cannot be guaranteed by international legal mechanisms or collective institutions. Peace can only be maintained through the creation of a balance of power among nations. As Goodrich

---

[58] Bertrand Russell, *Which Way to Peace?* (Plymouth, Great Britain: Michael Joseph Ltd, 1937), 68.

noted, however, the specific failures of the League in the 1930s were not the result of inadequacies in the balance of power or flaws in the architecture of the League. They were the result of the shortsightedness, confusion, and political incompetence of the government leaders of the time. "It was not the assumptions that were wrong or the system that was defective; rather, it was a human failure, the inability of peoples and governments to develop and carry out" policies that were in their own best interests.[59] The problem was not that the concept of international organization was tried and found wanting. The concept was never really tried.

[59] Goodrich, *The United Nations*, 17–18.

4

Facing fascism

The appeasement of Nazi Germany at Munich in 1938 has cast a long and enduring shadow over international affairs and the debate about pacifism. According to conventional interpretations pacifism led to appeasement and isolationism, which left Britain and other countries vulnerable to fascist aggression. Walter Lippmann wrote, "The preachment and the practice of pacifists in Britain and America ... were the cause of the failure to keep pace with the growth of German and Japanese armaments. They led to the policy of so-called appeasement."[1] Reinhold Niebuhr held similar views. "Nazi tyranny was allowed to grow ... because so many citizens of a Christian civilization were prevented by these (pacifist) scruples from resisting the monster when there was yet time."[2] Neville Chamberlain was forced to yield to Hitler's demands, according to this view, because of the pervasiveness and influence of pacifist pressure. Variations on this theme have permeated debates about war and peace ever since. In August 2006 US Defense Secretary Donald Rumsfeld evoked the memory of appeasement to challenge critics of Bush administration policy in Iraq. The world today faces "similar challenges in ... the rising threat of a new type of fascism," Rumsfeld claimed, warning that "some seem not to have learned history's lessons."[3]

The claim that pacifists were responsible for the political vacillations and mistakes that led to World War II is profoundly mistaken. Cecelia Lynch demonstrated in her masterful account *Beyond Appeasement* that the majority of those associated with interwar peace campaigns were opposed to appeasement and favored a forceful response to fascist aggression. As Martin

---

[1] Walter Lippmann, *US Foreign Policy: Shield of the Republic* (Boston: Little, Brown & Co., 1943), 53.
[2] Quoted in G. H. C. Macgregor, *The New Testament Basis of Pacifism and the Relevance of the Impossible Ideal* (Nyack, NY: Fellowship Publications, 1954), 126.
[3] Donald Rumsfeld, "Transcript: Rumsfeld's speech to the American Legion" (address, 88th Annual American Legion National Convention, Salt Lake City, Utah, 29 August 2006). Available online at Stars and Stripes, www.estripes.com/article.asp?section=104&article=38796&archive=true (accessed 23 October 2006).

Ceadel wrote, the isolationists, defeatists, and appeasers of the interwar era were not members of the peace movement but "fellow travelers" of that movement.[4] British, French, and US officials sometimes pandered to the widespread peace sentiment of the time, but they refused to adopt peace movement proposals that might have prevented war. As militarism advanced in Manchuria, Abyssinia (hereafter referred to as Ethiopia), Spain, and Czechoslovakia, peace groups criticized the inaction of Western governments and demanded a more forceful response. Internationalists in Britain, led by the LNU, were particularly active in opposing appeasement. Peace advocates in Britain, France, the United States, and other countries embraced an internationalist outlook and urged their governments to utilize the collective security machinery of the League of Nations. Many supported the use of coercive sanctions, including military measures, to counter the growing fascist threat.

To be sure some pacifists tried desperately to retain their purity. They rejected the use of military force under any circumstance. A few remained absolute pacifists even after Nazi armies attacked Poland and the Low Countries. In 1940 a handful of US peace advocates went so far as to ally with right-wing nationalists in the America First Committee. Isolationism, which emerged among nationalist Republicans, found converts on the left among those who could not accept the prospect of another world war. By the late 1930s, however, most of those who had previously embraced pacifism found themselves supporting the use of force against the rising Nazi menace. The advocates of absolute pacifism dwindled to a minuscule presence within society and were a minority even within the peace community. As Lynch wrote,

Most pacifists, despite their determination not to be involved in war preparations, opposed the appeasement of Italy . . . condemned Hitler's racist domestic policies, condemned German and Italian assistance to General Franco's forces in Spain, and expressed unease about Germany's foreign policy intentions.[5]

Most peace advocates were opposed to inaction and defeatism and were willing to support forceful action to protect nations threatened by war.

In this chapter I trace the trajectory of pacifism and internationalism in the interwar era and examine how peace advocates responded to the

[4] Martin Ceadel, "A Legitimate Peace Movement: The Case of Interwar Britain, 1918–1945," in *Challenge to Mars: Essays on Pacifism from 1918 to 1945*, ed. Peter Brock and Thomas P. Socknat, 134–48 (Toronto: University of Toronto Press, 1999), 135.

[5] Cecelia Lynch, *Beyond Appeasement: Interpreting Interwar Peace Movements in World Politics* (Ithaca, NY: Cornell University Press, 1999), 111.

excruciating dilemmas of confronting fascism while attempting to remain true to nonviolent principles. The period witnessed important expressions of absolute pacifism, but it featured even stronger and more broadly supported expressions of support for collective security, as confirmed in the remarkable Peace Ballot campaign of 1934–5 in Britain. Peace advocates and internationalists were often ahead of their governments in urging vigorous action to punish and deter fascist aggression. As the options for preventing war dwindled pacifism increasingly gave way to internationalism, which was interpreted narrowly under the circumstances as multilateral armed resistance to Hitler. Some radical pacifists tried to articulate a social justice perspective as an alternative to isolationism or military internationalism, but their voices were drowned out in the din of approaching war. The only option left was military struggle against fascism.

PEACE MOVEMENT REBORN

From the ashes of World War I new forms of peace activism emerged. Radical antimilitarist groups came to the fore, while the earlier more conservative peace societies declined. The previous emphasis on stability and order gave way to a concern for social reform and economic justice. The growing involvement of women gave new energy and political dynamism to the antiwar cause. Disillusionment with war spread throughout society. In literature, film, and the graphic arts the horrors of the recent bloodletting were graphically depicted and decried. Revelations of government deceit and incompetence fed the antimilitarist wave. Leading intellectuals, religious leaders, and scientists united in rejecting war. New peace leadership appeared, drawn from women's groups, social reform movements, and religious advocates of the Social Gospel.[6] These new leaders saw war as the product of imperialism and frustrated national ambition. They advocated self-determination and greater democratic control over political decision making as the keys to peace.

One of the most prominent of the new peace leaders was Jane Addams, who rose to fame in the late nineteenth century as founder of Hull House in Chicago and a leading social reformer on behalf of the poor. Addams's interest in peace and international affairs emerged in 1898 when she joined the growing anti-imperialist movement. She condemned militarism as a form of theft from the poor and considered her antiwar activism a logical

[6] Charles Chatfield, *The American Peace Movement: Ideals and Activism* (New York: Twayne Publishers, 1992), 31.

extension of her concern for social justice. Addams was a committed suffragist who believed that the political empowerment of women would help to reduce the frequency of war and advance the cause of the social reform. During World War I she helped to organize an International Congress of Women in the Hague that sought to end the conflict through mediation. Addams also joined suffragist leader Carrie Chapman Catt in creating the WPP.[7] This led to the creation in 1919 of the Women's International League for Peace and Freedom (WILPF), perhaps the world's first explicitly feminist-pacifist organization, which has remained active to the present. In 1931 Addams was awarded the Nobel Peace Prize.

Women played an increasingly prominent role in mobilizing peace sentiment. After winning the vote in 1920 women activists in the United States turned greater attention to the cause of preventing war. Some feminist leaders saw the growing peace movement as a unifying cause that could bind up the differences that emerged when some suffragists supported US entry into World War I. Once the war was over all could agree on the value of campaigning to prevent such a disaster in the future. The struggle for peace, which had divided the movement in 1917, thus became a unifying cause in the 1920s and 1930s. In Britain the political influence of women increased significantly following the Equal Franchise Act of 1928. The new law extended the vote to millions of women, who voted for the first time in the 1929 general election. In Britain and the United States working for peace became a focal point for women's newly acquired voting power. Feminism and pacifism increasingly converged.

During and after World War I several organizations dedicated to absolute pacifism emerged. In December 1914 a group of Christian pacifists dissatisfied with the pro-war stance of the mainline Protestant churches met in Cambridge, England, to form the Fellowship of Reconciliation (FOR) under the leadership of Quaker Henry T. Hodgkin.[8] A year later an FOR group formed in the United States. Among those who joined the fledgling pacifist fellowship was the young minister Norman Thomas, who believed that "war and Christianity are incompatible."[9] FOR has remained an active voice of religiously based absolute pacifism to the present.

---

[7] Charles DeBenedetti, *The Peace Reform in American History* (Bloomington, IN: Indiana University Press, 1980), 93–4.

[8] Peter Brock and Nigel Young, *Pacifism in the Twentieth Century* (Syracuse, NY: Syracuse University Press, 1999), 24.

[9] James C. Duram, "In Defense of Conscience: Norman Thomas as an Exponent of Christian Pacifism during World War I," *Journal of Presbyterian History* 52, no. 1 (spring 1974): 24.

In 1915 opponents of US involvement in the war formed the Anti-Preparedness Committee, which later evolved into the AUAM. This group worked against US involvement in the European war, opposed military intervention in Mexico in 1916, and criticized the increasingly repressive political climate in the United States as the war drew nearer. The AUAM later helped to create the National Council for Prevention of War, which was one of the most significant US peace organizations of the interwar era. To protect the rights of conscientious objectors and defend First Amendment freedoms AUAM formed a Civil Liberties Bureau, which later became the American Civil Liberties Union (in 1920) and has remained a stalwart defender of democratic freedoms to the present. The American Friends Service Committee (AFSC) was founded in 1917 to provide young Quakers and other conscientious objectors with an opportunity to serve those in need during World War I. In subsequent decades the AFSC broadened its humanitarian mission and increasingly focused on relieving the tensions that lead to armed conflict. The organization has served as a mainstay of public campaigns to oppose war and promote disarmament ever since. In 1924 veteran feminists and antiwar campaigners Tracy Mygatt, Frances Witherspoon, and Jessie Wallace Hughan founded the War Resisters League (WRL) as the US branch of War Resisters' International. The WRL began as a registry for those who refused to participate in war and after World War II evolved into an activist organization for nonviolent resistance. Although never a very large organization, with membership in the USA of only a few tens of thousands at its peak, the WRL nonetheless exerted considerable influence during times of antiwar mobilization and it remains active today.

PLEDGING WAR RESISTANCE

In the latter half of the 1920s a sense of moral outrage and repugnance at the folly of war became widespread and a significant movement for absolute pacifism developed. In 1925 Arthur Ponsonby launched his famous Peace Letter campaign, seeking signatures on a pledge to "refuse to support or render war service to any Government which resorts to arms." Ponsonby's appeal was enormously popular and brought in more than 128,000 signed pledges, which he delivered to the government in December 1927.[10] Ponsonby appealed for support on the basis of what he considered a new

[10] Martin Ceadel, *Pacifism in Britain 1914–1945: The Defining of a Faith* (Oxford: Clarendon Press, 1980), 80.

form of "utilitarian pacifism." War was objectionable not only on religious, moral, and humanitarian grounds, but on the basis of practical considerations as well. The recent world war had proved, Ponsonby contended, that the horrendous costs of modern war far exceeded any conceivable benefit that might result. This perspective was similar to that of scientific pacifism, which predicted at the turn of the century that industrialized war would lead to such mass slaughter that losses would inevitably outweigh gains. Utilitarian concerns thus combined with moral appeals in a broad public rejection of war.

As the movement for pacifism grew Albert Einstein lent his enormous prestige to the call for war resistance. He actively supported campaigns for conscientious objection and the refusal of military service. Einstein's espousal of war resistance reinforced a growing movement for absolute pacifism on British and US campuses. In 1930 he joined with Jane Addams, Sigmund Freud, Thomas Mann, H. G. Wells, Rabindranath Tagore, and other prominent intellectuals in an appeal against conscription and the military training of youth. He counseled "thoughtful, well-meaning and conscientious" people to accept a "solemn and unconditional obligation not to participate in any war."[11] During a December 1930 speech at the Ritz Carlton Hotel in New York Einstein offered his famous "two per cent" solution to the problem of war:

> Even if only two per cent of those assigned to perform military service should announce their refusal to fight, as well as urge means other than war of settling international disputes, governments would be powerless, they would not dare send such a large number of people to jail.

Einstein's speech generated considerable enthusiasm among pacifists. In the United States buttons reading "two per cent" began appearing on campuses and in communities.[12]

Not all pacifists were enthusiastic about Einstein's "two per cent" solution. The preeminent French pacifist Romain Rolland shared Einstein's commitment to war resistance but criticized the "deceptive promise" and "puerile assurances" of his plan for individual refusal. Given the increasingly industrial and technical nature of war and the development of air power and weapons of advanced destructiveness, Roland observed, it "becomes a matter of complete indifference to governments whether two or ten per cent of the population refuses military service."[13] Rolland was remarkably prescient in anticipating the trend toward technological warfare and

---

[11] Albert Einstein, *Einstein on Peace* (New York: Simon and Schuster, 1960), 91.
[12] *Ibid.*, 117–18.   [13] *Ibid.*, 119, 232.

recognizing that individualized resistance would never reach sufficient scale to cripple the war machine. He was an admirer of Einstein but also a devoted follower of Gandhi, and he advocated mass nonviolent action as an alternative means of preventing war and achieving social justice.

In February 1933 the call for refusing military service became the subject of a famous resolution at the Oxford Union. The specific proposal presented to the Union during one of its weekly debates was "That this House will in no circumstances fight for King and country."[14] The resolution was adopted by a vote of 275 to 153. The same resolution was debated and approved at other British universities, indicating considerable support for an absolute pacifist position among British students. Winston Churchill later decried the Oxford pledge as that "ever-shameful resolution," which supposedly displayed "decadent, degenerate Britain" to the calculating totalitarians in Germany, Russia, and Japan.[15] In truth the pledge was simply one modest expression of the widespread revulsion against war that existed in Britain at the time. The incident was blown out of proportion by the press and by the failed attempt of Randolph Churchill and other conservative Oxonians to expunge the "red" resolution. The broad support for the Oxford pledge reflected a deepening sense of revulsion at the narrow nationalism and uncritical patriotism that many saw as the root causes of war.

A similar movement emerged among students in the United States. Hundreds of thousands of US college students signed a pledge that they would not "support the United States government in any war it may conduct." This movement was led by young socialists and communists, who were able to work together in a rare united effort to mobilize the widespread youth pacifist sentiment that existed at the time. In April 1934 nearly 20,000 students across the country left their classrooms in a student strike to protest the mounting threat of war. The following year the student strike was even larger, as more than 150,000 protesters gathered on 130 campuses across the country.[16] In New York 10,000 youths demonstrated on campuses with placards that read "Life is Short Enough" and "Build Schools – Not Battleships."[17] The student pacifist movement continued for several years thereafter and was folded into the Emergency Peace Campaign that began in 1936.

---

[14] Quoted in Brock and Young, *Pacifism in the Twentieth Century*, 120.
[15] Winston S. Churchill, *The Second World War*, vol. I, *The Gathering Storm* (Cambridge, MA: Houghton Mifflin, 1948), 85.
[16] DeBenedetti, *The Peace Reform in American History*, 127.
[17] Robert Divine, *The Illusion of Neutrality* (Chicago, IL: University of Chicago Press, 1962), 84.

Absolute pacifism also emerged in France. As in Britain and other countries the horrors of the world war and the threat posed by the new technologies of aerial bombing and chemical weaponry prompted some to reject war totally. The internationalist/just war tradition of the APD remained the dominant perspective among French peace advocates, but a new form of "integral pacifism" emerged in the *Ligue internationale des combatants de la paix* (LICP), founded in 1930. The evils of modern war were greater than any gains that it might achieve, LICP leaders argued. They supported the principle of collective security and the use of economic sanctions but opposed military action. They emphasized the Gandhian method of civil resistance as the preferred means of national defense. The LICP grew rapidly for a few years and gained a following not only in Paris but throughout the provinces, claiming some 20,000 members at its peak. Integral pacifism was a passionate outcry against war, but it was essentially antipolitical and offered no convincing strategy for countering the rising threat of fascist aggression.[18] "With each succeeding crisis in the thirties," wrote Norman Ingram, "the sands of *intégralité* poured faster through the pacifist hourglass towards September 1939." Integral pacifism became increasingly untenable after Hitler came to power and it declined sharply in the second half of the decade.[19]

The largest and most influential absolute pacifist movement developed in Britain. The Peace Pledge Union (PPU) was founded and led by Rev. "Dick" Sheppard, former vicar of St. Martin-in-the-Fields in London. Sheppard began his effort in October 1934 with a letter to the press appealing for signatures on a pledge that read, "I renounce war, and I will never support or sanction another."[20] Sheppard was inspired not only by Ponsonby's earlier effort but also by a similar appeal issued the year before in New York by the influential US religious leader, Rev. Harry Emerson Fosdick. The response to Sheppard's appeal was strong, gaining 30,000 signatures in just a few months. In July 1935 Sheppard chaired a meeting of 7,000 pledge signers in the Albert Hall. A year later he decided to establish the PPU as an organization; it came into existence in May 1936 and eventually attracted 136,000 signers.[21]

---

[18] Norman Ingram, "Defending the Rights of Man: The Ligue des droits de l'homme and the Problem of Peace," in *Challenge to Mars*, 117–33, 128–9.

[19] Norman Ingram, *The Politics of Dissent: Pacifism in France 1919–1939* (Oxford: Clarendon Press, 1991), 70–3, 127–8, 134, 138–40, 285.

[20] Brock and Young, *Pacifism in the Twentieth Century*, 131.

[21] Ceadel, *Pacifism in Britain 1914–1945*, 80.

The PPU served for a time as the epicenter of radical pacifism in Britain. Sheppard was not only an inspiring preacher and a gifted broadcaster (one of the first to use the electronic airwaves) but a talented organizer. Local PPU groups emerged throughout the country, numbering 800 at the height of the campaign.[22] The weekly newspaper, *Peace News*, began publication in 1936 and remains in circulation today. The movement attracted a broad array of supporters and sponsors, including artists and writers, retired officials, political figures (especially members of the Independent Labour Party), and many members of the clergy and lay activists. The union attracted not only absolute pacifists but a range of peace advocates with varying political perspectives, many of whom increasingly recognized the need for a firm stand against Hitler. As the Nazi threat grew and the danger of war increased the PPU began to lose support and dwindled to a remnant of its former self.

REVOLUTIONARY ANTIMILITARISM

Signing individual pledges against war was not enough, some pacifists argued. It was also necessary to organize mass action to resist war and fascism. The principal advocate of this perspective was the Dutch anti-militarist Bart de Ligt. An ordained minister of the Netherlands Reformed Church, he counseled war resistance during World War I (for which he was imprisoned) and was a leader of the Union of Christian Socialists and the International Anti-Militarist Bureau. His theory of nonviolent resistance to war embodied many of the ideas that Gandhi developed independently in South Africa and India. Preventing war requires not merely individual refusal, de Ligt wrote, but collective mass action. Not only would-be soldiers but all workers must refuse to provide their service and labor to the militarist system. The goal should be not only "down with weapons" but also down with hammers and tools.[23] De Ligt urged pacifists and revolutionaries to make greater use of the methods of nonviolent resistance: civil disobedience, noncooperation, boycotts, strikes, and collective refusal to pay taxes or serve in the army. If the masses practice these methods, he insisted, "no power on earth can resist them."[24]

De Ligt's ideas developed not only from moral reasoning but from pragmatic considerations. As weapons and war grow ever more lethal and

---

[22] Brock and Young, *Pacifism in the Twentieth Century*, 132.
[23] Herman Noordegraaf, "The Anarchopacifism of Bart de Ligt," in *Challenge to Mars*, 89–100, 92.
[24] Bart de Ligt, *The Conquest of Violence: An Essay on War and Revolution* (New York: E. P. Dutton & Company, 1938), 163.

all-encompassing, nonviolent means of resistance become the primary and most effective means of fighting for justice and peace. The same is true for the methods of political revolution. De Ligt was sympathetic to the Russian revolution but opposed the Bolshevik methods of war and terror. He advocated a "revolution of the revolution," the overthrow of corrupt and oppressive regimes not through armed struggle but through nonviolent resistance.[25] In these ideas de Ligt anticipated the theories of revolutionary nonviolence that were developed by Barbara Deming and others in the 1960s and that have been applied with increasing frequency in the decades since.

De Ligt worked tirelessly during the 1930s to prevent the impending world war. He called for a "permanent mobilization not only against war . . . but against all its causes, whether moral, political, social or economic."[26] His *Plan of Campaign against War and All Preparation for War* was proposed to the War Resisters International in 1934 and translated into several languages.[27] It called for individual refusal and collective action against war. It contained demands for political, economic, and social justice to establish a stable peace. De Ligt's plan was widely studied and discussed, but the anarcho-pacifist groups who attempted to implement it had little influence. Many on the left were increasingly committed to armed struggle against fascism, especially as the Spanish civil war unfolded, while a growing number of pacifists recognized the need for forceful sanctions against the rising fascist threat.

THE PEACE BALLOT

The majority of those who considered themselves pacifist in the 1930s were pragmatists not absolutists. Most supported a collective security response to Mussolini and Hitler. They were more interested in supporting the League of Nations and advocating disarmament than in signing pledges of individual war resistance. This is evident in the large public backing in Britain for the LNU, which claimed one million supporters in 1933, although the number of paid subscribers peaked at a little over 400,000 in 1931.[28] The number of LNU followers far exceeded those of the PPU.

---

[25] Noordegraaf, "The Anarchopacifism of Bart de Ligt," 95.   [26] De Ligt, *The Conquest of Violence*, 201.
[27] Bart de Ligt, *Plan of Campaign Against All War and All Preparation for War (First Proposed to the International Conference of the War Resisters' International at Welwyn, Herts, England, July, 1934)* (London: Peace Pledge Union, 1939).
[28] Donald S. Birn, *The League of Nations Union 1918–1945* (Oxford: Clarendon Press, 1981), 130.

The LNU was responsible for one of the largest and most successful mobilizations of peace sentiment in history, the Peace Ballot campaign. This nationwide private referendum began in November 1934 and concluded in June 1935. More than 38 percent of the adult British population took part, a total of 11,640,000 people. Martin Ceadel described it as "undoubtedly the most impressive single enterprise launched by any modern British 'cause' or promotional group."[29] As official sponsor of the vote the LNU mobilized half a million volunteers to take ballots door to door in homes and communities throughout the country. This in itself was a monumental feat, which further confirmed the overwhelming public desire for peace that existed at the time. Officially known as the National Declaration on the League of Nations and Armaments, the Peace Ballot demonstrated strong public support for participation in the League and for the reduction and control of armaments. The ballot also revealed broad endorsement for the principles of collective security, expressed through support for the use of sanctions, including even military measures, in response to aggression by one nation against another. The results showed that absolute pacifism – the rejection of any forceful response to aggression – was a minority position.

The impetus for the campaign was the widespread public disappointment that followed the collapse of the 1932–3 World Disarmament Conference in Geneva. In the wake of the failure of government leaders to agree on steps for disarmament, peace advocates searched for a way to demonstrate public support for the reduction of armaments and for regulation of the munitions industry. As public concern about the threat of aerial warfare increased many also sought to build support for abolishing bombers. Within the LNU a parallel concern emerged to demonstrate public support for collective security as an alternative to isolationism and absolute pacifism. Lord Cecil and other LNU leaders hoped that the proposed Peace Ballot would demonstrate public support for the League and encourage a strong government response to the threat of aggression. Criticisms of the campaign from the Conservative Party and major newspapers only served to increase public interest and support. As Cecil noted, Tory attacks had "the effect of bringing over to our side many doubters who previously were uncertain as to their participation."[30]

---

[29] Martin Ceadel, "The First British Referendum: The Peace Ballot, 1934–5," *English Historical Review* 95, no. 377 (October 1980): 810.
[30] Quoted in Ceadel, "The First British Referendum," 827.

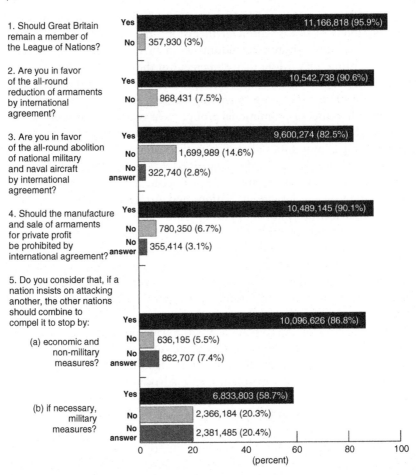

Source: Ceadel, "The First British Referendum," 825.

The Peace Ballot, 1934–5: official results

LNU leaders were extremely gratified by the ballot results. The vote helped to orient many peace activists more favorably toward collective security.[31] As Ceadel noted, the result "reveal[ed] that the connotations of the League of Nations were almost wholly favourable, that multilateral

[31] Lynch, *Beyond Appeasement*, 112.

disarmament was accepted to be the ideal way of preventing war, and that the private arms trade was an object of widespread suspicion." The public response to the fifth question, which had two parts, was more ambiguous but nonetheless showed support for collective security, including the use of military sanctions. As Ceadel observed, the 58.7 percent endorsement for military sanctions "falls short of a ringing call for defiance of all aggressors," but it nonetheless indicated a widespread public willingness, even among peace supporters, to stand up to international aggressors, by military force if necessary.[32] As the London *Daily Herald* noted: "one fact stands out with inescapable clearness. The solid mass of British public opinion demands a policy based not on isolation, not on particular alliances or particular antagonisms, but on the collective system which is embodied in the League."[33]

The results of the ballot were released at a triumphant rally in the Albert Hall, just as the Ethiopia crisis broke in July 1935. The ballot's strong expression of public support for collective security put pressure on the Baldwin cabinet to take a forceful stand against Italy's aggression – or at least to appear to be taking such a stand. As Lynch and Ceadel observed, the ballot results clearly influenced the government's handling of the crisis. Whitehall's decision to impose partial economic sanctions on Italy and press for similar action at the League of Nations was taken "with public opinion in mind." The ballot results also made the question of collective security an issue in the general election that year. The government promised voters that it would back a strong collective security policy. They made this pledge, in Ceadel's words, because of a "feeling, rarely experienced so clearly . . . that the government had a morally-binding mandate for collective security."[34]

AGAINST APPEASEMENT

Throughout the 1930s peace activists were harsh critics of fascist aggression and urged strong international efforts to halt the rising threat. During the initial Manchuria crisis in 1931 radical pacifists and internationalists alike condemned Tokyo's actions and urged Western governments to respond vigorously through the League of Nations.[35] The member governments on the League Council were unwilling to take forceful action, however. They denied Chinese pleas for help and instead established the Lytton

---

[32] Ceadel, "The First British Referendum," 832–3.   [33] Quoted in *ibid.*, 835.   [34] *Ibid.*, 837.
[35] Lynch, *Beyond Appeasement*, 159.

Commission to investigate whether Japan had indeed committed aggression. The commission reported in the affirmative a year later but still the Council dallied. Citizen groups responded to the League's inaction by advocating sanctions and promoting consumer boycotts of Japanese goods.[36] The FOR and other US groups urged the Hoover administration to impose sanctions.[37] The National Council for Prevention of War supported legislation to ban commercial and financial transactions with Japan or any state that violated the Pact of Paris. The WILPF urged the imposition of an arms embargo on wartime belligerents. In Congress the House Foreign Affairs Committee initially approved an arms embargo Bill, but pressure from the arms industry and the armed services killed the measure. In January 1932 the Hoover administration responded to the growing public pressure for action by enunciating the Stimson doctrine, which declared that the United States would not recognize any territorial changes achieved through military aggression. This was a positive step, many peace advocates agreed, but most wanted more forceful action. The US statement of non-recognition had no impact on Japan, which proceeded to consolidate its position in Manchuria and landed troops in Shanghai.

During the Ethiopia crisis of 1935–6 peace groups again demanded a forceful international response to Italian aggression. They sharply condemned the inaction of Western governments and demanded that the League of Nations impose sanctions. In France both the APD and the LICP urged the application of vigorous League of Nations sanctions.[38] In several countries pacifist and socialist groups called for boycotts, strikes, and nonviolent direct action to block shipments to Italy.[39] In Britain the LNU, the WILPF, and many other groups urged Whitehall to take the lead in mobilizing pressure against Italy. Because of the results of the Peace Ballot Prime Minister Baldwin and Foreign Secretary Hoare were under pressure to act. Said the previous foreign secretary Austen Chamberlain, "If we edged out of collective action of this kind, a great wave of opinion would sweep the Government out of power."[40] In the United States the National Council for Prevention of War and other groups also supported League of Nations action. Pacifist and internationalist groups joined together in urging that the Roosevelt administration impose sanctions and cut off the flow of arms to Italy.

---

[36] Chatfield, *The American Peace Movement*, 62.
[37] DeBenedetti, *The Peace Reform in American History*, 125–6.
[38] Ingram, *The Politics of Dissent*, 103, 215. [39] De Ligt, *The Conquest of Violence*, 230.
[40] Quoted in Lynch, *Beyond Appeasement*, 114.

In response to these pressures the United States agreed to halt arms exports to Italy and urged a "moral embargo" on trade and the supply of raw materials. The British government went to the League of Nations and in November 1935 convinced the Council to adopt a resolution urging the imposition of sanctions. League measures were never implemented, however, as few governments were willing to incur the costs and risks of enforcing the measures. A cut-off of oil supplies could have crippled Mussolini's war machine and hobbled Italy's economy, but enforcement would have required a naval blockade. Neither Britain nor France was prepared for such a show of force. Diplomats in Paris and London feared that pressuring Mussolini would drive Italy into an alliance with Germany. Economic interests further weakened the will for sanctions. Despite the Roosevelt administration's appeal for a moral embargo, US corporations increased their trade with Italy. Shipments of oil and strategic materials such as copper, iron, and scrap steel rose sharply. The White House acted to cut off government financing for such trade, but the shipments continued. As historian Robert Divine observed, "It seemed as if American businessmen were intent on proving [Senator Gerald] Nye's thesis that they favored profits above peace."[41] Business groups in other countries also sought to cash in on Italy's war needs. In the end the French government stalled, the United States stood on the sidelines, and the British government was unwilling to press forward on its own.

IMPERIAL FAILURE

The LNU and other peace groups in the United States and Europe were bitterly disappointed by the capitulation to Italy and the League's failure to act. They were further shocked by the December 1935 revelation that Foreign Secretary Hoare and his French counterpart, Pierre Laval, had negotiated a secret agreement to appease Mussolini and grant Italy control over two-thirds of Ethiopian territory. News of the pact caused a furor. Public outrage at the scandal was so intense that Baldwin was forced to sack Hoare "exclusively in deference to public displeasure," as Ceadel phrased it.[42] Laval was also forced out of office. (He later headed the Vichy government and actively assisted the Nazis in deporting Jews and left-wing activists to concentration camps.) The British and French governments disclaimed any intention to reward Italian aggression, but they did just that when they refused to act decisively against Mussolini's invasion and then subsequently

---

[41] Divine, *The Illusion of Neutrality*, 128–30. [42] Ceadel, "The First British Referendum," 837.

accepted his territorial conquest. "Never let the fact be forgotten," wrote US peace leader Kirby Page, "that the governments of Great Britain and France entered into an agreement with Mussolini by which they consented to the handing over to Italy of a huge portion of Ethiopia."[43]

Many peace activists attributed the pusillanimity of Britain and France to economic and imperial self-interest. As the Danish antimilitarist Ellen Hörup observed, when London declared its supposed support for League sanctions the Anglo-Persian oil company continued to ship oil to Mussolini's forces in Ethiopia. In November 1935, when French Foreign Minister Laval urged the League to postpone sanctions, French exporters sharply increased their shipments of oil. "The events of the autumn have shown us financial imperialism hand-in-hand with political imperialism," Hörup argued.

> None of the Great Powers have the slightest interest in overthrowing Mussolini. On the contrary, they all prefer Fascism to Socialism . . . The action of the League of Nations was bluff . . . and during all this bluff the war . . . continued in Ethiopia unaffected, in Fascist style, with bombs upon the defenceless and unarmed . . .[44]

Britain and France seemed more interested in preserving their colonies than in risking military action to deter fascism. Their commitment of substantial military forces in overseas colonies left fewer troops available to resist Hitler's encroachments in Europe. In 1938 nearly half of the British army was stationed in the colonies, the largest contingent – more than 55,000 – in India and Burma.[45] The deployment of a major share of Britain's military might in the colonies was a financial drain and a diversion of forces that might have been used to stand up to Italy and Germany. As Lynch observed "the situation would have been different if policing the Empire had not occupied the bulk of the British military."[46] At the normative level Britain and France lacked the moral authority to condemn Japanese and Italian assertions of imperial prerogative when they themselves maintained far-flung empires in India, Egypt, Indochina, and beyond. Kirby Page said, "So long as the system of empire is upheld and endeavors made by Great Britain, France, and the United States to continue the full enjoyment of the fruits of conquest, there can be no restoration for Ethiopia, and no security for China."[47] The colonial policies of Britain and France undermined their material and moral standing in the struggle against fascism.

---

[43] Kirby Page, *Must We Go to War?* (New York: Farrar & Rinehart, Inc., 1937), vii.
[44] Quoted in de Ligt, *The Conquest of Violence*, 235.
[45] Brian Bond, *British Military Policy between the Two World Wars* (Oxford: Clarendon Press, 1980), 119.
[46] Lynch, *Beyond Appeasement*, 123.   [47] Page, *Must We Go to War?*, vii.

The failure to confront Italian aggression in Ethiopia is often considered the death knell of the League of Nations. In fact the League was crippled from its very inception by the failure of the United States to participate and by the unwillingness of major governments, especially Britain and France, to utilize the League's machinery of mandatory arbitration and collective security. The betrayal of Ethiopia merely sealed its fate and sent the organization into rigor mortis. The Ethiopia crisis also marked the end of the pretense that British or French political leaders were willing to accept the principles of collective security or would work with other governments to deter aggression. In November 1936 the British government ended its support for the League's collective security procedures, making official what had been plainly evident in fact. In a speech echoing the sentiments of US isolationism, Baldwin declared "I am not going to get this country into war with anybody for the League of Nations . . ."[48]

As governments backpedaled on their commitment to the League civil society groups intensified their efforts to uphold the principles of peace. In 1936 pacifist and internationalist groups formed the International Peace Campaign (IPC) as a last desperate attempt to organize public support for disarmament and against war. The campaign was a response to the Ethiopia crisis and the betrayal by Britain and other governments of the widespread international sentiment for forceful measures against Italy. The IPC coalition extended to forty-three countries and brought together representatives of educational, religious, labor, and other organizations with a combined membership of some 400 million people.[49] The campaign was initiated by Lord Cecil of the LNU in Britain and by the French radical Socialist deputy and later minister of the Popular Front government Pierre Cot. The campaign was known on the continent as the *Rassemblement universel de la paix pour le droit* (RUP). It was an uneasy alliance of conservative internationalist groups, religiously inspired pacifist organizations, and left-leaning unions and popular front groups.[50] It focused on two central demands: international disarmament, and "establishment within the framework of the League of Nations of effective machinery for remedying international conditions which might lead to war." Approximately 16 million people signed petitions in support of these demands. It was one of the largest international peace campaigns in history and a vivid expression of

---

[48] Quoted in Lynch, *Beyond Appeasement*, 117.   [49] Birn, *The League of Nations Union 1918–1945*, 173.
[50] Peter Farrugia, "The Conviction of Things Not Seen: Christian Pacifism in France, 1919–1945," in *Challenge to Mars*, 101–16, 107.

the degree of public alarm about the danger of renewed war.[51] It flared brightly for a couple of years but foundered on the shoals of the Spanish civil war and the mounting threat of world war.

THE NEUTRALITY DEBATE

For many Americans during the interwar era preserving peace meant staying out of military conflicts in Europe and Asia. US political culture had a long tradition of neutrality. The founders of the republic had advised keeping distant from foreign wars. In his farewell address, George Washington famously urged Americans to avoid foreign entanglements, "to steer clear of permanent alliances with any portion of the foreign world."[52] Thomas Jefferson wanted the new republic "never to take active part in the quarrels of Europe."[53] Traditionally the United States allowed unrestricted trade with nations at war. When the United States entered World War I, however, the tradition of neutrality was cast aside, and trade with Germany was banned. After the war reports that US corporations had financed and armed both sides in the conflict created a determination among many Americans to ban all trade with belligerents. A growing number of people supported a policy of remaining neutral and embargoing all belligerents as a way of preventing economic interests from dragging the nation into war again.

While most Americans favored noninvolvement in foreign conflicts, they differed on whether neutrality should be absolute or discriminate. Pacifists and isolationists wanted to impose a policy of strict neutrality, which would require the United States to impose an arms embargo and other sanctions against all parties engaged in armed conflict, victims and aggressors alike. This position implied moral equivalence among belligerents, as if there were no difference between a country that launched a war for conquest and one that fought for self-defense. Internationalists and many progressive peace advocates favored a more discriminating approach. They were troubled by the idea of absolute neutrality. How could one be neutral in the struggle between defenseless Ethiopia and aggressive Italy? Remaining aloof in the face of gross injustice or military aggression seemed unacceptable morally

[51] Christian Louis Lange, "The Nobel Peace Prize 1937 Presentation Speech," 10 December 1937. Available online at the Nobel Foundation, http://nobelprize.org/nobel_prizes/peace/laureates/1937/press.html (accessed 8 January 2007).

[52] George Washington, "Farewell Address" (1796). Available online at the US Department of State, http://usinfo.state.gov/usa/infousa/facts/democrac/49.htm (accessed 13 March 2006).

[53] Thomas Jefferson to James Monroe, 11 June 1823. Available online at the School of Cooperative Individualism, www.cooperativeindividualism.org/jefferson_f_03.html (accessed 13 March 2006).

and politically. They believed that the United States had a responsibility to take a stand against aggression. While it was important to stay out of armed conflicts, internationalists and progressives agreed, it was necessary at times to choose sides. This meant that sanctions should be imposed against aggressors but not their victims.

The National Council for Prevention of War favored absolute neutrality but also developed an internationalist stance in support of cooperative efforts to prevent war. The council claimed that "measures withholding aid from all belligerents in any conflict" would help to keep the United States out of foreign conflicts and "act as a deterrent to war."[54] As council leader Frederick Libby explained: "We support this [neutrality] legislation, while at the same time we cherish no illusions that efforts to keep out of a general war are any substitute for the prevention of war through the World Court and a revised League of Nations."[55] The council called attention to economic exploitation and imperialism as root causes of war and urged the United States to support self-determination for oppressed people and equality of status for all nations.

The Roosevelt administration initially opposed neutrality legislation, but the momentum for keeping the United States out of foreign conflicts and controlling the munitions industry was so great that the White House had to yield to political reality. The Neutrality Act that passed Congress in August 1935 was a compromise. It imposed arms embargoes on all belligerents in time of war, but it gave the president discretionary power to determine when a war was taking place and thus when embargoes would be applied. The Act also created a National Munitions Control Board to license and supervise all arms shipments.[56] Peace supporters generally supported the Neutrality Act, but many were troubled by the isolationist tendencies reflected in the legislation. The Federal Council of Churches stated, "The churches, in supporting neutrality, are not to be understood as endorsing an isolationist policy."[57] National peace groups also sought to distinguish their position from isolationism, but in practice their support of neutrality legislation placed them in tactical alliance with Senate isolationists.

THE EMERGENCY PEACE CAMPAIGN

In 1935–6 pacifist organizations in the United States joined together to create a broadly based effort to keep the United States out of war. Founding

---

[54] Quoted in Lynch, *Beyond Appeasement*, 161.   [55] Quoted in Divine, *The Illusion of Neutrality*, 93.
[56] Chatfield, *The American Peace Movement*, 64.   [57] Quoted in Divine, *The Illusion of Neutrality*, 119.

groups in the Emergency Peace Campaign included the FOR, the AFSC, the National Council for Prevention of War, and the WILPF. The program of the Emergency Peace Campaign emphasized international cooperation, equitable economic development, and the strengthening of international law, but its overriding objective was to promote neutrality as a way of keeping the United States out of war. The campaign encompassed a broad coalition including the National Grange, the Farmer's Union, the United Mine Workers, churches, women's organizations, and university based groups.[58] The campaign sponsored meetings and study conferences in hundreds of cities in 1936. Thousands of religious teachers and ministers agreed to give talks, and labor and farm groups sponsored educational programs.[59] It was an impressive mobilizing effort that represented the broadest US peace movement campaign of the interwar era. In 1937 the Emergency Peace Campaign launched an even more ambitious effort, the No-Foreign-War Crusade. It began with a national radio broadcast featuring Eleanor Roosevelt, Admiral Richard Byrd, and Rev. Harry Emerson Fosdick and reached 2,000 towns and 500 college campuses and many religious, labor, and leaders. According to DeBenedetti, the crusade "raised pacifist influence in the antiwar movement of the thirties to its highest level."[60] The Emergency Peace Campaign achieved a partial victory when Congress renewed and strengthened the Neutrality Act in May 1937, extending the neutrality mandate to civil wars and adding strategic materials to the embargo list.

One of the most extraordinary indications of the degree of neutralist sentiment in the United States in the 1930s was the near-passage of the Ludlow amendment in 1938. Sponsored by Indiana Republican Congressman Louis Ludlow, the legislation proposed a constitutional amendment that would require a national referendum for a declaration of war, except in the event of an invasion of the United States. Ludlow introduced his proposal in the House of Representatives in 1935 and for several years thereafter, but it did not come to a vote until 1938, when it reached the floor of the House on what DeBenedetti termed "a crest of antiwar enthusiasm."[61] The vote came in the midst of deepening public concern that the Roosevelt administration was tilting away from strict neutrality and leading the country into war. The National Council for Prevention of War and other peace groups supported the amendment and lobbied to bring it to a vote. The Gallup poll showed 73 percent of the public in favor. The measure seemed assured of passage until

[58] Lynch, *Beyond Appeasement*, 163.   [59] Chatfield, *The American Peace Movement*, 67.
[60] DeBenedetti, *The Peace Reform in American History*, 130–2.   [61] *Ibid.*, 132.

the White House mounted a major fight against it, arguing that its adoption would undermine the conduct of US foreign policy. The amendment was defeated but only by the slim margin of 209 to 188. As historian Charles Chatfield observed, "Even with the utmost effort, the administration prevented the amendment from coming to a floor vote in the House by only 21 votes."[62]

LOSING SPAIN

The continuing US debate on neutrality overlapped with the Spanish civil war, which broke out in July 1936 and became a crucial battleground in the struggle against fascism. Germany and Italy provided substantial backing for General Francisco Franco's military coup. The Soviet Union and many on the left supported the loyalists of the Spanish Republic. Britain and France refused to intervene and did nothing to prevent outside intervention. Moderate peace groups such as the APD refused to support the republican cause and opposed the imposition of sanctions.[63] The policy of nonintervention gave the advantage to Franco, since his forces controlled the seaports and received more technical assistance from the fascist states than the republic received from Moscow. The US Congress adopted an arms embargo resolution that cut off military support to the beleaguered republic but that did not stop Hitler and Mussolini from aiding Franco. Senator John Bernard of Minnesota complained that the measure was a sham intended to "choke off democratic Spain . . . at a time while it is being assailed by the Fascist hordes of Europe."[64] The arms embargo was not truly neutral, critics argued, when it had the effect of aiding the fascists and hastening the defeat of democratic Spain.

As evidence mounted that Germany and Italy were providing weapons and even troops to aid Franco's forces, sympathy for the republic increased. Most major peace and internationalist groups in the United States and Europe urged their governments to support the republic. Thousands of Americans signed up for the Lincoln Brigade and joined the fighting in Spain. Thousands more rallied behind the republic and supported political efforts to repeal the arms embargo. Support for lifting the embargo came from many quarters, including former Secretary of State Henry Stimson,

---

[62] Chatfield, *The American Peace Movement*, 68.   [63] Ingram, *The Politics of Dissent*, 107.

[64] Representative John T. Bernard of Minnesota, extension of remarks, "Spanish Embargo Act – Why I Voted 'No,'" on 21 January 1937, in the US House of Representatives, 75th Cong., 1st sess., *Appendix to the Congressional Record* 81, pt. 9:65–7.

Norman Thomas, Albert Einstein, and many educators and Protestant Church leaders. A Bill to lift the arms embargo was introduced in the Senate. A group of 800 women marched in Washington and delivered a petition to the State Department calling for repeal.[65] The Roosevelt administration was sympathetic to these appeals but chose not to act. The president did not want to break ranks with Britain and France and was afraid of offending his many Catholic constituents who were influenced by the Vatican, which favored Franco over the left-leaning republic.[66] Reinhold Niebuhr wrote at the time, "It is now quite clear that Franco's victory was the first, and may have been the decisive, defeat of the democracies" as the world war began. He blamed the allied failure in Spain on "Tory class interests" in Britain and Roosevelt's dependence on the Catholic vote in the USA.[67]

For many pacifists Spain was a turning point, as illustrated by the odyssey of British Member of Parliament Ellen Wilkinson. A former communist and member of the WILPF, Wilkinson returned from a visit to Spain in 1937 convinced that it was the central battleground in the international struggle against fascism. She resigned from the PPU and later served as a member of the wartime government. Like other peace advocates at the time, "her antifascism proved stronger than her pacifism."[68]

THE END OF "PACIFISM"

The contradictions between internationalist support for collective security and pacifist rejection of armed force became acute in 1938 as the Nazi regime moved against Austria and Czechoslovakia. Internationalists within the LNU urged the British government to place its military forces at the disposal of the League of Nations to resist further aggression. This was a forlorn gesture, since by then there was no hope that the moribund League could respond. During the crisis over Czechoslovakia the LNU urged Whitehall to stand up to Hitler and sharply criticized the policy of "seeking peace by surrender to force."[69] As Chamberlain left for Munich the LNU leadership called for Britain to join with France and Russia in warning that

---

[65] F. Jay Taylor, *The United States and the Spanish Civil War* (New York: Octagon Books, 1971), 168–9.
[66] Divine, *The Illusion of Neutrality*, 226–7; Arnold A. Offner, *American Appeasement: United States Foreign Policy and Germany, 1933–38* (Cambridge, MA: Harvard University Press, 1969), 159.
[67] Reinhold Niebuhr, *Christianity and Power Politics* (New York: Charles Scribner's Sons, 1952), 71, 120–1.
[68] Josephine Eglin, "Women Pacifists in Interwar Britain," in *Challenge to Mars*, 149–68, 151.
[69] Birn, *The League of Nations Union 1918–1945*, 193–4.

an invasion of Czechoslovakia meant war. The pacifists of the PPU reacted differently. They argued for political and economic concessions to Germany and proposed a world conference to create a more equitable international order. The PPU leaders insisted that they were advocating fundamental transformations in the international system not defeatism, but in fact their position amounted to appeasement. Many pacifists, like Britain's leaders, clung to the naïve belief that it was still possible to negotiate with Hitler. They misunderstood the diabolical nature of the Nazi regime and believed that reasonable concessions would satisfy Hitler's ambitions.

When Chamberlain returned with "peace in our time," some peace advocates reluctantly accepted the agreement as "an inglorious peace," in Vera Brittain's words; but many others condemned it.[70] The WILPF declared that the Munich settlement "cannot be called peace because it is not founded on justice."[71] In India Gandhi accused England and France of cowardice. They have "quailed before the combined violence of Germany and Italy," he wrote. "Europe has sold her soul."[72] Gandhi argued for resistance to fascism through "the use of nonviolence as a weapon," although he offered no specific ideas how this might be done, for which he was criticized by prominent Jewish intellectuals such as Martin Buber and Judah Magnes. In France the APD condemned the agreement as an attack on Czech sovereignty. Its leader Theodore Ruyssen warned that it would only increase the likelihood of war. Some integral pacifists defended the agreement, but the ranks of pure pacifism were rapidly dwindling. Ruyssen and many others recognized that war was now inevitable. Their only hope was that the coming conflict would destroy fascism and that the principles of collective security might rise from the ashes to gain greater political recognition and support.[73]

In the United States support for pure pacifism rapidly diminished. Internationalists and progressives worried that the campaign for neutrality was weakening the will to resist fascist aggression. James Shotwell and supporters of the League of Nations Association launched the Committee for Concerted Peace Efforts, which worked to defeat the Ludlow

[70] Vera Brittain, "Pacifism after Munich," in *Testament of a Generation: The Journalism of Vera Brittain and Winifred Holtby*, ed. Vera Brittain *et al.*, 228–31 (London: Virago, 1985), 229.

[71] Lynch, *Beyond Appeasement*, 119.

[72] M. K. Gandhi, "Logical Consequence," 10 August 1938, from *The Collected Works of Mahatma Gandhi* 74, no. 151 (Patiala House, Tilak Marg, New Delhi: Publications Division, Ministry of Information and Broadcasting, Government of India, 1999): 98–100; CD-ROM, continuous collection.

[73] Ingram, *The Politics of Dissent*, 116–18.

amendment and promoted selective arms embargoes against aggressor states.[74] Progressives abandoned the Emergency Peace Campaign, which began to unravel in late 1937. Many of those who previously called themselves pacifist became uneasy with the term and were uncomfortable allying themselves with conservatives and right-wing isolationists in support of the Ludlow amendment. Major organizations that had supported the neutrality campaign, including the American Association of University Women and the National Council of Jewish Women, ended their affiliation with the National Council for Prevention of War. Peace groups found themselves increasingly isolated from the mainstream coalition they had helped to build just a few years before.

Pacifist leaders made one last desperate attempt to keep the United States out of war. In 1938 the National Council, the WILPF and other groups joined with the Socialist Party to form the Keep America Out of War Congress. In 1940 the congress began to fall under the influence of the right-wing America First Committee.[75] It was, in Lynch's words, a "tenuous, uneasy, and short-lived alliance" that put pacifists in company with right-wing nationalists who in some cases were Nazi sympathizers.[76] After the Japanese attack on Pearl Harbor the congress hastily disbanded, marking an ignominious end to a dubious attempt by some pacifists to avoid war at all costs, even at the expense of allying with proto-fascists.

The dwindling pacifist movement faced a fundamental contradiction as it campaigned to prevent war in the late 1930s. It tried to project an internationalist message, even as it campaigned to keep the United States aloof from the world crisis. Pacifists tried to project an internationalist perspective. They called for a "social change" strategy of greater engagement in the world to address the underlying political and economic equalities that contribute to war. They opposed imperialism and economic exploitation and supported self-determination for oppressed peoples and nations. Their overriding political objective, however, was keeping the United States out of war. Their longer-range internationalist agenda received less attention and in any case was not relevant to the immediate challenge of confronting fascist aggression.

By 1938 many internationalists and progressive peace advocates agreed with Einstein's call for military preparations to resist Nazism. "While the goals of pacifism remain unchanged," he wrote, "the methods of achieving peace must necessarily be adapted to changing circumstances." Sound

---

[74] Chatfield, *The American Peace Movement*, 68.
[75] DeBenedetti, *The Peace Reform in American History*, 133.   [76] Lynch, *Beyond Appeasement*, 168–9.

pacifism, he argued, includes the right to resist butchery and the obligation to face international challenges.[77] For the majority of those who supported peace, internationalism came to be understood as collective military action against aggression, while pacifism was identified primarily with isolationism. This was not what pacifists intended. They tried to advocate a position that was simultaneously internationalist and antiwar, but the worsening crisis left no room for such nuance and made their stance increasingly untenable. As Chatfield wrote, "pacifist internationalism lost its political relevance long before the nation went to war."[78] The term pacifism increasingly acquired a pejorative, even treasonous, connotation. It became synonymous with inaction and defeatism in the face of the enemy. Pacifism's earlier calls for sanctions and vigorous action against fascist aggression were forgotten. This was the end of pacifism as it had been previously understood. A few religious sects and radical groups still used the term, but for all others it became tainted. Even Einstein condemned "unsound, irresponsible pacifism," claiming in a 1941 letter that it contributed to the defeat of France and to England's ordeal.[79]

Despite their intense efforts to prevent war peace advocates were blamed for allowing it to happen. This was a misinterpretation of history that ignored the demands of the majority of peace advocates for resistance to fascism. It gave pacifists more influence than they actually possessed at the time and diverted attention from the actions of those actually responsible for the mistakes that were made. The decisions to accommodate and appease fascism were made by the leaders of Britain, France, and the United States, not by pacifists. These political elites were influenced more by right-wing sympathies, economic self-interest, imperial ambitions, and Catholic conservatism than by the pressures of pacifism. To be sure, peace advocates wanted to keep their countries out of war, but they were not neutral in the face of the acts of aggression that began with Manchuria in 1931 and continued right up to the outbreak of world war in 1939. Many peace advocates supported sanctions, arms embargoes, and, as the Peace Ballot results showed, even collective military action against aggressors. They advocated resistance to Mussolini and defense of the Spanish republic. They considered themselves internationalists and urged self-determination and economic justice for oppressed peoples. Theirs may have been a utopian

---

[77] Einstein, *Einstein on Peace*, 250, 276.   [78] Chatfield, *The American Peace Movement*, 70.
[79] Einstein, *Einstein on Peace*, 319.

view in light of the harsh political realities of the time, but it was not the cause of war. They were perhaps naïve in believing too long in the League of Nations, and mistaken in supporting neutrality legislation and aligning with isolationists. They were reluctant to admit the inevitability of war; but this did not make them responsible for its outbreak.

5

Debating disarmament

The historical indictment against pacifism includes the charge that disarmament efforts during the interwar years restricted Western preparedness, allowing Germany and Japan to gain a decisive military advantage that emboldened aggression. Eugene V. Rostow blamed the naval disarmament agreements of that era for "inhibiting the possibility of military preparedness ... through which Britain and France could easily have deterred the war."[1] Norman Podhoretz asserted that the interwar disarmament process "resulted in cutbacks by the democratic side and increases by the totalitarian side."[2] The presumed lesson of history is that disarmament leads to weakness and invites aggression, while military build-ups bring strength and provide security. There is another lesson from history, however, that was widely accepted in the years after World War I: multilateral disarmament can help to prevent war, while military build-ups generate destabilizing arms races and create pressures for militarization. For peace advocates – internationalists and pacifists alike – the struggle against arms accumulation has been an essential part of the strategy for peace. Beginning in the interwar era and continuing especially during the cold war, the demand for disarmament moved to the center of the peace agenda.

The theory of disarmament as a strategy for peace rests on the assumption that large military establishments and excessive levels of weaponry increase the tendency of governments to use military force as the primary instrument of statecraft. When military power is the principal tool of foreign policy, decision makers tend to view international issues through the prism of military action. As the popular saying goes, when your primary tool is a hammer every problem looks like a nail. Weapons makers and military elites generate pressures for maintaining arms production regardless of actual

[1] Quoted in Peter Van Den Dungen, "Critics and Criticisms of the British Peace Movement," in *Campaigns for Peace: British Peace Movements in the Twentieth Century*, ed. Richard Taylor and Nigel Young (Manchester: Manchester University Press, 1987), 268.
[2] Norman Podhoretz, "Appeasement by any Other Name," *Commentary* 76, no. 1 (July 1983): 29.

security conditions. Arms build-ups by one state often prompt reciprocal build-ups by another. This feeds an arms race dynamic and increases political tensions that can lead to war. The case for disarmament also rests on social justice grounds. Economist Seymour Melman argued that the presence of a "permanent war economy" distorts industrial decision making and diverts resources from human needs and civilian innovation toward unproductive military purposes.[3] Said Archbishop Desmond Tutu in his 1984 Nobel Peace Prize speech,

nations are engaged in a mad arms race, spending billions of dollars wastefully on instruments of destruction, when millions are starving. And . . . just a fraction of what is expended so obscenely . . . would make the difference in enabling God's children to fill their stomachs, be educated, and given the chance to lead fulfilled and happy lives.[4]

This chapter tells the story of the debate about disarmament in the pre-nuclear era. I examine the beginnings of disarmament concerns in the nineteenth century and trace the growing interest in arms limitation in the years before World War I. Disarmament efforts were a minor issue in the nineteenth century in part because weapons levels were not as ubiquitous and lethal as they are now. Over time, however, as the destructiveness of war increased and the harmful consequences of militarization became more evident, the importance of disarmament increased. In the nineteenth century arbitration and the codification of international law dominated the peace agenda, but in the twentieth century disarmament rose to the fore. World War I gave a decisive boost to the disarmament cause when revelations of profiteering and influence peddling by weapons makers aroused public anger toward military industrialists. Many blamed the war on the greed of powerful "merchants of death." I review this backlash against munitions makers after the Great War, which moved disarmament to the center of the antiwar agenda and helped build support for the pacifist cause. In the 1920s and 1930s disarmament campaigns attracted the support of millions of people throughout the world, especially in Europe and the United States. I review the history and role of the peace movement in promoting the naval disarmament conferences of the 1920s and the World Disarmament Conference in the early 1930s. I conclude by addressing the realist critique of disarmament

---

[3] Seymour Melman, *The Permanent War Economy: American Capitalism in Decline* (New York: Simon & Schuster, 1985).

[4] Desmond M. Tutu, "Nobel Lecture," Oslo, Norway, 11 December 1984, in *Statements: The Nobel Peace Prize Lecture: Desmond M. Tutu* (New York: Anson Phelps Stokes Institute for African, Afro-American, and American Indian Affairs, 1986), 37.

and the links between arms reduction and the larger imperative of enhancing international cooperation and peace. The history and implications of nuclear disarmament are examined in following chapters.

EARLY RELUCTANCE

Although criticisms of excessive arms spending were voiced frequently at nineteenth-century peace congresses, demands for disarmament were heard only rarely. Peace leaders were reluctant to address arms limitation issues. Bertha von Suttner wrote that "friends of peace should not take up the armaments question: this can only follow from a preceding understanding and creation of a legal order."[5] She and other peace advocates believed that a juridical system for conflict prevention had to precede arms reduction. Disarmament could occur only after the development of an effective arbitration system and strengthened mechanisms of international law. Similar views were expressed by Senator d'Estournelles de Constant of the French Chamber of Deputies in 1903:

Disarmament is the last step of pacific organization. Before achieving disarmament, the reduction of arms must occur; and before that, the limitation of arms; and that limitation will have to be first preceded by a general accord among the powers.[6]

Some pacifists worried that the demand for disarmament would be seen as an unpatriotic attack against the armed forces, which would undermine public support for peace societies. Frédéric Passy argued: "while disarmament was obviously the distant aim of our efforts and our hopes, the moment had not come to ask for it." In 1896 Princess Gabrielle Wiesniewska of Poland founded one of the world's first organizations specifically devoted to disarmament, the *Alliance universelle des femmes pour le désarmement*. The group's advocacy of arms reduction was so controversial, however, that its mission and name were soon changed to the *Alliance des femmes pour la paix*.[7]

Although few were willing to advocate disarmament in the nineteenth century, many peace supporters criticized the costs of militarization. In 1848 the French economist Émile de Girardin documented the enormous costs of military expenditures in France and other countries. He criticized the misuse of capital that could otherwise help to build railroads and factories

---

[5] Sandi E. Cooper, *Patriotic Pacifism: Waging War on War in Europe, 1815–1914* (New York: Oxford University Press, 1991), 117.
[6] Quoted in *ibid.*, 127.   [7] *Ibid.*, 117–18.

and provide for public education. His colleague Frédéric Bastiat wrote that militarism imposed its heaviest burden on the unemployed and the working poor. Eugénie Niboyet, a member of the Paris-based *Société de la morale chrétienne*, argued that reduced military spending would benefit society and spur economic development. Progress, she observed, "has no need of cannons or rifles to advance; the conquests of industry are achieved without striking a blow."[8]

The reluctance of early peace societies to address disarmament also reflected the influence of nationalism within the peace movement. Many peace advocates actively sympathized with the nationalist rebellions against autocratic rule in Europe. These were just struggles, most agreed, and the rebels needed more arms not fewer. Nationalists warned that limiting arms would benefit already well-armed repressive states and weaken the national liberation struggles in Italy, Hungary, and Spain. A universal ban on arms would hurt the weakest most. This was the same dilemma that troubled peace advocates in the 1930s during the debate about neutrality in the United States. Similar questions surfaced in the 1990s during the international arms embargo against former Yugoslavia. The ban on arms exports to former Yugoslavia hampered the ability of the Bosnian government to defend itself and worked to the benefit of the already well-armed Serbian aggressors. In response officials in the Clinton administration and in Congress urged the USA to lift the embargo.[9]

DISARMAMENT TO THE FORE

It was not until the turn of the twentieth century that peace advocates began to campaign actively for disarmament. A key influence was the work of Ivan Bloch (also known as Jean de Bloch), whose 1899 six-volume study, *The Future of War*,[10] meticulously examined the lethal consequences of industrialized war. Weapons were becoming so destructive, Bloch and others argued, that they had to be placed under control. The call for arms control sounded most vigorously in France. The campaign was led by radicals and socialist Members of Parliament, including Jean Jaurès, Francis de Pressensé, François Fournier, and Maurice Allard. French peace advocates played a key role in placing arms limitation issues on the agenda of the 1906

---

[8] Quoted in *ibid.*, 21, 26–7.
[9] Robert W. Tucker and David C. Hendrickson, "America and Bosnia," *The National Interest*, no. 23 (fall 1993): 14–27.
[10] Jan Bloch, *The Future of War in its Technical, Economic, and Political Relations* (New York: Garland, 1899).

meeting of the Interparliamentary Union in London. They did so in the hope that this would assure consideration of the issue at the forthcoming 1907 Hague Peace Conference. Pacifists and socialists joined forces in critiquing the wastefulness of military spending. They called for the redirection of government resources from weapons production to economic development as a means of improving the living conditions of workers and the poor. The demand for reduced military spending remained controversial, however, and inevitably brought criticism that its proponents were acting as German agents.

In the years preceding World War I peace scholars and activists in several countries documented the increasingly blatant and pernicious influence of weapons makers in fueling the arms race and arousing militaristic nationalism. At the Universal Peace Congress held at the Hague in 1913, British socialist G. H. Perris produced a report on European war industries that documented linkages and interlocking directorates among major munitions firms in Britain, Germany, and France. Drawing upon his own investigations in Britain as well as the research of Karl Liebknecht in Germany and Francis Delaisi in France, Perris showed that these industries were reaping huge profits and were using their wealth and power to manipulate public fear of foreign enemies – while at the same time helping to arm these enemies. Delaisi documented the efforts of the Krupp and Creusot industrial groups in Germany and France respectively to bankroll large-scale nationalist media campaigns and curry favor with leading political figures.[11] The military industrialists funded advertising and media efforts which advocated increased arms expenditures and longer terms of military service. They influenced newspapers to encourage nationalistic editorial policies. They provided financial support for the campaigns of elected officials who supported ever larger military budgets. In these and other ways, prewar critics argued, the self-interest of the major weapons manufacturers created nationalistic ardor and an arms race that pushed the nations of Europe toward catastrophe.

Peace advocates also criticized the role of finance capital. Resolutions at the 1913 Universal Peace Congress opposed war loans and denounced financiers in London and Paris as criminal participants "in the incitement to murder." Speakers at the congress sharply criticized loans to governments in southeastern Europe that sustained the Balkan wars. If nations in the region had not been able to borrow money, it was argued, they would have been unable to maintain war. The French delegate Jeanne Mélin

---

[11] Cooper, *Patriotic Pacifism*, 135–7.

complained of the inability of women to obtain loans. She contrasted the largess of banks lending money for war with their miserly rejection of funding for social needs at home.[12]

In the last years before the Great War, the peace movement shed its timidity and began to speak out sharply against militarization and war profiteering. Internationalists joined with progressive peace advocates in calling for greater efforts to restrain the accelerating arms race. They developed proposals for mutual arms reduction among the major powers that would enhance international security. In all of this they anticipated the emphasis on disarmament that was to result from the tragedy of 1914.

CHALLENGING THE "MERCHANTS OF DEATH"

In the aftermath of the Great War many blamed the carnage on the greed of the munitions makers and the influence of big navy lobbying groups in Washington, Paris, London, Tokyo, and Berlin. The critique of the prewar arms race came not just from pacifists but from senior government officials. The former British Foreign Secretary Sir Edward Grey wrote, "Great armaments lead inevitably to war."[13] Admiral of the Fleet Lord Wester Wemyss said in a memorandum to the Admiralty in 1919: "Every firm engaged in the production of armaments and munitions . . . naturally wants the largest output" and has

a direct interest in the inflation of the Navy and Army Estimates and in war scares . . . So long as this subterranean conspiracy against peace is allowed to continue, the possibility of any serious concerted reduction of armaments will be remote.[14]

Lord Welby, Britain's Principal Permanent Secretary to the Treasury, was especially harsh in condemning the arms complex to the House of Commons in March of 1914: "We are in the hands of an organisation of crooks. They are politicians, generals, manufacturers of armaments and journalists. All of them are anxious for unlimited expenditure, and go on inventing scares to terrify the public."[15] The same sentiment was expressed more than a decade later by President Franklin Roosevelt in a 1934 message to Congress:

---

[12] *Ibid.*, 135–7.

[13] Viscount Grey of Fallodon, KG, *Twenty-Five Years 1892–1916*, vol. I (New York: Frederick A. Stokes Co., 1925), 89.

[14] Quoted in Aldous Huxley, ed., *An Encyclopædia of Pacifism* (New York: Harper & Brothers, 1937), 2.

[15] Philip Noel-Baker, *The Private Manufacture of Armaments* (New York: Oxford University Press, 1937), 445.

The peoples of many countries are being taxed to the point of poverty and starvation ... to enable government to engage in a mad race in armaments ... This grave menace to the peace of the world is due in no small measure to the uncontrolled activities of the manufacturers and merchants of engines of destruction.[16]

Such condemnation of arms manufacturers was reinforced in the early 1920s by a League of Nations inquiry into the origins of the war. The League report confirmed that private weapons firms had "fomented war scares, bribed government officials, and circulated false, inflammatory reports on various nations' military strength, to stimulate arms spending."[17] Animosity against the arms industry was raised further in the 1930s by the Nye Committee hearings in the US Senate and the report of the Royal Commission in Great Britain in 1935, which provided further evidence of profiteering, bribery, and price fixing. These reports convinced many that the war benefited only the arms manufacturers. They deepened an already pervasive public distrust of the motivations for war.

Officially known as the Senate Hearings on the Munitions Industry, the Nye Committee hearings caused what Charles DeBenedetti termed "a national sensation" in the United States.[18] When the proceedings opened in September 1934 journalists were already calling them "historic." The investigation continued for eighteen months, through ninety-three hearings and testimony from more than two hundred witnesses.[19] Arms manufacturers were grilled about the enormous profits they reaped in a war that left more than 50,000 US troops dead. The proceedings were widely publicized by a US press corps eager to believe the worst about the perfidy of major industrialists. The hearings came in the depths of the Great Depression and were fed by and helped to nourish an unprecedented wave of anticorporate sentiment.

The Nye Committee hearings were largely a peace movement initiative. Dorothy Detzer of the WILPF played the pivotal role in convincing Gerald P. Nye, the Republican Senator from North Dakota, to chair an investigation into the arms industry. Detzer was a skilled lobbyist and a key organizer

---

[16] Quoted in Norman Cousins, *The Pathology of Power* (New York: W. W. Norton and Company, 1987), 84.

[17] *Ibid.*

[18] Charles DeBenedetti, *The Peace Reform in American History* (Bloomington, IN: Indiana University Press, 1980), 126.

[19] US Senate, 1921–1940, September 4, 1934, "Merchants of Death", www.senate.gov/artandhistory/history/minute/merchants_of_death.htm (accessed 2 June 2006). Quoted from Arthur M. Schlesinger, Jr. and Roger Bruns, eds., *Congress Investigates: A Documented History, 1792–1974* (New York: Chelsea House Publishers, 1975).

in the international disarmament movement during the 1920s and 1930s. Detzer and pacifist leaders Frederick Libby and Nevin Sayre provided major support for the hearings. They uncovered evidence for the committee and publicized its findings. They made sure that the committee fully investigated the arms industry and that its findings were widely communicated to journalists throughout the country. The Nye Committee hearings documented price fixing, the bribing of public officials, collusion between US and British firms, and excess profits from the sale of arms to both sides in the war.[20] The hearings did not provide definitive proof of a conspiracy to foment war, but they conveyed the impression of a private munitions industry that dragged the nation into war for the sake of private profit. The investigation also revealed violations of US neutrality law, which motivated congressional efforts to enact the 1935 Neutrality Act and tighten restrictions on arms sales to belligerent nations. The hearings gave impetus to the rise of pacifist movements, which pressed ever more strongly for disarmament and neutrality.

THE NAVAL DISARMAMENT TREATIES

The Covenant of the League of Nations included a mandate for disarmament. In Article 8 the signatories recognized that "the maintenance of peace requires the reduction of national armaments to the lowest point consistent with national safety." The article stated:

The Members of the League agree that the manufacture by private enterprise of munitions and implements of war is open to grave objections. The Council [of the League] shall advise how the evil effects attendant upon such manufacture can be prevented . . ."[21]

The Council was instructed to formulate plans for the reduction of arms to be considered and reviewed at least every ten years. Peace advocates interpreted this article as a mandate for disarmament and began to mobilize pressure for the convening of a world disarmament conference to implement the required general reduction of armaments. The Versailles Treaty prohibited Germany from acquiring what were defined as "aggressive" weapons, including tanks, heavy guns, military aircraft, submarines, large battleships, and poison gas. Peace advocates seized upon this provision of

---

[20] Charles Chatfield, *The American Peace Movement: Ideals and Activism* (New York: Twayne Publishers, 1992), 63–4.
[21] "The Covenant of the League of Nations," appendix A, in Leland M. Goodrich, *The United Nations* (New York: Thomas Y. Crowell, 1959), 338.

the otherwise despised Versailles agreement. They called for universalizing the ban on aggressive weapons and for actualizing the commitment to disarmament. For liberal opinion disarmament was to be the linchpin of the new era of international cooperation and collective security.[22]

Government leaders had different ideas, however, and had no intention of reducing armament levels. Soon after the guns fell silent officials in London, Tokyo, Washington, and other capitals announced plans to continue naval shipbuilding. In the United States pacifists were incensed when the War Department proposed compulsory military service in 1919 and a major expansion of naval shipbuilding in 1920. The dormant AUAM reawakened and joined with leaders of the women's movement to build a public campaign for disarmament. Internationalists in the LEP expressed concern that renewed arms build-ups would undermine international cooperation. Isolationist members of Congress also raised concerns about the federal government's turn toward militarism so soon after the recent war. Senator William Borah took the lead in proposing an international conference to limit naval shipbuilding. The public response to Borah's initiative was positive, and support for the proposed disarmament conference increased. Progressives and internationalists lobbied for the conference as a step toward fulfilling the disarmament mandate of the League of Nations, hoping that US leadership in such a conference would improve the prospects for eventual US membership of the League. Borah and isolationist Republicans in the Senate supported the proposed conference for exactly the opposite reason, as an alternative to the League. In May 1921 the Senate approved Borah's amendment to the naval appropriations Bill calling on the president to invite other countries to a naval disarmament conference. The Harding administration, initially cool to the proposed conference, bowed to political reality and agreed to invite nine nations to Washington for negotiations, which opened on Armistice Day in November 1921.

Peace groups mounted a major lobbying campaign at the Washington conference. They formed the National Council on Limitation of Armaments, which served as a clearinghouse for citizen efforts. The National Council was directed by Frederick Libby, an influential and highly effective Quaker activist, with major support in subsequent years from Dorothy Detzer. The National Council developed into a broad coalition that included not only the major peace groups but a wide range of organizations, from the Veterans of Foreign Wars to the Federal Council of

---

[22] Donald S. Birn, *The League of Nations Union 1918–1945* (Oxford: Clarendon Press, 1981), 35.

Churches and the National League of Women Voters.[23] The Council campaigned for disarmament throughout the 1920s and later became the National Council for Prevention of War. DeBenedetti described the campaign in support of the Washington disarmament conference as "the finest achievement of positive citizen peace action in the interwar period."[24] Cecelia Lynch called it a "successful and important beginning for peace groups." The campaign generated six million letters, telegrams, and petitions and helped to create a climate of political support that facilitated the negotiation of significant arms reduction agreements.[25] The results were a partial victory for the peace movement.

The most important agreement was the Five Power Naval Limitation Treaty, signed in February 1922, in which the major powers took the unprecedented step of voluntarily agreeing to mutual limitations of major armaments. The five major powers agreed to a moratorium on the construction of battleships for ten years and established fixed ceilings on capital ship tonnage, with Britain and the United States in the first rank, Japan in the second, and France and Italy in the third. The United States, Britain, and Japan agreed to scrap more than sixty warships that were already built or under construction.

The Washington conference was followed in 1930 by the London naval disarmament conference. Women's groups in Britain took the lead in mobilizing public support for the conference. Eighteen organizations, including the WILPF, joined together to form the British Peace Crusade, which claimed to represent more than two million people. The Crusade campaigned vigorously for further arms reduction in delegation meetings with high-level US and British officials. These and other citizen efforts helped to encourage further arms reduction agreements at the London conference. The major powers extended the moratorium on battleship construction until 1936 and established ceilings on other major classes of warships, including cruisers, destroyers, and submarines. Peace groups were generally pleased with the results of the conference, although they worried that the new ceilings allowed an overall net build-up in the number of ships.[26]

The naval disarmament efforts of the interwar years achieved some modest progress in placing partial restrictions on warship production, but

---

[23] Chatfield, *The American Peace Movement*, 56–7.
[24] DeBenedetti, *The Peace Reform in American History*, 112.
[25] Cecelia Lynch, *Beyond Appeasement: Interpreting Interwar Peace Movements in World Politics* (Ithaca, NY: Cornell University Press, 1999), 133, 135.
[26] *Ibid.*, 97–9.

they could not be sustained. The rise of fascist aggression led to worsening political tensions and dashed the hope that disarmament efforts could prevent war. Japan announced its withdrawal from the treaties in 1934. The other principals no longer considered themselves bound by the treaty limits, and the era of negotiated naval disarmament came to an end.[27] Although of limited duration and impact, the Washington and London disarmament agreements nonetheless represented a significant advance in international peacemaking. They were the first successful disarmament agreements in modern history. The major powers were able to reach diplomatic accord in restraining one of the principal factors that many felt had caused war. The treaties confirmed the value of multilateral diplomacy and set a precedent for the nuclear disarmament agreements that emerged during the cold war.

WORLD DISARMAMENT CONFERENCE

Although supportive of the naval disarmament process, peace advocates continued to agitate for a broader, more universal disarmament process. They called for the reduction of all deadly weapon systems, especially bombers, which were soon to display their lethal effect in the Japanese assault against Shanghai in early 1932, and later in the German attack against Guernica during the Spanish civil war. Pacifists continued to campaign for a general disarmament conference under the authority of the League of Nations. They wanted to strengthen the League and build support for international cooperation and collective security to replace competing international alliances. While lobbying to encourage progress at the Washington and London conferences, therefore, peace groups kept up a steady drumbeat of support for a world disarmament conference.

Much more so than the naval disarmament conferences, the World Disarmament Conference that opened under League of Nations auspices in Geneva in February 1932 was a gathering that peace advocates welcomed with enthusiasm, and which they considered a result of their effort. Lynch described the campaign for the World Disarmament Conference as the "largest, best organized, and most intense transnational effort by peace movements to voice their demands during the interwar period."[28] Women's groups played an especially significant role in building support for the conference, but churches, university groups, trade unions, and many

[27] Seyom Brown, *The Causes and Prevention of War*, 2nd edn (New York: St. Martin's Press, 1994), 202.
[28] Lynch, *Beyond Appeasement*, 183.

other organizations also participated. In Britain the WILPF took the lead in gathering more than 2 million signatures on a disarmament petition. Similar petition drives took place in other countries.

The conference chair was former British Foreign Secretary Arthur Henderson, a disarmament advocate who agreed to convene a special opening ceremony that would display the depth and intensity of public support for disarmament and the League of Nations. During the ceremony "a procession of peace groups" presented "with great fanfare a total of twelve million petitions in favor of disarmament in front of League officials and government delegations."[29] It was a crowning moment for the attempt of peace groups to build support for disarmament and strengthen the role of the League of Nations.

In preparation for the conference the International Federation of League of Nations Societies developed a set of principles for disarmament known as the "Budapest proposals." These called for a general prohibition against the categories of aggressive weapons that were denied to Germany: tanks, heavy mobile guns, bombers, submarines, and chemical weapons. They also included a call for a 25 percent across the board cut in arms expenditures worldwide and a parallel "proportionate reduction" of all categories of weapons. Many peace and internationalist groups supported these proposals and also urged the abolition of bombers and aerial weapons. The LNU in London encouraged the British government to "lead by example" through unilateral arms reduction.

Britain, France, and other major powers were skeptical of such proposals and were reluctant to engage in a general disarmament process that might limit their military capabilities. They saw disarmament not as a universal process to eliminate weapons and the threat of war, but as a means of regulating the competition in arms and protecting their special status as major powers. The pressure of public opinion forced them to take action toward arms limitation, but they were determined to avoid the kind of universal disarmament that was demanded by peace advocates and envisioned in the League Covenant. On the eve of the Geneva conference the British government claimed that it should be exempted from further reductions because of its "responsibilities" in maintaining the empire. London advocated arms cuts by other governments but claimed that it was "unable to offer further reductions" itself.[30]

Despite the reluctance of governments, political momentum for the World Disarmament Conference was overwhelming. A senior official in

[29] *Ibid.*, 186.   [30] *Ibid.*, 100–1.

London complained that the cabinet was being "dragged unwillingly along" by the weight of public opinion. The British government responded to these pressures by agreeing to a set of proposals for the Geneva conference that included a ban on submarines and bombers, but that allowed the use of bombers for "police" purposes in the colonies. British peace groups were outraged by this claim of imperial privilege. A delegation of religious leaders told government officials that "there is much unrest in church circles that nothing adequate is being done" to reflect the widespread public support for disarmament.[31] The government subsequently modified its position slightly, but it continued to insist on the right to build and use bombers in the colonies.

THE COLLAPSE OF DISARMAMENT

The World Disarmament Conference met in the shadow of rising fascist political power in Japan, Germany, and Italy. It ultimately collapsed in failure over confusion and uncertainty about how to address the mounting militarist danger. The first shock came before the conference even began when Japan attacked Shanghai and proceeded with the virtual annexation of its puppet regime in Manchuria. Peace groups responded to these outrages by demanding League of Nations action against Japan. They criticized the British government and other Western powers for selling arms to Japan and doing nothing to counter Tokyo's aggression. They pointed to the bombing of Shanghai as validation of their concerns about the horrific consequences of aerial warfare. Their demands for an enforceable international ban on bombing and more vigorous general disarmament efforts intensified.

As the Geneva conference extended into 1933 with no tangible results, disillusionment set in. Hitler's rise to power alarmed many and posed excruciating dilemmas for peace movements, as for governments. Since 1919 peace advocates had condemned the unequal terms of the Versailles Treaty and had called for granting Germany equality of status with other nations. They recognized that the punitive provisions of the treaty were not only unfair but politically counterproductive and that German resentments were feeding militarism and revanchism. Throughout the 1920s pacifist and internationalist groups lobbied for the acceptance of Germany as an equal partner with other nations. Progress was made in this direction with the Locarno Treaties of 1925, which guaranteed the Franco-German border, and with Germany's entry into the League in 1926. Peace groups favored

[31] *Ibid.*, 103–5.

granting Germany equal status in armaments in the hope that this would remove any justification for German rearmament. Parity in armaments within the context of a world disarmament agreement would be the best way of both satisfying German national claims and reducing the threat of an arms race that could lead to war. In Britain Lord Cecil and the LNU argued that a universal arms limitation agreement would make it more difficult for Germany to seek special privileges. London's reluctance to consider general disarmament, LNU leaders insisted, was dangerous and counterproductive. The failure of the disarmament process would weaken the position of moderates in Germany and strengthen the rearmament demands of German nationalists.

The rising Nazi party was not satisfied with mere equality of status, of course. Hitler used the discrimination to which Germany was subjected as an excuse to justify expansionist military aims. Even before the Nazis took power in March 1933, the Berlin government demanded a revision of the naval disarmament agreements to grant Germany the same privileges offered the other major powers. In October 1933 Hitler announced that Germany was leaving the World Disarmament Conference and withdrawing from the League of Nations in protest over the refusal of the major powers to grant military parity. Germany's action and Japan's subsequent withdrawal from the Washington and London naval accords brought an end to the multilateral disarmament process. These ominous developments were harbingers of the resurgent militarism that was soon to engulf the world.

DISARMAMENT AT FAULT?

The political mistakes that led to World War II were many, but they were not the fault of the 1922 and 1930 naval disarmament treaties or the attempt to negotiate a world disarmament agreement. The naval agreements, while they lasted, constrained the Japanese as much as the British and US fleets. British, French, and US leaders were indeed ill prepared and unwilling to confront fascist aggression in the 1930s, but their pusillanimity was not the result of any weakness in naval armament. Britain and the United States remained well ahead of Germany in naval capability before and during World War II. A general disarmament agreement as envisioned in 1933 might have constrained the German military build-up. While it is unlikely that Hitler would have accepted restraints on his military ambitions, the reluctance of the Western powers made it easier for him to walk out and begin the process of militarization. The decisions to accommodate fascist aggression and delay rearmament were made by government leaders, not by peace activists. Pacifist groups certainly had their faults, as noted in the previous chapter. They held on too long to the hope that the League of Nations could be relied upon to protect the peace, and that Hitler could be placated. The limitations of peace advocacy during the interwar era were many, but working for disarmament was not one of them. It is a distortion of history to blame the outbreak of World War II on the movement for disarmament.

A more legitimate criticism is that peace advocates placed too much faith in disarmament as a means of preventing war. The theory that blamed World War I primarily on the "merchants of death" was incomplete. Excessive military expenditure and an overabundance of arms were indeed factors in making armed conflict more likely and deadly, but they were not the only or the principal causes of war. The lesson of the interwar disarmament process is not that disarmament brings weakness, but that disarmament by itself is insufficient to guarantee peace. An exclusive emphasis on levels of weaponry is not a sufficient strategy for preventing war.

As Hans Morgenthau famously observed, "[people] do not fight because they have arms. They have arms because they deem it necessary to fight." The prevention of war requires more than merely lowering armament levels. The competition for arms is a function of the competition for power, wrote Morgenthau, and "a mutually satisfactory settlement of the power contest is a precondition for disarmament."[32] Australian political scientist Hedley Bull wrote that arms races are both a cause and a consequence of international tension. "The fact that the arms race contributes to political tension does not diminish the difficulty that it cannot be brought to an end without the ending of this tension."[33] The arms race is a symptom of a deeper malady, and it can be cured only by treating the underlying disease.

Yet disarmament efforts can help to address those underlying causes of war by providing a framework for political bargaining and tension reduction. The naval disarmament treaties established patterns of mutual agreement and communication among the great powers that for more than a decade restrained excessive arms spending and improved mutual understanding on military security issues. The problem with the disarmament process, peace advocates argued, was not that it went too far but that it did

---

[32] Hans J. Morgenthau, "Does Disarmament Mean Peace?," in *Arms and Foreign Policy in the Nuclear Age*, ed. Milton L. Rakove, 417–23 (New York: Oxford University Press, 1972), 422.

[33] Hedley Bull, "Disarmament and the International System," in *Theories of Peace and Security: A Reader in Contemporary Strategic Thought*, ed. John Garnett (London: Macmillan, 1970), 138.

not go far enough. Disarmament efforts in the interwar era showed that mutual arms limitation can reduce the levels of weaponry that might serve as a temptation for political leaders to wage war. The naval disarmament agreements temporarily tamed military rivalries and opened the door to improved interstate cooperation. This result was also evident during the nuclear era. Periods of significant arms limitation were associated with détente in the 1970s and the end of the cold war in the late 1980s. The advantages of disarmament can be ephemeral, however, and are easily subverted when major states seek unilateral advantage. Disarmament can make a meaningful contribution to peace but only if it is sustained and accompanied by other peacemaking efforts.

6

Confronting the cold war

World War II taught pacifists and internationalists bitter lessons about attempting to secure peace in a broken world. No one could accept any longer the enlightenment dream that society was evolving naturally toward peace. Not after the collective madness of virtually the entire world at war, which left more than 50 million dead and ended with the dropping of the atomic bomb. Not with the subsequent rise of a cold war nuclear arms race that threatened to annihilate hundreds of millions and perhaps extinguish life itself. The bloody record of the twentieth century, wrote Jonathan Schell, showed that violence "was capable of fantastic mutation and expansion," as if "an evil god had turned human society into an infernal laboratory to explore the utmost extremes of violence."[1]

Albert Camus diagnosed the dilemma of the age in his essay "Neither Victims nor Executioners." The horrors of world war "killed something in us," shattering our self-confidence. The quest for utopias and the doctrine of ends justifying means had led to mass murder. The challenge for the future was to develop more modest political aims, "free of messianism and disencumbered of nostalgia for an earthly paradise" – to seek a world in which murder would no longer be legitimized, where the resort to violent means could be tamed. To prevent annihilation, he wrote, we must pursue international democracy. We must resist dictatorship "by means which are not in contradiction with the end we seek."[2]

In the initial postwar years Camus's plea for a less violent future fell on deaf ears. Political realism was the reigning philosophy, with Reinhold Niebuhr and Hans Morgenthau the dominant intellectual voices of the era. The rise of totalitarianism and the horrors of world war seemed to

---

[1] Jonathan Schell, *The Unconquerable World: Power, Nonviolence, and the Will of the People* (New York: Metropolitan Books, 2003), 3.
[2] Albert Camus, *Neither Victims nor Executioners* (Philadelphia: New Society Publishers, 1986), 27–8, 33, 44–5.

confirm the brutish *realpolitik* character of international relations. The experience of world war convinced many of the value of military power and the necessity of confronting aggression with armed force. Political leaders in Washington equated peace with the extension of US military power. The intensifying struggle against Soviet communism justified the creation of a national security state and the expansion of US military intervention around the world. Similar militarist tendencies were evident in the Soviet Union, France, and Britain, and in nationalist and revolutionary communist regimes in the developing world.

Internationalism remained a powerful force, however, and emerged to reassert itself from the ashes of war. Political leaders recognized the need for more effective international mechanisms to keep and enforce the peace. They sought to create a world organization that, in the words of the UN Charter, would "save succeeding generations from the scourge of war." They were determined not to repeat the failures of the League of Nations. For Franklin D. Roosevelt this meant assuring political support for US participation. For the great powers generally the goal was establishing a world body that would serve their needs, which meant a UN structure dominated by the Security Council and the veto power of the permanent five. Peace advocates saw flaws in such an arrangement but most acknowledged the necessity of conceding to political realism. They supported the new United Nations in the hope that it would prevent renewed world war.

These were difficult years for the peace movement, which sank to its lowest ebb of the century.[3] Pacifism was equated with appeasement and was falsely associated with communism. Yet even in these dark years the voice of peace called forth with alternatives to the problems of war and militarization. All sectors of the peace community supported the United Nations, although many sought to reform the organization and strengthen its human rights and peacemaking functions. Some pacifists and liberal internationalists supported Einstein's vision of supranational government, as a movement for world federalism emerged. Alarms were raised about the militarization of US policy and the excessive influence of the arms sector in promoting the use of force. Far from protecting the peace, pacifists warned, US military policy exacerbated cold war tensions and threatened to embroil the USA in constant war. This chapter examines these and related developments in the years after World War II. It concludes with a review of the influential report *Speak Truth to Power*, in which leading peace

---

[3] Charles DeBenedetti, *The Peace Reform in American History* (Bloomington, IN: Indiana University Press, 1980), 156.

advocates diagnosed the dilemmas of the nuclear age and prescribed a new form of more responsible and realistic pacifism to confront the deepening dangers of the cold war era.

CREATING THE UNITED NATIONS

Soon after the outbreak of World War II internationalists and peace advocates in the United States, Britain, and other countries began to mobilize on behalf of a postwar international organization to keep the peace. In the United States James Shotwell and leaders of the former League of Nations Association formed a Commission to Study the Organization of Peace. The commission was supported by the American Association of University Women, the Church Peace Union, the Young Women's Christian Association, and other mainstream groups.[4] The commission's first annual report in 1940 called for US participation in the fight against fascism and urged support for the creation of a postwar international security system that could prevent future aggression. In 1940 the Federal Council of Churches created a Commission on a Just and Durable Peace. Led by future secretary of state John Foster Dulles, a prominent Presbyterian and lay leader, the commission urged active US support for and participation in a postwar international organization as an essential requirement for peace.[5] In Britain the LNU emphasized that the collapse of the previous League was due not to any inherent problems with the concept of international organization but to the failure of major governments to support and utilize the structures for peace that had been created.[6] The LNU joined with other British groups soon after the outbreak of war to campaign for the creation of a future international organization.

The movement for a postwar international organization received a major boost in the United States with the 1939 publication of Clarence Streit's *Union Now*.[7] Streit's book called for the United States and Britain to form a federation of democratic states that would gradually evolve into a global union. *Union Now* generated keen interest in the United States and sold a quarter million copies within two years. In 1941 supporters of Streit's vision

---

[4] *Ibid.*, 135.
[5] Charles Chatfield, *The American Peace Movement: Ideals and Activism* (New York: Twayne Publishers, 1992), 85–7.
[6] Cecelia Lynch, *Beyond Appeasement: Interpreting Interwar Peace Movements in World Politics* (Ithaca, NY: Cornell University Press, 1999), 193.
[7] Clarence K. Streit, *Union Now: A Proposal for a Federal Union of the Democracies of the North Atlantic* (New York: Harper & Bros., 1939).

created a new organization, the Federal Union, which established sixty chapters around the country. The concept of an Anglo-American partnership for international harmony was articulated most persuasively in 1943 with the publication of Wendell Wilkie's *One World*. The former Republican presidential candidate argued that the United States must assume global leadership in creating a more peaceful world. *One World* was an anecdotal account of his world travels that included an impassioned "sermon on internationalism" urging Americans to support the creation of an inclusive United Nations Council. The first printing of the book sold out in two days, and 200,000 copies were purchased within a week. According to DeBenedetti, "Wilkie's testimonial to world interdependence enjoyed the most fantastic sales in American publishing history."[8]

By 1942 the isolationism that had characterized US public opinion in the late 1930s gave way to support for internationalism. An opinion poll in mid-1942 showed 73 percent of Americans favoring US participation in a postwar international organization, compared to 50 percent in 1941 and 33 percent in 1937.[9] This support for internationalism was accompanied by a revival of interest in Woodrow Wilson, as evidenced by the 1944 Hollywood film *Wilson* by Darryl F. Zanuck. It was now almost universally agreed that US rejection of the League of Nations in 1919 had been a mistake, and that the hopes for peace after the war would depend on a US commitment to the creation of an effective international organization.

Internationalist groups played an active role in building public support for a postwar organization. In the United States the newly formed United Nations Association absorbed what was left of the earlier League of Nations Association and organized local committees and study groups to build public understanding and support for a postwar organization. Several other civic and religious groups organized similar campaigns, some with a legislative emphasis. James Shotwell, Clark Eichelberger, and other internationalists formed an umbrella group, Americans United for World Organization, which arranged educational programs among women's organizations, labor groups, business associations, churches, and farm groups. Americans United coordinated its work with the US State Department, which credited the coalition with "markedly increasing [the] number of comments from individuals throughout the country" endorsing the plan for

---

[8] DeBenedetti, *The Peace Reform in American History*, 142.
[9] Robert A. Divine, *Second Chance: The Triumph of Internationalism in America during World War II* (New York: Atheneum, 1967), 68–9.

creating the United Nations.[10] Members of Congress reported a heavy flow of constituent messages supporting the creation of a new international organization after the war. In 1943 newly elected Representative J. William Fulbright introduced a resolution in the House of Representatives urging US participation in a postwar collective security organization. In the Senate a similar resolution supporting the creation of a world organization passed with only five dissenting votes.[11] Peace groups actively supported the campaign for a new international organization and urged that it be based on principles of universality and equality of status. They also urged greater attention to economic and humanitarian concerns in the design of the new organization. The WILPF argued for greater democratic participation in any future international system and emphasized the need to overcome global economic inequalities to prevent future war.

The State Department encouraged this process and reported in a 1948 internal memo:

one of the significant factors which has sustained this popular abandonment of isolationism has been the work of the international relations organizations. They wield an influence much greater than is suggested by their numbers (100,000–200,000 adults) since they include, or reach, citizens who translate their interest in foreign policy into significant action.[12]

Dozens of leaders from trade unions, African-American groups, women's organizations, and religious bodies were present in San Francisco in 1945 for the founding of the United Nations. Among the forty-two organizations invited to serve as "consultants" at the San Francisco conference were Americans United, the Federal Council of Churches, the National Association for the Advancement of Colored People, the United Auto Workers, and the American Association of University Women. Religious groups were particularly active in San Francisco. They issued a "tri-faith" statement which advocated an international Bill of civil and human rights, the strengthening of international law, and a greater commitment to arms limitation.

The citizen groups that attended the San Francisco conference lobbied vigorously for the inclusion of human rights provisions in the UN Charter. The horrors of Nazi barbarism had convinced many that human rights and fundamental freedoms were necessary requirements if peace, security, and justice were to be achieved.[13] The Charter included an affirmation of

---

[10] Quoted in Lynch, *Beyond Appeasement*, 200. [11] Chatfield, *The American Peace Movement*, 88–9.
[12] Cited in Lynch, *Beyond Appeasement*, 205–6.
[13] Leland M. Goodrich, *The United Nations* (New York: Thomas Y. Crowell, 1959), 244.

"respect for human rights and for fundamental freedoms" and called for the creation of a Human Rights Commission. Citizen groups also urged greater attention to self-determination for colonized peoples and advocated stronger provisions for equitable economic development.

The US and British governments were initially vague about the details of a postwar international organization. Washington and London preferred a concert of major powers working under the loose authority of an international council. Roosevelt was skeptical about entrusting US security to a new international organization. He spoke instead of a "four policemen" scheme, in which the United States, Britain, the Soviet Union, and China would work together in a great power condominium to enforce the peace. Churchill favored a loose alliance system based on regional councils that would preserve the prerogatives of the great powers. Citizen groups strongly favored a more structured approach, however. As public involvement increased and the discourse broadened, proposals for a great power concert or for regional spheres of influence were adjusted to incorporate universalist principles. According to Lynch, the initial preferences of Churchill and Roosevelt were "modified to take into account a broader normative agenda."[14]

The resulting structure of the United Nations was a compromise between the *realpolitik* of great power domination and the public desire for democratic internationalism. The Charter established a powerful Security Council with veto power for the permanent five, but it also embodied principles of universal participation and included an explicit commitment to human rights and social and economic development. Peace advocates were supportive but were concerned about the flawed design of the new organization. The veto power would prevent the United Nations from constraining aggressive acts by the great powers or intervening in conflicts that directly affected their interests. Since the concerns and perceived national interests of the permanent five extended over much of the earth, this meant that the United Nations would be severely crippled and unable to act in many parts of the world. As the cold war emerged and the US-Soviet rivalry extended to virtually every continent, the United Nations was indeed relegated to the sidelines during its initial decades. Peace advocates also criticized the inadequate powers accorded the General Assembly, which violated the principles of universality and equality of status upon which the United Nations was supposedly founded. They actively supported the United Nations nonetheless, while

[14] Lynch, *Beyond Appeasement*, 199.

working to make it more democratic and inclusive. Many agreed with the sentiments expressed by President Julius Nyerere of Tanzania, "we have to rejoice in the very imperfect United Nations and have to work to strengthen it."[15]

THE RISE OF WORLD FEDERALISM

The worldwide shock at the dropping of atomic bombs compounded the concern many peace advocates felt at the inadequacies of the United Nations and gave impetus to a significant movement for world federalism. The destructive power unleashed at Hiroshima and Nagasaki fundamentally altered the nature of international security. In an age of atomic energy, wrote Norman Cousins, "the foundations of the old sovereignties have been shattered." For better or worse, all nations stand virtually unarmed in the presence of the bomb. We are all "at the mercy of one another, and shall have to devise a common security or suffer a common cataclysm." The UN Charter, wrote Cousins, is "a feeble and antiquated instrument for dealing with the problems of an Atomic Age." The need for world government existed long before Hiroshima and Nagasaki, but it became unmistakably clear "in the glare brighter than sunlight produced by the assault on the atom." The old notions of sovereignty became "vestigial obstructions in the circulatory system of the world."[16]

The concept of world government was always implicit in the theory of international cooperation and was a subject of debate among philosophers over the centuries. A tension existed between those like Kant who envisioned sovereign nations coming together in a loose voluntary association and others like Einstein who believed that nations must transcend sovereignty to create a genuine world government. The former aimed toward a system of collective security, in which nations pool their separate military capabilities to enforce collective judgments, while the latter implied the creation of a single world authority with a monopoly over all uses of force in the external relations of nations. In practice internationalism came to embody the former meaning, but for many peace advocates, especially in the years immediately after World War II, the latter concept of a federal union of nations was seen as vital to peace and human survival. H. G. Wells was a pioneer in popularizing the federalist argument. His 1914 novel

---

[15] Julius K. Nyerere, *Freedom and Unity: Uhuru na umoja: A Selection from Writings and Speeches, 1952–65* (London: Oxford University Press, 1967), 19.
[16] Norman Cousins, *Modern Man is Obsolete* (New York: Viking Press, 1946), 40–1 and 22–3.

The World Set Free envisioned a battle fought with "atomic bombs," in which the survivors formed a world government that brought an end to war. In 1928 he wrote *The Open Conspiracy* to outline his thinking about world government. In 1933 he elaborated these ideas in *The Shape of Things to Come*. "The directive idea of my life," he recalled, "was the creative World-State."[17]

The world federalism movement began to garner public support during the 1940s and especially after the war. Einstein played a significant role in its promotion. He was a supporter of the United Nations but hoped that it could be transformed into a genuine world government. He advocated "a *supra*national, not *inter*national, organization, resting on law and vested with adequate military power to enforce the law."[18] In a 1946 radio address he said,

> our only hope for survival lies in the creation of the world government capable of resolving conflicts among nations by judicial verdict . . . No person or nation can be regarded as pacifist unless they agree that all military power should be concentrated in the hands of a supranational authority, and unless they renounce force as a means of safeguarding their interests against other nations.

The key to peace, he argued in February 1950, is to

> do away with mutual fear and distrust. Solemn renunciation of the policy of violence, not only with respect to weapons of mass destruction, is without doubt necessary. Such renunciation, however, will be effective only if a supranational judicial and executive agency is established at the same time, with power to settle questions of immediate concern to the security of nations.[19]

The organized campaign for federalism was launched immediately after the atomic bombings in Japan. In the United States several federalist organizations emerged. Future US Senator Harris Wofford, Jr. helped to create a student federalist movement. Another future senator, Alan Cranston of California, was an energetic and active supporter of the federalist movement. In August 1947 a Gallup poll reported 56 percent of respondents in favor of transforming the United Nations into a world government, with just 30 percent opposed.[20] In April 1947 several federalist organizations merged to form the United World Federalists. Its motto was

---

[17] H. G. Wells, *H. G. Wells in Love: Postscript to an Experiment in Autobiography*, ed. G. P. Wells (Boston: Little, Brown and Co., 1984), 235.

[18] Albert Einstein, *Einstein on Peace* (New York: Simon and Schuster, 1960), 415.

[19] *Ibid.*, 379, 522.

[20] Lawrence S. Wittner, *One World or None: A History of the World Nuclear Disarmament Movement Through 1953*, vol. I of *The Struggle against the Bomb* (Stanford: Stanford University Press, 1993), 71.

"world peace through world law."[21] By 1949 United World Federalists had more than 46,000 members and 720 chapters. It had the endorsement of forty-five national organizations, including farm, veterans, labor, and religious groups.[22]

In Britain the federalist movement was led by Henry Usborne, whose Crusade for World Government sponsored meetings and educational fora in communities throughout the country. The Crusade eventually gained some 15,000 registered supporters. Usborne was a Labour Member of Parliament, and he introduced a motion affirming Britain's readiness to federate with other nations. The resolution had the support of nearly a hundred Members of Parliament by the end of the year but never came to a vote.[23] In Japan the famed writer and social reformer Kagawa Toyohiko joined with other prominent public figures to endorse federalism. A Parliamentary Committee for World Federation claimed 180 members of the Diet, including Prime Minister Yoshida Shigeru.[24]

The world federalism movement peaked in 1949, when federalist societies existed in eighteen nations, with an international headquarters in Paris. In the United States more than twenty state legislatures approved petitions urging Congress to initiate plans for transforming the United Nations into a world government.[25] In two states where such referenda appeared on the ballot, Massachusetts and Connecticut, voters overwhelmingly approved the proposal. A resolution in Congress declaring world federation "a fundamental objective" of US foreign policy attracted 111 cosponsors in the House and 21 in the Senate.[26]

COLD WAR COLLAPSE

After rising to great heights the world federalism movement came crashing down abruptly in the wake of the Korean War and the cold war political atmosphere that gripped the United States and other countries. The victory of the communist movement in China was misinterpreted as evidence of a spreading monolithic totalitarianism that threatened to engulf the world. The development of the H-bomb and the sharp rise in East–West military tensions disillusioned many liberals and internationalists. Hopes for a more peaceful and cooperative postwar order disappeared. Fear and hysteria gripped public consciousness, as substantial majorities in Europe and the

---

[21] DeBenedetti, *The Peace Reform in American History*, 149.   [22] Wittner, *One World or None*, 70.
[23] *Ibid.*, 93, 95.   [24] *Ibid.*, 51.   [25] Chatfield, *The American Peace Movement*, 95.
[26] Wittner, *One World or None*, 70–1.

United States favored the development and possession of nuclear weapons to deter the Soviet threat. Anticommunism spread like a virus, undermining the universalist principles of federalism. Visions of one world gave way to the grim reality of a planet divided in two, separated by an iron curtain. In the United States Senator Joseph McCarthy fanned the flames of paranoia by charging that leftists in government had "lost" China. The hand of Moscow was suspected in liberal internationalist causes, especially those that advocated cooperation with communist states. The increasingly rigid anticommunism and intolerant political climate silenced many of those who had previously supported federalism. Most of the states that had passed measures favoring world government voted to rescind their earlier resolutions.

Liberal internationalists were swept up in the anticommunist wave. Many federalists and liberals began to equate internationalism with an interventionist foreign policy to deter the Soviet Union and the global communist threat. As DeBenedetti noted, the assumptions of federalism with its strong opposition to totalitarian aggression "coincided all too easily with the cold war premises of the emerging American national security state." Many believed that the communist threat in the 1950s was equivalent to the fascist threat of the 1930s, and that collective military force and even nuclear deterrence were necessary to prevent renewed tyranny. The world federalism movement thus foundered on the shoals of cold war internationalism.

Some of those who had greeted the bomb with horror now came to accept it as a necessary deterrent against the communist threat. In 1948 a Church of England report stated that "the possession of atomic weapons is generally necessary for national self-preservation."[27] In the United States the Federal Council of Churches, which in 1945 had condemned the use of the bomb, declared in 1950 that atomic weapons were necessary for defense and that their use was "justifiable" as retaliation against attacks on the United States or its allies by "atomic weapons or other weapons of parallel destructiveness."[28] In Britain, France, West Germany, and other countries, public opinion polls showed substantial majorities in support of the bomb and favoring the use of nuclear weapons either preemptively or in response to attack. Many agreed with Churchill that without the bomb, "it is certain that Europe would have been communized and . . . London . . . under bombardment."[29]

[27] *Ibid.*, 311.
[28] Federal Council of Churches, Special Commission, *The Christian Conscience and Weapons of Mass Destruction* (New York: Department of International Justice and Goodwill, 1950), 14.
[29] Wittner, *One World or None*, 311–13.

The Korean War was a turning point in tilting public opinion toward support of cold war policies. Many internationalists and peace advocates supported the US-led war in Korea, which was seen as a justified act of collective defense against aggression and which was endorsed by the UN Security Council and General Assembly. The National Executive Council of the United World Federalists backed the war and urged the United States to "muster its full strength in the cause of freedom." In Britain Henry Usborne of the Crusade for World Government declared himself "four square behind the United Nations" in the war.[30] In Japan the previously pacifist Socialist Party split over the war and divided into two separate parties. A few groups such as the WRL opposed the war and mounted meager protests, but they were a tiny minority. Later, some of those who had supported the war came to regret their decision. They were dismayed by General Douglas MacArthur's march to the north, the subsequent Chinese intervention, and the bloody two-year stalemate that followed. They were horrified by the ferocity of the war, which killed 39,000 US soldiers and left more than two million Chinese and Koreans dead, many of them civilians. The war caused severe damage to US society as well, reinforcing a pervasive cold war atmosphere that suffocated the spirit of federalism and antiwar dissent. The result of the Korean War, wrote Michael Howard, "was quite simply to militarise the United States."[31]

The very language of peace was corrupted by the cold war ideological struggle. The Soviet-dominated East described itself as defending "peace," while the US-dominated West emphasized the goal of "freedom." These two great principles, which philosophers had for so long sought to combine, now came to be regarded as polar opposites. They were manipulated and distorted as propaganda shibboleths, and in the process lost much of their meaning – the "peace" of the East predicated on submission to totalitarianism, the "freedom" of the West based on the threat of war. Peace advocacy was further debased by the spread of communist-front "peace" organizations backed by the Soviet Union, which discredited the peace agenda and made the very concept seem subversive. Vera Brittain complained that the communist-front groups were making peace a "dirty word." Pacifist groups found themselves labeled as communist fronts. The federalist movement, with its emphasis on world government, was particularly susceptible to such charges. The identification of peace with communism became so pervasive

---

[30] *Ibid.*, 316–17.
[31] Michael Howard, *War and the Liberal Conscience* (New Brunswick, NJ: Rutgers University Press, 1989), 124.

that some mainstream groups placed the word "peace" in quotation marks.[32] In these difficult circumstances a small number of determined pacifists kept alive the flicker of the absolutist faith. Groups such as the AFSC, the FOR, the WILPF, and the WRL continued to function, albeit at reduced levels. Some committed pacifists continued to speak out and engaged in nonviolent direct action against war and nuclear weapons, but mass-based peace activity in the United States became virtually nonexistent.

MILITARIZATION AND RESISTANCE IN JAPAN

One of the early casualties of the cold war was the previous US policy of pacifying postwar Japan. The United States imposed the pacifist Constitution in 1946 but soon thereafter began to undermine its prohibition against the maintenance of armed forces. US policy makers looked to Japan as a potential strategic ally in containing communism and maintaining US military dominance in the western Pacific. Following the outbreak of the Korean War, the United States and Japan signed a mutual security treaty. Washington urged Tokyo to form a National Police Reserve, which in 1954 became the Self-Defense Forces (SDF) and has since grown into one of the world's most formidable military forces. Over the decades the United States exerted relentless pressure for Japan to expand its military capabilities and adjust its policies to allow overseas deployments in support of US-led military interventions.

During the 1950s a substantial peace movement emerged in Japan. Its agenda focused on nuclear disarmament, support for Article 9 of the Constitution, and opposition to Japanese military subservience to the United States. When Washington and Tokyo announced the renegotiation of the security treaty in 1959, peace and disarmament groups organized a massive *Anpo Tōsō* public opposition campaign. Peace advocates opposed the treaty on the grounds that it would subordinate Japanese interests to US military purposes and would increase the chances of Japan becoming involved in war. They also opposed the treaty in the context of the growing international outcry against nuclear testing and the fear that the United States might base nuclear weapons in Japan.[33]

---

[32] Wittner, *One World or None*, 319–20.
[33] Lawrence S. Wittner, *Resisting the Bomb: A History of the World Nuclear Disarmament Movement, 1954–1970*, vol. II of *The Struggle against the Bomb* (Stanford: Stanford University Press, 1997), 245.

In March 1959 thirteen national organizations, including the disarmament federation *Gensuikyo*, the Socialist Party, and *Sohyo* (Japan's major labor federation), established a national coalition to oppose the revised security pact. As Parliament debated the treaty in the spring of 1960, resistance intensified. In May more than 300,000 people demonstrated against the treaty outside Parliament in Tokyo, the largest protest in postwar Japanese history up to that time.[34] In June members of *Zengakuren*, the national student federation, broke through security barricades and clashed with helmeted police wielding truncheons. A student at Tokyo University was killed during the demonstrations, which prompted further protests and led to additional beatings and police repression. More than a thousand people were injured during the clashes, sending shock waves through the nation.[35] The ruling Liberal Democratic Party ignored public opposition and rammed the treaty through the Diet, but the violent clashes and resulting public outcry led to a political crisis that forced Prime Minister Kishi Nobusuke from office. President Eisenhower canceled a scheduled visit to Japan.

Japanese peace advocates were unable to prevent renewal of the security treaty, but they were successful at the time in blocking attempts to revise the Constitution and helped to build a political consensus against renewed militarization. Public opinion polls showed strong public support for maintaining Article 9 and for utilizing peaceful diplomacy rather than military force in international affairs.[36] Support for maintaining Article 9 stood at between 70 and 90 percent in opinion polls conducted from the 1960s to the 1980s.[37] In recent decades, however, nationalist demands for constitutional revision have gained ground, as have US pressures for militarization. In 2003 the government of Prime Minister Koizumi Junichiro broke decisively with Japan's postwar tradition by deploying 600 noncombat SDF troops to Iraq for "humanitarian reconstruction assistance." Koizumi's successor Abe Shinzo vowed in 2006 that his government would proceed with rewriting the Constitution and revising Article 9. In 2007 the Diet approved legislation calling for a national referendum on amending the Constitution.[38]

---

[34] Mari Yamamoto, *Grassroots Pacifism in Post-war Japan: The Rebirth of a Nation* (London: RoutledgeCurzon, 2004), 215.

[35] Wittner, *Resisting the Bomb*, 243–4.

[36] Peter J. Katzenstein and Nobuo Okawara, *Japan's National Security: Structures, Norms and Policy Responses in a Changing World* (Ithaca, NY: East Asia Program, Cornell University, 1993), 108–10, 115–16.

[37] Yamamoto, *Grassroots Pacifism in Post-war Japan*, 215.

[38] Norimitsu Onishi, "Japan to Vote on Modifying Pacifist Charter Written by US," *New York Times*, 15 May 2007.

THE LEVIATHAN

During the cold war the patterns of political, economic, and social mobilization that arose during World War II were institutionalized, and a huge national security apparatus was established at the heart of the US political system. Over the decades the United States engaged in a vast program of military interventionism that has continued to the present. Through covert and overt military action and political manipulation, Washington destabilized governments and fomented military coups and wars in dozens of countries around the world. Conscription was reintroduced, the armed forces were expanded, military spending increased, and the development of nuclear arms and other weapons systems accelerated. The national security apparatus responsible for these policies became a state within a state, an "iron triangle" exerting a vice-like grip on the shaping of US foreign policy and laying claim to a substantial share of US government resources. Thus was created a self-perpetuating set of deeply rooted policies and institutions that reinforced the tendency to rely on military solutions to problems of international conflict. In 1961 President Dwight Eisenhower issued his famous warning: "In the councils of government, we must guard against the acquisition of unwarranted influence, whether sought or unsought, by the military-industrial complex." That concentration of misplaced power was already in place when Eisenhower spoke, and it has remained at the center of US policy ever since.[39]

In 1965 Marc Pilisuk and Thomas Hayden wrote the important article, "Is There a Military Industrial Complex Which Prevents Peace?", which helped to shape the thinking of Vietnam war opponents. Drawing on the theories of C. Wright Mills, the authors examined how the ascendance of corporate and military elites has shaped US decision making, creating "consensus relationships," common decision-making practices, and a set of unchallenged "core beliefs" that predominate on military related issues. The social structure and political culture of the United States have evolved

---

[39] Among the many books that have examined the "unwarranted influence" of military industrial elites are: Richard J. Barnet, *The Economy of Death* (New York: Atheneum, 1969); Tristram Coffin, *The Armed Society: Militarism in Modern America* (Baltimore, MD: Penguin Books, 1964); Fred J. Cook, *The Warfare State* (New York: Macmillan, 1962); J. William Fulbright, *The Arrogance of Power* (New York: Random House, 1966); Richard F. Kaufman, *The War Profiteers* (Indianapolis, IN: Bobbs-Merrill, 1970); Sidney Lens, *The Military-Industrial Complex* (Philadelphia, PA: Pilgrim Press, 1970); and Ralph L. Stavins et al., eds., *Washington Plans an Aggressive War* (New York: Vintage Books, 1971). More recent books include Chalmers A. Johnson, *The Sorrows of Empire: Militarism, Secrecy, and the End of the Republic* (New York: Metropolitan Books, 2004); and A. J. Bacevich, *The New American Militarism: How Americans are Seduced by War* (New York: Oxford University Press, 2005).

in a way that sustains the power of military industrial institutions and interests.[40] Pilisuk and Hayden concluded that "American society *is* a military-industrial complex." Economic and institutional interests have combined with cultural influences to shape policies and assumptions that prioritize the role of military power. Militarization has become a dominant presence in US political life, with grave costs and consequences for the prospects of peace. Anatol Rapaport described militarization as a war system, a set of perceptions, practices, and institutions displaying character-istics of autonomous adaptation and self-preservation.[41] This is an accurate portrayal of the military leviathan that has become deeply entrenched in US society and in the conduct of US foreign policy.

The US tendency to militarize international affairs has devalued diplomatic approaches and led to continuous military interventions and wars throughout the cold war era and beyond, up to the invasion and occupation of Iraq. In the years from 1950 through 2005 the United States used force to attack or intervene in the affairs of other nations dozens of times.[42] Vietnam was only the largest and most costly example of this policy of military intervention against developing nations. Washington also launched numerous covert actions in which the United States, principally through the Central Intelligence Agency (CIA), sponsored paramilitary forces and engaged in other forms of political and economic destabilization to overthrow or subvert governments and nationalist movements. This was a record of military intervention in the affairs of other nations unmatched in human history, surpassing even that of Britain during the height of its empire. It was a policy that fomented numerous armed conflicts and caused millions of deaths, and that soon sparked the reemergence of antiwar opposition.

SPEAKING TRUTH TO POWER

In the early years of the cold war a committee of pacifist leaders gathered under the auspices of the AFSC to explore alternatives to militarization. Led by Stephen G. Cary and including veteran peace advocates like James E. Bristol, William B. Edgerton, Robert Gilmore, Milton Mayer, A. J. Muste,

---

[40] Marc Pilisuk and Thomas Hayden, "Is There a Military Industrial Complex Which Prevents Peace? Consensus and Countervailing Power in Pluralistic Systems," *Journal of Social Issues* 21, no. 3 (July 1965): 67–117.

[41] Anatol Rapaport, *Peace: An Idea Whose Time Has Come* (Ann Arbor, MI: University of Michigan Press, 1992), 86, 107, 175.

[42] Richard F. Grimmett, "Instances of Use of United States Armed Forces Abroad, 1798–2006," *CRS Report for Congress*, Order Code RL32170, 8 January 2007. Available online at the Federation of American Scientists, www.fas.org/sgp/crs/natsec/RL32170.pdf (accessed 12 September 2007).

and Clarence Pickett, the group warned against the dangers of over-reliance on military power, defended the principles of nonviolence, and called for a new, more realistic movement to prevent war and protect human freedom. The committee argued that militarization was incompatible with liberty, incapable of providing security, and ineffective in dealing with communism and other social evils. Their report sought to give practical expression to pacifist beliefs, and to show their relevance in resolving the most pressing problems of totalitarianism and war in the modern world. The resulting 1955 publication, *Speak Truth to Power*, was an eloquent and insightful manifesto of alternatives to violence. It speaks with startling prescience fifty years later and remains one of the seminal documents of pacifist literature during the twentieth century.

Speak Truth to Power recounts the consequences of militarization for US foreign policy – constant military interventions, the readiness to use nuclear weapons, a preference for unilateral military action over cooperation with the UN, the diversion of economic resources from development assistance to military aid, and the distortion of diplomacy through over-reliance on military threats. The open-ended nature of the commitment to militarization prevents the pursuit of alternative diplomatic, economic, and social policies that are needed to prevent war. The constant preparation for war and large-scale investment in military readiness impose huge burdens on society, diverting economic, political, and psychological resources to destructive purposes. Militarization has a corrosive effect on social values and human freedom, the authors noted, distorting political culture and creating demands for loyalty and conformity that threaten liberty. Under these conditions, mass opinion is easily manipulated to fan the flames of nationalism and military jingoism. "The organizational, cultural, and spiritual framework of a society prepared to wage modern mass warfare is incompatible with the framework of a society that sustains democratic and human values." War mobilization "can only be carried out at the expense of the very democracy we seek to protect." Military power "is as corrupting to the [one] who possesses it as it is pitiless to its victims. It is just as devastating to its employer as it is to those who suffer under it."[43] Those who wield such power fall prey to the evils they deplore in others.

Cold war militarization led to the perversion of language. *Speak Truth to Power* called attention to the appalling misuse of the term "free world" to describe countries within the orbit of US influence. The phrase is applied to

---

[43] American Friends Service Committee, *Speak Truth to Power: A Quaker Search for an Alternative to Violence* (Philadelphia: American Friends Service Committee, 1955), 17–19, 25.

all nations, no matter how dictatorial and exploited, which are considered partners of the USA. The military dictatorships of South Korea and Pakistan, the impoverished and exploited nations of Africa and Central America – all were painted "free" under this broad brush. Within this distorted picture, communism was portrayed as implacably hostile – the evil empire, as Ronald Reagan later termed it. Left-leaning national liberation movements were painted as communist and targeted for attack. This was the devil theory at work, a rationalization in which communists and insurgents were systematically dehumanized and thus deemed fit for military destruction.

In recent years terrorism has replaced communism as the new frame of dehumanization. It has been used to lump together all those who are considered enemies. The victims of US bombing and attack in Iraq are branded terrorists, regardless of the specific circumstances involved. The so-called "global war on terror" is used to justify any and all measures – invasion, war, military occupation, torture, indefinite internment, warrantless wiretapping – whatever may be deemed necessary by government officials to defeat the "evil" enemy. Fighting terrorism offers a rationalization for what is otherwise unjustifiable, just as during the cold war the fight against communism provided the justification for the unthinkable.

The crisis of the modern era, the authors of *Speak Truth to Power* suggested, requires a reconsideration of realist assumptions and a new understanding of the principles of pacifism. More effective and humane strategies are needed for addressing the critical challenges of social evil. Too often in the past pacifists have decried the horrors of war but have not faced frankly the problem of resisting social evil. They have shied away from the difficult task of making their moral commitments applicable to the most pressing dilemmas of justice and security. Camus wrote of the need for people to break out of their fear and silence, to combine love and indignation in transcending the false choices of murder or enslavement.[44] This was the task to which peace leaders now set themselves – to build a revitalized, more realistic peace movement to overcome the twin evils of totalitarianism and militarization. They called for renewed dedication to the philosophy and active practice of nonviolence. The *Speak Truth to Power* report emerged at a time of low ebb in the history of peace advocacy, but it helped to chart an intellectual and moral path toward renewed citizen activism against war, especially the ultimate violence of nuclear war. Peace advocates soon found themselves riding a wave of rising public concern and involvement for disarmament.

---

[44] Camus, *Neither Victims nor Executioners*, 52–3.

7

Banning the bomb

With advent of the nuclear age the challenge of disarmament became enormously more urgent. At stake in the struggle to reduce armaments and prevent war was nothing less than *The Fate of the Earth*, as Jonathan Schell wrote, the very survival of human life.[1] Among the first to speak out against the new horror of self-destruction were the atomic scientists who built the bomb. Their efforts were followed in subsequent decades by waves of citizen activism in the late 1950s and early 1960s and then in the 1980s, which produced some of the largest mobilizations for peace in human history. These movements generated the political pressure for arms control in the 1960s and 1970s and for arms reduction at the end of the 1980s that brought an end to the cold war. They established a nuclear taboo in politics and culture that generated enduring pressure on the nuclear weapons states to reduce and deemphasize their reliance on nuclear weapons. This chapter summarizes the history of the struggle to ban the bomb and examines further implications of the relationship between disarmament and peace.

THE SHOCK OF DISCOVERY

The explosion of the first atomic bomb at the Trinity site in New Mexico on 16 July 1945 had a transforming impact on the scientists and military officials who witnessed it. Robert Jungk observed in *Brighter Than a Thousand Suns* that many of those present – who otherwise professed no religious faith – "recounted their experiences in words derived from the linguistic fields of myth and theology." General Thomas Farrell, deputy director of the Manhattan Project, described the "strong, sustained, awesome roar which warned of doomsday and made us feel that we puny things were blasphemous to dare tamper with the forces heretofore reserved to the Almighty." J. Robert Oppenheimer, director of the Los Alamos scientists and a savant

[1] Jonathan Schell, *The Fate of the Earth* (New York: Knopf, 1982).

of Eastern religion, reflected on passages from the *Bhagavad-Gita*, the sacred Hindu epic:

> If the radiance of a thousand suns
> were to burst into the sky,
> that would be like
> the splendor of the Mighty One

As the sinister mushroom cloud rose in the distance, Oppenheimer was reminded of another line from the *Gita*: "I am become Death, the shatterer of worlds."

The bombings of Hiroshima and Nagasaki left many of the atomic scientists disturbed and bewildered. The scientists suddenly found themselves in an unprecedented and unaccustomed position of public acclaim. As Jungk writes, "the godlike magnitude of their performance had given them the standing of mythical figures ... They were called titans and compared with Prometheus."[2] Yet many felt uneasy about the destructive power their discoveries had unleashed. Some began to contemplate how they might put their new-found status to use in urging international control of atomic energy. A few expressed the cautious hope, as biophysicist Eugene Rabinowitch phrased it, "that the fate of Hiroshima and Nagasaki would cause [humankind] to turn a new leaf." Rabinowitch invited fellow scientists to be part of a "conspiracy to preserve our civilization by scaring [people] into rationality."[3]

It is one of history's supreme ironies that Einstein, the great pacifist, played a key role in urging the development of atomic weapons. Einstein's August 1939 letter to President Roosevelt recommending the development of a US nuclear program became the basis for the creation of the Manhattan Project. At the end of the war Einstein regretted his action and felt that he and the atomic scientists had been deceived. He had supported the bomb only to guard against possible German development of such a weapon. He assumed that the United States would never use the bomb except to deter or retaliate against the use of such a weapon by another country. The bombing of a prostrate Japan on the verge of surrender was not what he had envisioned.

The feared German bomb never materialized. US military leaders had unequivocal proof well before the end of the war that Germany did not have a functioning atomic bomb program. When allied troops entered Germany after D-Day a special intelligence unit code-named Alsos followed close

---

[2] Robert Jungk, *Brighter than a Thousand Suns: A Personal History of the Atomic Scientists* (New York: Harcourt Brace & Company, 1958), 201, 221–2.
[3] Eugene Rabinowitch, "Five Years After," *Bulletin of the Atomic Scientists* 7, no. 1 (January 1951): 3.

behind to search for the suspected nuclear program. They tested Germany's rivers and found no evidence of the radionuclides that would signal the presence of uranium processing. They searched German-controlled research facilities in occupied France and Germany. They reviewed documents and interviewed scientists. They discovered that the German atomic research program was at least two years behind that of the United States, and that Germany possessed no factories for the production of enriched uranium or plutonium. By early 1945 it was clear that the dreaded German bomb did not exist.

The fruitless search for the phantom German atomic bomb in 1944–5 had an eerie parallel nearly sixty years later in the search for weapons of mass destruction in Iraq. In both cases teams of scientists and technicians scoured conquered territory to find evidence of menacing weapons. In both cases the investigating scientists came up empty handed. Research and development activities were discovered, but no evidence was found of a functioning atomic weapons program. Of course there were many differences between the two episodes. In the case of Germany, the menace of expansionist tyranny was very real and had plunged Europe and much of the world into war. Eminent nuclear physicists expressed genuine concerns about the possibility of a German bomb program. In the case of Iraq, by contrast, the government of Saddam Hussein was weakened by defeat in previous war and years of sanctions and did not threaten international security. Nuclear scientists expressed concerns about Iraq's nuclear ambitions, but emphasized that international monitors from the International Atomic Energy Agency had already verified the destruction of Baghdad's nuclear weapons program in the early 1990s. Few experts believed the Bush administration's claim that Iraq actually possessed weapons of mass destruction.

SCIENTISTS ORGANIZE

One of the first scientists to sound the alarm about the danger of atomic weapons was Leo Szilard. As early as September 1942 Szilard drafted a memo outlining the ominous implications of the work upon which they were embarked. "We cannot have peace in a world in which various sovereign nations have atomic bombs in the possession of their armies."[4] At the Metallurgical Laboratory at the University of Chicago, where the first

---

[4] Quoted in Lawrence S. Wittner, *One World or None: A History of the World Nuclear Disarmament Movement through 1953*, vol. I of *The Struggle against the Bomb* (Stanford, CA: Stanford University Press, 1993), 20.

nuclear chain reaction took place in December 1942, a committee of atomic scientists began addressing the political problems of controlling and harnessing nuclear energy. The committee produced a 1944 report, *Prospectus on Nucleonics*, which warned that attempts to achieve atomic supremacy could not bring lasting security. The report argued for the creation of "an international administration with police powers which can effectively control . . . the means of nucleonic warfare."[5]

In June 1945 the Chicago scientists produced a new report, largely written by Rabinowitch, which argued against the military use of the bomb against Japan. The report warned that there could be no effective defense against atomic weapons. It argued against bombing Japan because this could shatter the prospects for establishing the necessary degree of trust and mutual confidence to establish international control.

If the United States were to be the first to release this new means of indiscriminate destruction upon mankind, she would sacrifice public support throughout the world, precipitate the race for armaments, and prejudice the possibility of reaching an international agreement on the future control of such weapons

the scientists wrote.[6] The report argued for a public demonstration of the new weapon in a desert or on a barren island. It urged US leaders to renounce the use of such weapons in the future and to join in the establishment of an international control mechanism.

When the government rejected the scientists' reports and proceeded with the bombings of Japan, the scientists joined together to form the Federation of Atomic Scientists, which soon changed its name to the Federation of American Scientists (FAS). Their mission was to enlighten the public about the new atomic danger and apply pressure on political leaders for international control. By early 1946 the FAS claimed seventeen local groups with nearly 3,000 members, including 90 percent of the scientists who had worked on the bomb. At the same time Rabinowitch and some of his colleagues in Chicago founded a new publication, the *Bulletin of Atomic Scientists*, which was to become, and remains today, the premier journal and most authoritative source of information on the state of the nuclear danger. Featuring the distinctive "doomsday clock," designed by Edward Teller, the *Bulletin* by mid-1947 had a circulation of 20,000, including scientists in

[5] *Prospectus on Nucleonics* (the Jeffries Report), in *A Peril and a Hope: The Scientists' Movement in America: 1945–47*, ed. Alice Kimball Smith (Chicago, IL: University of Chicago Press, 1965), 554.

[6] James Franck *et al.*, "A Report to the Secretary of War (June 1945)," in *The Atomic Age: Scientists in National and World Affairs*, ed. Morton Grodzins and Eugene Rabinowitch, 19–27 (New York: Basic Books, 1963), 27.

seventeen countries. Szilard and Einstein organized the parallel Emergency Committee of Atomic Scientists to help raise funds for the movement. Einstein served as chair of the committee, which was endorsed by other prominent scientists, including Hans Bethe and Linus Pauling. Szilard was the active force behind the committee and played a crucial role in building the scientists' movement.[7]

The atomic scientists' most urgent demand was for international control of atomic energy. For a brief time in early 1946 they helped to convince an otherwise skeptical US government to consider eliminating atomic weapons and establishing a system of international control of nuclear energy. When the bombs were dropped on Japan President Truman had declared that Americans "must constitute ourselves trustees of this new force ... We thank God that it has come to us, instead of our enemies."[8] Within a few weeks, however, the administration began to consider a different approach. Future Secretary of State Dean Acheson drafted a message for the president in early October that declared "the hope of civilization lies in international arrangements looking, if possible, to the renunciation of the use and development of the atomic bomb."[9] In November US, British, and Canadian leaders issued a remarkable statement echoing many of the views of the scientists. There is no defense against atomic weapons, they declared, and no nation can maintain a monopoly on the new technology. The path to security lies in preventing war and establishing international control over this new power. The joint declaration of November 1945 was followed by the meeting of US, British, and Soviet foreign ministers on 27 December 1945, which supported the proposal for international control and called for the formation of an atomic energy commission under the authority of the United Nations. The very first resolution adopted by the UN General Assembly, meeting in London on 24 January 1946, called "for the elimination from national armaments of atomic weapons and of all other major weapons adaptable to mass destruction."[10] The resolution created a UN Atomic Energy Commission charged with developing immediate plans for: (1) control of atomic energy to the extent necessary to ensure its use only for peaceful purposes; (2) the elimination from national armaments of atomic weapons and of all other major weapons

---

[7] Wittner, *One World or None*, 60–1.

[8] Harry S. Truman, "Radio Report to the American People on the Potsdam Conference" (radio address, White House, Washington, DC, 9 August 1945).

[9] Quoted in Wittner, *One World or None*, 249.

[10] United Nations General Assembly, *Establishment of a Commission to Deal with the Problems Raised by the Discovery of Atomic Energy*, 1(I), London, 24 January 1946.

adaptable to mass destruction; and (3) effective safeguards by way of inspection and other means to protect complying states against the hazards of violations and evasions.

To formulate the details of the nuclear control policy adopted at the United Nations, Truman appointed a special committee headed by Acheson, with significant input from David Lilienthal, director of the Tennessee Valley Authority. In March 1946 the committee presented one of the most far-reaching proposals of the nuclear era, which became known as the Acheson–Lilienthal plan. The proposal offered a formula for controlling atomic energy and preventing a nuclear arms race. It provided for the creation of an international body, an Atomic Development Authority, which would maintain a monopoly on the production of fissile materials and distribute them only in "denatured" form for peaceful purposes. The plan called for the elimination of atomic weapons then in existence (i.e. US weapons) and the creation of a system of international ownership and inspection to prevent the further development of such weapons and to guard against violations. Oppenheimer wrote that the report "proposes that in the field of atomic energy there be set up a world government, that in this field there be renunciation of national sovereignty." The plan contained, he believed, "new and healthy avenues of approach [for] the problem of preventing war."[11] It was a remarkable reflection of pacifist insight in the development of public policy.

THE BARUCH PLAN

The success of the scientists and their allies was short lived, however, for Truman soon appointed financier Bernard Baruch to serve as the US representative to the UN Atomic Energy Commission and gave him a free hand to formulate the specific proposal that would be presented to the United Nations. When Oppenheimer, Lilienthal, and other scientists learned of Baruch's appointment, they were deeply disappointed. Baruch was known as a self-promoter and a hardliner who disdained the proposals of the scientists. Baruch's June 1946 address to the UN Atomic Energy Commission in New York began dramatically with an apocalyptic reference: "We are here to make a choice between the quick and the dead." He spoke grandly of abolishing war, but the specific proposal he offered significantly diminished the prospects for creating a more secure world. The Baruch plan differed substantially from its predecessor. His plan called for a

---

[11] Quoted in Wittner, *One World or None*, 250–1.

UN control body that would have the power to punish offending nations through enforceable sanctions, including military means. The destruction of existing (US) atomic weapons would come only at the end of the process, after the UN control body had conducted on-site inspections and had assured the dismantling of all nuclear capabilities in other countries. The United States would have retained its monopoly on nuclear weapons until after the last stages of the disarmament process, when nuclear programs in other countries were dismantled. Soviet Foreign Minister Andrei Gromyko promptly dismissed the Baruch plan and proposed instead that the United States destroy its existing nuclear stockpiles first, before creation of a system of international control. This was an equally one-sided proposal, from the opposite perspective, and would have allowed the Soviet Union to continue its rapidly developing nuclear program while the United States disarmed unilaterally. The two nations entered an immediate stalemate, which persisted for decades.

During the cold war and afterwards, a kind of historical mythology developed around the Baruch plan. Realists described Moscow's rejection of the plan as a sign of Soviet perfidy and a cause of the cold war. Arms controllers looked back upon the plan as a significant US initiative for the elimination of atomic weapons and international control of nuclear energy. Neither assumption was entirely correct. Stalin no doubt intended to pursue the development of nuclear weapons regardless of any diplomatic commitments, but the Baruch proposal was obviously one sided. It was an assertion of unilateral US advantage, not a serious proposal for the elimination of nuclear weapons or international control of atomic energy. From the very beginning of the atomic age the United States insisted on retaining its nuclear weapons while demanding that other countries give up theirs. This has remained the basis of US nonproliferation policy to the present, and is a continuing obstacle to progress toward genuine disarmament.

Washington's declared intention to eliminate nuclear weapons might have been taken more seriously if the United States had not been at that very moment building additional bombs and preparing to begin nuclear testing on Bikini Atoll in the Pacific. On the very day Baruch spoke, the US Congress passed and President Truman signed a Bill allowing the use of navy ships as targets in the coming atomic tests.[12] Several Senators objected to the resolution and the tests, arguing that the USA would be accused of double talk at the UN, but their concerns were swept aside. Two weeks

---

[12] Jonathan M. Weisgall, *Operation Crossroads: The Atomic Tests at Bikini Atoll* (Annapolis, MD: Naval Institute Press, 1994), 101–3.

later, on 1 July 1946, Test Able exploded over Bikini ending any further pretense of a US interest in eliminating nuclear weapons.

Meanwhile historical amnesia descended over the Acheson–Lilienthal plan and the first resolution of the United Nations that preceded it. Few historians acknowledged that for a few fleeting months in early 1946 the US government was committed to a plan for the elimination of nuclear weapons, and that the United States pledged to dismantle its existing nuclear capabilities in conjunction with the establishment of an international atomic control mechanism. The Acheson–Lilienthal plan had flaws, especially the lack of mechanisms for assuring international compliance, but it offered the promise of genuine diplomatic dialogue for the control of atomic weapons. The plan contained crucial provisions – a US commitment to eliminate its weapons in concert with the creation of an international control mechanism – that were then and remain today necessary foundations upon which to build international cooperation to prevent nuclear war.

In the wake of the collapse of the Baruch plan, and in the face of mounting hostility from an increasingly cold-war-minded US government, the atomic scientists movement waned. The political atmosphere for nuclear disarmament became increasingly oppressive. Fear and distrust began to strain relations and friendships among the scientists. The anti-communist hysteria of the time was directed especially toward the foreign-born scientists who had helped to discover the secrets of the atom. More than half of those who were labeled communists during the congressional hearings of the early 1950s were physicists and mathematicians. Hundreds of scientists were mercilessly hounded and dismissed from their jobs. By 1951 the Emergency Committee of Atomic Scientists dissolved, and the FAS dwindled to just 1,000 members.[13] The *Bulletin of Atomic Scientists* lost subscribers, but it continued to publish, and persisted to become a vital voice of sanity in the succeeding waves of disarmament activism which emerged in the late 1950s and again in the 1980s.

FOR NUCLEAR SANITY

Disarmament activism revived in the late 1950s in parallel with the increase in nuclear weapons testing, especially H-bomb explosions, and the consequent rise of public concerns about radioactive fallout. In the years from 1945 through 1963 the United States and the Soviet Union conducted more than 550 nuclear tests, most of them in the atmosphere, including nearly a

---

[13] Wittner, *One World or None*, 266–7, 326.

hundred nuclear explosions at the Nevada test site. Radioactive debris from these explosions drifted over nearby towns, especially St. George, Utah, and was carried aloft over much of the country. Approximately 250,000 US soldiers participated in military maneuvers at the test site, exposing themselves to high levels of radioactivity. Many later suffered from leukemia and cancer. In the 1980s the survivors and their families formed the Atomic Veterans Association, which lobbied for and eventually won government compensation for the radiation-induced illnesses and premature deaths that resulted from their exposure. Fears of radioactive fallout and nuclear war increased not only in the United States but throughout the world.

One of the strongest voices against the worsening nuclear peril in the 1950s was that of British philosopher Bertrand Russell, a veteran pacifist who had opposed the Boer War, supported conscientious objectors during World War I, campaigned for peace during the interwar years, and endorsed the world federalist movement after World War II. In 1955 Russell joined with Einstein and other renowned international scientists in issuing an appeal for governments to acknowledge the suicidal nature of nuclear weapons and work for peace. In 1957 Linus Pauling issued a statement signed by 11,000 scientists, including 2,000 Americans, calling for a ban on atmospheric testing.[14] That same year atomic scientists from several countries, including the Soviet Union, gathered at a conference center in Pugwash, Nova Scotia for the start of annual meetings that provided a unique opportunity for dialogue between Western scientists and their counterparts in the East. The Pugwash movement remains active today and in 1995 won the Nobel Peace Prize. Receiving the award for the scientists movement was Joseph Rotblat, the Polish-born physicist who had resigned from the Manhattan Project when he learned that the German bomb did not exist (he was the only scientist to do so) and who remained a stalwart campaigner for nuclear disarmament until his death in 2005 at the age of ninety-six.

It was during this time of nuclear awakening that two of the most important antinuclear organizations of the cold war era emerged, CND in Britain and SANE in the United States. CND was launched at a large public meeting at Central Hall, Westminster in February 1958. Addressing that inaugural meeting were Russell, Canon L. John Collins (the first chair of CND), playwright J. B. Priestley, former military commander Stephen King-Hall, Labour Member of Parliament Michael Foot, and historian

---

[14] Charles DeBenedetti, *The Peace Reform in American History* (Bloomington, IN: Indiana University Press, 1980), 160.

A. J. P. Taylor. During 1958 and the years following, CND flourished, drawing support from youth, the Churches, and rank and file members of the Labour Party. By 1960 CND had more than 450 local groups. A CND demonstration that year in Trafalgar Square attracted more than 60,000 people, the largest public rally held in London in more than a hundred years.[15]

SANE was formed in the United States in 1957. Founders included writer Norman Cousins, Clarence Pickett of the AFSC, Norman Thomas of the Socialist Party, and Homer Jack, a Unitarian minister from Chicago. The name SANE was inspired by the work of the famed psychoanalyst and author Erich Fromm, whose book *The Sane Society* was highly influential at the time and who urged citizens to lift a "voice of sanity" against nuclear fear. SANE attracted the support of other peace groups and endorsements from prominent public figures, including Rev. Harry Emerson Fosdick, Paul Tillich, James Shotwell, Eleanor Roosevelt, and Cleveland Amory. Through a series of creative full-page advertisements in the *New York Times* (including one that featured Dr. Benjamin Spock worrying about the effects of fallout on children), SANE gained public attention and popular support. Within a year the organization had 150 local committees and some 25,000 members. Its most prominent chapter emerged in Hollywood, where actor Steve Allen gathered nearly 150 artists and entertainers to create the Hollywood for SANE committee.[16]

CND and SANE had many similarities (CND's newsletter was entitled *Sanity*), and they waxed and waned in parallel over the decades, as anti-nuclear activism rose in the late 1950s and early 1960s, declined subsequently, and then rose to even greater heights in the late 1970s and early 1980s. The two groups differed in political approaches, however. CND from the outset was more explicit in supporting the demand for unilateral disarmament. In 1960 CND supporters mounted a successful effort to win official Labour Party endorsement of a resolution urging "the unilateral renunciation of the testing, manufacture, stockpiling and basing of all nuclear weapons in Great Britain."[17] The victory for unilateralism was short lived, however, as the Labour Party reversed its position the following year. The CND program also included demands for multilateral objectives, such as a nuclear test ban

[15] Lawrence S. Wittner, *Resisting the Bomb: A History of the World Nuclear Disarmament Movement, 1954–1970*, vol. II of *The Struggle against the Bomb* (Stanford, CA: Stanford University Press, 1997), 47, 185.

[16] Milton S. Katz, *Ban the Bomb: A History of SANE, the Committee for a Sane Nuclear Policy, 1957–1985* (New York: Greenwood Press, 1986), 24, 42.

[17] Quoted in Wittner, *Resisting the Bomb*, 186.

treaty and the creation of nuclear-free zones, but the principle of unilateral-ism remained part of the CND program. Independent initiatives could stimulate mutual disarmament, CND leaders emphasized, by helping to reduce tensions and sparking a process of reciprocal reduction.

SANE's political program was more moderate than that of CND, focus-ing on an end to nuclear testing. SANE emphasized that its program was "not unilateralist," although it supported "political and military initiatives by the US to break the present impasse," which it hoped would encourage a "peace race" to replace the arms race. SANE's political methods focused on public education and political and legislative action aimed at decision makers in Washington. Although concentrating on testing issues SANE also supported broader disarmament goals. A national conference in October 1959 adopted a program that included "comprehensive disarma-ment, a strong UN capable of enforcing world law, and the transition to a peacetime economy."[18]

Other disarmament groups formed at the time. In 1961 Dagmar Wilson joined with other women to create Women Strike for Peace, which con-sciously projected an image of "housewives" resisting nuclear destruction to save their children. In 1962 Leo Szilard founded the Council for a Livable World as a political action committee to support pro-disarmament candi-dates. Throughout the United States and in many other countries, anti-nuclear activism increased. In Africa political leaders were outraged in 1960 when France detonated three nuclear bombs in the Sahara. Tanzania's Julius Nyerere decried the "humiliation under which we in Africa still labour ... [when] a government can sit in Paris and decide what piece of Africa they are going to use for testing their hydrogen bomb!"[19] In Ghana the government froze French assets and Kwame Nkrumah threatened a mass nonviolent march into the testing zone.[20]

THE BEGINNING OF ARMS CONTROL

As the public outcry against radioactive fallout intensified in the early 1960s government leaders were forced to respond. Political pressure for a test ban treaty was especially strong in Britain, where Prime Minister Harold Macmillan told President Kennedy that public pressures against testing

[18] Quoted in *ibid.*, 247.
[19] Julius K. Nyerere, *Freedom and Unity: Uhuru na umoja: A Selection from Writings and Speeches, 1952–65* (London: Oxford University Press, 1967), 69.
[20] Kwame Nkrumah, *I Speak of Freedom: A Statement of African Ideology* (New York: Praeger, 1962), 214–15.

were running high and that the British cabinet "wished for some new disarmament initiative to be taken and given wide publicity." The public clamor for an end to testing convinced US and Soviet leaders that, as Lawrence Wittner observed, "nuclear arms control measures made good politics."[21] A diplomatic breakthrough came in 1963, thanks partly to the intermediary role of SANE co-chair Norman Cousins, who met separately with Kennedy and Khrushchev to identify mutually acceptable terms. The resulting test ban treaty was a political landmark, the first nuclear disarmament agreement. It was also a triumph for public health and the environment, ending the radioactive poisoning of the earth's atmosphere. The treaty helped to reduce US-Soviet tensions, but it did not stop the arms race. Nuclear testing went underground and in fact accelerated. More nuclear explosions were conducted in the years after the test ban treaty than before. Nonetheless the agreement was a beginning of the arms control process, and it established a precedent that eventually culminated in significant nuclear disarmament nearly three decades later. When the treaty was signed Kennedy expressed "deep gratification" to Cousins and other disarmament advocates for "mobilizing American public opinion in favor of a test-ban."[22]

The signing of the test ban treaty was a significant victory for the ban the bomb movement and gave a boost to the cause of nuclear pacifism. The weight of public pressure was a major factor in the political calculations of political leaders at the time. As Wittner wrote,

the antinuclear movement ... constrained the major actors and helped shape the choices they made ... Antinuclear sentiment eased the dangerous international confrontation, slowed the nuclear arms race, and provided the basis for the unprecedented nuclear arms control agreements that were to follow.[23]

US, British, and Soviet leaders could not ignore the worldwide protest against radioactive fallout and the growing demands for a halt to nuclear testing. The cause of nuclear disarmament gained new legitimacy and public support. The cruciform symbol of CND "became as well known as the Union Jack," wrote Collins, and earned an enduring place in popular culture as the universal peace sign.[24] New organizations emerged and continued to function after the signing of the test ban treaty to carry on the fight for disarmament. The stage was set for the dramatic upsurge in disarmament activism that began fifteen years later.

---

[21] Wittner, *Resisting the Bomb*, 394–5, 415.   [22] Quoted in *ibid.*, 418.
[23] Ibid., 383.   [24] Canon L. John Collins, *Faith Under Fire* (London: Leslie Frewin, 1966), 310.

NUCLEAR PACIFISM IN JAPAN

Opposition to nuclear weapons spread far beyond Europe and North America, as Wittner documented in his magisterial three-volume study on the world nuclear disarmament movement. Nowhere was support for the nuclear disarmament movement stronger or more persistent than in Japan, which has special authority and motivation on this issue as the only nation to have suffered nuclear attack. The annual commemorative ceremonies at Hiroshima and Nagasaki became not only rituals for memorializing the dead but fervent pleas for nuclear disarmament and world peace. They affirmed a unique Japanese mission to work for the elimination of atomic weapons, and expressed the hope that the ordeal of those two cities might somehow be redeemed through a worldwide commitment to end war.[25]

Japanese antinuclear sentiment began to crystallize in 1954, when several Japanese fishermen aboard the ironically named *Lucky Dragon* were severely contaminated (one was killed) by radioactive fallout from a US nuclear test conducted at Bikini Atoll. The episode galvanized public opinion and sparked widespread antinuclear protest. Nearly 20 million signatures were collected on petitions calling for disarmament and an end to nuclear tests. Both the upper and lower chambers of Parliament adopted unanimous resolutions calling for a ban on nuclear weapons. Most prefectural governments and some 250 municipalities passed similar resolutions.[26] For the first time in Japanese history the peace movement gained widespread support and respectability within society and was able to influence government decision makers.

In the late 1950s, in response to the worldwide crisis over nuclear testing and radioactive fallout, the nuclear disarmament movement intensified. *Gensuikyo*, affiliated with the Socialist Party, became the leading force behind the mobilization of antinuclear sentiment and gained the endorsement of prominent Japanese leaders from all walks of life. In 1958 Kagawa Toyohiko joined with Albert Schweitzer and Bertrand Russell in an open letter to world leaders urging a suspension of nuclear tests.[27] More than a thousand Japanese scientists signed Linus Pauling's petition against nuclear testing. Public opinion polls showed some 90 percent of the population

---

[25] Robert Kisala, *Prophets of Peace: Pacifism and Cultural Identity in Japan's New Religions* (Honolulu: University of Hawai'i Press, 1999), 175.

[26] Mari Yamamoto, *Grassroots Pacifism in Post-war Japan: The Rebirth of a Nation* (London: RoutledgeCurzon, 2004), 167.

[27] Robert Schildgen, *Toyohiko Kagawa: Apostle of Love and Social Justice* (Berkeley, CA: Centenary Books, 1988), 281.

opposed to nuclear testing and supporting a worldwide ban on nuclear weapons. The student federation *Zengakuren* organized hundreds of thousands of students to participate in public rallies and boycotts of classes. Protests were directed at both US and Soviet nuclear testing. *Zengakuren* activists unfurled a banner in Moscow's Red Square denouncing Soviet nuclear tests, and they organized massive rallies outside the Soviet Embassy in Tokyo.[28]

Antinuclear activism surged again in the 1980s. In preparation for the Second UN Special Session on Disarmament, which convened in New York in the spring of 1982, the major Japanese peace and disarmament groups joined together with a wide range of mainstream civil society groups to form the Japanese National Liaison Committee for Nuclear and General Disarmament. The Liaison Committee collected nearly 29 million signatures on a nuclear disarmament petition, which was presented to the United Nations in June 1982, at the time of the giant rally for disarmament in New York's Central Park which attracted nearly one million people. An antinuclear petition organized by the Union of New Religions was signed by more than 36 million people. Some 200,000 people participated in a disarmament rally in Hiroshima in March 1982, and 400,000 demonstrated in Tokyo in May of that year. More than 1,400 local governments passed resolutions urging the Japanese government to promote disarmament at the UN Special Session.[29]

THE RISE OF THE NUCLEAR FREEZE

The nuclear freeze and disarmament movements of the late 1970s and 1980s were a response to the accelerating nuclear build-up of the Soviet Union and the United States. The specific catalyst was the deployment by the Soviet Union of new intermediate range nuclear missiles (the SS-20) in eastern Europe in the late 1970s and the corresponding deployment by the United States in NATO countries of Cruise and Pershing II missiles. The Soviet invasion of Afghanistan added to an already tense political climate and sparked a renewed cold war response in the United States which paved the way for the election of Ronald Reagan. Some European governments also

---

[28] Wittner, *Resisting the Bomb*, 42–3, 242–3.
[29] Lawrence S. Wittner, *Toward Nuclear Abolition: A History of the World Nuclear Disarmament Movement, 1971 to the Present*, vol. III of *The Struggle against the Bomb* (Stanford: Stanford University Press, 2003), 203–4.

hardened their policies toward the Soviet Union, although the people of Europe generally rejected the atmosphere of renewed cold war hostility.

Like the previous ban-the-bomb movement, the antinuclear campaigns of the late 1970s were rooted in environmental consciousness and growing public concerns about radiation and the fragility of nuclear technology. The accident at the Three Mile Island nuclear reactor in Pennsylvania in March 1979 gave a decisive boost to the antinuclear cause and accelerated the organizing that led to the nuclear weapons freeze campaign. In Germany the movement against nuclear power in the 1970s laid the foundation for the massive campaign against nuclear missiles in the 1980s. As public opposition to nuclear technology increased, a visceral fear of radiation spread throughout society. The "primitive fear" that Cousins had identified at the dawn of the atomic age reemerged and deepened.[30]

During the early 1980s nuclear fear reached unprecedented levels. Opinion surveys found a huge jump in the percentage of people fearing nuclear war. According to the Gallup poll of September 1981, 70 percent of Americans surveyed felt that nuclear war was a real possibility, and 30 percent felt that the chances of such a conflict were "good" or "certain."[31] In Europe the fear of nuclear war was even greater. The percentage of Europeans believing that nuclear war was "probable in the next 10 years" rose from just over 10 percent in 1977 to more than 30 percent in 1980. In West Germany fear of nuclear war rose from 17 percent in July 1979 to a startling 48 percent in January 1980.[32] Daniel Yankelovich and John Doble wrote in *Foreign Affairs* that "a great change . . . has transformed the outlook of the American electorate," and the public is "determined to stop what they see as a drift toward nuclear confrontation."[33] This "sea change" was marked most significantly by widespread public doubt about the chances of surviving a nuclear war. Whereas in 1955 only 27 percent of the public thought humankind would be destroyed in an all-out nuclear war, thirty years later 89 percent agreed with that statement.

The new disarmament movements were also a response to the crisis in nuclear disarmament. The negotiated arms control agreements of the 1970s did not slow the arms race or reduce the nuclear danger but in fact allowed

---

[30] Norman Cousins, *Modern Man is Obsolete* (New York: Viking Press, 1945), 7.
[31] "Poll Finds 7 out of 10 Imagining Outbreak of Soviet Nuclear War," *Washington Post*, 27 September 1981, A17.
[32] Thomas R. Rochon, *Mobilizing for Peace: The Antinuclear Movements in Western Europe* (Princeton, NJ: Princeton University Press, 1988), 46–7.
[33] Daniel Yankelovich and John Doble, "The Public Mood: Nuclear Weapons and the U.S.S.R.," *Foreign Affairs* 63, no. 1 (fall 1984): 33–5.

for the build-up of weapons on both sides. In the United States disarmament activists and liberal members of Congress grew increasingly frustrated with the Strategic Arms Limitation Treaty (SALT) process and began to search for a new approach that could reduce nuclear dangers and break the momentum of the continuing nuclear build-up. The idea of a US-Soviet nuclear freeze had been proposed in the early 1970s by Gerard Smith, chief US negotiator for the SALT I treaty. The concept was raised again and developed in more detail by Richard Barnet of the Institute for Policy Studies in the spring 1979 issue of *Foreign Affairs*.[34] During the US Senate debate on the SALT II treaty that year, Senators Mark Hatfield and George McGovern introduced an amendment calling for a US-Soviet freeze on strategic nuclear weapons. These ideas soon crystallized into the proposal for a nuclear moratorium, which became the nuclear weapons freeze.

In 1980 Randall Forsberg, director of the Institute for Defense and Disarmament Studies in Massachusetts, issued the "Call to Halt the Arms Race." This was the founding manifesto of the nuclear weapons freeze campaign. Forsberg later published a feature article elaborating the rationale for a nuclear freeze in *Scientific American*.[35] The freeze proposal was breathtakingly simple yet profoundly significant in its political implications. It urged the United States and the Soviet Union to accept an immediate, verifiable halt to the testing, production, and deployment of new nuclear weapons and their delivery systems.[36] This modest formulation became the basis for the nuclear weapons freeze campaign and sparked one of the largest peace mobilizations in US history.

The great political value of the freeze concept was its accessibility to the average citizen. It was "user friendly." Supporters did not need a PhD in physics or a degree in international relations to understand and accept its logic. It was eagerly embraced by a public anxious for a way out of the worsening nuclear dilemma. The enormous popularity of nuclear disarmament in the 1980s transformed the politics of the nuclear debate. Previously an obscure and highly technical field reserved for experts, nearly all of them white males, nuclear policy making now became the province of ordinary citizens. The debate over nuclear weapons and military strategy was radically democratized. The discussion of nuclear policy was removed from the

---

[34] Richard Barnet, "U.S.-Soviet Relations: The Need for a Comprehensive Approach," *Foreign Affairs* 57, no. 4 (spring 1979): 779–95.

[35] Randall Forsberg, "A Bilateral Nuclear-Weapon Freeze," *Scientific American* 247, no. 5 (November 1982): 52–61.

[36] Pam Solo, *From Protest to Policy: Beyond the Freeze to Common Security* (Cambridge, MA: Ballinger Publishing, 1988), 45.

cloistered boardrooms of military strategists and taken to the city square. Ordinary citizens demanded a say in the most vital of all issues, the prevention of nuclear war and the survival of the human race. The anti-nuclear movements of Europe, although not adopting the nuclear freeze proposal *per se*, developed their own version of a demand for mutual disarmament. Their slogan was "no to SS-20s and Cruise and Pershing missiles." This call for an end to nuclear deployments on both sides captured the essential symmetry of the freeze concept.

The demand for mutual disarmament by the Soviet Union and the United States was of profound political significance. Western peace advocates were able to transcend the limitations of previous campaigns that directed protests primarily against US nuclear weapons. By directing their political demands equally at Moscow and Washington the disarmament activists of the 1980s dispelled the political stereotypes that had hindered earlier peace movements. They were able to overcome lingering suspicions from the early days of the cold war that disarmament activists were dupes of the Soviet Union. The demand for mutual disarmament enabled the peace movement to achieve a decisive breakthrough in political credibility.

GOD AGAINST THE BOMB

One of the most distinctive features of the disarmament debate during the 1980s was the extensive involvement of the religious community. The engagement of the churches cast a "mantle of respectability" over the peace movement and gave new legitimacy to discussions of disarmament.[37] When religious leaders spoke out for reversal of the arms race, it became easier and more acceptable for others to express similar views. The backing of the religious community made peace a mainstream issue and gave credibility and momentum to the disarmament movement. The enhanced legitimacy arising from this support strengthened peace activism and helped to generate the political pressure that ultimately led to changes in nuclear policy.

Veteran religious peace activists like William Sloane Coffin, Jr. and Jim Wallis played a decisive role in building the disarmament and nuclear freeze campaigns of the 1980s. As senior minister of New York's prestigious Riverside Church, Coffin initiated a disarmament program that reached thousands of clergy and laity across the United States. *Sojourners* editor Wallis was on the founding committee of the nuclear weapons freeze

---

[37] William Sloane Coffin, interview by the author, 3 December 1990.

campaign. Along with Coffin he played an important role in articulating the moral and religious argument for disarmament. Religious peace organizations like Pax Christi, the FOR, and the AFSC were major players in the developing disarmament movement.

By far the most significant statement from US religious leaders during the 1980s was the pastoral letter of the US Catholic Conference of Bishops, *The Challenge of Peace: God's Promise and Our Response*, issued in May 1983. Written by Father J. Bryan Hehir for a committee of bishops chaired by Joseph Cardinal Bernardin of Chicago, with significant input from Bishop Thomas Gumbleton of Detroit, the bishops' pastoral letter had a profound impact on public discourse. The letter from the normally conservative Catholic hierarchy challenged the very foundations of US nuclear policy and specifically opposed key elements of the Reagan administration's military build-up.

While avoiding the phrase "nuclear freeze," the bishops declared their support for "immediate bilateral agreements to halt the testing, production and deployment of nuclear weapons systems." They endorsed a policy of no first use and a comprehensive nuclear test ban treaty. The bishops condemned any initiation of nuclear war and opposed even retaliatory strikes that would threaten innocent life. The logic of this position should have led the bishops to reject any possession of nuclear weapons and to oppose the doctrine of nuclear deterrence itself, since these are predicated on the threat of nuclear weapons use. The bishops chose instead to offer an interim "strictly conditioned" acceptance of nuclear deterrence, with the provision that "nuclear deterrence should be used as a step on the way toward progressive disarmament."[38] The influential Catholic journal *Commonweal* called the Catholic pastoral letter a "watershed event" not only for the Church but for society as a whole.[39] George Kennan wrote in the *New York Times* that the bishops' letter was "the most profound and searching inquiry yet conducted by any responsible collective body into the relations of nuclear weaponry, and indeed of modern war in general."[40]

Many other religious bodies and church denominations issued statements condemning nuclear weapons during the 1980s. Most of the Protestant churches went further than the Catholic bishops in condemning the very existence of nuclear weapons. The uneasy acceptance of nuclear

---

[38] National Conference of Catholic Bishops, *The Challenge of Peace: God's Promise and Our Response, A Pastoral Letter on War & Peace* (Washington, DC: United States Catholic Conference, 1983), 58–9.
[39] "The Pastoral and The New Moment," *Commonweal* 110, no. 10 (20 May 1983): 291–2.
[40] George F. Kennan, "The Bishops' Letter," *New York Times*, 1 May 1983, E21.

deterrence that had characterized the Protestant tradition prior to the 1980s gave way in many instances to explicit endorsement of disarmament. Not only the use but the very possession of nuclear weapons became unacceptable. The US Lutheran Church and the Lutheran Church of America passed resolutions urging the elimination of nuclear weapons. The executive ministers of the US Baptist Church called the existence of nuclear weapons and the willingness to use them "a direct affront to our Christian beliefs." At the World Council of Churches assembly in Vancouver in 1983, delegates proclaimed:

We believe that the time has come when the churches must unequivocally declare that the production and deployment as well as the use of nuclear weapons are a crime against humanity and that such activities must be condemned on ethical and theological grounds.[41]

Many pastoral letters were issued during the 1980s but none was more far-reaching in its condemnation of nuclear policy than that of the United Methodist Church. The Methodist document, *In Defense of Creation*, went beyond the Catholic letter in a number of respects. It was more radical in its critique of nuclear policy and explicitly rejected not only the arms race but the whole concept of deterrence. Addressing the ambiguity left by their Catholic colleagues, the Methodist bishops declared that nuclear deterrence "must no longer receive the churches' blessing, even as a temporary warrant." The Methodist statement also addressed the economic consequences of the arms race: "Justice is forsaken in the squandering of wealth in the arms race while a holocaust of hunger, malnutrition, disease, and violent death is destroying the world's poorest peoples."[42] The Methodist bishops supported a comprehensive test ban, a ban on space weapons, and no first use of nuclear weapons.

The Jewish community also spoke out for disarmament in the 1980s. The Union of American Hebrew Congregations, led by rabbis Alexander Schindler and David Saperstein, was an early supporter of the nuclear weapons freeze proposal and sponsored local educational forums in synagogues and among community groups across the country. Even conservative Jewish groups spoke out against the nuclear threat. In April 1982 the Rabbinical Assembly of America issued a statement endorsing the nuclear freeze. In February 1983 the Synagogue Council of America, an umbrella

---

[41] David Gill, ed., *Gathered for Life: Official Report, VI Assembly World Council of Churches* (Grand Rapids, MI: Eerdmans, 1983), 137.

[42] The United Methodist Council of Bishops, *In Defense of Creation: The Nuclear Crisis and a Just Peace* (Nashville, TN: Graded Press, 1986), 48, 15.

group embracing all branches of Judaism, adopted a resolution urging that the United States and the Soviet Union "implement a bilateral mutual cessation of the production and deployment of nuclear weapons."[43]

The involvement of the religious community in the nuclear debate in the 1980s played a major role in generating public pressure and support for nuclear disarmament. The clergy who issued pastoral letters and declarations against the nuclear danger awakened public consciousness and encouraged citizen activism. This religious community involvement was decisive in shaping the political climate and building public support for peace and disarmament.

A PRAIRIE FIRE

The nuclear weapons freeze movement swept through the United States in the 1980s like the proverbial prairie fire. It began with a ballot initiative in western Massachusetts in the 1980 election. The proposal for a bilateral nuclear freeze was endorsed by 59 percent of voters in rural districts who went heavily for Ronald Reagan. The freeze proposal thus demonstrated its ability to win voter approval among conservatives as well as liberals. Hundreds of local town meetings in Vermont and other New England states subsequently voted to endorse the freeze. By 1982 the freeze had been endorsed by eleven state legislatures, more than two hundred city councils, and forty county governments.[44] Support for the freeze poured in from prominent academic scholars and former government officials. More than 150 national organizations endorsed the freeze, including the US Conference of Mayors, the Young Women's Christian Association, the American Nurses Association, and more than two dozen of the largest US trade unions.[45]

The most dramatic expressions of support for disarmament came in 1982. On June 12 nearly a million people marched to New York's Central Park to protest the nuclear arms race. It was the largest peace demonstration in US history. That year disarmament organizers and sympathetic public officials also placed the nuclear freeze proposition on the ballot in numerous locations. A quarter of the US electorate voted in what amounted to an informal national referendum on the nuclear arms race. It was the largest electoral mobilization for peace in US history. The vote in California was especially significant, not only because of the state's size and leadership in establishing

---

[43] L. Bruce van Voorst, "The Churches and Nuclear Deterrence," *Foreign Affairs* 61, no. 4 (spring 1983): 845.

[44] Neal R. Peirce and William R. Anderson, "Nuclear Freeze Proponents Mobilize on Local Referenda, House Elections," *National Journal* 14, no. 38 (18 September 1982): 1602–5.

[45] Solo, *From Protest to Policy*, 66.

national trends but because the White House mounted a major campaign of opposition. The freeze resolution won by a 52–48 margin in an election where Republicans swept statewide races. Nationwide the freeze resolution was approved in eight out of nine states and in many of the country's largest cities. Across the nation, 18 million Americans voted on the freeze, with 10.7 million, or 60 percent, voting in favor. As Representative Ed Markey, the principal freeze leader in Congress, observed, "it was the closest our country has ever come to a national plebiscite on nuclear arms control." Disarmament activists translated their proposal for mutual disarmament into "political muscle at the ballot box, delivering to the White House a resounding vote of no-confidence in its nuclear buildup."[46]

Nuclear freeze referenda 1982

	Percentage		Votes	
	Yes	No	Yes	No
States				
Arizona	41	59	262,012	379,759
California	52.5	47.5	3,778,331	3,414,987
Massachusetts	74	26	1,221,710	437,905
Michigan	58	42	1,508,659	1,159,263
Montana	56	44	–	–
New Jersey	76	24	1,780,862	575,527
North Dakota	58	42	113,523	80,765
Oregon	61.5	38.5	572,000	357,586
Rhode Island	59	41	161,852	112,011
Selected cities				
Chicago	75	25	404,173	135,325
Denver	62	38	93,630	56,981
Philadelphia	75.5	24.5	231,787	75,149
Washington, DC	70	30	77,521	33,369
Total nationwide	60	40	10,729,922	7,120,915

Source: Nuclear Weapons Freeze Campaign.

FERMENT IN EUROPE

As the nuclear freeze campaign attracted growing support in the United States an unprecedented wave of antinuclear activism spread across western

---

[46] Ed Markey, interview by the author, 28 August 1991.

Europe. The Soviet and NATO decisions to deploy new intermediate range nuclear missiles on the continent sparked the largest peace movement mobilization in modern European history. In the fall of 1981 and then again in October 1983 Europeans took to the streets by the millions to protest the nuclear arms race. Throughout western Europe opposition to the new missiles reached enormous proportions, and the peace movement enjoyed unprecedented popularity. According to a 1982 poll approval of the peace movement in the major NATO countries ranged from a low of 55 percent to a high of 81 percent. The result was intense political opposition to NATO and Soviet missiles, and powerful pressures not only against the intermediate range weapons but against the entire cold war system of East–West nuclear competition.

In October 1981 more than 250,000 people gathered in Bonn, 100,000 marched in Brussels, 250,000 demonstrated in London, and half a million people took to the streets in several cities in Italy. A month later nearly half a million people jammed the streets of Amsterdam. A huge banner carried through the streets of Paris captured the movement's message: "Neither Pershings nor SS-20s."[47] In Milan a banner read "No to the Pentagon! No to the Kremlin!"[48] At nearly all of the rallies and mass demonstrations held that year and two years later in 1983, protesters called for the elimination of both Soviet and NATO nuclear weapons. The major organizations involved, such as the Interchurch Peace Council in the Netherlands and CND in Britain, criticized Soviet as well as NATO policy. To be sure, the emphasis was on Western policy, since the demonstrators were citizens of NATO countries and were speaking primarily to their own governments, but Soviet policies were openly criticized as well.

One of the most significant antinuclear peace mobilizations of the 1980s was the women's peace camp at Greenham Common in Britain. In September 1981 members of the group Women for Life on Earth marched to the Greenham Common military base, which was scheduled to receive NATO missiles. The women decided to remain and kept up a continuous peace presence at the base for several years. The women's peace camp attracted significant media attention and prompted the creation of other peace camps at more than a dozen sites in Britain and elsewhere in Europe. A similar camp was established in the United States at Rome Air Force base near Seneca, New York, site of the founding conference of the women's

[47] Frank J. Prial, "50,000 March in Paris to Protest Weapons Buildup," *New York Times*, 26 October 1981, A11.
[48] "100,000 in a Milan Peace March," *New York Times*, 1 November 1981, 6.

suffrage movement more than a hundred years earlier. In December 1982 nearly 30,000 women representing various peace camps and other peace organizations descended upon Greenham Common for a major protest against nuclear weapons.[49] The encampment at Greenham Common became an inspiration to the antinuclear cause, especially to the women who played a leadership role in building the disarmament movement.

The culmination of the historic peace mobilization of the 1980s came in October 1983 when nearly 3 million people poured into the streets of cities all across western Europe to protest nuclear missile deployments and to demand an end to the arms race. In London more than 300,000 people assembled in Hyde Park for what the *New York Times* called the "the largest protest against nuclear weapons in British history."[50] Similar mobilizations of hundreds of thousands of people took place in Rome, Vienna, Brussels, Stockholm, Paris, Dublin, Copenhagen, and other cities.[51] The largest crowd assembled in the Hague, as nearly one million people filled the streets of the Dutch capital.[52] The biggest turnout of protesters occurred in West Germany, when on a single day, 400,000 marched in Bonn, 400,000 in Hamburg, 250,000 in Stuttgart, and 100,000 in West Berlin. In addition, more than 200,000 people participated in an extraordinary human chain that stretched continuously for sixty-four miles from the US army headquarters in Stuttgart to the missile base at Neu Ulm.[53] The October 1983 demonstrations were the largest mobilization of peace sentiment in human history up to that time (the worldwide mobilization against war in Iraq in February 2003 was even larger).

Despite the massive outpouring of disarmament activism, NATO governments disregarded public opinion and proceeded with the deployment of Cruise and Pershing intermediate range nuclear missiles. On the surface it appeared that the peace movement had lost the battle against new nuclear weapons, and that all the massive mobilization of protest had been for naught. Yet the peace movement eventually prevailed in the larger political struggle against new nuclear weapons in Europe and the overall arms race. The Reagan administration responded to the antinuclear ferment in 1981 by

---

[49] Alice Cook and Gwyn Kirk, *Greenham Women Everywhere: Dreams, Ideas and Actions from the Women's Peace Movement* (Cambridge, MA: South End Press, 1983), 32.

[50] R. W. Apple, Jr., "Missile Protesters Jam Central London," *New York Times*, 23 October 1983, A16.

[51] James A. Markham, "Vast Crowds Hold Rallies in Europe against US Arms," *New York Times*, 23 October 1983, A1; and Jon Nordheimer, "500,000 Join Dutch Antimissile Rally," *New York Times*, 30 October 1983, 3.

[52] Rochon, *Mobilizing for Peace*, 6; and Maarten Huygen, "Dateline Holland: NATO's Pyrrhic Victory," *Foreign Affairs* 62 (12 November 1984): 176.

[53] Rochon, *Mobilizing for Peace*, 6.

proposing the "zero option" plan, which called for the elimination of all intermediate range nuclear weapons in Europe. Reagan supported the zero option, contrary to the advice of military officials, because it appealed to his desire to see nuclear weapons eliminated.[54] Some of his White House aides saw political value in the proposal as a way of coopting peace movement demands. An administration official told disarmament supporter Mary Kaldor, "We got the idea from your banners . . . the ones that say 'No cruise, No Pershing, No SS-20s.'"[55] The White House fully expected that Brezhnev-era Soviet leaders would reject the plan, which they did. Even Mikhail Gorbachev was initially skeptical and tried to link Soviet acceptance of the plan to limits on the US Strategic Defense Initiative, which Reagan flatly refused. In 1987 Gorbachev unexpectedly dropped the demand for SDI linkage and accepted the zero option without conditions. NATO leaders had to accept the offer, despite serious misgivings from Henry Kissinger and other conservative leaders and former officials. In the end the peace position prevailed. Peace advocates crafted the message ("No to Soviet and NATO missiles") and created the antinuclear political climate that helped to produce the 1987 INF treaty, which led to the ending of the cold war.

WHO WON?

According to the conventional wisdom, the policies of peace-through-strength brought about the collapse of the Soviet Union. As Margaret Thatcher famously said "Ronald Reagan won the Cold War without firing a shot."[56] President George H. W. Bush made a similar claim in his State of the Union address in January 1992. It was the US military build-up, Western officials declared, especially Reagan's cherished SDI, that broke the back of Soviet power and forced the Kremlin to sue for peace. This theory of cold war triumphalism has had an enduring impact on US strategic think-ing, reinforcing the realist faith in the dominant influence of military power. US political leaders believe that more of the same – military build-ups, wars of intervention, and coercive diplomacy – can bring further victories for Western interests. This belief in the transformative effect of military might is at the core of political thinking in Washington and was part of the

---

[54] Paul Lettow, *Ronald Reagan and His Quest to Abolish Nuclear Weapons* (New York: Random House, 2005), 60.

[55] Mary Kaldor, "'We Got the Idea from Your Banners,'" *New Statesman* 113, no. 2920 (13 March 1987): 14–15.

[56] Quoted in Dinesh D'Souza, "How Reagan Won the Cold War," *National Review* 49, no. 22 (24 November 1997): 38.

mentality that led to the war in Iraq. The consequences of misinterpreting history can be severe.

The cold war was ended not by military build-ups but by Mikhail Gorbachev's "new thinking," which broke decisively with the logic of militarism, and by the pressures of disarmament activism, which created a political climate conducive to arms reduction and East–West understanding. Reagan deserved credit for accepting Soviet concessions and proposing sweeping nuclear reductions (including at Reykjavik the elimination of all nuclear weapons), but the leading role belonged to Gorbachev and to the people of Europe, West and East, who demanded political change. The Soviet system collapsed when millions of citizens and human rights campaigners in the East took to the streets in the historic "velvet revolution" of 1989. George Kennan described the triumphalist interpretation as "silly and childish." Military pressures from the West during the cold war were usually counterproductive and had the effect of reinforcing Soviet repression and militarism. "The general effect of cold war extremism was to delay rather than hasten the great change that overtook the Soviet Union at the end of the 1980s," Kennan observed.[57] As the Russian poet Yevgenii Yevtushenko put it, "your hardliners help our hardliners, and our hardliners help your hardliners."[58] The Soviet leaders responsible for changing Kremlin policy described the triumphalist interpretation as "absolute nonsense," according to Georgi Arbatov, and "a very big delusion," in the words of Gorbachev.[59] Alexander Yakovlev, the principal architect of *perestroika*, said that US hardline policies "played no role. None. I can tell you with the fullest responsibility. Gorbachev and I were ready for changes in our policy regardless of whether the American President was Reagan, or . . . someone more liberal."[60] The pressures that brought change in the East came mainly from within, not without.

Missing from the conventional debates about who won the cold war is a recognition of the role of the peace movement. The first President Bush made a special point of attempting to dismiss the influence of antinuclear activism. On three occasions during the televised presidential and vice-presidential debates of October 1992, Bush and his running mate, Dan

---

[57] George Kennan, *At a Century's Ending: Reflections, 1982–1995* (New York: W. W. Norton, 1996), 185; George F. Kennan, "The G.O.P. Won the Cold War? Ridiculous," *New York Times*, 28 October 1992.

[58] *Moscow News*, 23–30 October 1988.

[59] Georgi Arbatov, *The System: An Insider's Life in Soviet Politics* (New York: Random House, 1992), 321; "A Very Big Delusion," *The New Yorker* 68, 37, no. 2 (2 November 1992): 4.

[60] Quoted in Wittner, *Toward Nuclear Abolition*, 487.

Quayle, denounced the nuclear freeze movement. In fact disarmament activism in the West played an important role in generating political pressures for an end to the cold war. Even before the advent of Gorbachev, the nuclear freeze movement began transforming the Reagan administration's approach to nuclear policy.[61] Arms control supporters in Congress forced the administration to adopt a more flexible negotiating approach toward the Soviet Union, and the White House began tailoring its rhetoric and declaratory policy to address the new climate of public opinion that the movement helped to create. The decision to begin arms control negotiations (contrary to the administration's initial intentions), the shaping of the zero option and other bargaining positions at the Geneva talks, the stalemating of the MX missile program, the rejection of civil defense planning, the development of a formidable arms control lobby within Congress – all of these developments were the result of peace movement activism and occurred before Gorbachev came to power. Continued peace pressures placed constraints on the SDI, cut off funding for nuclear testing, and restricted US military intervention in Central America. The global public mood in favor of disarmament provided encouragement for Gorbachev's initiatives and played a role in perhaps the most crucial Kremlin decision, delinking the issue of intermediate-range missiles in Europe from the question of the SDI. As Gorbachev declared at a meeting of Soviet officials, "untying the package on the medium-range missiles ... will be our response to the state of public opinion in the world."[62] This was the decisive step that opened the floodgates to negotiated arms reduction. The pressures generated by the disarmament movement pushed the political system toward nuclear restraint and helped to change the course of history.

LESSONS FROM THE END OF THE COLD WAR

The way in which the cold war ended provides validation for both realist and liberal interpretations of international relations. It confirmed the realist view that weapons levels are secondary to the state of political relations among nations in determining the prospects for peace. It also showed that conciliatory gestures can generate positive reciprocity between nations and enhance international security. Morgenthau and other realist writers were correct in arguing that politics is more important than disarmament in creating the conditions for peace. The East–West arms race came to a halt not through protracted disarmament negotiations but through a rapid

[61] *Ibid.*, 403, 446.   [62] Quoted in *ibid.*, 397.

improvement in political relations between the two blocs. Arms control efforts during most of the cold war era produced some modest results, but they did not prevent war (Korea, Vietnam, Afghanistan), did little to alter the underlying political mistrust between East and West, and did not even reverse the competition in nuclear weapons. It was not until a reform-minded and more trustworthy Soviet leadership came to power, and Western leaders recognized the advantages of accepting Soviet concessions, that icy political relations melted and the prospects for peaceful cooperation advanced. When political trust and understanding improved the vast apparatus of ideological hostility that had been built up over forty years disappeared with breathtaking speed. Dramatic arms reductions that few would have considered conceivable a few years before followed in rapid succession. All of this was made possible by a reduction of tensions and improvement in East–West political relations.

While political factors rather than disarmament negotiations were the decisive factor in ending the cold war, the formal agreements that brought about these changes were adopted within the framework of traditional arms control bargaining. The process of arms negotiation provided the legal framework within which the United States and the Soviet Union could reach agreement. Throughout much of the cold war arms control negotiations exerted a stabilizing influence in an otherwise terrifying atmosphere of nuclear confrontation. This in itself was an important contribution to the prospects for peace. In the late 1980s this framework of arms negotiation provided the setting in which the revolutionary initiatives of Gorbachev could break through to reduce political tensions and bring an end to the cold war.

If the ending of the cold war confirmed key principles of political realism, it also vindicated one of the core beliefs of the disarmament movement – that unilateral initiatives can reduce tensions and spur mutual arms reduction. Throughout the cold war British disarmament leaders urged independent action to reduce tensions and stimulate reciprocal action by the Soviet Union. Unilateral disarmament was a cornerstone of the program of CND. A 1962 report by the British Council of Churches called for independent renunciation of nuclear weapons as a "unilateral stage within a multilateral process." It emphasized the importance of "carrying out unilateral acts in a way that would increase the chance that they would be reciprocated, thus improving the international climate, and starting a process of building confidence and trust."[63]

---

[63] *The Church and the Bomb: Nuclear Weapons and the Christian Conscience. The Report of a Working Party under the Chairmanship of the Bishop of Salisbury* (London: Hodder and Stoughton, 1982), 133, 139.

The concept of unilateral initiatives has solid grounding in political theory and practice. Hedley Bull noted that the most significant acts of disarmament tend to occur spontaneously (and often unilaterally) in response to periods of detente and a lowering of political pressures.[64] Cooperation theorists have emphasized what can be termed the power of positive reciprocity. Robert Axelrod and others found that the most stable basis for cooperation is the simple tit-for-tat process, in which one party responds in kind to the gestures of the other.[65] Game theory experiments show that the most successful strategy for gaining maximum benefit for both parties is to open with a cooperative move and thereafter respond in kind to the other player's actions; cooperative gestures always generate the most favorable outcomes. US political scientist Charles Osgood highlighted the role of unilateral initiatives in his famous GRIT strategy (graduated reciprocation in tension-reduction).[66] Unilateral initiatives could play a constructive role in lowering hostilities, Osgood argued, and could pave the way for more cooperative political relations. President John F. Kennedy applied Osgood's ideas in 1963 when he announced a unilateral halt to atmospheric nuclear testing, which led to the signing of the partial test ban treaty later that year.[67]

The peace initiatives of Gorbachev were a spectacular enactment of the Osgood strategy, which Louis Kriesberg termed "super-GRIT."[68] Taking a leaf from Kennedy's political script two decades before, Gorbachev ordered a halt to Soviet underground nuclear testing in August 1985. This bold initiative, coinciding with the fortieth anniversary of the Hiroshima bombing, placed enormous pressure on the Reagan administration and the West. Peace movements in the United States and Europe seized upon the Soviet gesture to lobby intensively for a reciprocal response. The Reagan administration initially rebuffed the Soviet gestures, but by 1987, as Gorbachev made ever more significant concessions, Washington finally said "yes" to Moscow's "da." Disarmament initiatives and strategic concessions from the Soviet Union proved decisive in easing political tensions and reducing the dangers of the East–West nuclear stand-off.

---

[64] Hedley Bull, "Disarmament and the International System," in *Theories of Peace and Security: A Reader In Contemporary Strategic Thought*, ed. John Garnett, 136–48 (London: Macmillan, 1970), 136–8.

[65] Robert Axelrod, *The Evolution of Cooperation* (New York: Basic Books, 1984).

[66] Charles E. Osgood, *An Alternative to War or Surrender* (Urbana, Il.: University of Illinois Press, 1962).

[67] Richard Wendell Fogg, "Dealing with Conflict: A Repertoire of Creative, Peaceful Approaches," *Journal of Conflict Resolution* 29, no. 2 (June 1985): 334.

[68] Louis Kriesberg, *Constructive Conflicts: From Escalation to Resolution*, 2nd edn (Lanham, MD: Rowman & Littlefield, 2003), 221.

A further example of the power of positive reciprocity occurred a few years later when President George H. W. Bush announced the unilateral demobilization of US tactical nuclear weapons from ships and submarines and the removal and dismantling of nuclear artillery and short-range missiles in Europe.[69] This bold initiative in September 1991 was promptly reciprocated by Gorbachev, who announced a similar and even more sweeping withdrawal and dismantling of tactical nuclear weapons from Soviet land forces and naval vessels.[70] These reciprocal reductions resulted in the largest single act of denuclearization in history, removing some 12,500 nuclear weapons from deployment.[71] Contrary to the conventional wisdom, unilateral initiatives proved highly effective in reducing the nuclear danger. The greatest advances for peace occur when political leaders make conciliatory gestures that reduce tensions and prompt reciprocation. Citizen movements play a decisive supporting role when they create the favorable political climate that encourages these initiatives.

[69] S. Budiansky and B. Auster, "An Assault on Nuclear Arms," *US News & World Report* 3, no. 15 (7 October 1991): 24–8.

[70] "Nuclear Weapons: Going, Going," *The Economist* 321, no. 7728 (12 October 1991): 54.

[71] "NRDC Nuclear Notebook: Russian Nuclear Forces, 2002," *Bulletin of the Atomic Scientists* 58, no. 4 (July/August 2002): 70; "NRDC Nuclear Notebook: US Nuclear Forces, 2002," *Bulletin of the Atomic Scientists* 58, no. 3 (May/June 2002): 71; Joshua Handler, "The 1991–1992 PNIs and the Elimination, Storage, and Security of Tactical Nuclear Weapons," in *Tactical Nuclear Weapons: Emergent Threats in an Evolving Security Environment*, ed. Brian Alexander and Alistair Millar, 20–41 (Washington, DC: Brassey's, 2003).

8

Refusing war

In recent decades the struggle for peace has increasingly taken on an antiwar character. Waves of disarmament activism have alternated with massive antiwar campaigns in an era of almost permanent peace mobilization. Movements against unpopular wars have multiplied and reached unprecedented scale, most dramatically in response to US aggression in Vietnam and Iraq. These movements are a reaction to the process of militarization that crystallized in the cold war era. As peace advocates had warned, the permanent mobilization for war that emerged in the wake of World War II reinforced the predisposition of political leaders to use military force and created greater institutional capacities to intervene in the affairs of other countries. Militarist tendencies developed in a number of major powers, but US military interventionism was most frequent and had the greatest global impact. When these interventions were particularly costly and egregious, as in Vietnam and Iraq, antiwar mobilizations reached massive scale and acted to constrain warmaking options. This is a new phenomenon in history, one that has made the peace movement a more important and controversial political actor. Antiwar protest, actual or prospective, has become a consideration in the calculations of government leaders and has started to emerge as a potential influence in the global politics of peace.

The scale of antiwar protest is largely determined by the nature of the particular conflict in question. The wars against Vietnam and Iraq were so obviously unjust that they prompted massive opposition. In the case of Iraq mass protest emerged before the war even began. In some situations, such as the US intervention in Panama in 1989, wars are concluded so quickly that there is little opportunity for opposition. Some uses of military force are less controversial and have greater international support. During Bosnia's ordeal in the early 1990s some peace and human rights activists supported NATO military intervention to stem ethnic cleansing. When NATO finally acted in 1994 there were no mass protests. The 1998 NATO intervention in Kosovo and bombing of Serbia generated only minor antiwar protest.

Antiwar movements are expressions of pragmatic pacifism, responses to specific unjust military actions that are deemed unacceptable by large numbers of people.

The antiwar movements of the modern era are rooted in a long tradition of anti-imperialist struggles dating back to the nineteenth century. Antecedents include the fight against the US war in Mexico during the 1840s and US intervention in Central America in the 1930s, and anti-imperialist movements at the turn of the twentieth century against the US war in the Philippines and King Leopold's brutal policies in the Congo, which took an estimated 5 to 8 million lives.[1] In China and Korea people struggled for decades against European and Japanese domination. In France peace advocates protested the takeover of Algeria in the 1830s and the invasion and occupation of Indochina a few decades later. In the 1880s Frédéric Passy stood in the Chamber of Deputies to condemn France's conquest of Tonkin China and the hypocrisy and racism of European colonization. He reminded his listeners that the Annamese were a sophisticated and cultured people with a long and proud tradition of resisting foreign conquest.[2] Their history included a thousand years of struggle against Chinese domination, and would later add thirty years of bitter fighting to defeat French and later US military intervention.

In this chapter I examine contemporary antiwar issues, focusing on the Vietnam and Iraq experiences. The antiwar movement influenced the policies of the Johnson and Nixon administrations in numerous ways, exerting constant pressure for negotiation and military withdrawal, and constraining military escalation.[3] Peace activism gave impetus to congressional efforts to cut off funding in the last months of the war. Peace activism spread to the ranks of the military, reflected in the emergence of a GI and veterans antiwar movement (in which I participated) and in the deterioration of morale and the will to fight. The war gave rise to widespread conscientious objection, which the chapter examines in an historical context. The chapter also examines the unprecedented global mobilization against the invasion of Iraq. Although the antiwar movement was unable to prevent the invasion, it influenced political outcomes in several countries and interacted uniquely with deliberations at the UN Security Council, enhancing the legitimacy of the United Nations. The movement emerged

---

[1] Ch. Didier Gondola, *The History of Congo* (Westport, CT: Greenwood Press, 2002), 59–63.
[2] Sandi E. Cooper, *Patriotic Pacifism: Waging War on War in Europe, 1815–1914* (New York: Oxford University Press, 1991), 53, 178.
[3] Melvin Small, *Johnson, Nixon, and the Doves* (New Brunswick, NJ: Rutgers University Press, 1988), 226–31.

in part from opposition to the so-called "global war on terror," as activists sought to craft alternative strategies for countering terrorism based on principles of nonviolence and conflict transformation.

VIETNAM: A TRIANGULAR MOVEMENT

The Vietnam antiwar movement was the largest, most sustained, and most powerful peace campaign in human history. For a decade, as the US war against Indochina escalated, reached its furious peak, and then gradually wound down, millions of citizens in the United States and around the world campaigned continuously and intensely to bring the slaughter to an end. Antiwar protests occurred on every continent, fueling political radicalization and the development of a counterculture that shaped global values and consciousness. The antiwar struggle in the United States was plagued by divisiveness, as political differences manifested themselves and were magnified in the crucible of an unprecedented mass movement. Three distinct tendencies emerged – a "new left" rooted in student radicalism and traditional pacifist organizations such as the WRL, an "old left" movement dominated by Trotskyist groups, and a liberal wing involving more moderate groups such as SANE and Americans for Democratic Action. Despite the frustrations and anguish antiwar protesters experienced in attempting to stop a seemingly intractable war, the peace movement had a significant impact in constraining, de-escalating, and ending the war.[4]

Activism for social justice and peace was already on the rise when US military escalation in Indochina accelerated in the months following alleged attacks in the Tonkin Gulf in August 1964. The US civil rights movement inspired faith in the power of nonviolent protest and motivated a growing number of people, whites as well as blacks, to join the struggle for justice. The ban-the-bomb movement mobilized tens of thousands of people for marches and demonstrations against nuclear testing and in favor of disarmament. In the 1960s groups such as the Student Peace Union and Students for a Democratic Society (SDS) emerged to make explicit connections between ending cold war militarism and promoting domestic justice and democracy. Student activists rejected the methods and beliefs of earlier communist-associated groups from the 1930s, favoring action over theory, inclusiveness over sectarianism, and decentralization over

---

[4] Tom Wells, *The War Within: America's Battle over Vietnam* (Berkeley, CA: University of California Press, 1994), 4.

consolidation. In April 1965 SDS organized the first mass protest against the war, which brought 25,000 demonstrators to Washington.[5] SDS was an important catalyst in sparking antiwar protest, but its relative role in the overall movement declined as the ranks of protesters swelled and as activists focused on other issues, such as organizing for justice in urban ghettos. New left activism continued to grow, however, inspired by the methods and message of Dr. Martin Luther King, Jr. and by advocates of revolutionary nonviolence like David Dellinger and Barbara Deming.

The huge surge of peace activism in the 1960s and 1970s provided an opportunity for old left groups such as the Trotskyist Socialist Workers Party (SWP) and its affiliate, the Young Socialist Alliance, to gain influence and recruit new members. The SWP sought not only to stop the war but to create a larger radical movement for socialist revolution. It rejected the Democratic and Republican parties as tools of the ruling class and tried to build support for its own political party and sectarian agenda. SWP members insisted on organizing large, legal demonstrations as the sole tactic for building the antiwar movement. This "robotlike promotion of mass demonstrations," as historian Tom Wells described it, was the signature SWP contribution to the movement.[6] As opposition to the war grew and the demonstrations became larger the SWP was able to exert influence far beyond its actual support within the movement. The SWP also gained ground when some new left activists adopted adventurist and mindlessly confrontational tactics that turned off potential supporters and fueled the "law and order" political reaction of the right. In 1970 SWP leaders formed a separate national organization, the National Peace Action Coalition, to replace the new left New Mobilization Committee to End the War in Vietnam (known as "the Mobe") and to compete with its successor, the People's Coalition for Peace and Justice. This divisiveness and sectarianism within the movement impeded the antiwar cause.

The third wing of the antiwar movement consisted of liberals and moderates who attempted to apply pressure on Congress, communicate effectively with the media, and use the electoral system to bring the war to an end. The liberal groups sought to project a moderate, mainstream image to the media in the hope of building a political majority against the war. SANE organized one of the first protests against the war when it joined with Americans for Democratic Action in November 1964 to organize a

---

[5] Charles DeBenedetti, *The Peace Reform in American History* (Bloomington, IN: Indiana University Press, 1980), 169, 173; Wells, *The War Within*, 25–6.

[6] Wells, *The War Within*, 18.

demonstration of 300 people in front of the White House urging a negotiated peace. In June 1965 SANE and other liberal groups gathered more
than 18,000 people in New York's Madison Square Garden for an
"Emergency Rally on Vietnam," at which Hans Morgenthau joined with
Benjamin Spock, Senator Wayne Morse, Coretta Scott King, and others to
call for a ceasefire and a negotiated settlement. In November 1965 SANE
joined with the Catholic Peace Fellowship and the newly formed Clergy and
Laymen (later Laity) Concerned About Vietnam to organize a demonstration of 35,000 people in Washington.[7] The liberal antiwar position advocated de-escalation leading to negotiations, while more radical groups
within the movement called for an end to bombing and a withdrawal of
US troops. Historians differ on which elements of the movement had the
greatest impact. DeBenedetti favored the liberal wing of the movement and
believed that radical and leftist tendencies hurt the antiwar cause.[8] Wells
concentrated on the radical elements of the movement but also acknowledged the diversity of the movement, examining the multifaceted ways in
which each tendency exerted influence. In the end each element of the
movement made a contribution toward ending the war.

CHALLENGING PRESIDENTS, CONSTRAINING ESCALATION

The year 1968 was a decisive turning point for the war in Vietnam. US
policy was shaken to the core by the conjunction of the cataclysmic Tet
offensive by the Vietnamese resistance that put the lie to claims of US
success, and the peace movement's "Dump Johnson" policy in the New
Hampshire presidential primary. The liberal activists who planned the
electoral challenge to Johnson in 1967 faced formidable odds and could
never have imagined that the first primary vote would occur just a few weeks
after a major reversal of US fortunes during the Tet uprising. The "Dump
Johnson" movement was led by Allard Lowenstein of Americans for
Democratic Action, who was convinced that progress in Vietnam would
not occur until the warmaking president was removed from office. The
indefatigable Lowenstein mobilized hundreds of volunteers for the campaign and convinced Eugene McCarthy, the droll former professor, poet,
and senator from Minnesota, to lead the charge. McCarthy was a dull and

---

[7] Milton S. Katz, *Ban the Bomb: A History of SANE, the Committee for a Sane Nuclear Policy, 1957–1985*
(New York: Greenwood Press, 1986), 96–7; DeBenedetti, *The Peace Reform in American History*, 173.
[8] Charles Chatfield, "At the Hands of Historians: The Antiwar Movement of the Vietnam Era," *Peace
and Change* 29, nos. 3 and 4 (July 2004): 497.

uninspiring speaker and many doubted his electability, but large numbers
of young people trekked to snowy New Hampshire to urge local voters to
support the senator as a way to end the war. When the ballots were tallied in
March 1968, McCarthy polled an incredible 42 percent of the vote, compared to 49.5 percent for the president who was a write-in candidate.[9]
McCarthy lost the vote count but won what DeBenedetti termed "an
astonishing psychological victory" that stunned Johnson and the political
establishment in Washington.[10] McCarthy's demonstration of Johnson's
political vulnerability opened the way for Senator Robert Kennedy to enter
the primaries as a more effective and electable antiwar candidate. It also
contributed to Johnson's announcement in late March that he would not
run for reelection and would begin negotiations on ending the war. The
president announced a bombing halt and rejected the Pentagon's request
for 206,000 more troops, thus halting the process of military escalation. It
would take several more agonizing years for the United States to withdraw,
but this was the beginning of the end.

An equally powerful challenge to presidential prerogative occurred in the
fall of 1969 through the Vietnam moratorium movement. The antiwar
movement reached a nadir in early 1969 after the election of Richard
Nixon, with many activists frustrated and disillusioned at their seeming
inability to halt the carnage. Former McCarthy campaign activists Sam
Brown, Marge Sklencar, and David Hawk conceived the idea of a different
kind of peace action that would inspire renewed commitment and bring the
antiwar cause to mainstream USA, while providing an alternative to the
tired formula of mass rallies. They called for people to take action in their
communities and at their workplaces rather than in Washington, to pause
and interrupt business as usual on October 15 to help end the war. The
moratorium idea caught on like wildfire and gained the endorsement of a
wide range of organizations, including the Central Conference of American
Rabbis, the Ripon Society, and major unions such as the Teamsters and
the United Auto Workers. John Kenneth Galbraith, Hans Morgenthau,
W. Averell Harriman, and other prominent intellectuals and former officials endorsed the idea, as did twenty-four Democratic members of the US
Senate. The Vietnam Moratorium Committee had a paid staff of thirty-one
and a network of 7,500 field organizers.[11] The October 15 actions were

---

[9] Charles DeBenedetti, Charles Chatfield assisting author, *An American Ordeal: The Antiwar Movement of the Vietnam Era* (Syracuse, NY: Syracuse University Press, 1990), 200–1, 211–12.

[10] DeBenedetti, *The Peace Reform in American History*, 181–2.

[11] DeBenedetti and Chatfield, *An American Ordeal*, 253.

hugely successful, engaging millions of Americans in local activities that ranged from a gathering of 100,000 people on the Boston Common, to prayer vigils in hundreds of small towns, to the wearing of peace signs and arm bands by troops in Vietnam. The moratorium events were, in DeBenedetti's words, "the largest mass volunteer actions in American history."[12] They had an impact on Nixon's conduct of the war and helped to prevent a major escalation of military violence.

Nixon's supposed plan for peace in Vietnam, which he promised in the 1968 campaign, turned out to be a threat of massive military escalation if North Vietnam did not sue for peace on US terms. He explained his plan to senior aide H. R. Haldeman as the "madman theory:" a threat of major military escalation by an unpredictable president obsessed about communism.[13] In 1969 Nixon instructed Henry Kissinger to deliver just such a warning to the Vietnamese and their Russian supporters, giving Hanoi until November to sue for peace or face the consequences. The administration began preparation for Operation Duck Hook, a huge, rapid expansion of military pressure, including mining the harbors of Haiphong and bombing in the northern part of Vietnam and along the Chinese border. The administration also placed nuclear forces on alert and ordered B-52 bombers with nuclear weapons to fly north over Alaska to circle outside Soviet air space in what was called Operation Giant Lance.[14] The Vietnamese and Soviets were not swayed by these military threats, and they called the president's bluff. Nixon knew at this point that his plan would fail, for he could not afford the political risks of carrying out his threat of military escalation in the face of deepening skepticism about the war and a rising tide of antiwar activism.

The president claimed to be unimpressed by the ubiquitous moratorium events and the giant November 15 rally in Washington that followed. In truth the White House was extremely concerned and feared that the prospect of further demonstrations and public resistance made it impossible to carry out the planned military escalation.[15] Nixon later admitted that antiwar protests undermined his ultimatum to the north: "these highly publicized efforts aimed at forcing me to end the war were seriously

---

[12] DeBenedetti, *The Peace Reform in American History*, 184.
[13] H. R. Haldeman, *The Ends of Power* (New York: Times Books, 1978), 98.
[14] Scott Sagan, "The Vietnam War and Richard Nixon's Secret Nuclear Alert" (transcript, *Torn Curtain: The Secret History of the Cold War*, Episode 3, Radio National, *ABC News*, 28 May 2006). Available online at ABC Online, www.abc.net.au/rn/history/hindsight/features/torn/episode3.htm (accessed 14 February 2007).
[15] See the account of these events in Daniel Ellsberg, "Introduction: Call to Mutiny," in *Protest and Survive*, ed. E. P. Thompson and Dan Smith (New York: Monthly Review Press, 1981), xv–xvi.

undermining my behind-the-scenes attempts to do just that." He noted the "irony" that "protest[s] for peace ... destroyed whatever small possibility may still have existed of ending the war in 1969." This was an admission that antiwar resistance prevented a major military escalation and constrained US military options: "although publicly I continued to ignore the raging antiwar controversy, I had to face the fact that it had probably destroyed the credibility of my ultimatum to Hanoi."[16]

SOCIAL DISRUPTION AND POLITICAL COSTS

As demonstrations against the war continued and became ever larger – 300,000 in New York in April 1967, 500,000 in Washington in November 1969 and again in April 1971, with parallel huge protests in San Francisco – frustration and anguish over the movement's inability to end the relentless killing in Vietnam increased.[17] Some activists adopted more confrontational and disruptive tactics. The Oakland Stop the Draft Week actions of October 1967, the turbulent demonstrators at the Democratic national convention in Chicago in August 1968, the "days of rage" of October 1969, the massive campus uprising that followed the May 1970 killings of students at Kent State University, and the May 1971 May Day action of mass civil disobedience in Washington, DC (which led to the arrest of 12,000 people, the largest mass jailing in US history) – these and other actions contributed to an atmosphere of lawlessness and anarchy. Although polls showed more than 70 percent of the public opposed to the war by 1971, surveys also found substantial percentages opposed to antiwar demonstrations.[18] Draft card burnings, disrespect for the flag, and the hippie culture all contributed to the sense of malaise that many conservative middle-class Americans felt, and which Nixon and other politicians manipulated and exploited.

Disruptive action had negative consequences but it also had the beneficial effect (from the point of view of the peace movement) of raising the social costs of continuing the war. The growing atmosphere of divisiveness created deep misgivings within the establishment and strengthened the resolve of political leaders to end the war as a way of reducing social tensions. The confrontational methods of the antiwar movement also fed

---

[16] Richard Nixon, *RN: The Memoirs of Richard Nixon* (New York: Grosset & Dunlap, 1978), 401, 403.
[17] Estimates of crowd sizes from Wells, *The War Within, passim*; and DeBenedetti, *The Peace Reform in American History*, 179, 185.
[18] DeBenedetti, *The Peace Reform in American History*, 189; Wells, *The War Within*, 283, 299, 511, 525.

the paranoia of the White House and motivated the illegal actions that led to Watergate, Nixon's resignation, and the political turnaround of the 1974 mid-term elections. This in turn solidified the congressional majority in favor of ending further financial support for the war, which sealed the fate of the puppet regime in Saigon. The antiwar movement inadvertently created opportunities for political backlash, but in the end it generated sufficient pressure to force an end to the war.

After the war some military officials argued that US forces were stabbed in the back by liberal politicians and the media. General H. Norman Schwarzkopf said in a 1992 interview that the United States lost the war in Vietnam because "we didn't use our full military power. We were fighting with one hand tied behind our back."[19] In fact Vietnam was a full-scale war of savage ferocity that involved the near total commitment of US ground and air forces. The United States dropped 7.5 million tons of bombs and shells on Indochina, more than three times the munitions used in all the theaters of World War II combined. Estimates of the total number of Indochinese killed reach as high as 3 million.[20] The United States faced the impossible task of reversing a deeply entrenched, popularly supported national revolution that had already succeeded in defeating the French and that fiercely resisted US intervention. The war was unwinnable militarily and a lost cause politically. Like the invasion of Iraq thirty years later, the US intervention in Vietnam was based on deception, violated legal and moral principles, and lacked political support domestically and internationally. US warmakers faced determined and vocal antiwar opposition at home, including among their own soldiers, which ultimately succeeded in bringing the military nightmare to an end. Former CIA director William Colby described the antiwar movement as an "invisible participant" in the Paris peace negotiations.[21] It was an apt comment, for the antiwar movement did much to push the United States to the bargaining table and limit military options. For the peace movement it was an extraordinary accomplishment, however long and difficult, which helped to change the course of history.

[19] H. Norman Schwarzkopf, interview by Academy of Achievement, Las Vegas, Nevada, 26 June 1992. Available online at Academy of Achievement, www.achievement.org/autodoc/page/schoint-1 (accessed 14 February 2007).

[20] As a percentage of population, these Vietnamese losses were twice as high as those suffered by the Japanese during World War II. See John E. Mueller, "The Search for the 'Breaking Point' in Vietnam: The Statistics of a Deadly Quarrel," *International Studies Quarterly* 24, no. 4 (December 1980): 497–519.

[21] William Colby, *Lost Victory: A Firsthand Account of America's Sixteen-Year Involvement in Vietnam* (Chicago, IL: Contemporary Books, 1989), 336–7.

RESISTANCE IN THE MILITARY

One of the most remarkable and least known dimensions of the antiwar movement was the resistance that developed within the military itself. The Vietnam era witnessed pervasive opposition to military conscription, unprecedented GI resistance within the armed forces, and a dramatic campaign of antiwar veterans. Never before in US history, and rarely in the history of the world, has an army in the midst of war faced such widespread antiwar opposition within the ranks. The combination of these multiple manifestations of military resistance crippled the conscription system, undermined the morale and fighting ability of the armed forces, and deepened public opposition to the war.

Conscription was never popular in the USA, but the Vietnam War sparked the largest wave of public opposition to the draft since the Civil War. The opposition to conscription was fueled in part by widespread perceptions of the system's unfairness. Military deferments for college students prompted many to prolong their studies. Wealthy and well-connected youth usually could obtain a deferment from the draft, or like George W. Bush, could find a place in the National Guard to avoid service in Vietnam. As a result the burden of conscription fell disproportionately on poor and working-class youth. Avoiding the military draft became a preoccupation of millions of people, as more than half of the 27 million men eligible for the draft during the Vietnam era were deferred, exempted, or disqualified. Millions of young men claimed phantom disabilities, flocked to exempt occupations and schools, married and had children early, or employed other means of dodging the draft.

Distinct from the millions who dodged the draft were the many thousands who resisted the conscription system and actively opposed the war. The draft resistance movement was the cutting edge of the antiwar movement in 1967–8, according to historian Michael Foley. Thousands of young men turned in their draft cards in highly visible and dramatic events coordinated across the country in October 1967 and April 1968.[22] Although organized draft resistance events subsequently subsided individual draft resistance continued and expanded. Martin Anderson, head of Nixon's task force on the all-volunteer force, warned in 1970 that the number of draft resisters was expanding "at an alarming rate" and that the government was "almost powerless to apprehend and prosecute

---

[22] Michael S. Foley, *Confronting the War Machine: Draft Resistance during the Vietnam War* (Chapel Hill, NC: University of North Carolina Press, 2003), 9, 135, 262.

them."[23] Approximately 570,000 young men were classified as draft offenders during the Vietnam era. Of that number, over 209,517 were accused of draft violations, 8,750 were convicted, and 3,250 were imprisoned.[24] The massive number of draft resisters and the growing network of lawyers and counselors assisting them overwhelmed the courts and clogged the selective service appeals system. An estimated 60,000 to 100,000 chose exile to avoid the draft, most of them fleeing to Canada and Sweden.[25]

Many of those who went into the military also opposed the war. The GI antiwar movement included the publication of nearly 300 "underground" newspapers. Dozens of protest actions by low-ranking troops occurred at bases and on ships around the world. More defiant forms of GI resistance also occurred, ranging from desertion and refusal of orders to outright mutinies and assaults against commanders ("fraggings") in Vietnam. GI coffeehouses were opened as centers of antiwar activity in towns near more than a dozen major military bases, ranging from Killeen, Texas (Fort Hood) to Fayetteville, North Carolina (Fort Bragg). In November 1969, a few days before the giant moratorium rally in Washington DC, a full page advertisement calling for an end to the war appeared in the *New York Times*, signed by 1,366 active duty GIs. An army-sponsored survey during the height of the GI movement in 1970–1 found that one out of four enlisted persons participated in some form of dissident activity.[26]

Dramatic proof of the collapse of the army in Vietnam was the prevalence of combat refusal. In my research for *Soldiers in Revolt* I uncovered evidence of ten instances in which groups of soldiers refused to fight. Shelby Stanton's subsequent *The Rise and Fall of an American Army: US Ground Forces in Vietnam, 1965–1973* revealed that combat refusal was much more prevalent. Drawing from unit archives, Stanton reported that during 1970 there were thirty-five instances of combat refusal in the army's elite First Cavalry Division, some involving entire units.[27] If other combat divisions in Vietnam had similar rates, the total number of combat refusals during the latter years of the war must have numbered in the hundreds. These figures

---

[23] *Ibid.*, 344.

[24] Lawrence M. Baskir and William A. Strauss, *Chance and Circumstance: The Draft, the War and the Vietnam Generation* (New York: Alfred Knopf, 1978), 69.

[25] "Draft Resistance and Evasion," in *The Oxford Companion to American Military History*, ed. John Whiteclay Chambers II (New York: Oxford University Press, 1999), 238.

[26] R. William Rae, Stephen B. Forman, and Howard C. Olson, *Future Impact of Dissident Elements within the Army*, Technical Paper RAC-TP-441 (McLean, VA: Research Analysis Corporation, January 1972), 25.

[27] Shelby L. Stanton, *The Rise and Fall of an American Army: US Ground Forces in Vietnam, 1965–1973* (Novato, CA: Presidio Press, 1985), 349.

do not include the more frequent incidents of combat avoidance, in which units consciously avoided engagement with the enemy. When commanders in Vietnam sent units into the field they could not be certain how the troops would respond. In the face of pervasive resistance and noncooperation in the ranks, US combat effectiveness in Vietnam melted away.

The veterans returning from Vietnam formed one of the most important organizations of the era, Vietnam Veterans against the War, VVAW, whose most famous member was former Navy lieutenant, later senator and presidential candidate John Kerry. With the authority of having fought the war the antiwar veterans had greater credibility and legitimacy than civilian peace activists and were therefore more effective in demanding an end to US involvement. By 1971 VVAW boasted nearly 20,000 members, including 2,000 soldiers serving in Vietnam.[28] The Nixon administration was deeply concerned about the antiwar veterans and mounted a major campaign to subvert their movement. H. R. Haldeman complained that media coverage of the veterans' demonstrations was "killing us" and that the White House was "getting pretty well chopped up."[29] Attorney General John Mitchell described VVAW as the single most dangerous group in the United States.[30] VVAW was subjected to relentless attack by the administration. The Watergate crisis originated from the White House campaign of espionage and dirty tricks against VVAW and other antiwar groups. The plot to burgle the offices of the Democratic Party was meant in part to find links between VVAW and party leaders. The administration's campaign to smear and subvert antiwar veterans thus contributed to the undoing of the Nixon presidency, which further undermined political support for military assistance to the Saigon government.

The soldier and veteran movements made an important contribution to the antiwar effort. They gave expression to an unprecedented revulsion against war in the ranks of the military. When even those who served in the army and fought the war rose up in revolt, political leaders had to take notice. The antiwar GIs and veterans thus performed a historic service to their nation in bringing the USA's longest and most divisive war to a close. The veterans were, as they envisioned themselves, true patriots in the tradition of Thomas Paine. They were "winter soldiers" who did not shrink

---

[28] Andrew E. Hunt, *The Turning: A History of Vietnam Veterans Against the War* (New York: New York University Press, 1999), 119.

[29] H. R. Haldeman, *The Haldeman Diaries: Inside the Nixon White House* (New York: G. P. Putnam's Sons, 1994), 218.

[30] Richard Stacewicz, *Winter Soldiers: An Oral History of the Vietnam Veterans Against the War* (New York: Twayne Publishers, 1997), 336.

from devotion to their country, who served it doubly as warriors and then as advocates of peace.

THE RISE OF CONSCIENTIOUS OBJECTION

The Vietnam era witnessed an unprecedented increase in the number of conscientious objectors to military service. In the early stages of the war legal and administrative restrictions limited the availability of objection, but a series of legal challenges and court rulings eventually forced the Selective Service System to relax its standards. During the course of the war 170,000 men were classified as conscientious objectors.[31] Toward the end of the war the level of conscientious objection rose to extraordinary levels. More than 61,000 registered as conscientious objectors in 1971. The following year, the last for the draft, conscientious objectors outnumbered military conscripts.

Large-scale conscientious objection to war first developed during World War I, when the military conscription laws in the United States and Britain allowed exemptions from combat duty for members of pacifist religious sects and in Britain for those opposed to war on the basis of deeply held moral beliefs. In Britain applicants for conscientious objection were required to appear before local tribunals, where they sometimes faced hostile questioning. In the United States objectors approved by local draft boards were required to report to army camps and perform noncombatant service in the military, usually in the medical corps. Absolute objectors who opposed noncombatant service as indirect support for war had no legal recourse and often went to jail. The number of young men who succeeded in registering as conscientious objectors was relatively small in both countries, 16,000 in Britain and nearly 4,000 in the United States, although much larger numbers applied for objector status. In Britain the No Conscription Fellowship emerged as the libertarian voice of absolute pacifists opposed to military conscription. Among absolute objectors in the United States was Roger Baldwin, founder of the American Civil Liberties Union, who described military conscription as "a flat contradiction of all our cherished ideals of individual freedom, democratic liberty, and Christian teaching."[32] Absolutists like Baldwin believed that alternative service was unfair socially and ineffective politically as a means of challenging militarism, since the burden of military service would simply fall on

---

[31] "Conscription," in *The Oxford Companion to American Military History*, 181.
[32] Quoted in Norman Thomas, *Is Conscience a Crime?* (New York: Vanguard, 1927), 27.

someone else, usually less fortunate, and would not deprive the state of the needed cannon fodder for war.

During World War II the United States and Britain permitted conscientious objection. In Britain most of the objectors were church-goers from pacifist religious groups. Only 60,000 men and 1,000 women applied for objector status out of approximately 8 million who served in the armed forces during the war. Nearly two-thirds of the applicants were assigned to alternative service or noncombatant duty within the military. In the USA objector status was permitted only for those who "by religious training and belief" objected to participation in all war. Unlike in World War I applicants were not required to belong to specific pacifist denominations, and for the first time objectors could perform alternative service outside the military. The number of conscientious objectors in the USA during the war was quite limited. The official Selective Service System estimate is approximately 72,000, but scholars place the real number closer to 100,000.[33] More than half of the objectors performed noncombatant service in the military. The three historic peace churches – Quakers, Mennonites, and Brethren – cooperated with the government in establishing a Civilian Public Service (CPS) program of nonmilitary alternative service primarily involving soil conservation and forestry duties in camps sponsored and financed by the churches but under overall Selective Service System direction. Approximately 12,000 objectors served in CPS camps during the war years.

Conscientious objection during World War II was also permitted in three British dominions – Australia, New Zealand, and Canada. Australia was the most tolerant of objectors and allowed both noncombatant and civilian alternative service. In New Zealand the system was more restrictive, permitting only absolute opposition to all war and requiring some form of national service. In Canada objectors were assigned initially to civilian service camps in remote areas but were later allowed to perform noncombatant service in the military. The total number of objectors in all three countries was less than 20,000. Canada had the largest number, 11,000, three-quarters of whom were Mennonites.[34]

Conscientious objection in the United States changed significantly during the Vietnam War, as court rulings allowed for a broader interpretation of the "religious training and belief" requirement. The 1965 Supreme Court

---

[33] Peter Brock and Nigel Young, *Pacifism in the Twentieth Century* (Toronto: University of Toronto Press, 1999), 175.
[34] *Ibid.*, 205.

ruling in the case of Daniel Seeger stated that the test of belief was not solely affirmation of a Supreme Being, but a sincere and meaningful faith commitment that occupied a central place in one's life. In the 1970 case of Elliott Welsh the Court went further and ruled that objection could be based on strongly held moral and ethical beliefs, without reference to religion. These were important legal victories for the conscientious objector movement that created a broader basis for moral objection to war. The courts did not recognize the right of selective objection, however. The many young people who opposed the Vietnam War but not all uses of military force had no legal recourse to exemption. In denying the principle of selective objection the courts maintained a strict legal distinction between pacifist objection to all war and objection based on just war criteria.

In recent decades conscientious objection has undergone further transformation and worldwide expansion. The right to conscientious objection has spread to every country in Europe and has achieved unprecedented levels of social acceptance. In countries such as the United States, where volunteer service has replaced conscription, conscientious objection among civilians has disappeared, although it has continued among active duty soldiers at relatively low levels. During the 1980s and 1990s, groups such as Amnesty International and the European Congress of Conscripts Organizations (ECCO) successfully lobbied the European Parliament to include the right to refuse military service in the basic human rights framework and legal code of the European Union. All member countries, including the central and east European states joining after the cold war, were required to allow conscientious objection to military service. The trend toward supplementing religious grounds for objection with more secular ethical concerns also continued and spread to other countries.[35] In Germany, Finland, and other northern European countries applicants for conscientious objection are not required to prove religious motivation or appear before a hearing board. They simply check a box on a written form and in most cases are automatically certified as conscientious objectors on the basis of their personal declaration.

Germany became the epicenter of contemporary conscientious objection. The Basic Law or Constitution of the West German state in 1949 established the right to conscientious objection even before a new army was created. Article 4 declared "No one shall be forced to do war service with arms against his conscience." This was an extraordinary gesture of deference to pacifism, parallel to the Japanese Constitution's prohibition against the

---

[35] Charles C. Moskos and John Whiteclay Chambers II, eds., *The New Conscientious Objection: From Sacred to Secular Resistance* (New York and Oxford: Oxford University Press, 1993).

use of military force in international conflict. In both instances the establishment of constitutional principles of pacifism was a reaction against the militarism that caused World War II. Germany's Military Service Act of 1959 allowed conscientious objection for those who opposed particular wars as well as all war. This was a landmark decision that bridged the gap between absolutism and just war principles and established a legal basis for selective objection. Objector applications in Germany remained relatively modest until the late 1960s, when they began to increase, rising from approximately 6,000 in 1967 to 35,000 in 1973, and 68,000 in 1983.[36] Mounting pressures on the conscription system led to the decision in the mid-1980s to streamline procedures for approving conscientious objector requests. This opened the floodgates for further increases in the number of objectors, which in 2002 reached an unprecedented 189,000.[37] German conscientious objectors are required to serve in the *Zivildienst* performing low paid labor in the social sector.

As conscientious objector status became commonplace and easy to obtain in Germany and other European countries, the experience of refusing military service changed fundamentally. Gone were the sacrifice and drama associated with conscientious objection in earlier historical periods. Mostly absent was the experience of courageously standing up for one's convictions and saying no to war. The young people who choose civilian service over military duty today in Germany or Finland bear little resemblance to the harried conscientious objectors and war resisters of World War I or the Vietnam era. On the other hand, the very pervasiveness of conscientious objection reflects a widespread social presumption against military service and the use of military force. Even when the choice is relatively easy and casual, the decision to avoid military service by so many indicates a general disregard for the ways of the warrior. It suggests widespread acceptance within European society of the basic values and orientation of pacifism.

THE MOVEMENT AGAINST WAR IN IRAQ

In 1991, exulting over the success of the US-led war that drove Iraqi forces out of Kuwait, President George Bush declared, "we've kicked the Vietnam

---

[36] David Cortright and Max Watts, *Left Face: Soldier Unions and Resistance Movements in Modern Armies* (Westport, CT: Greenwood Press, 1991), 143.

[37] Brock and Young, *Pacifism in the Twentieth Century*, 307. German conscientious objection statistics available at the *Bundesamt für den Zivildienst*, www. zivilditnst.cle (accessed 8 August 2007).

syndrome once and for all."[38] The president thus expressed the hope and belief of US leaders that the antiwar upsurge of the Vietnam era had been an isolated episode, an aberration from the established pattern of US politics, and that wars of intervention could proceed in the future without the impediment of large-scale public resistance. The president's statement overlooked the fact that many Americans opposed the use of military force in the Gulf War. Hundreds of thousands of people demonstrated in cities around the United States and Washington, DC in the fall of 1990 and January 1991 against war in the Gulf. Many major religious bodies, including the US Catholic Conference of Bishops, called for alternatives to the use of force. Many believed that sanctions and diplomacy, if pursued consistently and vigorously, could have succeeded in reversing Iraqi aggression. Because the Gulf War was over in forty-three days, protests did not continue.

By the standards of just war theory the Gulf War had greater legitimacy than the Vietnam War, since the use of "all necessary means" was authorized by UN Security Council Resolution 678. This was not the case with the invasion of Iraq twelve years later. The Iraq War was opposed by nearly every government and most of the people of the world. The US-led invasion aroused worldwide antiwar protests even larger than those of the Vietnam era. It laid the foundation for what could be termed an "Iraq syndrome," an unprecedented increase in worldwide opposition to US foreign and military policy. The global reaction to the war, wrote Francis Fukuyama, "succeeded in uniting much of the world in a frenzy of anti-Americanism."[39]

As an unprovoked war of choice, fought without legal justification or UN authorization, the Iraq invasion utterly failed to meet moral standards for the justifiable use of force. The war was condemned by religious leaders throughout the world. National conferences of Catholic bishops in Europe, Asia, and Africa joined the Vatican in issuing statements against the war. In December 2002 Archbishop Renato Martino, head of the Pontifical Council for Justice and Peace, called the proposed military action in Iraq a "war of aggression."[40] Nearly every mainline Christian denominational body in the United States, including the US Catholic Conference of

---

[38] George H. W. Bush, "Remarks to the American Legislative Exchange Council" (Old Executive Office Building, Washington, DC, 1 March 1991). Available online at the George Bush Presidential Library and Museum, http://bushlibrary.tamu.edu/research/papers/1991/91030102.html (accessed 14 February 2007).

[39] Francis Fukuyama, "After Neoconservatism," *New York Times Magazine*, 19 February 2006.

[40] Archbishop Renato Martino, quoted in "Without Disarmament, Peace is Disarmed, says Archbishop Martino," ZENIT, 17 December 2002. Available online at ZENIT, http://zenit.org/english/

Bishops and the major Protestant Churches, publicly opposed the war. Many religious leaders and members of local congregations participated in antiwar activities. Church-based opposition to war was broader in the case of Iraq than in any previous conflict in modern history. Faith-based activists were major players in the principal US coalitions against the war, United for Peace and Justice and Win Without War. Traditional religious peace groups – including the Catholic pacifist organization Pax Christi and groups within the Friends, Mennonite, and Brethren communities – played a leadership role in raising awareness and organizing antiwar opposition.

The campaign against the invasion of Iraq was the largest, most intensive mobilization of antiwar sentiment in history.[41] On 15 February 2003 in hundreds of cities across the globe an estimated 10 million people demonstrated against war. It was the largest single day of antiwar protest ever organized. More than a million people jammed the center of London, and equal numbers demonstrated in Rome and Barcelona. Crowds of hundreds of thousands gathered in New York, Madrid, Berlin, Sydney, and dozens of other cities.[42] In the course of just a few months the peace movement in the United States reached levels of mobilization that, during the Vietnam era, took years to develop. The Iraq campaign was more international in character than any previous antiwar movement, as protests were coordinated throughout the world and activists understood themselves to be part of a truly global struggle. In dozens of countries national coalitions were created, encompassing a wide range of movements and organizations. The coalitions set up websites that were linked to each other, and many adopted the same slogan and graphic design, a missile crossed out with the words "stop the war."

---

visualizza.phtml?sid=29125 (accessed 14 February 2007); and Gerard O'Connell, "Bullets in Iraq, But all Quiet on the Vatican Front," *Our Sunday Visitor*, 13 April 2003, http://www.osvpublishing.com/periodicals/showarticle.asp?pid=793 (accessed 2 December 2003).

41 Barbara Epstein, "Notes on the Antiwar Movement," *Monthly Review* 55, no. 3 (July–August 2003): 109.

42 Estimates of the numbers of demonstrators and antiwar events are drawn from the website of United for Peace and Justice, the largest grassroots peace coalition in the United States. United for Peace and Justice, "The World Says No to War," 15 February 2003. Available online at United for Peace and Justice, www.unitedforpeace.org/feb15.html (accessed 24 November 2003). In San Francisco, police and organizers estimated the crowd at 200,000, but a careful analysis by the *San Francisco Chronicle*, employing an innovative aerial observation method, put the crowd at approximately 65,000. See "Counting Crowds: Using Aerial Photography to Estimate the Size of Sunday's Peace March in S.F.," *San Francisco Chronicle*, 21 February 2003. Available online at SFGate, http://sfgate.com/cgi-bin/article.cgi?f=/c/a/2003/02/21/MN20213.DTL (accessed 14 February 2007). For newspaper accounts of the protests, see Angelique Chrisafis *et al.*, "Threat of War: Millions Worldwide Rally for Peace," *Guardian* (London), 17 February 2003, 6; Glenn Frankel, "Millions Worldwide Protest Iraq War," *Washington Post*, 16 February 2003, A1; Alan Cowell, "1.5 Million Demonstrators in Cities Across Europe Oppose a War Against Iraq," *New York Times*, 16 February 2003, A20.

More important than the number and extent of these demonstrations was the political character of the antiwar opposition. Rejection of US policy was especially strong in countries where governments supported the US war effort. In Great Britain, Spain, and Italy, citizens said "no" while their political leaders were saying "yes." In Spain and Italy opinion polls showed more than 80 percent of the public opposed to participation in the US-led war.[43] In Germany antiwar sentiment played a decisive role in Chancellor Gerhard Schroeder's come-from-behind electoral victory in September 2002. In Turkey, with antiwar opposition running at 86 percent in the polls, political leaders turned aside billions of dollars in US financial inducements and refused the Bush administration's request to use the country as a base and transit corridor for US invasion forces. Ankara's rejection had a direct impact on military planning, forcing the Pentagon to change its attack plan and redeploy forces to the south of Iraq. Public revulsion over Spain's participation in the war and the government's mishandling of the initial reaction to the Madrid terrorist bombing led to the March 2004 election of socialist José Luis Rodríguez Zapatero, who promptly implemented his campaign pledge to withdraw Spanish troops from Iraq. Throughout the world public opposition to the war prevented Washington from obtaining meaningful military contributions to its ersatz coalition in Iraq.

A few days after the February 2003 demonstrations, *New York Times* reporter Patrick Tyler conferred "superpower" status on the antiwar movement. The huge antiwar demonstrations were indications, wrote Tyler, of "two superpowers on the planet: the United States and world public opinion." The White House faced a "tenacious new adversary" which was generating massive opposition to the administration's war policy and left the world's largest military power virtually alone in the international community.[44] Antiwar commentators quickly adopted the phrase and proclaimed their movement "the other superpower." Jonathan Schell wrote in *The Nation* of the movement's "immense power" in winning the hearts and wills of the majority of the world's people.[45] Even UN Secretary-General Kofi Annan used the phrase in referring to antiwar

---

[43] Polling numbers drawn from The Pew Global Attitudes Project, "America's image further erodes, Europeans want weaker ties: But post-war Iraq will be better off, most say," 18 March 2003. Polling conducted and reported by the Pew Research Center for the People & the Press. Available online at The Pew Research Center, http://www.people-press.org (accessed 14 February 2007).

[44] Patrick E. Tyler, "Threats and Responses: News Analysis; A New Power in the Streets," *New York Times*, 17 February 2003, A1.

[45] Jonathan Schell, "The Other Superpower," *The Nation* (27 March 2003). Available online at *The Nation*, www.thenation.com/doc.mhtml?i=20030414&s=schell (accessed 14 February 2007).

opinion.[46] A new form of global social movement emerged, an unprecedented expression of collective consciousness and action bound together through the Internet.

WINNING WHILE LOSING

Despite the unprecedented scale and scope of the Iraq antiwar movement, the United States and Britain ignored the pervasive opposition to war and rolled ahead with their pre-planned invasion. Given the Bush administration's determination to remove Saddam Hussein by force, the movement probably had little chance of halting the march to war. Nor did peace advocates have much time to organize: less than six months from when the major antiwar coalitions emerged in the fall of 2002 until the start of war.

Although the antiwar movement did not stop the invasion, it nonetheless had significant impact. The influence of the global opposition to war was evident in the Security Council debate prior to the invasion. When the Bush administration went to the Security Council in the fall of 2002, it won backing for a tougher weapons inspection regime but not for military action. Resolution 1441 established rigorous conditions for renewed weapons inspection, which the Baghdad regime promptly accepted, but it contained no language that could be interpreted as authorizing the use of military force. When the United States and Britain returned to the Security Council in February 2003 to seek authority for war, they were decisively rebuffed. Not only France, Germany, and Russia, but six other nonpermanent members – Chile, Mexico, Cameroon, Guinea, Angola, and Pakistan – refused to support the US proposal. Washington made determined efforts to twist arms, sending diplomatic missions to make threats and offer inducements, but its lobbying efforts produced only two other supporters, Spain and Bulgaria. Rather than face the embarrassment of such a meager showing, Washington withdrew its proposed resolution. This was a major victory for the global antiwar movement. The strength of worldwide opposition prevented the Bush and Blair governments from gaining Security Council support and forced them to proceed without international authorization. The importance of the Security Council rebuff to the United States is enormous. It was, according to Immanuel Wallerstein, "the first time since the United Nations was founded that the United States, on an issue that mattered to it, could not get a majority on the Security

---

[46] Geoffrey Nunberg, "The Nation: Search Engine Society; As Google Goes, So Goes the Nation," *New York Times*, 18 May 2003, Section 4, 4.

Council."[47] This was widely recognized as a humiliating political defeat for the supposed lone superpower. It represented a major loss of legitimacy and a weakening of US political prestige.

The interplay between the antiwar movement and the United Nations deserves special comment. Most UN officials and Security Council members were opposed to the war but were powerless to stop it. The UN Security Council by its very design is a captive of the permanent members, and when its most powerful members are bent on military aggression, the United Nations has no capacity to prevent them from acting. The most important power of the Security Council is its authority to confer international legitimacy. When it withholds consent, as it did in Iraq, it denies legitimacy. It was able to do so because of the worldwide antiwar movement. A creative dialectic developed between the Security Council and global civil society. The public opposition to war hinged largely on the lack of UN authorization. The objection of UN diplomats in turn depended on the strength of antiwar opposition. The stronger the antiwar movement in the United States, Germany, France, and other countries, the greater the determination of officials at the United Nations to resist Bush administration pressures. The stronger the objections at the United Nations, the greater the legitimacy and impact of the antiwar movement. It was a unique and unprecedented form of global political synergy. By defending the United Nations, despite its many shortcomings, and insisting upon international authorization for the use of force, the peace movement helped to build the opposition to war and strengthened respect for international law. Bush administration officials later criticized the Security Council for supposedly "failing its responsibilities." Many peace advocates considered the episode a shining moment for the United Nations. By standing up to political pressures from the United States, the Security Council displayed rare political courage and integrity. It was one of the United Nations' finest hours.

Movements can win even when they appear to lose. Although the antiwar movement did not prevent the invasion of Iraq it helped to set the terms of the debate internationally and exerted decisive influence on public opinion. The Bush administration rammed through its war policy, but it was unable to win the larger and more important struggle for hearts and minds. As was the case during the Vietnam War, the White House lost the war politically before it ever began militarily. As the occupation dragged on, creating a

[47] Immanuel Wallerstein, "US Weakness and the Struggle for Hegemony," *Monthly Review* 55, no. 3 (July–August 2003): 28.

"fiasco" as reporter Thomas Ricks described it, opposition to US policy steadily increased.[48] As in Vietnam antiwar sentiment spread even to the ranks of the military, with thousands of service members sending an "appeal for redress" to members of Congress urging US withdrawal. War is never solely about military results, said Clausewitz, but is an extension of politics, a means of realizing political aims. For the Bush White House the war was a disaster that failed to achieve its declared aims and weakened the administration's political standing at home and abroad.

For the peace movement antiwar campaigns are never solely about immediate results. They are part of a longer historical effort to vindicate the principles of realistic pacifism and lay the foundations of a more cooperative and peaceful future. During the Iraq debate the peace movement achieved unprecedented credibility and legitimacy. It received overwhelming support from civil society, especially the religious community, and largely avoided the backlash effects and internal sectarianism that hindered the Vietnam era movement. The movement's political arguments against the war were vindicated by official deceit and incompetence and by the horrendous aftermath of the invasion and occupation. Peace movement support for the United Nations and insistence on Security Council authorization for the use of force served as a partial counterweight to the Bush administration's circumvention of the United Nations and was an attempt to give greater legitimacy to the world body, despite its many flaws. The Iraq antiwar campaign elevated the role of global civil society as an increasingly important voice in determining matters of war and peace. In all of these ways it created new possibilities for avoiding unjustified wars in the future.

COUNTERING THE "WAR ON TERROR"

In the aftermath of the September 2001 attacks, as the Bush administration declared an open-ended "war on terror," peace and human rights activists called for a different kind of response to the terrorist attacks. They argued for a counterterrorism strategy based on cooperative law enforcement rather than unilateral war. The proper response to the criminal attacks of Al Qaida was not war, they emphasized, but a vigorous, multilateral police effort to apprehend perpetrators and prevent future attacks. Religious leaders led by Rev. Jim Wallis of Sojourners and Rev. Bob Edgar of the National Council of Churches circulated a statement appealing for "sober restraint" and warning against indiscriminate retaliation that would cause more loss of

---

[48] Thomas E. Ricks, *Fiasco: The American Military Adventure in Iraq* (New York: Penguin Press, 2006).

innocent life. "Let us deny [the terrorists] their victory by refusing to submit to a world created in their image," the declaration read. The statement was eventually signed by more than 4,000 religious leaders and was published in the *New York Times* in November 2001.

Wallis challenged peace advocates to take the threat of terrorism seriously and to develop effective nonviolent strategies for countering it. "For non-violence to be credible," he wrote, "it must answer the questions that violence claims to answer, but in a better way."[49] The theories of nonvio-lence provide a solid foundation for crafting effective policies against terrorism. Nonviolence is fundamentally a strategy for justice, a means of overcoming oppression and abuse, of which terrorism is surely a most extreme example. The principles of nonviolence are fully compatible with vigorous law enforcement efforts to track down and prosecute those respon-sible for mass murder. This requires action by courts and police forces and may involve the limited use of force.

Some absolute pacifists object even to limited forms of coercion, but most peace advocates accept the use of police force, provided it is con-strained, narrowly targeted against known criminals, and conducted within the rule of law. John Howard Yoder argued that policing is distinct from and ethically more justifiable than war.[50] Political scientist Robert Johansen has proposed ways to use international courts and multilateral policing to achieve justice and protect the innocent while strengthening the rule of law.[51] Theologian Gerald Schlabach has integrated these concepts into a theory of "just policing."[52] These approaches stretch but do not contradict the core philosophy of nonviolence, which seeks to preserve peace but also uphold justice. The presumption is always against the use of force, but extreme circumstances may arise – such as countering terrorist attacks – where the demands of justice require some limited use of police power. Cooperative law enforcement and intelligence sharing among governments are effective and lawful means of reducing the operational capacity of terrorist networks and protecting the innocent from attack.

The alternative strategy for countering terrorism also rests upon the theory and practice of conflict transformation, which seeks to ameliorate

[49] Jim Wallis, *God's Politics: Why the Right Gets It Wrong and the Left Doesn't Get It* (San Francisco: HarperCollins, 2005), 163.
[50] John Howard Yoder, *The Politics of Jesus*, 2nd edn (Grand Rapids: MI: Eerdmans, 1994), 204.
[51] Robert C. Johansen, "Enforcement without Military Combat: Toward an International Civilian Police," in *Globalization and Global Governance*, ed. Raimo Väyrynen, 173–98 (Lanham, MD: Rowman & Littlefield, 1999).
[52] Gerald Schlabach, "Just Policing, Not War," *America* 189, no. 1 (7–14 July 2003): 19–21.

the underlying dynamics that lead to violent extremism. To prevent armed violence it is necessary to understand why communities are in conflict and to resolve the grievances and conditions that fuel militancy. In countering the terrorist threat, this means recognizing the injustices that motivate support for extremist groups and enabling affected communities to resolve grievances through democratic political means rather than terrorist violence. The goal should be to separate militants from their support base by resolving the political injustices that terrorists exploit. In overcoming terrorism it is vital to differentiate between hard core militants and those who support them – to undermine the social base of Al Qaida-related groups by driving a wedge between militants and their potential sympathizers.

This approach should not be confused with appeasement or a defeatist justification of terrorist crimes. The point is not to excuse criminal acts but to learn why they occur and to use this knowledge to prevent future attacks. A nonviolent strategy does not mean appeasing hard core militants. Rather, it seeks to reduce the appeal of extremist methods by addressing legitimate grievances and providing channels of nonviolent political engagement for those who sympathize with the declared political aims. A two-level response is needed: determined law enforcement pressure against terrorist criminals, and active engagement with affected communities to resolve underlying grievances. Michael Walzer wrote, counterterrorism "must be aimed systematically at the terrorists themselves, never at the people for whom the terrorists claim to be acting."[53] Military attacks against potential sympathizers can be counterproductive and may drive third parties toward militancy. Legally based police action is by its nature more discriminating and is more effective politically because it minimizes backlash effects.

To overcome terrorism, concluded a UN working group in 2002, "it is necessary to understand its political nature as well as its basic criminality and psychology."[54] This means recognizing and addressing the legitimate political grievances that terrorist groups exploit – such as Israeli oppression of the Palestinians, US military encroachments into Muslim countries, and the military occupation of Iraq. These are grievances that generate widespread political frustration and bitterness in many Arab and Muslim countries, including among people who condemn terrorism and Al Qaida's brutal methods. Many in the Arab and Muslim world seek greater democracy and human rights within their own countries and resent US support for

[53] Michael Walzer, *Arguing about War* (New Haven, CT: Yale University Press, 2004), 60–1.
[54] United Nations General Assembly, Security Council, *Report of the Policy Working Group on the United Nations and Terrorism*, A/57/273-S/2002/875, New York, August 6, 2002, para. 13.

repressive regimes. These political concerns are widely shared throughout the world. They also coincide with the agenda of the peace and human rights community. Many peace and justice groups were actively campaigning to support the rights of the Palestinian people and oppose US military interventionism long before September 2001. Peace movements throughout the world continue to support these just demands, even as they condemn those who employ terrorist means to achieve them. No cause, however legitimate, can justify terrorism and the killing of innocent people. Nonviolent means are available both to achieve justice and counter violent extremism. The best way to undercut support for jihadist violence, peace advocates emphasize, is to support democracy and human rights, and to oppose militarization and oppression. These are the means of preventing violence and terror.

PART II

Themes

9

Religion

Throughout the ages religion has served as both catalyst to conflict and inspiration for peace. The ambivalence of the sacred, as Scott Appleby termed it, is one of history's great enigmas. Many of the most vicious and intractable wars have been cloaked in religious garb. Yet religion also provides valuable resources for peacemaking. Within each of the great religions there is "a moral trajectory challenging adherents to greater acts of compassion, forgiveness, and reconciliation," Appleby wrote, an "internal evolution" that offers hope for religiously inspired peacemaking.[1]

All major religions have imperatives to love others and avoid the taking of human life. In Buddhism the rejection of killing is the first of the Five Precepts. Hinduism declares "the killing of living beings is not conducive to heaven."[2] Jainism rejects the taking of any form of life: "if someone kills living things . . . his sin increases."[3] The Qur'an states "slay not the life that God has made sacred."[4] The Bible teaches "you shall not murder."[5] This reverence for life and desire to avoid harm is the first of what theologian Mark Juergensmeyer identified as the three major aspects of nonviolence within world religions. The second is the ideal of social harmony and living peacefully with others, frequently emphasized in the Old Testament and the Qur'an. Third is the willingness to sacrifice and suffer for the sake of expiating sin and avoiding injury to others, which is common in the Abrahamic traditions.[6]

---

[1] R. Scott Appleby, *The Ambivalence of the Sacred: Religion, Violence, and Reconciliation* (Lanham, MD: Rowman & Littlefield, 2000), 31.

[2] *Manusmrti* 5.48.   [3] *Sutrakritanga* 1.1.

[4] Qur'an 6:151. All Qur'an translations from Reza Aslan, *No god but God: The Origins, Evolution, and Future of Islam* (New York: Random House, 2005).

[5] Exodus 20:13 (all Biblical scripture quoted from the New International Version).

[6] David Noel Freedman and Michael J. McClymond, "Religious Traditions, Violence, and Nonviolence," in vol. III of *Encyclopedia of Violence, Peace, & Conflict*, ed. Lester Kurtz, 229–39 (San Diego, CA: Academic Press, 1999), 236.

At the core of the great religions is the injunction to care for the other, especially for the one in need. Buddhism and Hinduism are founded on principles of compassion and empathy for those who suffer. Islam emerged out of the Prophet's call to restore the tribal ethic of social egalitarianism and to end the mistreatment of the weak and vulnerable.[7] In the New Testament Jesus is depicted throughout as caring for and ministering to the needy. Compassion for the stranger is the litmus test of ethical conduct in all great religions. So is the capacity to forgive, to repent and overcome past transgressions. The key to conflict prevention is extending the moral boundaries of one's community and expressing compassion toward others.

There are many other religious principles that provide a foundation for creative peacemaking. Nonviolent values pervade the Eastern religious traditions of Buddhism, Hinduism, and Jainism and echo through the Gospel of Jesus. The religious emphasis on personal discipline and self-restraint also has value for peacemaking. It provides a basis for constraining the impulses of vengeance and retaliation that arise from violent conflict. The power of imagination within religion provides another basis for peace-making. The moral imagination, to use John Paul Lederach's term, is necessary to envision a more just and peaceful order, to dream of a society that attempts to reflect religious teaching.[8]

This chapter explores the contributions of religion to peacemaking. I examine how the spiritual longing for meaning and transcendence is linked by many to principles of love and peace. After reviewing Jain and Buddhist traditions, I discuss Islam and the concepts of *jihad* and *salaam*, evoking struggle on the one hand and social harmony on the other. Judaism has a similar duality of divinely sanctioned war and a teaching of peace through justice, defined as *shalom*. Christians derive their commitment to peace from Jesus's commandment to love all including enemies. The early Christian commitment to pacifism was absolute, but Christ's words were soon reinterpreted in church teaching and replaced by the just war tradition. Support for pacifism and peacemaking remained, however, and reemerged with the founding of the peace churches in the sixteenth and seventeenth centuries and the rise of social Christianity in the late nineteenth and early twentieth centuries. The chapter concludes with an overview of the continuing debate between the realist and pacifist traditions

---

[7] Aslan, *No god but God*, 29 and 40.
[8] John Paul Lederach, *The Moral Imagination: The Art and Soul of Building Peace* (New York: Oxford University Press, 2005); Marc Gopin, *Between Eden and Armageddon: The Future of World Religions, Violence, and Peacemaking* (New York: Oxford University Press, 2000), 20–3.

within Christianity through an examination of the writings of Reinhold Niebuhr and John Howard Yoder.

EASTERN TRADITIONS

I begin with a brief glance at Eastern religious traditions and the emergence of core principles of nonviolence within Hinduism, Jainism, and Buddhism. This quick survey overlooks a great deal within the Eastern traditions, from Taoism and the ancient Chinese sages to contemporary Baha'ism. It does not mean to suggest that Eastern traditions are inherently nonviolent. Militant tendencies exist in the East as elsewhere. My purpose is not to deny these realities but to focus narrowly on Eastern religious ideas and practices that inform the principles of peacemaking.

The teachings of Hinduism include nonviolence, renunciation of want, selfless duty, and the harmony of all life. The theology of immanence within Hinduism connects the soul of the individual with the divine soul that is present in all creation. The atman (individual self) is identified with brahma (supreme being), the innermost self linked to the divine spirit of the universe. The practices of yoga were designed to increase awareness of the divine light within. The core statement of this belief, "Thou art That," appeared in the *Upanishads* in approximately 800 BCE.[9] The *Bhagavad Gita* appeared a few centuries later to identify selflessness as the core ideal of religious practice. Although Arjuna the protagonist of the *Gita* is a warrior, he is advised by Khrishna to cast off all desires and be indifferent to gain or loss. The highest form of spirituality is detachment from the fruits of labor. The object of life is unity with the divine presence that permeates the world.

The non-Vedic creeds of Jainism and Buddhism exerted significant influence on Hinduism and have helped to shape the broader evolution of nonviolent thinking. The principle of *ahimsa* or nonharm spread from the sixth century BCE in India through the teachings of Mahavira, the founder of Jainism, and Siddhartha Gautama, the founder of Buddhism. Killing is strictly prohibited in Buddhism, which preaches freedom from hate, fear, and self-delusion in order to achieve enlightenment.[10] The Noble Truths describe life as constant suffering, the result of wants and attachments to the material world. The path to fulfillment is *metta*, boundless love, the giving of oneself without concern for reward.

[9] K. M. Sen, *Hinduism* (Baltimore, MD: Penguin, 1961), 19.
[10] Paul R. Fleischman, *The Buddha Taught Nonviolence, Not Pacifism* (Seattle, WA: Pariyatti Press, 2002), 10.

Buddhism and the principles of nonviolence became official public policy through the reign of Aśoka, who ruled in the years *c.* 265–238 BCE[11] over a vast Mauryan empire that covered most of India and extended into present day Afghanistan. H. G. Wells described Aśoka as "one of the great monarchs of history," a warrior who later renounced violence, embraced Buddhism, devoted himself to the Eightfold Path, and made unique contributions to the public welfare and education of the people under his rule. His famous Rock Edicts and Pillar Edicts carried statements and instructions encouraging right livelihood and providing information about his life and deeds. Aśoka advocated the principle of "conquest by *dharma*" (right living) to replace the traditional concept of military conquest. He organized the digging of wells, the planting of trees, and the building of hospitals and public gardens. According to scholar Romila Tharpar, Aśoka devoted the machinery of the state towards the practical realization of the ideal of good life.[12] He was particularly active in supporting the spread of Buddhism, building stupas and monasteries and sending missionaries throughout his realm and beyond – while at the same time adopting a policy of respect and tolerance toward other religions. His foreign policy was based on friendship, free trade, and cultural exchange with others. Wells enthused, "amidst the tens of thousands of names of monarchs that crowd the columns of history . . . the name of Asoka shines . . . almost alone, a star."[13]

Buddhism has been criticized for being preoccupied with spiritual concerns and ignoring social issues.[14] The Noble Truth that life is suffering can be interpreted as an endorsement or acceptance of the status quo. In recent decades a new tradition of Engaged Buddhism has emerged through the activism and writings of Thich Nhat Hanh of Vietnam, Aung San Suu Kyi of Burma, Maha Ghosananda of Cambodia, and the Dalai Lama.[15] The engaged Buddhists draw inspiration from the principle of *metta*, which they interpret as active compassion and bringing relief to those in suffering. Engaged Buddhists believe it is as important to do good as it is to refrain from doing evil. The Dalai Lama said that human interests were inextricably

---

[11] Also given as *c.* 273–232, "Aśoka," in *The New Encyclopædia Britannica*, vol. I, *Micropædia* (Chicago: Encyclopædia Britannica, Inc., 2005), 635.

[12] Romila Thapar, *Aśoka and the Decline of the Mauryas*, 2nd edn (Delhi: Oxford University Press, 1973), 181, 201.

[13] H. G. Wells, *The Outline of History: Being a Plain History of Life and Mankind* (New York: Macmillan, 1921), 432.

[14] Appleby, *The Ambivalence of the Sacred*, 132.

[15] This discussion draws from the insights of the author's former student. Sarah Wheaton, "Engaged Buddhism: The Development of Nonviolent Social Change in Buddhist Thought" (research paper, University of Notre Dame, Notre Dame, IN, 23 November 2005).

linked because all people depended on common social bonds and the natural environment in order to survive. As scholar Sallie King wrote, "our happiness can only exist within a shared matrix."[16] During the 1960s Thich Nhat Hanh was an activist for peace who was critical not only of the Saigon government and the US war but the brutality and intolerance of the communist-led resistance. During the 1990s Maha Ghosananda led thousands of Buddhist monks, nuns, and laypeople on marches to support reconciliation and encourage participation in UN-sponsored elections. Since the late 1980s Aung San Suu Kyi has led a movement for democracy entirely through nonviolent means. Suu Kyi's social engagement is based partly on her interpretation of the traditional concept of karma:

Some people think of karma as destiny or fate and that there's nothing they can do about it. It's simply what is going to happen because of their past deeds ... But karma is not that at all. It's doing, it's action. So you are creating your own karma all the time.[17]

Karma is the accumulation not only of past but present deeds, which implies the need for positive action in the here and now.

One of the most significant Buddhist reform organizations is *Sōka Gakkai* ("value-creating society"), which was founded in Japan in the 1930s but grew after the war into a substantial organization with some 8 million members and its own political party, *Kōmeitō*, known in the West as the "clean government" party. *Sōka Gakkai* is based on the theory of life force, developed by its second president Toda Jōsei. The theory posits the existence of a pervasive, all-encompassing force that permeates the universe and is the source of health, prosperity, social harmony, and happiness. Each human being is part of this life force and thus has immutable, supreme value. Any attempt to relativize the value of life, to make it subordinate to any other interest, is contrary to the order of the universe and can only harm human welfare and peace.[18] This belief in the interconnectedness of life leads to a spirit of empathy and benevolence toward others and forms the foundation for *Sōka Gakkai*'s commitment to social justice and peace. *Sōka Gakkai* has been a leading force for nuclear disarmament and a strong supporter of the United Nations and international cooperation. It is a

---

[16] Sallie B. King, *Being Benevolence: The Social Ethics of Engaged Buddhism* (Honolulu: University of Hawai'i Press, 2005), 13.

[17] Aung San Suu Kyi, *The Voice of Hope: Conversations with Alan Clements* (New York: Seven Stories, 1997), 124–5.

[18] Robert Kisala, *Prophets of Peace: Pacifism and Cultural Identity in Japan's New Religions* (Honolulu: University of Hawai'i Press, 1999), 79, 86.

prime example of Engaged Buddhism serving as an inspiration for peace activism.

STUDY WAR NO MORE

The Hebrew Bible contains prominent passages emphasizing the importance of war in achieving God's will, but it also contains many references to peace and the values of nonviolence. The traditional interpretation that contrasts the harsh and wrathful God of the Old Testament with the loving and merciful God of the New is a misperception. The rabbinic interpretation saw peace as a central part of God's purpose for humankind.[19] Compassion and love for others are central themes of the Old Testament, most famously in the passage of Leviticus to "love your neighbor as yourself."[20] As scholar Marc Gopin noted, the sources in Judaism that address questions of war occupy only a handful of pages in the sacred texts and halakhic literature, while references to peacemaking values such as repentance, forgiveness, and reconciliation are ubiquitous. The term *shalom* is mentioned more than 2,500 times in classical Jewish sources.[21] As in Islam the term is considered a definition of God and has a multi-dimensional meaning that defines peace as wholeness, truth, justice, righteousness, and grace. It is a complex and sophisticated concept that defines peace as the achievement of all human values in harmony.[22] *Shalom* embodies the conditions and values that are necessary for the prevention of war, including social justice, self-determination, economic well being, human rights, and the use of nonviolent means to resolve conflict.

Judaism teaches that war results from the denial of justice, when people allow "monstrous immoralities to fester instead of eradicating them. The only way to prevent the ultimate explosion," wrote scholar Roland Gittelsohn, "is to avoid or erase the iniquities that cause it."[23] War is permitted in the Hebrew Bible, but it is always in the context of the struggle against injustice and immorality. To avoid war, the torah teaches, establish conditions of justice.

In Exodus Yahweh is depicted as a warrior against Pharaoh, destroying his legions in the sea. God wages war, while humans are passive and must

---

[19] John Ferguson, *War and Peace in the World's Religions* (New York: Oxford University Press, 1978), 86–7.
[20] Lev. 19:18.   [21] Gopin, *Between Eden and Armageddon*, 77.
[22] Steven S. Schwarzschild, "Shalom," in *The Challenge of Shalom: The Jewish Tradition of Peace and Justice*, ed. Murray Polner and Naomi Goodman (Philadelphia, PA: New Society Publishers, 1994), 18.
[23] Roland B. Gittelsohn, "Pacifist," in *The Challenge of Shalom*, 219.

trust in the lord. "I am a jealous God," the Old Testament says in several places (Exodus 20:5). God is also depicted as exclusivist, offering protection to his chosen people, while excluding and sometimes justifying violence against others.[24] The ethic of social compassion is strong but it applies primarily within the tribe, according to this interpretation. Yet there is also a more universalist message in the torah, a compassion that embraces all humans, and a profound respect for the peacemaker.

Judaism's emphasis on ethical behavior and universal benevolence provides a strong foundation for peacemaking. The concept of holistic peace through social justice is especially important in the latter books of Isaiah and Jeremiah. Roland Bainton described the theme of the second chapter of Isaiah as that of redemptive pacifism through the suffering of God's servants. Humankind could achieve peace and be reconciled to divine truth by doing justice, loving mercy, and walking humbly with the Lord.[25]

In Isaiah and Micah the ultimate messianic vision for the fulfillment of divine purpose is portrayed as a time when humans will turn their swords into plowshares and study war no more. That famous passage contains not only an injunction against war but a sophisticated outline of the requirements for a more just and peaceful international order. Out of Zion, says Isaiah, "shall go forth teaching and the word of the Lord . . . [who] shall judge between the nations, and shall arbitrate for many peoples." They shall "beat swords into plowshares and their spears into pruning hooks." Then comes the vision of a world where "nation will not take up sword against nation, nor will they train for war any more."[26] As theologian Reuven Kimelman observed, the ordering of these sentences links the vision of disarmament to a process of moral instruction, international arbitration, and economic conversion.[27] Disarmament becomes possible when national conflicts can be adjudicated properly in an international tribunal. It is not enough to desist from going to war. Nations must also cease the education for war and agree to the negotiation and resolution of conflicts. They must address the economics of war. To "beat swords into plowshares" requires a process of conversion, to redirect economic activity from producing instruments of destruction to creating means of human development. Micah

---

[24] Regina M. Schwartz, *The Curse of Cain: The Violent Legacy of Monotheism* (Chicago, IL: University of Chicago Press, 1997), xi.

[25] Roland H. Bainton, *Christian Attitudes toward War and Peace: A Historical Survey and Critical Re-evaluation* (New York: Abingdon Press, 1960), 31.

[26] Isaiah 2: 3–4.

[27] Reuven Kimelman, "Judaism, War, and Weapons of Mass Destruction," in *Ethics and Weapons of Mass Destruction: Religious and Secular Perspectives*, ed. Sohail H. Hashmi and Steven P. Lee (New York: Cambridge University Press, 2004), 379–80.

repeats the passage and adds that every person shall sit under his own vine and fig tree, suggesting the need for economic security as a further requirement for peace. And "no one will make them afraid;" they will have freedom from fear.[28] In these succinct sentences Isaiah and Micah encapsulate a profound vision of the foundations of peace, one that has inspired people of the Abrahamic tradition through the centuries.

SALAAM AND JIHAD

Islam lacks a consistent teaching or practice of pacifism and is often misunderstood as a religion of the sword that justifies the use of violence to spread the faith. While the principles of nonviolence are not well developed within Islam, a few minority pacifist sects exist, including the *Maziyariyah* and *Ahmadiyah* movements. Concepts of peace are at the core of Muslim teaching. The term *salaam*, etymologically related to the Hebrew *shalom*, envisions a peaceful, harmonious social order of justice toward all without violence or conflict. In Arabic *salaam* is translated as peace and is considered one of the holy names of God.[29] The Sufi tradition of mysticism embodies many principles that are compatible with nonviolence. The Sufis emphasize the inner struggle to perfect one's love of God and to achieve harmony and compassion with others. To be one with nature and God is to be in a state of peace. Sufis consider Islam a religion of universalism, tolerance, peace, and reconciliation.

Islam teaches that life is sacred and that the believer has a duty to uphold truth and justice. Egalitarianism and social justice are core principles of Islam. As writer Reza Aslan noted, "benevolence and care for the poor were the first and most enduring virtues preached by Muhammad in Mecca."[30] According to the Qur'an piety lies

not in turning your face East or West in prayer ... but in distributing your wealth out of love for God to your needy kin; to the orphans, to the vagrants, and to the mendicants; it lies in freeing the slaves, in observing your devotions, and in giving alms to the poor.[31]

Pursuing justice in the face of oppression and suffering is the personal and collective duty of every Muslim. It is impossible for a Muslim to practice his or her faith without a commitment to social welfare. The concept of

---

[28] Micah 4: 2–4.
[29] Seyyed Hossein Nasr, *The Heart of Islam: Enduring Values for Humanity* (San Francisco, CA: HarperSanFrancisco, 2002), 217.
[30] Aslan, *No god but God*, 60.   [31] Qur'an 2:177.

withdrawal from the concerns of society has no place within Islam. For Muslims peace is not merely the absence of war or organized violence. It is also the presence of justice and the creation of conditions in which humans can realize their full potential.[32]

No concept in Islam is more frequently misunderstood and misinterpreted than *jihad*. The term literally means struggle or striving, an exertion or great effort. Its primary religious connotation is the struggle of the soul to overcome evil and sin, to submit completely to God's will and strive for moral perfection. This inward or spiritual struggle is defined as greater *jihad*. Because the inner struggle for holiness is inseparable from the outward struggle for social justice, *jihad* also has a secondary connotation. This lesser *jihad* calls the believer to struggle against oppression and tyranny, by military means if necessary. This concept of militant struggle is used by contemporary Islamic extremists to justify armed violence and terrorism for the supposed purpose of defending Islam. Al Qaida and other extremist groups manipulate and exploit Islam, wrote Aslan, "to give religious sanction to what are in actuality social and political agendas."[33] This was not how Mohammed intended the term, nor how many Islamic scholars through the ages have interpreted it. Jihad cannot be simply equated with military struggle, although its association with violence is undeniable.[34] Its primary meaning is spiritual struggle to achieve complete submission to God.

The Qur'an clearly allows the use of force, as evident in passages instructing believers to "slay the polytheists wherever you confront them"[35] and "carry the struggle to the hypocrites who deny the faith."[36] Not just the Qur'an but also the *sunnah* and *hadith* provide ample foundation for a tradition of justified violence.[37] So does the experience of the Prophet as military leader during the Medina period. These traditions have been used by some Islamic scholars to assert the principle of religious war

---

[32] Abdul Aziz Said, Nathan C. Funk, and Ayse S. Kadayifci, "Introduction: Islamic Approaches to Peace and Conflict Resolution," in *Peace and Conflict Resolution in Islam: Precept and Practice* (Lanham, MD: University Press of America, 2001), 7.

[33] Aslan, *No god but God*, 81.

[34] In about two-thirds of the instances in which the verb *jahada* or its derivatives appear in the Qur'an, it is associated with warfare. Freedman and McClymond, "Religious Traditions," 235.

[35] Qur'an 9:5.   [36] Qur'an 9:73.

[37] According to Ronnie Hassan, the *Sunnah* was "established during [the Prophet Muhammed's] life for all to follow and to pass on for generations . . . a set of practices that the Prophet taught the Muslims to follow;" and *Hadith* "is a narration of the words or acts of the Prophet, as perceived and transmitted by one or more persons who heard or saw the Prophet saying or performing these acts." See Ronnie Hassan, "*Hadith* and *Sunnah* – Two Different Concepts," *Understanding Islam*, 28 March 2003. Available online at Understanding Islam, www.understanding-islam.com/related/text.asp?type=article&aid=186&ssc (accessed 8 March 2007).

to convert unbelievers. Over the last century Islamists have seized upon this interpretation to promote a militant interpretation of *jihad*. In Saudi Arabia Palestinian scholar Abdullah Azzam (1941–1989) taught a violent version of *jihad* that influenced the founding of the Palestinian militant group Hamas and that had exceptional impact on one of his students in particular, Osama bin Laden.[38]

Many Islamic scholars have contested this justification of holy war as a distortion of the Prophet's teachings. They point to the cardinal principle in the Qur'an that "there can be no compulsion in religion."[39] On this point the Qur'an is unequivocal: "The truth is from your Lord; believe it if you like, or do not."[40] The message to non-Muslims is, "To you your religion, to me mine."[41] These passages counsel tolerance and patience toward other faiths and in no way provide justification for religious war. The Qur'an places limits on the use of force. The concept of lesser *jihad* can be considered a rudimentary just war theory.[42] According to this interpretation, the Qur'an prohibited aggression and all but strictly defensive wars. It established previously unrecognized distinctions between combatants and noncombatants. The Qur'an teaches "do not begin hostilities; God does not like the aggressor."[43] Killing is permitted only in response to murder or in the case of "villainy in the land." Permission to fight is given only to those who are oppressed or who have been driven from their homes.[44]

Although violence is permitted for just cause in Islam, some Muslim reformers have interpreted *jihad* in the context of nonviolence and have advocated the use of peaceful means to overcome oppression. They find inspiration for this approach in Qur'anic teachings that extol patience and forgiveness. The Qur'an acknowledges the right of retribution but states "those who forgive the injury and make reconciliation will be rewarded by God."[45]

One of history's most important Muslim practitioners of nonviolent action was Abdul Ghaffar Khan, a prominent ally of Gandhi from the Pashtun region of northwest Pakistan who led a significant mass movement of nonviolent direct action among people with a fierce warrior ethic. Khan was inspired by Gandhi, but he was committed to nonviolence before he met the Mahatma. He was motivated primarily by his interpretation of the Qur'an and *hadith*.[46] He combined the principle of struggling against injustice with the call for patience and endurance. He told his followers:

---

[38] Aslan, *No god but God*, 86.   [39] Qur'an 2:256.   [40] Qur'an 18:29.   [41] Qur'an 109:6.
[42] Aslan, *No god but God*, 81.   [43] Qur'an 2:190.   [44] Qur'an 22:39.   [45] Qur'an 42:40.
[46] Mukulika Banerjee, *The Pathan Unarmed: Opposition & Memory in the North West Frontier* (Karachi: Oxford University Press, 2000), 146.

I am going to give you such a weapon that the police and the army will not be able to stand against it. It is the weapon of the Prophet, but you are not aware of it. That weapon is patience and righteousness. No power on earth can stand against it ... tell your brethren that there is an army of God, and its weapon is patience.[47]

Khan created the *Khudai Khidmatgar*, the "Servants of God," as a nonviolent army of determined nonviolent resistance against British rule. Eventually numbering some 100,000 members, the *Khudai Khidmatgar* employed rigorous training methods to instill discipline, physical stamina, and courage. Members wore military-style uniforms with distinctive red shorts and marched in regimental-style formations, while maintaining strict nonviolent discipline. The *Khudai Khidmatgars* participated in resistance campaigns, performed poverty relief and humanitarian services, and contributed significantly to the ultimate success of the freedom movement.[48] When Khan died in 1988, vast crowds gathered in his honor throughout northwest Pakistan. Indian Prime Minister Rajiv Gandhi attended the funeral, and a one-day ceasefire was declared in the Soviet-Afghan war raging nearby.[49] All came to pay homage to the person who channeled the Muslim principle of *jihad* into a remarkable movement of nonviolent resistance against injustice. The example of Khan and the *Khudai Khidmatgar* stands as a model for those who would seek to struggle for justice while remaining true to the meaning of *salaam*.

CHRISTIANITY

The doctrinal basis for the Christian commitment to pacifism is explicitly stated in various New Testament passages:

You have heard that it was said, "Love your neighbor and hate your enemy." But I tell you: Love your enemies and pray for those who persecute you.[50]

Do not be overcome by evil, but overcome evil with good.[51]

These and related passages have been the subject of endless exegesis by countless theologians and religious teachers over the centuries, but to the earliest Christians and many since, they stand as an unequivocal command to love all unconditionally and are a prohibition against war. Early Christians rejected the bearing of arms and military service even at the

---

[47] Abdul Ghaffar Kahn quoted in Robert C. Johansen, "Radical Islam and Nonviolence: A Case Study of Religious Empowerment and Constraint among Pashtuns," *Journal of Peace Research* 34, no. 1 (February 1997): 58.

[48] Eknath Easwaran, *A Man to Match His Mountains: Badshahkhan, Nonviolent Soldier of Islam* (Petaluma, CA: Nilgiri Press, 1984), 111–13, 121–8, 168–9.

[49] Banerjee, *The Pathan Unarmed*, 8.   [50] Matthew 5:43–4.   [51] Romans 12: 21.

cost of a martyr's death. According to Bainton, there is no evidence of Christians serving in the emperor's army prior to the years 170–80 CE.[52] References to participation in the military increase in the years after that, but it was not until the conversion of Constantine in the early fourth century that military service was fully accepted among Christians. Citations advocating pacifism can be found in the writings of Tertullian, Origen, and Lactantius, and in the testimonies of martyrs Justin, Maximilian, and Marcellus.[53] The early Christians opposed war not only on the basis of Christ's love commandment, but because they considered the oath to the emperor that was required of soldiers a form of idolatry.[54] On a more practical level many early Christians found it difficult to justify serving in an army that persecuted the followers of Jesus.

As the Christian Church crystallized into an established institution the early commitment to pacifism fell by the wayside. When Christianity became a state religion through Constantine, the Church accepted military service as a duty of citizenship. The role of Christianity changed from that of persecuted sect to official belief system. The emergent Church hierarchy fully embraced the imperial system, and only baptized Christians could serve in the Roman army. Ambrose and Augustine codified this accommodation with power into the doctrine of just war, which Grotius and Aquinas later developed further. The classical Roman code of conduct in battle, inherited from Cicero, was reinterpreted in a Christian context to serve as a justification for war. Christians were taught to distinguish between the commitment to love at a personal level and the acceptance of the use of force in political affairs. Augustine claimed on the basis of Old Testament teachings that war is an instrument of divine judgment upon wickedness. He reconciled this with the obviously divergent teachings of the New Testament by insisting that the commandment of love can only be applied in personal relations. The tradition of pacifism was kept alive, but it was confined to the margins of society where minority sects sought to live by Jesus's nonviolent creed. These included the Waldensians beginning in 1170, St. Francis of Assisi (1181–1226) and his Franciscan order, the Lollards of fifteenth-century England, the Hussites and Taborites in the Czech Republic, and their Moravian successors. The most significant of these minority movements were the Anabaptists and Quakers.

---

[52] Bainton, *Christian Attitudes toward War and Peace*, 71–2.
[53] J. R. Burkholder and Karl Holl, "Pacifism," in *The Encyclopedia of Christianity*, vol. IV, ed. Erwin Fahlbusch *et al.* (Grand Rapids, MI: Eerdmans, 2005), 2.
[54] David G. Hunter, "A Decade of Research on Early Christians and Military Service," *Religious Studies Review* 18, no. 2 (April 1992): 87–93.

ANABAPTISTS AND QUAKERS

The Protestant reformation unleashed a torrent of separatism and violence within Europe, but it also gave birth to the Anabaptist tradition and a movement to recapture the irenic principles at the heart of the Christian Gospel. In the sixteenth century Conrad Grebel, Menno Simons, and other Christian reformers created a distinct religious community based on the practice of adult baptism and a commitment to the literal interpretation of Christ's call to "resist not evil." They were greatly influenced by Erasmus, whose famous *Complaint of Peace* (written in 1516) railed against the wickedness of war and the "sinister spectacle" of bishops and cardinals arousing the faithful to battle.[55] Erasmus combined religious analysis and rational humanism in an eloquent rebuke of war and defense of Christ's message of peace. "When one considers the whole life of Jesus," he wrote, "what is it if not an uninterrupted lesson in peace and mutual love?"[56] Erasmus's interpretation of Christ inspired the Mennonites, who used his translation and *Annotations* of the New Testament as their Gospel text.[57] The Anabaptists rejected all forms of armed violence as a sin against God and refused to serve as soldiers or to participate in war. Because government authority is based on coercion and the threat of violence, they believed, the affairs of state were inherently sinful and corrupt. They were deeply pessimistic about human nature and had little faith in the possibility of secular social reform. They rejected the established political order but made little attempt to change it. Most withdrew from state affairs in quasi-anarchist fashion into mostly agricultural communities.

After their emergence in northern Switzerland and southern Germany in the sixteenth century and the persecution they suffered in the religious wars of that era, the Mennonites emigrated in considerable number to North America in search of land and religious freedom. As they settled in the United States and Canada over the centuries, they remained a people apart, carefully sustaining their pacifist beliefs and their rejection of the state's warmaking authority. They preferred to live a quiet existence as farmers in rural communities and to register as conscientious objectors to military service. By the second half of the twentieth century, however, withdrawal from the challenges of war and armed violence became less viable.

[55] José Chapiro and Desiderius Erasmus, *Erasmus and Our Struggle for Peace* (Boston, The Beacon Press, 1950), 161.

[56] Quoted in Chapiro and Erasmus, *Erasmus and Our Struggle for Peace*, 145.

[57] Abraham Friesen, *Erasmus, the Anabaptists and the Great Commission* (Grand Rapids, MI: Eerdmans, 1998), 38.

Mennonite communities were no longer as isolated as they once were. Their lives increasingly intertwined with mainstream society. Some Mennonites became uncomfortable with the limitations of the traditional doctrine of nonresistance. Standing aside from the epic struggle against fascism during World War II, or from the movements for civil rights and peace in subsequent decades, no longer seemed morally justified. J. Lawrence Burkholder and others questioned the pursuit of moral perfectionism in an imperfect world. The problem with traditional Mennonite ethics, Burkholder wrote, was that it "had failed to come to terms with this social reality."[58] In 1972 John Howard Yoder published his provocative and highly influential book, *The Politics of Jesus*,[59] which argued that Christians were called to act against injustice and violence. Mennonites became increasingly engaged in working for peace. Some participated actively in antiwar movements, while others became mediators and created international conciliation programs. In recent decades Mennonites have become a major force in organized movements for peace and conciliation around the world.

The Quakers, or the Society of Friends, shared the Mennonite commitment to uncompromising Christian love, but they sought to transform the world rather than withdraw from it. Arising in Cromwell's England in the mid-seventeenth century, the Friends stressed the inner light of personal revelation, guided by the Christian Gospel, as their basis for the rejection of war and violence. They sought to reform society and bring moral principles into the public square. Through the teachings of founder George Fox and other early Friends, the Quakers developed a distinct religious tradition that included a strong pacifist commitment. In the eighteenth and nineteenth centuries the Friends adopted a biblically oriented emphasis on the Christian teaching of nonresistance and uncompromising love. In the twentieth century Quaker pacifists renewed their emphasis on the Inner Light as the primary basis for their rejection of war and armed violence.

Unlike other pacifists Quakers did not shy away from confronting social evil. Theirs was an outward looking creed that sought to influence politics and social policy.[60] From their earliest origins, they developed a tradition of "speaking truth to power." William Penn, the Quaker founder of

---

[58] J. Lawrence Burkholder, "The Limits of Perfection: Autobiographical Reflections," in *The Limits of Perfection: A Conversation with J. Lawrence Burkholder*, ed. Rodney J. Sawatsky and Scott Holland (Waterloo, Ontario: Institute of Anabaptist and Mennonite Studies, Conrad Grebel College, 1993), 32–3.

[59] John Howard Yoder, *The Politics of Jesus* (Grand Rapids, MI: Eerdmans, 1972).

[60] Peter Brock and Nigel Young, *Pacifism in the Twentieth Century* (Syracuse, NY: Syracuse University Press, 1999), 7, 9.

Pennsylvania, said that "true godliness" does not turn men out of the world but "excites their endeavours to mend it."[61] From 1682 until 1756 the Quakers dominated the political life of provincial Pennsylvania in the so-called "holy experiment," a partly successful attempt to establish government on the basis of Christian principles of love and charity. Penn and his successors were particularly effective in maintaining cordial relations with the native first American communities of the colony. Quakers in England and the USA were leaders in major social reform movements for free trade, the abolition of slavery, and women's suffrage. They were active in rejecting the military encroachments of the Crown and speaking out against war. William Penn's 1693 *Essay towards the Present and Future Peace of Europe* was one of the earliest treatises on international peace. In the early nineteenth century Quakers in Britain and the USA were among the first to promote the cause of peace and war prevention, and they were founders and leaders of the earliest peace societies. Quakers have been at the forefront of nearly every major peace movement in modern US and British history. They have been pioneers in the field of peace research and helped to establish some of the earliest conciliation and conflict transformation programs.

TOLSTOY'S ANARCHIST PACIFISM

One of history's most forceful advocates of pacifism was Leo Tolstoy. Tolstoy was important because of his correspondence with and influence upon Gandhi and because of his stature as one of the world's most prominent novelists, which gave his writings wide reach. In the latter years of his life this former Russian military officer and member of the landed aristocracy experienced a profound spiritual crisis and religious conversion that led him to become an absolute pacifist. His reading of the New Testament and especially the Sermon on the Mount convinced him that his previous life of military service and economic privilege had been sinful. He renounced wealth, became a vegetarian, and condemned war. Christ's command to "resist not evil" is the central obligation of moral behavior, he wrote. Christ's injunctions are not perfectionist ideals that are unrealizable in a sinful world, Tolstoy argued, but firm rules that must be followed if humankind is to save itself from damnation. Only unconditional obedience to Christ's commandment of love can bring salvation. Since the institutions of government ultimately rest on powers of violent coercion,

---

[61] Quoted in Marjorie Sykes, *Quakers in India: A Forgotten Century* (London: George Allen & Unwin, 1980), 106.

the state is inherently sinful, he believed, which led him to adopt an anarchist position calling for political noncooperation. In such writings as *A Confession* (1879), *What I Believe* (1884), *The Kingdom of God Is within You* (1893), and his last novel *Resurrection* (1899), Tolstoy wrote incessantly and often didactically of his commitment to anarchist pacifism. As Peter Brock commented, "The passion and totalness with which Tolstoy henceforward espoused pacifism reflects perhaps the difficulty which the author of *War and Peace* experienced in renouncing patriotism and military glory."[62]

Tolstoy was uncompromising in his commitment to war resistance. Refusing to serve in the military was a Christian obligation, he argued, and the surest means of undermining state authority and bringing about a nonviolent world. He regarded conscription as "the apotheosis of state tyranny," to use Brock's words, the crucible where the sinful demands of the state clash most dramatically with the principles of religion.[63] He was a vigorous supporter of conscientious objection and opposed even alternative civilian service. In his "Notes for Soldiers" Tolstoy called upon military recruits to renounce "the ungodly and shameful calling of a soldier."[64] Tolstoy believed that individual war resistance was the only legitimate and most certain means of achieving a more peaceful world. He was dismissive of the established peace societies and scornful of the Hague Peace Conferences of 1899 and 1907. He considered arbitration and disarmament efforts futile, a diversion from the primary task of promoting worldwide refusal of military service.

Tolstoy never developed a coherent political program or organizational plan for spreading his strategy of war resistance. The challenge of translating his ideas into effective social action was left to others, especially Gandhi, who read and was greatly impressed by Tolstoy's writings, particularly the 1909 "Letter to a Hindu." Tolstoy wrote that the people of India were responsible for their own oppression because they allowed British colonial domination to continue. Gandhi interpreted Tolstoy's message as "slavery consists in submitting."[65] Gandhi went on to develop the Tolstoyan ideas of noncooperation into a philosophy and method of mass social action to overcome injustice. Tolstoy's writings had influence throughout the world,

---

[62] Peter Brock, *A Brief History of Pacifism from Jesus to Tolstoy*, 2nd edn (Toronto: Distributed by Syracuse University Press, 1992), 72.

[63] Peter Brock, *Freedom from War: Nonsectarian Pacifism 1814–1914* (Toronto: University of Toronto Press, 1991), 199.

[64] Leo Tolstoy, *Tolstoy's Writings on Civil Disobedience and Non-Violence* (New York: Bergman Publishers, 1967), 46.

[65] Quoted in Raghavan Iyer, ed., *The Essential Writings of Mahatma Gandhi* (New Delhi: Oxford University Press, 1990), 74.

including among peace advocates in Japan who opposed their country's 1904–5 war with Russia. Abe Isoo, future member of the Diet, reported that his reading of *The Kingdom of God Is within You* exerted "tremendous influence" on his commitment to social justice.[66] Abe and other Japanese intellectuals were attracted not only by Tolstoy's uncompromising opposition to war but by his belief in personal moral regeneration, which appealed to their neo-Confucian ethic, and by his rejection of privileges born of social injustice and militarism. Tolstoy's call for individual war refusal reverberated widely in the early 1930s in Britain and the United States when hundreds of thousands of people signed peace pledges vowing never to participate in war. Echoes of Tolstoyan resistance also emerged during the Vietnam era, as hundreds of thousands of young Americans rejected the military draft, and some of us who served in the military spoke out against the war as part of the GI peace movement.

SOCIAL CHRISTIANITY

The spread of peace societies in the late nineteenth and early twentieth centuries was deeply influenced by the rise of social Christianity and the Social Gospel movement. In response to the upheavals of industrialization and the challenges of socialism, many Protestants and Catholics found renewed meaning in Christ's call to minister to the needy and seek reconciliation with enemies. Theologically social Christianity asserted the immanence of God in the world and the presence of the divine spirit in every person. Its optimistic humanism was in stark contrast to Calvinist orthodoxy, which spoke of a transcendent God and viewed humans as condemned to sin and damnation. The leading voice of social Christianity in the United States was Walter Rauschenbusch, the Protestant minister who served a congregation of often unemployed workers in New York's Hell's Kitchen area in the early 1890s. Rauschenbusch presented a socialist critique of capitalism based on the teachings of Christ, arguing that "the Kingdom of God includes the economic life; for it means the progressive transformation of all human affairs by the thought and spirit of Christ." In Britain the Christian Social Union was founded in 1889 "to apply the moral truths and principles of Christianity to the social and economic difficulties of the

---

[66] Cyril H. Powles, "Abe Isoo: The Utility Man," in *Pacifism in Japan: The Christian and Socialist Tradition*, in *Pacifism in Japan: The Christian and his Socialist Tradition*, ed. Nobuya Bamba and John F. Howes (Vancouver: University of British Columbia Press, 1978), 147–8.

present time."[67] It was a religious duty, social Christians argued, to work for reform in domestic society and for peace internationally. In the United States the major Protestant denominations increasingly embraced social Christianity and established social service programs. In 1908 thirty denominations formed the Federal Council of Churches, which carries on the Social Gospel tradition today as the National Council of Churches.

Social Christianity continued to exert influence throughout the twentieth century. Many Protestants believed that Christianity must serve as a guide not only for personal salvation but for social and political reform and the prevention of war. Most Protestant reformers recognized the reality of social evil and the corrupt and violent nature of conventional politics, but they believed that progress toward a more peaceful society was possible. In the United States they filled the pages of the influential journal *The Christian Century* with appeals for peace. In the years after World War I, various denominations issued declarations supporting the League of Nations and opposing war and rearmament. Pacifism became a kind of "party line" within liberal Protestantism during the 1920s.[68] It was in this heady atmosphere that the brilliant young theologian Reinhold Niebuhr initially affirmed his pacifist faith and for a few years agreed to serve as chair of the FOR – before rejecting pacifism and becoming the foremost voice of Christian realism.

CATHOLIC PEACEMAKING

Catholic social teaching evolved in the late nineteenth century in parallel with social Christianity to address questions of social justice and the rights of labor. Pope Leo XIII's groundbreaking encyclical *Rerum Novarum*, issued in 1891, primarily addressed economic issues but also expressed new perspectives on peace. The Vatican called for a new international order in which peace would be based on justice and love rather than military alliances and weapons. The encyclical called for a reevaluation of the principle of defensive war in light of advances in the technology and destructiveness of war.[69] *Rerum Novarum* was the first in a long line of Catholic Church pronouncements establishing the tenets of Catholic social teaching, which Appleby summarized as: (1) the common good, the pursuit

---

[67] John Atherton, "Introduction: Christian Social Ethics in Context," in *Christian Social Ethics: A Reader* (Cleveland, OH: The Pilgrim Press, 1994), 18, 24–5, 27.

[68] Charles DeBenedetti, *The Peace Reform in American History* (Bloomington, IN: Indiana University Press, 1980), 116.

[69] Patricia McNeal, *Harder than War: Catholic Peacemaking in Twentieth-Century America* (New Brunswick, NJ: Rutgers University Press, 1992), 2.

of policies that serve the larger public community not just the Church; (2) solidarity, the commitment to achieve justice for all people; (3) subsidiarity, the dictum that central government should not decide what locally based bodies can determine for themselves; (4) the preferential option for the poor, to lift up the condition of "the least of these;" (5) the priority and inviolability of human rights, including the right to life and to political and economic justice; and (6) a preferential option for the family as the basic social unit.[70] These principles and the commitment to engage with the secular order brought Catholicism squarely into the debate about justice and peace.

As the influence of social Christianity spread in Europe and North America, Catholic support for the pacifist cause increased. In 1906 the Vatican sent a message of greeting and encouragement to the Universal Peace Congress being held that year in Milan. Working to avoid war, wrote Pope Pius X, "conforms to the precepts of the Gospel."[71] In France Catholic clergy and laity founded the Gratry Society, named for a liberal nineteenth-century abbot, Alphonse Gratry, who had been active in the *Ligue internationale et permanente de la paix*. Members of the Gratry Society urged believers to express their faith through an active commitment to political and social justice, with a special emphasis on preventing war. Although a majority of Catholic priests remained aloof or hostile to the cause of peace, a Catholic peace movement slowly emerged in France and other countries. In 1910 the International Catholic Peace League was founded with branches in France, Spain, Switzerland, and Belgium.[72]

The peace witness of Pope Benedict XV (1914–22) gave legitimacy to emerging Catholic peace efforts. Benedict opposed war in any form and rejected the theory of just war as historically outmoded and theologically inadequate. He earned the sobriquet "pontiff of peace" and was described as the most pacifist pope in modern history.[73] In Germany a Catholic peace association emerged under the leadership of Dominican priest Franziskus Stratmann. British Catholics formed the Catholic Council for International Peace. The Netherlands Roman Catholic Society for the Promotion of Peace emerged in 1912.[74] In France Catholic reformer Marc Sangnier advocated a "pacifism of action" that focused on building friendship

[70] Appleby, *The Ambivalence of the Sacred*, 42.
[71] Quoted in Roger Chickering, *Imperial Germany and a World Without War: The Peace Movement and German Society, 1892–1914* (Princeton, NJ: Princeton University Press, 1975), 380.
[72] *Ibid.*, 195, 380–1.
[73] Ronald G. Musto, *The Catholic Peace Tradition* (Maryknoll, NY: Orbis Books, 1986), 171.
[74] Jonkheer B. De Jong Van Beek En Donk, "History of the Peace Movement in the Netherlands," first published in 1915, in Sandi E. Cooper, "Introduction," in *Peace Activities in Belgium and the Netherlands*, ed. Sandi E. Cooper (New York: Garland Publishing, 1972), 29.

between the French and German people. The 1926 Bierville Congress he led gained the official backing of the Catholic Church and was endorsed by 117 prominent political figures, including Paul Painlevé, minister of war, and Édouard Herriot, minister of public instruction. Approximately 6,000 people attended, including 3,221 Germans and 1,768 French.[75]

In the United States Father John Ryan organized the Catholic Association for International Peace (CAIP), the first American Catholic peace organization. CAIP promoted the League of Nations and the World Court and encouraged international engagement to advance justice.[76] In the 1930s Dorothy Day and Peter Maurin founded the Catholic Worker movement, which ministered to the needy during the Great Depression and espoused absolute pacifism even into World War II. Day continued to work for peace and social justice until her death in 1980. The Catholic Worker movement has remained active to the present as a voice of pacifism and service to the poor.

The evolution of peace within Catholicism reached a culmination in 1962 and 1963 with the convening of the second Vatican Council and the release of Pope John XXIII's encyclical, *Pacem in Terris*. This groundbreaking document firmly linked the quest for peace to the defense of human rights and the pursuit of justice and greater equality among nations. It was the first papal encyclical addressed to all people of good will, not merely Catholics. Conflicts should be settled through negotiation, it argued, not armed struggle. It called for recognition of the "universal common good" and greater acknowledgment of the interdependence of all nations. The well-being of one country was linked to that of all others. In the interest of human dignity and life, the encyclical declared, the arms race should cease, weapons stockpiles should be reduced, nuclear weapons should be banned, and all nations should agree on a fitting program of disarmament. The document expressed "ardent desire" that the United Nations "may become ever more equal to the magnitude and nobility of its tasks."[77] John XXIII's encyclical and the documents of Vatican II deepened the Church's commitment to social justice, human rights, and peace, and confirmed the principle that Christian commitments apply in matters of society as in personal life.

[75] Peter Farrugia, "French Religious Opposition to War, 1919–1939: The Contribution of Henri Roser and Marc Sangnier," *French History* 6, no. 3 (September 1992), 294–5.

[76] McNeal, *Harder than War*, 10–12.

[77] *Pacem in Terris*, Encyclical of Pope John XXIII, promulgated 11 April, 1963, para. 145. Available online at Papal Encyclicals, www.papalencyclicals.net/John23/j23pacem.htm (accessed 12 June 2007).

The commitment to social engagement emerging from the Vatican Council sparked the rise of liberation theology, which was particularly influential in Latin America in the 1970s and 1980s. Liberation theology emphasized the social mission of the church in fulfilling Jesus's call to serve the needy and free the oppressed. At their conference in Medellín, Colombia, in 1968, the Latin American bishops spoke of the church "listening to the cry of the poor and becoming the interpreter of their anguish."[78] The development of liberation theology received a decisive boost and gained its name with the 1971 publication of *Teología de la liberación* by Peruvian theologian Gustavo Gutiérrez. According to the proponents of liberation theology, the Gospel calls believers to nonviolent action on behalf of the poor and oppressed. Although the Vatican expressed sympathy for the goals of the movement, papal officials warned against its Marxist tendencies and sharply rejected materialist interpretations of the Gospel. Pope John Paul II campaigned vigorously against liberation theology, as did his successor Benedict XVI – although the movement's call to social action on behalf of the poor lived on among Catholics and Protestants alike.

NIEBUHR'S CHALLENGE

No modern theologian has exerted more influence on the debate about war and peace than Reinhold Niebuhr. His trenchant insights into the dilemmas of applying moral principles in the immoral realm of politics have profoundly influenced the thinking of contemporary politicians and theologians alike. Hans Morgenthau described Niebuhr as the greatest political philosopher of America.[79] Martin Luther King, Jr. considered Niebuhr a prime influence on his intellectual formation.[80] John Howard Yoder termed Niebuhr's philosophy the "principal system of thought" with which pacifism must come to grips.[81] Niebuhr is often cited in support of a narrow interpretation of political realism, but his writings reveal a deep commitment to social justice and the principles of democracy. They also contain an important but often overlooked tribute to the nonviolent methods of

---

[78] Leonardo Boff and Clovodis Boff, *Introducing Liberation Theology* (Maryknoll, NY: Orbis Books, 1988), 76.

[79] Richard Harries, *Reinhold Niebuhr and the Issues of our Time* (Grand Rapids, MI: Eerdmans, 1986), 1.

[80] Martin Luther King, Jr., *Stride Toward Freedom: The Montgomery Story* (New York: Harper & Brothers, 1958), 98–9.

[81] John Howard Yoder, "Reinhold Niebuhr and Christian Pacifism," *Mennonite Quarterly Review* 29, no. 2 (April 1955): 101.

Gandhi. In these pages I attempt to rescue Niebuhr from the militarists, while acknowledging his critique of pure pacifism and his insistence on a more pragmatic and contingent understanding of the prospects for peace.

In 1932 Niebuhr published *Moral Man and Immoral Society*, which developed the major themes of his life work – the pervasiveness of sin individually and socially, the inherent immorality of political action, and the necessity of coercion to overcome injustice and tyranny. Niebuhr considered social reform a moral imperative. He had been a champion of the rights of organized labor during his pastorate in Detroit in the 1920s and was a firm supporter of civil rights for African Americans. Niebuhr considered Christ's "law of love" an uncompromising obligation of the Christian faith. Yet he was critical of the false optimism that had previously characterized much of Western liberalism. Niebuhr emphasized the unavoidable realities of human sinfulness – the imperfections of human nature and the limitations of what can be achieved in the struggle for social justice. As World War II approached he sharpened his critique of pacifism and argued for rearmament and military resistance to Hitler. In the last decades of his life Niebuhr became the oracle of cold war liberalism, justifying the military and nuclear containment of the Soviet Union, while retaining his commitment to racial and economic justice.

The fundamental fallacy of pacifism, according to Niebuhr, is its faith in human perfectibility and its rejection of the Christian doctrine of original sin. The full meaning of Christianity is expressed not only in the law of love but in the fact of human sinfulness. The absolutists "do not see that sin introduces an element of conflict into the world and that even the most loving relations are not free of it."[82] The selfishness of human communities is inevitable, he wrote. "Where it is inordinate it can be checked only by competing assertions of interests; and these can be effective only if coercive methods are added to moral and rational persuasion."[83] Given the inherent egotism and sinfulness of humans, justice can be achieved only by "a certain degree of coercion on the one hand, and by resistance to coercion and tyranny on the other hand." Political action seeks to achieve relative justice amid human selfishness and sin and should not be confused with the divine ethic which embodies perfection. The political life of society "must constantly steer between the Scylla of anarchy [war] and the Charybdis of

---

[82] Reinhold Niebuhr, "Why the Christian Church is not Pacifist," in *Christianity and Power Politics* (New York: Charles Scribner's Sons, 1940), 14.

[83] Reinhold Niebuhr, *Moral Man and Immoral Society: A Study in Ethics and Politics* (New York: Charles Scribner's Sons, 1932, 1960), 272.

tyranny." Niebuhr criticized those who refused to accept the necessity of military force against Nazi barbarism. Complacency or neutrality in the struggle against fascism was morally unacceptable. He condemned the "confused religious absolutism" of pacifists who rejected forceful action against Hitler. Inaction in such circumstances "means that a morally perverse preference is given to tyranny."[84]

The origins of sin, according to Niebuhr, are found in the dualism of human nature. We are finite beings constrained physically by the circumstances of time and place. Yet our consciousness transcends the limits of self and strives to achieve perfection and permanence against the finitude of existence. We confuse our only partial grasp of the truth with "the authority of the absolute." We stubbornly defend our own interests under the illusion that they represent universal values. Our egoism tempts us toward righteousness and a desire to impose our views on others. Niebuhr termed this the "permanent spiritual problem of man."[85] It is the sin of pride, the false belief that humans can realize absolute truth. The greatest evil often comes from religiously inspired zealots, who believe they have found God's truth and are determined to impose it on others with divinely sanctioned fury.

While Niebuhr sharply criticized pure pacifism, he also rebuked those who would seek to justify war on the basis of the Christian Gospel. Christ's injunctions to "resist not evil" and "love your enemies" are "uncompromising and absolute," Niebuhr wrote. Christ's love ethic is the "law of life." It is "drawn from, and relevant to, every moral experience," the guide of our total human experience.[86] There is nothing in the words or actions of Christ and his disciples that could be construed as providing justification for war, he argued. The efforts of some theologians to rationalize military force through reference to the Gospel are "futile and pathetic." In these beliefs Niebuhr had much in common with pacifist theologians. John Howard Yoder described the identification of the Christian Church with the affairs of state as "Constantinian heresy" and wrote that any attempt to justify war from the words of Jesus is "condemned to failure."[87] The invocation of divine guidance for the ungodly act of war is a reflection of what Niebuhr termed "the pathos of modern spirituality."[88] All wars are accompanied by

[84] Niebuhr, "Why the Christian Church is not Pacifist," 14–16.
[85] Reinhold Niebuhr, *Christianity and Power Politics* (New York: Charles Scribner's Sons, 1940), 156–7.
[86] Quoted in G. H. C. MacGregor, *The New Testament Basis of Pacifism and the Relevance of an Impossible Ideal* (Nyack, NY: Fellowship Publications, 1954), 127–8.
[87] John Howard Yoder, "Peace without Eschatology?" in John Howard Yoder, *The Royal Priesthood: Essays Ecclesiological and Ecumenical*, ed. Michael G. Cartwright (Scottdale, PA: Herald Press, 1998), 157 and 161.
[88] Quoted in MacGregor, *The New Testament Basis of Pacifism*, 130.

vast amounts of hypocrisy and self-deception. Each side in a conflict seeks to identify its cause with God's will. It is another form of sinful pride, of presuming to have divine sanction.

The Niebuhrian doctrine of human sinfulness emphasizes mutual responsibility for war. It rejects any sense of moral righteousness. Wars are "partly the consequence of the sins of society," Niebuhr wrote. They are conflicts between sinners, not between the righteous and the wicked. The rise of Nazism was rooted in the vindictiveness of the Peace of Versailles. The imperialism of fascism, Niebuhr cautioned, was different only in degree and not in kind from the imperial impulse in all life. "Our own sin is always partly the cause of the sins against which we must contend."[89] Niebuhr was sympathetic to the pacifist cause, even as he disagreed with its idealism. His ideas were sometimes manipulated to justify a form of intransigent militarism far beyond what he would have intended. He was a critic of the decision to drop the atomic bombs in 1945 and, although a supporter of nuclear deterrence, advocated a policy of no first use. In the years before his death he was a skeptic of the war in Vietnam.[90] The misuse and misinterpretation of Niebuhr's thought reflects the very egoism and unrestrained self-interest he warned against in his writings. Realism shorn of any pacifist influence too easily becomes an apology for militarism and imperial ambition. The concerns of pacifism are a necessary and prudent constraint on those who in the name of realism are all too ready to unleash the scourge of war.

BEYOND PERFECTIONISM

Many have responded to Niebuhr over the decades, but no one has defended pacifism more convincingly and authoritatively than John Howard Yoder. In *The Politics of Jesus* Yoder directly challenged the assertion that Jesus was neutral on matters of social justice. Yoder's central thesis was that "the ministry and the claims of Jesus are best understood as presenting ... not the avoidance of political options, but one particular social-political-ethical option."[91] The direction of that political option is clear from the message of the Gospel. It is to bring justice and mercy to the poor and the afflicted, to practice reconciliation and unconditional love

---

[89] Niebuhr, "Why the Christian Church is not Pacifist," 24.
[90] Reinhold Niebuhr and Hans Morgenthau, "The Ethics of War and Peace in the Nuclear Age," *War/Peace Report* 7, no. 2 (February 1967): 7.
[91] Yoder, *The Politics of Jesus*, 11.

toward others. Jesus is not only relevant but normative for a contemporary Christian social ethic, Yoder argued. The words and deeds of Jesus show a "coherent, conscious social-political character and direction."[92] They are a call to lift up the lowly, free the captive, and practice love toward all, even enemies. These were radical ideas that posed a direct political challenge to the Roman rulers of Palestine and that pose a continuing challenge to political authority today. Jesus was not just a moralist whose teachings had some political implications, wrote Yoder, but the "bearer of a new possibility of human, social, and therefore political relationships."[93]

Jesus introduced a radical new way of challenging unjust authority. As Walter Wink and other analysts have argued, Christ commanded his followers not only to "resist not evil" but also to "overcome evil with good." In Matthew's version of the Sermon on the Mount, the passive language of nonresistance is followed immediately by the proactive command to "love your enemies; do good to those who hate you." This is not a call for submission but for active, self-sacrificing love to overcome evil. As Yoder noted, the voluntary suffering of Jesus on the cross was the "political alternative to both insurrection and quietism."[94] Jesus rejected violence but also counseled loving defiance of injustice. Christ's command to turn the other cheek was not an invitation to passivity, Wink emphasized, but an invocation of active and creative defiance of oppressive authority. It offered an example of how the oppressed can defy and resist the powerful while maintaining human dignity and a spirit of love. Returning love for hate is "heaping burning coals" on the head of the oppressor. It is a way of denying the oppressor's power to humiliate.[95] Nonresistance and nonviolent resistance to evil are not polar opposites. They are intimately intertwined and fully compatible as the complete Christian ethic of love. The message of the Gospel of John, according to Yoder, is that "the cross and not the sword, suffering and not brute power determines the meaning of history."[96]

Niebuhr was correct to note the impossibility of perfectionism, Yoder agreed, but the goal of Christian social ethics is not perfection but a less imperfect world. The Lord's Prayer declares "thy will be done on earth as in heaven." The challenges of redemption are in the real world, where the ideals of personal and social morality meet the reality of sin. The apostle Paul calls humans to be "fellow workers with God" in moving the world

---

[92] *Ibid.*, 112.   [93] *Ibid.*, 52.   [94] *Ibid.*, 36.
[95] Walter Wink, *Engaging The Powers: Discernment and Resistance in a World of Domination* (Minneapolis, MN: Fortress Press, 1992), 176, 185.
[96] Yoder, *The Politics of Jesus*, 232.

closer to the kingdom. The commandment to love, wrote Scottish theologian G. H. C. MacGregor, is "binding here and now, even though we know that it cannot be completely fulfilled" in an imperfect world.[97] The fact that we cannot achieve perfect love in an "immoral society" is not an argument for failing to apply the law of love in political life. The Christian demands not a condition of absolute peace, wrote Yoder, but a social order that encourages good and restrains evil, that makes an imperfect world more tolerable. The purpose of Christian ethics is not to achieve impossible utopias but to strive for what Yoder termed "progress in tolerability."[98] By denouncing particular evils and devising remedies for social problems, it is possible to create not a perfect world, but one that can please God and be useful to other humans. As Yoder wrote, "sin is vanquished every time a Christian in the power of God chooses the better instead of the good . . . love instead of compromise . . . That this triumph over sin is incomplete changes in no way the fact that it is possible."[99]

Niebuhr's writings acknowledged the importance of striving for limited forms of social progress. He reconciled the commitment to social justice with his philosophical critique of perfectionism by emphasizing the concepts of discriminate judgment and relative justice. There are degrees of evil, and it is both possible and necessary to decide which is less, which is more tolerable. Discriminate judgment makes choices among less than perfect options to achieve relative justice. It weighs the good of achieving a just end against the harm that may be caused by the use of coercive means. This perspective is fully compatible with the Social Gospel view that social action can achieve partial progress toward justice. It is rooted in both pacifist and just war traditions. It requires the rigorous application of strict ethical standards before making the decision to employ coercive means. It sets limits on when and how military force can be applied. Yoder argued that a consistent application of Niebuhr's ethical framework "would lead in our day to a pragmatic . . . pacifism and to the advocacy of nonviolent means of resistance."[100]

THE NONVIOLENT ALTERNATIVE

As Yoder noted, the logic of Niebuhr's argument pointed toward nonviolent action as a bridge between injustice and moral purity. *Moral Man and*

---

[97] MacGregor, *The New Testament Basis of Pacifism*, 140–1.
[98] Yoder, "Peace without Eschatology?," 160.
[99] Yoder, "Reinhold Niebuhr and Christian Pacifism," 116.
[100] Yoder, "Peace without Eschatology?," 166.

Immoral Society contained an important analysis of Gandhian nonviolence. Niebuhr described Gandhi as "the greatest modern exponent of nonviolence."[101] He considered Gandhi's nonviolent methods morally superior means of exerting pressure to achieve social justice. Actions such as mass civil disobedience, strikes, and boycotts are not entirely free of coercion, Niebuhr noted, but they are far less sinful than the destruction and violence of war. Through mass noncooperation and actions that disrupt business as usual, nonviolent resisters limit the adversary's freedom of movement. By intervening in the social, economic, and political functioning of an oppressive system, nonviolent campaigners undermine illegitimate authority and create new realities that must be accommodated. Nonviolent action is capable of altering the relations of power and physically intervening to prevent oppressive action. Such actions are more than an attempt to persuade. They apply coercive pressure to undermine and impede the exercise of unjust authority.

Niebuhr emphasized the moral advantages of nonviolence. The Gandhian method helps to break the cycle of hatred and mutual recrimination that flows from the use of violence. The nonviolent method, he wrote, "reduces these animosities to a minimum and therefore preserves a certain objectivity in analysing the issues of the dispute." This "spiritual discipline against resentment" allows the parties to a conflict to acknowledge each other, and to discriminate between the evils of an unjust social situation and the individuals who are involved in it. Nonviolent resistance, Niebuhr observed, "is a type of coercion which offers the largest opportunities for a harmonious relationship with the moral and rational factors in social life."[102] It is an instrument of "moral goodwill" that can "obviate the dangers of incessant wars." It is a particularly strategic instrument for oppressed communities struggling to win freedom. In a statement of stunning prescience Niebuhr forecast in 1932 the evolution of this method in the United States:

The emancipation of the Negro race in America probably waits upon the adequate development of this kind of social and political strategy . . . The technique of nonviolence . . . will, if persisted in with the same patience and discipline attained by Mr. Gandhi and his followers, achieve a degree of justice which neither pure moral suasion nor violence could gain.[103]

Martin Luther King, Jr. undoubtedly read these words and through the movement he helped to lead proved them correct.

---

[101] Niebuhr, *Moral Man and Immoral Society*, 242.
[102] *Ibid.*, 248, 250–1.   [103] *Ibid.*, 252, 254.

Niebuhr concluded his analysis on nonviolent action with an appeal to the religious community: "There is no problem of political life to which religious imagination can make a larger contribution than this problem of developing non-violent resistance."[104] It requires the "sublime madness" of religious faith, he argued, to achieve the proper attitude of humility and forgiveness that is needed to wage nonviolent struggle. It takes faith to sustain the willingness to sacrifice and the capacity to forgive that are the foundation of the nonviolent method. Unfortunately, neither Niebuhr nor the religious communities to whom he appealed heeded this call to develop the non-violent method. Niebuhr never returned substantively to the problem of nonviolence in his voluminous writings. As the clouds of war and totalitarianism darkened the world, he directed his powerful intellect against the false optimism of the liberal conscience. Perhaps if he had followed up on his earlier inquiry into nonviolence, he might have helped to elucidate the Gandhian method as a third way, between war and pure pacifism, for achieving justice while remaining true to the Christian law of love.

[104] *Ibid.*, 254.

10

A force more powerful

Pacifism and nonviolence are often considered synonymous, but they are conceptually and politically distinct. The nonviolent method was conceived by Gandhi as a means of struggling against oppression and injustice, not as a solution to the problem of war. Some pure pacifists rejected the Gandhian method because it used "pressure methods to force the government's hands."[1] Most of those who have participated in nonviolent action campaigns over recent decades do not consider themselves pacifist. They support nonviolent resistance in the manner of Nehru, who wrote in his autobiography, we "accepted that method . . . not only as the right method but as the most effective one for our purpose."[2] The Gandhian method offers a pragmatic alternative to absolute pacifism, a way of overcoming injustice and realizing political objectives while remaining true to moral principles.

The distinctions between pacifism and nonviolence illuminate the limitations of pacifism. Withdrawing from the struggle against oppression is not a moral position, Walzer wrote. The weakness of the lamb, Nietzsche argued, is an invitation to slaughter. Gandhi rejected passivity and developed his method as an active form of struggle. In so doing he helped to bridge the gap between pure pacifism and resistance to evil by turning religious principles into methods of social change. As Martin Luther King, Jr. wrote, "Gandhi was probably the first person in history to lift the love ethic of Jesus above mere interaction between individuals to a powerful and effective social force on a large scale."[3] What impressed King and other followers of Gandhi was not only the success of nonviolent resistance in winning independence for India but its ability to achieve victory without

---

[1] Guy F. Hershberger, *War, Peace, and Nonresistance* (Scottdale, PA: Herald Press, 1946), 220.
[2] Jawaharlal Nehru, *Toward Freedom: The Autobiography of Jawaharlal Nehru* (New York: John Day, 1941), 80.
[3] Martin Luther King, Jr., *Stride Toward Freedom: The Montgomery Story* (New York: Harper & Row, 1958), 97.

stirring the rancor and bitterness that often result from revolutionary change. The peaceful and even amicable way in which the British handed over power in 1947 was in some respects as significant as the winning of independence itself. This double victory reinforced the belief that the nonviolent method could reconcile the twin requirements of love and resistance to evil.

Realists often dismiss nonviolence as naïve and unworkable. Nonviolence has been tried and found wanting, they claim. Writer and activist Barbara Deming argued to the contrary, "It has *not* been tried. We have hardly begun to try it. The people who dismiss it ... do not understand what it could be."[4] Gandhi said at the end of his life that the "technique of unconquerable non-violence of the strong has not been discovered as yet."[5] Organized nonviolence is a new and still undeveloped method of achieving political change. Only at the beginning of the twentieth century, with Gandhi's campaigns of mass noncooperation in South Africa and India, did nonviolent action begin to emerge as a viable means of social change. It is a method still "in the process of invention," wrote Deming.[6] Scholar Gene Sharp examined in detail the history of nonviolent action and the strategies and mechanisms by which it brings about social change.[7] While examples of nonviolent action can be found throughout history, as Sharp documented, only in the last century has nonviolent action made significant contributions to political change. Sharp's works have been translated into many languages and have been used to train nonviolent activists around the world, from Burma to Serbia. In recent decades the Gandhian method of strategic nonviolent action has been applied and enlarged upon in a growing number of countries.

Examples of major nonviolent successes are many. In Ghana Kwame Nkrumah led a decade-long campaign that brought political independence in 1957 through "positive action" – political agitation, public education, strikes, boycotts, and mass noncooperation. More recent examples include the "people power" movement of the Philippines in 1986, the "velvet revolution" in central and eastern Europe in the late 1980s, elements of the South African freedom movement, the flowering of democracy in Chile

---

[4] Barbara Deming, "On Revolution and Equilibrium," in *Revolution & Equilibrium* (New York: Grossman, 1971), 199.

[5] Quoted in Judith M. Brown, *Gandhi: Prisoner of Hope* (New Haven, CT: Yale University Press, 1989), 375.

[6] Deming, "On Revolution and Equilibrium," 198.

[7] See in particular Gene Sharp, *The Politics of Nonviolent Action* (Boston, MA: Porter Sargent, 1973) and *Waging Nonviolent Struggle: 20th Century Practice and 21st Century Potential* (Boston, MA: Porter Sargent, 2005).

and other Latin American countries during the 1980s and 1990s, the over-throw of Slobodan Milosevic in Serbia in 2000, and the Rose, Orange, and Tulip "revolutions" of Georgia, Ukraine, and Kyrgyzstan in 2003–5. There are examples of failure, as well, including the Tiananmen Square massacre of 1989, the isolation and collapse of the Kosovar nonviolent resistance struggle in the early 1990s, and the so far unsuccessful Burmese democracy movement. The overall record of success is nonetheless impressive. Walter Wink wrote, "Never before have citizens actualized this potential in such overwhelming numbers or to such stunning effect. And yet 'people power' is still in its infancy!"[8] Nonviolent resistance has indeed become "a force more powerful."[9] It offers a third way, distinct from war and inaction, for addressing the challenges of injustice. The alternative to war is not surrender or appeasement, but the fight for justice through nonviolent action.

In this chapter I examine the religious and philosophical principles underlying the Gandhian method, exploring how Gandhi synthesized Eastern and Western religious traditions, combining the insights of the *Bhagavad Gita* and the Sermon on the Mount. I describe the core concepts of *satyagraha*, the Gandhian method of mass action, and probe the ways in which nonviolent resistance is able to alter relations of political power and overcome injustice. I also review the influence of Gandhi's philosophy and method on King, Barbara Deming, and other nonviolent activists who adapted the Gandhian method to modern circumstances. The chapter concludes with an examination of the role of sacrifice and courage in the nonviolent method and a reinterpretation of the concept of "peace through strength."

RELIGIOUS ROOTS

Gandhi was deeply motivated by religious belief. From early childhood he was steeped in Hindu religious teaching. He was a devoted student of the *Gita*, the sacred Hindu scripture, and believed that its central message was detachment from material wants and pleasures. Gandhi was especially influenced by the Jain traditions of his native Gujarat region of western India. The Jain belief system incorporates the Buddhist principles of self-lessness, asceticism, and nonviolence. The Jains believe in noninjury to all

[8] Walter Wink, *Engaging the Powers: Discernment and Resistance in a World of Domination* (Minneapolis, MN: Fortress, 1992), 252.
[9] Peter Ackerman and Jack DuVall, *A Force More Powerful: A Century of Nonviolent Conflict* (New York: St. Martin's Press, 2000).

other living beings and practice strict vegetarianism and pacifism. The Jain and Buddhist traditions are predicated on the principle of *ahimsa*, or nonharm, which seeks to avoid injury to other living creatures.[10] It is better to suffer personal injury than to cause suffering to others. *Ahimsa* is not a passive concept, however. It implies a positive recognition of the right of every living being to strive for fulfillment and an obligation to uphold and protect that right. *Ahimsa* must go beyond mere noninjury, Gandhi believed, to include "action based on the refusal to do harm."[11] Ahimsa is positive love, the commitment to act to prevent injury to others.

Gandhi also studied Christianity and was significantly influenced by the teachings of Jesus, especially the Sermon on the Mount, which he considered of sublime beauty and importance. It was a Quaker in South Africa, Michael Coates, who introduced Gandhi to the Sermon on the Mount and helped him gain a deeper understanding of Jesus's gospel of love.[12] Gandhi kept a picture of Christ in his office in South Africa and on the wall of his ashram in India, and he often read passages from the Gospels before encounters with his Christian adversaries.[13] He considered Christ the "sower of the seed" of nonviolent philosophy. Gandhi's attraction to Christian nonviolence was reinforced by the writings of Tolstoy. The great novelist's conversion to absolute Christian pacifism appealed to Gandhi and corresponded with his own commitment to *ahimsa*. Tolstoy's call for noncooperation with illegitimate authority impressed Gandhi and matched his thinking about the need for defiance of British authority in India.

Gandhi's commitment to nonviolence derived primarily from his search for truth and spiritual meaning. As he contemplated the limits to human knowledge, he recognized the need for humility and tolerance in the search for truth. Only God is omniscient. Human knowledge is always conditional and relative. The quest for truth excludes the use of violence, said Gandhi, "because man is not capable of knowing the absolute truth and, therefore, not competent to punish."[14] We can never have the level of certainty about a perceived truth that would entitle us to commit violence on its behalf.

---

[10] K. M. Sen, *Hinduism* (New York: Penguin, 1961), 45.

[11] Quoted in Joan V. Bondurant, *Conquest of Violence: The Gandhian Philosophy of Conflict*, rev. edn (Princeton, NJ: Princeton University Press, 1988), 23.

[12] S. Radhakrishnan, ed., *Mahatma Gandhi: Essays and Reflections on His Life and Work* (Bombay: Jaico, 1956), 126.

[13] Louis Fischer, *The Life of Mahatma Gandhi* (New York: Harper & Row, 1950), 84, 333.

[14] Mahatma Gandhi, "Satyagraha, Civil Disobedience, Passive Resistance, Non-Co-operation," *Young India*, 23 March 1921, from *The Collected Works of Mahatma Gandhi* 22, no. 240 (23 November 1920– 5 April 1921) (Pitiala House, Tilak Marg, New Delhi: Publications Division, Ministry of Information and Broadcasting, Government of India, 1999), 451. CD-Rom, dynamic collection.

Because of the impossibility of absolute human knowledge, we have no right to impose our version of truth on another by physical force. "Without *ahimsa*," Gandhi said, "it is not possible to seek and find truth." Truth is to be found through the interplay of contending interpretations of reality and the synthesis of competing forces into a higher reality. Knowledge is forged in the crucible of nonviolent social contention and the objective consideration of alternative interpretations. "If there is dogma in the Gandhian philosophy," Joan Bondurant wrote, "it centers here: that the only test of truth is action based on the refusal to do harm."[15] In the Gandhian method, different perspectives and interests are harmonized through the medium of nonviolent social action into a higher truth.[16]

Gandhi's commitment to *ahimsa* and search for truth led him to emphasize the necessity of harmonizing ends and means. He believed that ends and means were not distinct categories of analysis but complementary components of the same reality. Gandhi reconciled ends and means as part of a common search for truth through the reconciliation of opposites. He placed greater emphasis on means than on ends. If ultimate truths are unknowable, he concluded, ultimate ends are also uncertain. The ends of human action are unpredictable, but the means employed are concrete and certain. Political philosopher Hannah Arendt came to a similar conclusion: "since the end of human action ... can never be reliably predicted, the means used to achieve political goals are more often than not of greater relevance to the future world than the intended goals."[17] In this sense, Bondurant observed, the Gandhian method is end creating rather than end serving.[18] As Gandhi said, "If one takes care of the means, the end will take care of itself."[19] Cesar Chavez had a similar view: "There is no such thing as means and ends. Everything that we do is an end, in itself, that we can never erase."[20] King likewise argued that "the end is preexistent in the means" and that truth and justice can only be achieved through moral means.[21]

---

[15] Bondurant, *Conquest of Violence*, 25.

[16] Robert J. Burrowes, *The Strategy of Nonviolent Defense: A Gandhian Approach* (Albany, NY: State University of New York Press, 1996), 108.

[17] Hannah Arendt, *On Violence* (New York: Harcourt Brace, 1970), 4.

[18] Bondurant, *Conquest of Violence*, 14.

[19] Mahatma Gandhi, "Working of Non-Violence," *Harijan*, 6 February 1939, from *The Collected Works of Mahatma Gandhi* 75, no. 47 (Pitiala House, Tilak Marg, New Delhi: Publications Division, Ministry of Information and Broadcasting, Government of India, 1999), 48. CD-Rom, dynamic collection.

[20] Quoted in Joan London and Henry Anderson, *So Shall Ye Reap* (New York: Thomas Y. Crowell, 1970), 183.

[21] Quoted in John J. Ansbro, *Martin Luther King, Jr.: The Making of a Mind* (Maryknoll, NY: Orbis Books, 1994), 185.

ACTION FOR CHANGE

Gandhi was not a philosopher but a strategist of social and political change. He cared little for grand theorizing and never attempted to organize his thoughts into a coherent philosophy. He was a doer more than a thinker. He defined his social action method as "soul force" or "truth force," a means of upholding truth through assertive social action. He sought to distinguish his method from "passive resistance," the term previously used, and still commonly misapplied in reference to mass noncooperation. There is nothing passive about resistance to social evil, Gandhi emphasized. He sought a social method that was active and forceful in overcoming injustice.

George Orwell was no great admirer of Gandhi, and reviled pacifism, but he recognized the unique strength and importance of Gandhi's new method. "Gandhi's attitude was not that of most Western pacifists," he wrote. "Satyagraha . . . was a sort of non-violent warfare, a way of defeating the enemy without hurting him and without feeling or arousing hatred."[22] Gandhi would have corrected Orwell to say that the goal is not defeating the adversary but achieving understanding and political accommodation, but otherwise he would have agreed with Orwell's description. The Gandhian method introduced a revolutionary new form of political struggle into human history. It provided a way of fighting against injustice without resorting to violence and without stirring the intense passions of hatred and revenge that usually accompany armed struggle. It combined the quest for religious truth with the struggle for social justice.

Satyagraha is a dynamic concept, involving constant action and a willingness to change and accept new understandings of truth. It goes far beyond mere pressure tactics or civil disobedience. It is an ethical search for truth through nonviolent action. It is a method of testing truth and transforming conflict through the power of love. It encompasses a broad range of actions designed to find truth through the interaction of contending social forces. Jim Wallis described the Gandhian method as a form of spiritual politics.[23] Gandhi engaged in political action not to achieve power for himself but to bring about social betterment. He engaged in political struggle because he wanted to end oppression and serve the needy. "I cannot render this service," he said, "without entering politics."[24] He considered

---

[22] George Orwell, "Reflections on Gandhi," in *A Collection of Essays* (New York: Harcourt Brace Jovanovich, 1946), 177.

[23] Jim Wallis, *The Soul of Politics: A Practical and Prophetic Vision for Change* (New York: Orbis Books, 1994).

[24] Brown, *Gandhi: Prisoner of Hope*, 190.

politics a form of religious commitment that transcended narrow self-interest and embraced the common good through a willingness to sacrifice.

Gandhi applied the principles of nonviolence in a unique and highly effective manner. Orwell wrote that "inside the saint, or near-saint, there was a very shrewd" political leader.[25] Gandhi's political method included three stages of activity – persuasion, sacrifice, and noncooperation. Before engaging in direct action Gandhi sought to persuade his adversaries through the presentation of facts and rational argument. According to historian Judith Brown, Gandhi showed "a meticulous concern for the collection of properly documented evidence."[26] When factual argument failed to persuade, as was often the case, Gandhi proceeded to the next stage, organizing dramatic acts of self-sacrifice. Through disciplined and nonviolent action and a willingness to suffer arrest or physical harm, Gandhi and his colleagues attempted to pierce the consciences of their adversaries. They also sought to reach third parties and win the political sympathies of those upon whom the exercise of political power depended. After dramatizing issues and arousing moral concern, Gandhi then moved to the final stage, mass noncooperation. Through boycotts and other forms of direct action, the Gandhian movement applied pressure on adversaries and forced them to change by withdrawing consent and undermining their ability to exercise power.

Martin Luther King, Jr. developed a similar typology of social action steps to guide his nonviolent action campaigns. In his incomparable "Letter from Birmingham City Jail," King identified the four essential steps of every nonviolent campaign, which can be paraphrased as follows: collect the facts, engage in negotiation and dialogue with the adversary, prepare for sacrifice, and take direct action.[27] Like Gandhi, King believed that the first step in every campaign is to collect the facts and publicize the issues. The next step is to present demands to the adversary in an attempt at negotiation and dialogue. When this initial interaction proves fruitless, as it usually does in the early stages of a campaign, the activists pause for reflection and preparation for more forceful action. Activists must "purify" themselves, said King, by preparing to sacrifice and pledging to maintain nonviolent discipline. Only after these steps have been taken does the campaign proceed to direct action, the fourth step. Through demonstrations, strikes, boycotts, and other forms of direct pressure, activists drive the process back to the

---

[25] Orwell, "Reflections on Gandhi," 171–2.   [26] Brown, *Gandhi: Prisoner of Hope*, 113.
[27] Martin Luther King, Jr., "Letter from Birmingham City Jail," in *A Testament of Hope: The Essential Writings and Speeches of Martin Luther King, Jr.*, ed. James M. Washington (San Francisco, CA: HarperSanFrancisco, 1991), 290.

bargaining table for the negotiation of a settlement. It is this creative combination of moral persuasion and social pressure that accounts for the effectiveness of the Gandhian method.

COERCION AND NONVIOLENCE

Notwithstanding Gandhi's emphasis on religious principles and moral persuasion, the nonviolent social action methods he pioneered inevitably involve a degree of political coercion. The concept of forcefulness was built into his method from the very outset. The Hindi word *agraha*, part of *satyagraha*, means "firmness" or "forcefully grasping." Gandhi's campaigns often employed boycotts, mass noncooperation, and other coercive tactics as a means of achieving political change through the force of social action. Gandhi was ambiguous about the role of coercion. He believed that humans were capable of spiritual and moral perfection, and he sought to persuade his adversaries through reason to do the right thing. As Judith Brown observed, this hope in the power of moral persuasion sustained Gandhi but it also imprisoned him, limiting his effectiveness as a political leader. Some analysts argue that he was too prone to compromise.[28] His controversial decision to call off the salt *satyagraha* campaign of 1930–1 for the mere promise of negotiations with the British was unpopular with his colleagues in the independence movement, especially when British officials refused to grant substantive concessions at the roundtable talks in London. Gandhi was so eager to negotiate that he would, in Stanley Wolpert's words, "retreat from the brink of victory."[29] Gandhi's uneasiness with coercion and his faith in the power of moral persuasion at times weakened the impact of his nonviolent campaigns.

Reinhold Niebuhr described Gandhi's attempts to deny coercive elements of nonviolent action as "pardonable confusion in the soul of a man who is trying to harmonise the insights of a saint with the necessities of statecraft." Elements of coercion are unavoidable, Niebuhr argued.

The selfishness of human communities must be regarded as an inevitability. Where it is inordinate it can be checked only by competing assertions of interest; and these can be effective only if coercive methods are added to moral and rational persuasion.[30]

[28] Peter Ackerman and Christopher Kruegler, *Strategic Nonviolent Conflict: The Dynamics of People Power in the Twentieth Century* (Westport, CT: Praeger, 1994), 201.
[29] Stanley Wolpert, *Gandhi's Passion: The Life and Legacy of Mahatma Gandhi* (New York: Oxford University Press, 2001), 4.
[30] Reinhold Niebuhr, *Moral Man and Immoral Society: A Study in Ethics and Politics* (New York: Charles Scribner's Sons, 1932), 243, 272.

Coercion becomes necessary when purely moral or rational pleas fall on deaf ears, as they so often do. Injustice cannot be willed away or removed solely through persuasion. It must be resisted by every moral means available, which may require the use of nonviolent compulsion.

King had none of Gandhi's ambiguity about coercive elements of nonviolence. Niebuhr's realistic Christianity was a "prime influence" on his thinking, and he spent much of his time in graduate school studying the implications of his philosophy.[31] He agreed with Niebuhr's emphasis on social evil, which he described as "stark, grim, and colossally real."[32] As an African American suffering the degrading abuses of racial segregation King was all too aware of the human capacity for evil. His personal experiences and his reading of Niebuhr and the Bible led him to a more nuanced approach to nonviolence. The Gospel commands us to be nonviolent, King agreed, but it also calls us to resist evil and injustice. He accepted Niebuhr's observation that self-interest constrains human reason. "Even the most rational men are never quite rational when their own interests are at stake," wrote Niebuhr. Power continues to exploit weakness until it is challenged by countervailing power.[33]

King integrated the thinking of Niebuhr and Gandhi into a perspective that he called "realistic pacifism." He retained a strong commitment to nonviolence, but this was tempered by a realization of the limitations of human nature.[34] It is utopian to believe that ethical appeals alone can bring justice. Social power must be applied in addition to moral reasoning if real political change is to occur. Ethical appeals remain important, King wrote, but these "must be undergirded by some form of constructive coercive power."[35] Power and love are usually considered polar opposites, King wrote. Love is identified with a resignation of power and power with a denial of love. "What is needed is a realization that power without love is reckless and abusive and that love without power is sentimental and anemic. Power at its best is love implementing the demands of justice."[36]

Deming shared King's belief in the need for a more pragmatic and realistic approach to the question of nonviolent coercion. Entrenched privilege cannot be overcome merely with persuasion, she argued. Pressure and forceful

---

[31] Taylor Branch, *Parting the Waters: America in the King Years, 1954–63* (New York: Touchstone, 1988), 87.

[32] Martin Luther King, Jr., *Strength to Love* (New York: Harper & Row, 1963), 58.

[33] Niebuhr, *Moral Man and Immoral Society*, 44, xii.   [34] King, Jr., *Stride Toward Freedom*, 99.

[35] Martin Luther King, Jr., *Where Do We Go from Here: Chaos or Community?* (New York: Harper & Row, 1967), 128–9.

[36] Martin Luther King, Jr., "Where Do We Go from Here: Chaos or Community?," in *A Testament of Hope: The Essential Writings and Speeches of Martin Luther King, Jr.*, ed. James M. Washington (San Francisco: HarperSanFrancisco, 1991), 577–8.

action are also necessary to bring about political change. In her seminal essay, "Revolution and Equilibrium," written at the height of the new left political ferment in 1968, Deming challenged nonviolent activists to adopt more effective means of disruption and noncooperation to challenge war and injustice. Nonviolent action is not merely prayerful protest, she wrote. It can and must be a form of coercion, a means of exerting political power. "To resort to power one need not be violent, and to speak to conscience one need not be meek. The most effective action *both* resorts to power *and* engages conscience."[37] Forceful nonviolent action employs strikes, boycotts, civil disobedience, and mass noncooperation to undermine the exercise of oppressive power. Deming and her colleague David Dellinger argued that these methods of "revolutionary nonviolence" were capable of challenging entrenched systems of oppression and were effective means of bringing about a more just and peaceful society.[38] The choice is not between accepting oppression and resorting to violent resistance. Forceful nonviolent action provides a third way. It allows us to be, in the words of Albert Camus, neither victim nor executioner.

THE POWER OF LOVE

Although King was a Niebuhrian realist, he was not completely pessimistic about human nature. King shared Gandhi's view that "no human being is so bad as to be beyond redemption."[39] He believed that even the most ardent segregationist had some potential for goodness and could be reached through the power of love. Like the force of magnetism, love has a unique power to attract. In some instances, it can draw the adversary to our side. Even when it does not affect the adversary, it attracts the support of bystanders and third parties and helps win support for the nonviolent cause. Love is the strongest form of human energy and has transformative power both personally and socially.

King emphasized the Christian concept of *agape* as that "overflowing love which is purely spontaneous, unmotivated, groundless, and creative."[40] It is "disinterested love," he wrote, love for the sake of love, the unrestrained giving of self. *Agape* is similar to the Hindu concept of nonattachment, which played such a central role in Gandhi's thinking. In the Eastern tradition spiritual fulfillment comes through complete selflessness and

[37] Deming, "On Revolution and Equilibrium," 203–4.
[38] Dave Dellinger, "Gandhi's Heirs," in *Revolutionary Nonviolence: Essays by Dave Dellinger* (Indianapolis, IN: Bobbs-Merrill, 1970), 201–4.
[39] Quoted in Ansbro, *Martin Luther King, Jr.*, 137–8.   [40] King, Jr., *Stride Toward Freedom*, 104.

detachment from the fruits of labor. Love and sacrifice are offered entirely for their own sake, without thought of reward. *Agape* is equally demanding, wrote King, the love of God working in the human heart. It is the capacity to love others not because of what they may do for or against us but because they are children of God. *Agape* is the means through which we seek to mold the human community in God's image. It enables us to love the person who commits evil even as we resist the evil being committed.

Like Gandhi, King conceived of this selfless love as proactive. *Agape* is not passive but active, an affirmative commitment. Christ's command to love, King wrote, is also a command to resist evil and work for justice. Just as Gandhi believed that the Hindu practice of *ahimsa* requires active opposition to evil, so King believed that the Christian concept of *agape* includes an obligation to work for social justice.

My study of Gandhi convinced me that true pacifism is not nonresistance to evil, but nonviolent resistance to evil. Between the two positions, there is a world of difference. Gandhi resisted evil with as much vigor and power as the violent resister, but he resisted with love instead of hate.

In the Gandhian method King found a positive means of overcoming injustice through the power of love, a method "passive physically, but strongly active spiritually."[41] It was the key to his realistic pacifism, a way of resisting social evil through assertive yet nonviolent means.

King incorporated Gandhian principles into his understanding and preaching of the Gospel. He saw nonviolence and the commandment to love as the essential core of Christ's teaching. As King came to understand the social implications of Christ's teaching, he placed increased emphasis on the obligation to care for the oppressed and overcome injustice. In this he was following the tradition of the Social Gospel movement, which held that Christ's message has a social as well as individual dimension. The writings of Walter Rauschenbusch left an "indelible imprint" on his thinking.[42] Rauschenbusch gave King a theological basis for the social concerns he acquired growing up as a sensitive African American confronting racial abuse. It is not enough merely to struggle against evil in our personal lives. Our faith also calls us to challenge social evil. Jesus identified with "the least of these" and frequently spoke of the needs of the downtrodden. In his first sermon at Nazareth, Jesus announced his ministry as bringing "good news to the poor." As Jim Wallis emphasized, the primary message of the Bible is deliverance for the poor and the oppressed.[43]

---

[41] *Ibid.*, 98, 102. [42] *Ibid.*, 91. [43] Wallis, *The Soul of Politics*, 149–51.

King was also strongly influenced by Jewish social theology, especially the writings of Abraham Joshua Heschel. In his seminal book *God in Search of Man*, Heschel argued that God is intimately involved in human affairs and is in search of humans to serve the divine purpose. Heschel developed a theology of "divine pathos" in which God is concerned with and acts through human history. Human beings serve God through the search for truth and the quest for a more compassionate society. When the divine spirit tugs at our conscience it is our moral duty to follow, to give ourselves selflessly to others. The commitment to social justice was, in Heschel's view, an act of worship. He practiced what he preached and was an active opponent of the Vietnam War and supporter of the civil rights movement. One of the iconic photos of the civil rights era shows Heschel, arm in arm with King, marching in the famous pilgrimage from Selma to Montgomery in March 1965. For Heschel that experience of marching with King had spiritual meaning: "I felt as though my legs were praying."[44]

While King believed that God is immanent in history he was careful to distinguish between the perfection of the divine and the imperfection of the human condition. He was too deeply schooled in Niebuhrian philosophy to ignore human sinfulness. The moral pilgrimage of life does not reach its ultimate destination, King wrote, and the kingdom of God always remains "not yet."[45] King transcended the facile optimism of pure pacifism and the excessive pessimism of Niebuhrian realism to fashion a creative synthesis. He combined a belief in the divine presence with an insistence on the necessary commitment of human beings to help bring about divine purpose. The struggle against the forces of evil helps to reveal God's purpose. It seeks to realize the "beloved community" by striving for greater love and justice on earth.[46]

SPIRIT AND METHOD

In Latin America nonviolent action is defined as *firmeza permanente*, "relentless persistence." The term echoes Gandhi's concept of *satyagraha*. It conveys the same sense of grasping forcefully for truth and implies

---

[44] Susannah Heschel, "Theological Affinities in the Writings of Abraham Joshua Heschel and Martin Luther King, Jr.," in *Black Zion: African American Religious Encounters with Judaism*, ed. Yvonne Chireau and Nathaniel Deutsch (New York: Oxford University Press, 2000).

[45] King Jr., *Strength to Love*, 64.

[46] Kenneth L. Smith and Ira G. Zepp, Jr., *Search for the Beloved Community: The Thinking of Martin Luther King Jr.* (Valley Forge, PA: Judson, 1998), 130.

constant action to overcome oppression. Argentinian Nobel Peace Prize winner Adolfo Pérez Esquivel wrote:

Nonviolence is not passivity or conformism ... It is a spirit of prophecy, for it denounces all sundering of a community of brothers and sisters and proclaims that this community can only be rebuilt through love. And it is a method – an organized set of ruptures in the civil order so as to disturb the system responsible for the injustices we see around us.[47]

The commitment to active nonviolence deepened after the 1968 Latin American bishops' conference in Medellín, Colombia, which sparked the birth of liberation theology and inspired numerous campaigns for political freedom and economic justice. The increased activism for social justice was rooted in the multiplication of "Christian base communities," which numbered more than 100,000 in Brazil alone during the 1980s, and which emerged throughout Latin America to proclaim Jesus's liberating message for the poor and the oppressed.[48]

The spread of nonviolence in Latin America owed much to the work of Jean and Hildegard Goss-Mayr, who spent many years as field secretaries of the international FOR sowing the seeds of nonviolence in Europe, Latin America, and beyond. In Latin America the Goss-Mayrs emphasized the Gospel commandment to serve the poor. They meticulously taught the methodology of Gandhian nonviolence and described King's campaigns against racial injustice in North America.[49] They began the work that led to the founding in the 1970s of SERPAJ, *Servicio Paz y Justicia en América Latina* (Service for Peace and Justice in Latin America), led by Pérez Esquivel. They influenced the thinking of the prominent Brazilian archbishop Dom Hélder Câmara, one of the continent's most important proponents of nonviolence. Hélder Câmara said that nonviolence was the weapon of the poor, a means of responding to oppression and injustice without causing greater violence.[50]

The practitioners of nonviolent action in Latin America combined a practical understanding of effective action methods with a deep spirit

[47] Adolfo Pérez Esquivel, *Christ in a Poncho: Testimonials of the Nonviolent Struggles in Latin America* (Maryknoll, NY: Orbis Books, 1983), 52.
[48] Philip McManus, "Introduction: In Search of the Shalom Society," in *Relentless Persistence: Nonviolent Action in Latin America*, ed. Philip McManus and Gerald Schlabach (Philadelphia, PA: New Society Publishers, 1991), 3.
[49] Ronald Pagnucco and John D. McCarthy, "Advocating Nonviolent Direct Action in Latin America: The Antecedents and Emergence of SERPAJ," in *Nonviolent Social Movements: A Geographical Perspective*, ed. Stephen Zunes, Lester R. Kurtz, and Sarah Beth Asher (Malden, MA: Blackwell Publishers, 1999), 240–2.
[50] "To Discover Our Humanity: Adolfo Pérez Esquivel," in *Relentless Persistence*, 242–3, 246.

of religious commitment. Underlying every nonviolent struggle, wrote Leonardo Boff, "is a powerful *mística*: the conviction that truth, justice, and love are ontological," that they are "objective forces tied to the very structure of reality." There is a transcendent moral order in the universe that endures regardless of how often it is violated.[51] By struggling for justice through nonviolent means, humans help to realize that divinely ordained moral order.

TWO HANDS

In the 1960s many third world revolutionaries and even some activists in the United States and other developed countries believed that justice could be achieved only through armed revolution. Nonviolent methods were considered too weak to overcome entrenched systems of oppression. Malcolm X famously called for resistance "by any means necessary." Frantz Fanon argued in *The Wretched of the Earth* that the "dizzying" effects of revolutionary violence were a liberating step toward freedom for the oppressed. Deming responded to Fanon and other advocates of violence by emphasizing the need to maintain "equilibrium" in the struggle for social justice. Nonviolent action is more effective than violence, she insisted, because it allows the movement for justice to maintain control over the conflict situation. Nonviolence achieves its success through the combination of avoiding harm to the adversary and applying pressure against his oppressive policies. This is what she called the "two hands" effect: respect for the person combined with defiance of his policies. Together they are "uniquely effective:"

> The more the real issues are dramatized, and the struggle raised above the personal, the more control those in nonviolent rebellion begin to gain over their adversary. For they are able at one and the same time to disrupt everything for him, making it impossible for him to operate within the system as usual, and to temper his response to this ... They have as it were two hands upon him – the one calming him, making him ask questions, as the other makes him move.[52]

By assuring the personal safety of the adversary and refusing to respond in kind to repression or attack, the nonviolent activist constrains or limits the level of violence in the dispute. The usual action–reaction cycle of escalating violence is broken. Niebuhr identified this "spiritual discipline against

---

[51] Leonardo Boff, "Active Nonviolence: The Political and Moral Power of the Poor," in *Relentless Persistence*, viii.
[52] Deming, "On Revolution and Equilibrium," 207–8.

resentment" as one of the greatest advantages of the nonviolent method.[53] Violent attack inevitably creates resentment and the desire for revenge. Nonviolence cuts across this tendency. It offers reassurance against personal harm. It reduces the desire for retaliation.

The unique duality of nonviolent action – concern for the person, but defiance of authority – throws the adversary off balance. The lack of retaliation by the victims of repression alters the usual emotional and psychological response pattern. The challenger's readiness to accept punishment without retaliation robs repressive methods of their effectiveness and can make them counterproductive. Sharp and others refer to this as "political ju-jitsu."[54] Just as the agile fighter causes the stronger opponent to lose physical balance, so the nonviolent challenger causes the adversary to lose moral and political footing. The adversary's coercive powers are of no use and may even be a detriment. Meanwhile the challenger maintains equilibrium and control. The result, said Deming, is to shake up the adversary and induce a process of questioning and reappraisal.

The success of a nonviolent campaign often depends on gaining the sympathy and political support of those who were previously uncommitted or neutral. The goal is to alter the political and moral dynamics of the struggle and thereby tip the balance of power toward the nonviolent challenger. If the adversary is unjustifiably harsh or repressive in responding to nonviolent action, support for the challengers may increase, while the adversary's own base of support shrinks. This is what Deming called the "special genius" of nonviolence,[55] what Chavez termed its "strange chemistry."[56] Sharp referred to it as the art of winning over uncommitted third parties.[57] The courage and commitment of the nonviolent challenger "moves the indifferent, unites the humble, and isolates the perverse," said Brazilian priest Domingos Barbé. "The secret of nonviolence is the spread of compassion in the hearts of the masses."[58] As Gandhi emphasized, power ultimately rests on the consent of the governed. Even in the most dictatorial regimes leaders depend on the support or acquiescence of the people to remain in power. That support can begin to erode when authorities abuse their power, and especially when they are unjustifiably brutal toward

[53] Niebuhr, *Moral Man and Immoral Society*, 248. [54] Sharp, *Waging Nonviolent Struggle*, 405–6.
[55] Deming, "On Revolution and Equilibrium," 211.
[56] Susan Ferriss and Ricardo Sandoval, *The Fight in the Fields: Cesar Chavez and the Farmworkers Movement*, ed. Diana Hembree (New York: Harcourt Brace & Company, 1997), 97.
[57] Sharp, *The Politics of Nonviolent Action*, part 3: 658.
[58] Domingos Barbé, "The Spiritual Basis of Nonviolence," in *Relentless Persistence: Nonviolent Action in Latin America*, ed. Philip McManus and Gerald Schlabach (Philadelphia, PA: New Society Publishers, 1991), 278.

dignified nonviolent challengers. When this occurs, people who were previously indifferent or on the sidelines may be moved to support the nonviolent challengers.

The exercise of excessive force often undermines the legitimacy of the adversary's authority. As Niebuhr wrote, unjustified brutality "rob[s] the opponent of the moral conceit" that identified his interest with the larger good of society. He described this as "the most important of all the imponderables in a social struggle."[59] When British police savagely beat nonviolent Indian protesters at the Dharasana salt works in May 1930, in full view of shocked reporters, the resulting worldwide indignation weakened the authority of the Raj and enhanced the moral stature of the Gandhian movement. The incident, wrote Louis Fischer, "made England powerless and India invincible."[60] In the wake of the great salt *satyagraha*, said Niebuhr, British fulminations about law and order lacked "moral unction." In the wake of these events, public sympathy within India and around the world shifted decisively against continued British rule. In the US civil rights movement as well, the ugly displays of segregationist violence in Selma and Birmingham, Alabama in the 1960s, directed against the disciplined nonviolence and courageous dignity of African American protesters, shocked the consciences of Americans and people around the world and rapidly undermined the power of southern hardliners, generating an overwhelming political consensus in favor of civil rights.

The significance of this third party effect can scarcely be overemphasized. It bridges the apparent gap between the spiritual emphasis of Gandhi and the more pragmatic and assertive approach of King, Deming, and other contemporary practitioners of nonviolent action. It combines both principled and pragmatic nonviolence. One need not assume, as Gandhi did, that humans are perfectible and will respond positively to generosity and moral persuasion. Even if some hearts are simply too cold and cannot be warmed even by the most loving and long-suffering appeals to conscience, nonviolence can still be effective. Even if the adversary remains absolutely unmoved personally, nonviolent action can appeal to the political sympathies of those upon whom the exercise of power depends. It can alter the adversary's political power base, thereby generating pressure for change in policy. The effectiveness of nonviolent action thus becomes less a question of moral persuasion and more a matter of influencing third-party opinion and undermining the adversary's legitimacy and public support. The essential considerations become tactical and strategic rather than philosophical.

---

[59] Niebuhr, *Moral Man and Immoral Society*, 250.   [60] Fischer, *The Life of Mahatma Gandhi*, 275.

The emphasis shifts to a pragmatic calculation of the most effective ways to divide the loyalties of the opponent's constituency and to win the sympathy and support of bystanders.

A TOOL AGAINST TYRANNY

A common misperception is that nonviolent action is incapable of achieving success against ruthless opponents. Nonviolence "takes too utopian a view of the enemy," wrote Martin Ceadel. Nonviolence works by appealing to the conscience of the adversary and can only succeed when opponents are relatively humane, as were the British in India.[61] Michael Walzer likewise challenged the efficacy of nonviolence, arguing that it was powerless against adversaries who employ brutal methods. When tyrants are prepared to assassinate civilian leaders, arrest and torture suspects, establish concentration camps, and forcibly remove large numbers of people, "nonviolent defense is no defense at all." Nonviolent action only succeeds, Walzer wrote, when the soldiers or political officials of the other side have a moral code that prevents them from wantonly killing unarmed civilians. Since tyrants like Hitler or Stalin obviously have no such code, the practice of nonviolence is unrealistic. It is either "a disguised form of surrender or a minimalist way of upholding communal values after a military defeat." In neither case is it a moral response to injustice.[62]

These criticisms reflect a common misunderstanding of how the nonviolent method works. Nonviolent action does indeed attempt to reach the heart of the oppressor, but its effectiveness does not depend upon an appeal to conscience. Rather, nonviolent resistance seeks to alter the political dynamics in a struggle by appealing to and winning sympathy from third parties and thereby undermining the power base of the oppressor. Nonviolence usually achieves its influence by exerting coercive pressure through social and political action. It utilizes boycotts, civil disobedience, and other forms of mass noncooperation to alter social dynamics and political power relations. It does not depend upon face-to-face persuasion or conversion of individual soldiers or political opponents. Its impact results from the pressure of effective mass action. Direct dialogue is often necessary to negotiate the resolution of a conflict, as Gandhi and King demonstrated, but this stage of struggle usually comes after other forms of direct action and

[61] Martin Ceadel, *Thinking about Peace and War* (New York: Oxford University Press, 1987), 157.
[62] Michael Walzer, *Just and Unjust Wars: A Moral Argument with Historical Illustrations*, 2nd edn (New York: Basic Books, 1977), 331–3.

mass noncooperation have created conditions conducive to bargaining. Nonviolent action succeeds when it erodes the public consent that sustains corrupt power.

The dissidents of eastern and central Europe rejected violence, wrote Václav Havel, not because it was too radical "but on the contrary, because it does not seem radical enough." They believed that "a future secured by violence might actually be worse than what exists now . . . [and] would be fatally stigmatized by the very means used to secure it."[63] Havel spoke of "living in truth" and the profound courage that is required to overcome complacency and oppression – the need for people "to say aloud what they think, to express their solidarity with their fellow citizens, to create as they want and simply to live in harmony with their better 'self'," in contrast to defining themselves "in terms of something else."[64] Havel described the dissident movement as an "existential revolution" that would provide hope for the "moral reconstitution of society . . . [and] the rehabilitation of values like trust, openness, responsibility, solidarity, love."[65] As Jonathan Schell observed, both Havel and Gandhi chose the word truth as the touchstone of their philosophy. They shared the conviction that "the prime human obligation is to act fearlessly and publicly in accord with one's beliefs." The velvet revolution that Havel helped to lead was the most sweeping demonstration in history of the power of nonviolent action to achieve political change. When the nonviolent resisters were finished, wrote Schell, "a new law of the world had been written, and it read: Nonviolent action can be a source of revolutionary power."[66]

No one would argue that nonviolent resistance is effective in every setting, but there are examples of nonviolent success even in the most extreme circumstances. During World War II many Danes and Norwegians resisted Nazification through mass noncooperation.[67] The people of Le Chambon and other communities in Europe protected many Jews from extermination.[68] In February 1943 nonviolent resistance occurred

---

[63] Václav Havel, "The Power of the Powerless," in *Without Force or Lies: Voices from the Revolution of Central Europe in 1989–90*, ed. William M. Brinton and Alan Rinzler (San Francisco, CA: Mercury House, 1990), 99.

[64] Quoted in Jonathan Schell, *The Unconquerable World: Power, Nonviolence, and the Will of the People* (New York: Metropolitan Books, 2003), 197; Václav Havel, *Living in Truth*, ed. Jan Vladislav (London: Faber and Faber, 1986), 76.

[65] Havel, "The Power of the Powerless," 123.   [66] Schell, *The Unconquerable World*, 205–6.

[67] Sharp, *Waging Nonviolent Struggle*, 135–40; Ackerman and DuVall, "Denmark, the Netherlands, the Rosenstrasse: Resisting the Nazis," in *A Force More Powerful*, 207–39.

[68] Philip P. Hallie, *Lest Innocent Blood be Shed: The Story of the Village of Le Chambon and How Goodness Happened There* (New York: Harper and Row, 1979).

even in the heart of Berlin, when thousands of non-Jewish wives gathered illegally on *Rosenstrasse* near Nazi headquarters to demand the release of their arrested Jewish husbands.[69] Nonviolent resistance to Soviet domination took many forms during the cold war and ultimately brought down the dictatorial system in the velvet revolution of 1989. Nonviolent action brought an end to the Milosevic regime in Serbia in 2000. These and other examples confirm that nonviolent resistance can succeed even under severe conditions.

COURAGE AND STRENGTH

Those who struggle nonviolently against repressive authority must be prepared to sacrifice. The readiness to suffer for the cause of justice is a key element of the Gandhian method and accounts for its political impact. Stanley Wolpert described Gandhi's life and method as a "pageant of his conscious courting of suffering."[70] The specter of innocent people facing arrest or unprovoked violence can be a powerful means of dramatizing injustice and overcoming moral indifference. The sacrifice of nonviolent resisters may spark a sympathetic response from bystanders, altering the political dynamics of a conflict. The willingness to suffer may also be a spiritual expression of love and selflessness. One of Gandhi's great insights was his understanding that change does not occur solely or even primarily through logical argument or reason. He said,

I have come to this fundamental conclusion that, if you want something really important to be done, you must not merely satisfy the reason, you must move the heart also. The appeal of reason is more to the head, but the penetration of the heart comes from suffering.[71]

The role of suffering in the Gandhian method has stirred scholarly debate. Sociologist Kurt Schock argued that "suffering is not an essential part of nonviolent resistance."[72] Peace scholar Michael Nagler wrote that personal sacrifice is integral to the method and that one cannot properly

---

[69] Nathan Stoltzfus, *Resistance of the Heart: Intermarriage and the Rosenstrasse Protest in Nazi Germany* (New York: W. W. Norton, 1996).

[70] Wolpert, *Gandhi's Passion*, 3.

[71] Mahatma Gandhi, "Speech at Birmingham Meeting," *Young India*, 11 May 1931, from *The Collected Works of Mahatma Gandhi* 54, no. 24 (Pitiala House, Tilak Marg, New Delhi: Publications Division, Ministry of Information and Broadcasting, Government of India, 1999), 48. CD-Rom, dynamic collection.

[72] Kurt Schock, *Unarmed Insurrections: People Power Movements in Nondemocracies* (Minneapolis, MN: University of Minnesota Press, 2005), 8.

speak of nonviolence without it.[73] Gene Sharp emphasized that nonviolent resisters may suffer hardships during political struggle and must be willing to face the repression that usually results from challenges to established authority. The point is not to invite suffering, according to Sharp, but to accept and withstand repression and continue struggling until mass non-cooperation undermines the adversary's power. Sharp thus downplayed the role of the "pageantry of suffering" that others have seen as vital to the transformative power of nonviolence. He recognized, though, that suffering can be a means of overcoming indifference and rationalization to convert or win over the adversary. He also noted that the brutalities of repression against nonviolent resisters may arouse a sympathetic response among third parties, which can split the ranks of the adversary and win political support for nonviolent challengers from previously uncommitted constituencies.[74]

Those who stand up to repressive authority will face hardships and may even suffer physical harm or death. Nonviolent action produces fewer casualties overall, but they are all on the side of the nonviolent campaign. The burden of physical suffering falls entirely on the challengers. For some this seems immoral, but the willingness to sacrifice is essential to nonviolence and the key to its success. As Sharp observed, when oppressors resort to violence, they are displaying weakness and desperation.[75] When nonviolent resisters are subjected to harsh treatment and yet refuse either to retaliate or retreat, they are showing strength. Their disciplined and dignified nonviolent suffering attracts political sympathy while the unjustified brutality of the adversary repels political support. In the nonviolent method conventional political calculations are turned upside down. Those who suffer physical harm often win, while those who employ physical force lose. In the nonviolent method achieving political victory has nothing to do with punishing the adversary. The goal is not to defeat or humiliate the opponent, said King, but to bring about reconciliation. As Deming wrote, "vengeance is not the point; change is . . . A liberation movement that is nonviolent sets the oppressor free as well as the oppressed."[76] The nonviolent movement achieves victory by overcoming enmity and changing power relationships between challenger and adversary.

In the Latin American tradition sacrifice in nonviolent struggle is linked to the theme of Christian redemption. Scripture teaches that there is no

---

[73] Michael N. Nagler, *Is There No Better Way? The Search for a Nonviolent Future* (Berkeley, CA: Berkeley Hills Books, 2001), 125.

[74] Sharp, *Waging Nonviolent Struggle*, 383–4, 410–12, 416.

[75] Sharp, *The Politics of Nonviolent Action*, part 3: 657–8.

[76] Deming, "On Revolution and Equilibrium," 209, 211.

salvation without the shedding of blood. The question is: whose blood? The answer, said Domingos Barbé, holds the key to what is truly revolutionary about nonviolence. The blood spilled is that of the innocent, of those who fight nonviolently against injustice. "This is the logic of the Cross, the heritage of Jesus, who died to remove sin from the world. However, the sacrifice of the just is so effective that far fewer die in nonviolent combat than in conventional war."[77] Miguel d'Escoto, the Nicaraguan priest and later member of the Sandinista government, made a similar point in 1978:

to preach the Cross is to preach nonviolence. Not the nonviolence of acquiescence, but the nonviolence of risking our life for the sake of preaching the demands of [fraternity]. When we do that, we suffer the retaliation of those who oppress others, and that is the Cross. When we suffer the Cross we participate in the birth pangs of Christ for the new humanity.[78]

The willingness to sacrifice and take risks is relevant to the practice of conflict transformation as well. The pioneering peace practitioner John Paul Lederach has emphasized that effective mediation requires cultural sensitivity, language skills, and trust between mediators and affected communities. These often involve a long-term commitment and a willingness to enter into situations that may be fraught with peril. In the 1980s Lederach conducted conciliation training workshops for Miskito indigenous communities in Nicaragua and found himself acting as an intermediary in politically charged negotiations with the Sandinista-led government. During those months he learned first hand the dangers of attempting to build peace while others are pursuing war. He was under surveillance by CIA operatives, and his enemies put a bounty on his head and nearly kidnapped his daughter.[79]

Gandhi repeatedly emphasized that nonviolent methods are for the strong, not the weak. It takes courage not to fight. It takes strength to suffer for a cause and not respond with violence. In an oft quoted but frequently misunderstood statement, Gandhi asserted that if there is only a choice between cowardice and violence, it is better to be violent. King had a similar view, "As much as I deplore violence, there is one evil that is worse than violence, and that's cowardice."[80] In these comments Gandhi and King did

[77] Barbé, "The Spiritual Basis of Nonviolence," 279.
[78] Miguel d'Escoto, M. M., "The Power of the Cross," *The Catholic Worker* 45, no. 2 (February 1979): 6.
[79] Personal communication, John Paul Lederach to author, 14 March 2007; Joseph S. Miller, "A History of the Mennonite Conciliation Service, International Conciliation Service, and Christian Peacemaker Teams," in *From the Ground Up: Mennonite Contributions to International Peacebuilding*, ed. Cynthia Sampson and John Paul Lederach (New York: Oxford University Press, 2000), 22.
[80] Quoted in Ansbro, *Martin Luther King, Jr.*, 140.

not mean to excuse violence but to emphasize the cardinal importance of courage. Only those who are prepared to sacrifice fully appreciate and express the power of nonviolence. Gandhi insisted on the highest standards of personal bravery. He believed that *satyagraha* was most effective when those practicing it were in a position to use physical force but consciously chose not to do so. Only by overcoming the fear of retaliation can we be free of the power of oppression. The ability to shed fear is the key to gaining freedom.

Using a position of strength to seek conciliation and peace is the essence of the nonviolent philosophy. It applies in interstate relations as well as in society. The powerful are in the best position to achieve peace and advance disarmament. Nietzsche wrote:

And perhaps a great day will come, when a people distinguished by war and victory . . . will voluntarily exclaim, "We will break the sword into pieces" . . . To disarm while being the best armed . . . that is the means to real peace.[81]

Nietzsche's quote gives a different twist to the often misused phrase "peace through strength." Choosing nonviolent means rather than military force is a way for the strong to achieve peace, to fight for the right without resorting to violence. The choices available for achieving justice and security are very much wider than conventionally assumed. In social action and in government policy, nonviolent means are available to protect the innocent, overcome oppression, and defend freedom. The great achievement of Gandhi, and the "genius" of his method, was to show that it is possible to confront social evil while remaining true to the principles of peace.

---

[81] Friedrich Nietzsche, *Sämtliche Werke. Kritische Studienausgabe*, ed. Giorgio Colli and Mazzino Montinari (New York: de Gruyter, 1980), II: 678–9.

11

Democracy

The rise of peace advocacy in the nineteenth century grew out of the theories of political liberalism and the Enlightenment belief in human perfectibility and social progress. Philosophers and economists of the eighteenth and nineteenth centuries believed that the spread of democracy and free trade would incline nations toward cooperation and peace. War would disappear, they claimed, when the ancient regime was replaced by the rising commercial middle class. Once people were liberated from the shackles of the past, the tyranny of privilege and prejudice would be replaced by what Thomas Jefferson termed "an aristocracy of talent and virtue."[1] War would be banished as an outdated anachronism of the old order, or so it was assumed.

In this chapter I examine the relationship between democracy and peace and probe the theoretical and empirical linkages between the two. Democracy is by definition a process in which citizens freely exercise their political rights and reconcile interests without resort to violence. The spread of democracy extends the arena of human affairs in which disputes are settled without violence. It establishes conditions that foster political cooperation. Nonviolence "is written into liberalism's genetic code," wrote Jonathan Schell. "In this basic respect, the long march of liberal democracy is a 'peace movement' – possibly the most important and successful of them all."[2]

My survey begins with a review of Enlightenment thinking and an examination of the theory of democracy and free trade as articulated by Richard Cobden and others. Perhaps the greatest philosophical contribution to the principles of peace was made by Immanuel Kant, whose analysis

---

[1] Quoted in Michael Howard, *The Invention of Peace and the Reinvention of War* (London: Profile Books, 2002), 28.

[2] Jonathan Schell, *The Unconquerable World: Power, Nonviolence, and the Will of the People* (New York: Metropolitan Books, 2003), 236, 240.

of the necessary conditions of peace has proved of enduring value for more than two centuries and has recently been confirmed in empirical studies. Contemporary understandings of human behavior and evidence of cooperative traits among humans reinforce Kant's moral imperatives. So do the findings of social science research on the importance of mutual democracy, commercial interdependence, and participation in international organizations as factors that incline states toward peaceful political relations. Studies of the empowerment of women help to broaden our understanding of democracy and the ways in which greater social equality can act as a restraint on the tendency to use military force. The evidence suggests that the philosophers were right to emphasize the importance of strengthening democracy as an effective strategy for reducing the likelihood of war. The relationship between democracy and peace is not linear, however, and is bounded by qualifications and limitations. The major democratic states – Britain, the United States, and France – have too often succumbed to imperial ambition, resorting to policies of armed intervention, economic exploitation and support for repressive regimes that have set back the cause of democracy in many parts of the developing world. Liberal democracy enhances peace only under specific conditions, and only when citizens exercise their democratic rights to assert greater public control over the use of military force.

EARLY VOICES

Enlightenment writers attributed the prevalence of war to the dominance of warrior classes, who waged battles to serve the interests of crown and manor, without regard for the rest of society. The rising power of the merchant classes would replace the rule of kings and nobles, removing the tendency toward war that was characteristic of the old order. One of the earliest to make this case was Émeric Crucé, who argued in *Le Nouveau Cynée* in 1623 that the creation of peace required a new social structure within nations. He advocated trade liberalization as a means of increasing the power of the merchant class, which he assumed would be less bellicose than the aristocracy. The spread of commerce would bring people together and help to promote mutual understanding and interdependence, he argued. It would reduce the power of feudal warriors and herald a new, more peaceful society.[3]

---

[3] Michael Howard, *War and the Liberal Conscience* (New Brunswick, NJ: Rutgers University Press, 1978), 20.

Montesquieu elaborated these ideas a century later. He built upon John Locke's view that the spread of commerce leads naturally to the development of a lawful society, and that such a society is inherently more orderly and less violent. Montesquieu believed that the spirit of commerce helped to soften and modify the struggle for power that is an inevitable part of the political order. "Commerce is the cure for the most destructive prejudices," he wrote in 1748.[4] "The natural effect of commerce is to lead to peace. Two nations that trade together become mutually dependent: if one has an interest in buying, the other has an interest in selling; and all unions are based on mutual needs."[5] Montesquieu's ideas influenced François Quesnay and the Physiocrats, who attacked mercantilism and advocated the free exchange of goods as the surest path to prosperity and peace. The right of people to rule themselves, think freely, and trade openly would create a future of progress and peace.

In the American colonies Thomas Paine was a passionate believer in the liberal democratic ideal. He asserted that war would fade when democratic societies replaced monarchies. "If commerce were permitted to act to the universal extent it is capable," Paine wrote, "it would extirpate the system of war."[6] He argued that "a delegation of power for the common benefit . . . promotes a system of peace."[7] A transfer of power from kings and lords to merchants and farmers would bring an end to wars.

Paine's contemporary Jeremy Bentham was a strong supporter of democracy, but he was more skeptical of the claim that it would automatically bring peace. In his 1789 *Plan for an Universal and Perpetual Peace*, Bentham advocated greater international cooperation and the promotion of democracy, but he cautioned against excessive optimism.[8] Allowing people to elect their own leaders would not guarantee peace. The sanction against war that an electorate might deliver was at best retrospective, and might be too late to prevent military aggression. Democratic governments would be as vulnerable to manipulation by powerful vested interests as any other regime, he presciently observed, and could be subverted by secrecy and deceit. Citizens must be educated and activated, Bentham emphasized, to restrain the tendencies toward violence that remain powerful even within representative

---

[4] Quoted in Michael W. Doyle, *Ways of War and Peace: Realism, Liberalism, and Socialism* (New York: W. W. Norton, 1997), 306.
[5] Quoted in Edward D. Mansfield and Brian M. Pollins, eds., *Economic Interdependence and International Conflict: New Perspectives on an Enduring Debate* (Ann Arbor, MI: University of Michigan Press, 2003), 3.
[6] Quoted in Doyle, *Ways of War and Peace*, 231.
[7] Quoted in Howard, *War and the Liberal Conscience*, 29. [8] Doyle, *Ways of War and Peace*, 226–8.

government. The pacifying influence of democracy depends on an informed and active citizenry capable of engaging in the political process to prevent war and preserve peace. Bentham's ideas presaged the development of peace societies and the public campaigns of education and advocacy that followed. They anticipated the contemporary understanding that democracy is strongest when it is leavened by public education and citizen activism.

DEMOCRACY AGAINST MILITARISM

In many countries movements for democracy were also movements for peace. In Japan supporters of the popular rights movement of the late nineteenth century were often opponents of militarism. Among these was Uchimura Kanzō, who argued against war not only on a moral basis but out of concern for the likely political consequence. He said of the looming war with Russia in 1904:

Our few remaining freedoms and constitution will disappear in smoke. Japan will become like a huge military camp. Its people will come to eat gunpowder instead of rice and reap sabres rather than peace.[9]

Early socialist leader Abe Isoo also linked his antiwar stance to support for democracy:

Democracy is stubbornly opposed to militarism. It is opposed on three counts: because arms actually protect capitalist class interests at the expense of the common people; because war aids in the exploitation of weak countries by strong powers, as arms are used to open up markets by force; and because militarism always grows into despotism, a retrogression from civilization to barbarism.[10]

Japan's 1947 postwar Constitution linked democracy, human rights, and peace. It embodied the liberal faith in democracy as an antidote to war. The Constitution's guarantee of democratic rights and creation of a strong parliamentary system were connected to the renunciation of war and the rejection of excessive armaments. By denying the right of the state to accumulate and use military power, the Constitution removed the principal instrument that nationalists and militarists had used in the past to dominate the people of Japan and other countries. It institutionalized a transfer of

[9] Quoted in John F. Howes, "Uchimura Kanzō: The Bible and War," in *Pacifism in Japan: The Christian and Socialist Tradition*, ed. Nobuya Bamba and John F. Howes (Vancouver: University of British Columbia Press, 1978), 106.
[10] Quoted in Cyril H. Powles, "Abe Isoo: The Utility Man," in *Pacifism in Japan*, 151.

power from the militarized state to elected representatives of the people. The exercise of democratic rights was to be the means of preserving peace.

The framers of the US Constitution considered war the enemy of democracy. Alexander Hamilton was a proponent of executive authority, but he was deeply concerned about the corrosive consequences of presidential power in foreign and military affairs. He wrote in *Federalist* 8, "It is of the nature of war to increase the executive at the expense of the legislative authority."[11] Hamilton famously warned: "The history of human conduct does not warrant that exalted opinion of human virtue which would make it wise to commit interests of so delicate and momentous a kind . . . to the sole disposal of . . . a president of the United States."[12] The framers assigned war making authority instead to Congress. Many Americans later assumed that the constitutional provision of president as "commander in chief" included authority to undertake military action, but this was not what the framers intended or what the Constitution provided. As Arthur Schlesinger, Jr. wrote: "Article I [of the US Constitution] gave Congress not only the appropriations power – itself a potent instrument of control – but also the power to declare war, to raise and support armies, [and] to provide and maintain a navy." Congress was to have sole power to authorize war and maintain armed forces.[13] The framers hoped that the functioning of representative democracy would restrain the impulse to war.

COBDEN: PEACE THROUGH FREE TRADE

One of history's most influential and articulate advocates of the liberal theory of peace was the English merchant and political leader Richard Cobden. Born into poverty in Sussex in 1804, Cobden entered the calico trade at age fifteen and established himself as a successful merchant near Manchester. He traveled widely and read extensively and became especially interested in economics and the principles of trade. His first pamphlets, published in the 1830s, marked him as a gifted writer. They also sketched the outlines of the ideas that were to dominate his life, and that were at the heart of British political debate: free trade, a noninterventionist foreign policy, extension of the franchise, and the separation of church and state. In 1838 Cobden joined the Anti-Corn Law League, and with his colleague

---

[11] Alexander Hamilton, "The Federalist No. 8," in *The Federalist with Letters of "Brutus,"* ed. Terence Ball (Cambridge: Cambridge University Press, 2003), 32.

[12] Alexander Hamilton, "The Federalist No. 75," in *The Federalist with Letters of "Brutus,"* 366.

[13] Arthur M. Schlesinger, Jr., *War and the American Presidency* (New York: W. W. Norton, 2004), 47–8.

John Bright became a leader in the historic campaign to end feudal-era restrictions on agricultural production. Cobden and Bright had a knack for explaining complicated economic arguments in simple, easy-to-understand language; they were among the most eloquent and influential orators of their era.[14] In 1841 Cobden was elected to Parliament, where he served for most of the next twenty years.

Cobden's interest in peace and nonintervention grew directly out of his advocacy of free trade. He wanted to reduce the economic and political power of the landed gentry, who still dominated British politics at the time. The nobles and lords steered the country toward wars and colonial exploits that benefited the few at the expense of the many. The sooner political power was transferred from the aristocracy to the middle class, he argued, the quicker society could move beyond war toward a more productive and peaceful future. Cobden believed that free trade would create prosperity at home and introduce a new era of international peace. "There is no human event that has happened in the world more calculated to promote the enduring interests of humanity than the establishment of the principle of free trade," he declared.[15] "The more any nation traffics abroad upon free and honest principles," he famously wrote, "the less it will be in danger of wars." Cobden argued that nations achieve greatness through the power of trade not military might. "Labour, improvements, and discoveries confer the greatest strength upon a people . . . by these alone, and not by the sword of the conqueror, can nations . . . hope to rise to supreme power and grandeur."[16]

Cobden's thinking reflected the influence of Adam Smith, history's most famous apostle of free trade. Smith supported free commerce as the surest means to individual liberty, social harmony, and cooperation among nations. Through free trade, Cobden and Smith believed, people who previously lived in a state of fear of their neighbors would achieve a new sense of security and become less bellicose toward their trading partners. Cobden also shared the enthusiasm for free trade of his contemporary John Stuart Mill, who wrote in 1848:

---

[14] "Cobden and Bright," *Historic World Leaders*, Gale Research, 1994. Reproduced in *Biography Resource Center*, Farmington Hills, MI: Thomson Gale. 2005, http://galenet.galegroup.com.lib-proxy-nd. edu/servlet/BioRC.

[15] *Ibid.*

[16] Richard Cobden, "From *The Political Writings of Richard Cobden*," in *International Relations in Political Thought: Texts from the Ancient Greeks to the First World War*, ed. Chris Brown, Terry Nardin, and Nicholas Rengger, 538–49 (Cambridge: Cambridge University Press, 2002), 542, 546.

It is commerce which is rapidly rendering war obsolete, by strengthening and multiplying the personal interests which are in natural opposition to it . . . it may be said without exaggeration that the great extent and rapid increase of international trade, in being the principal guarantee of the peace of the world, is the great permanent security for the uninterrupted progress . . . of the human race.[17]

Cobden was active in public life not only through his service in Parliament but in his role as a leading voice in the London Peace Society. He participated in many national and international meetings for peace, where he consistently advocated nonintervention in the affairs of other countries and opposed Britain's traditional balance-of-power diplomacy. During the US Civil War he and Bright defended the northern cause against those who wanted Britain to support the Confederacy. He also opposed British involvement in the Crimean War. In the late 1840s and 1850s Cobden launched an unsuccessful campaign to reduce British military spending. He emphasized that war and the heavy military expenditure that went with it consumed productive resources that were needed for the improvement of society. Excessive military spending also required high taxation, which could lead to social discontent and political turmoil.[18]

Cobden based his opposition to war not on religious or humanitarian concerns but on a rationalist calculation of what would best serve society's interests. His instincts were conservative. He wanted to preserve the interests of the rising commercial classes. He shied away from sweeping proposals for radical social change and focused instead on pragmatic suggestions to improve the public welfare. He was one of the first to introduce a motion in Parliament calling for the arbitration of international disputes.[19] He emphasized the practicality of his proposal:

My plan does not embrace the scheme of a congress of nations, or imply the belief in the millennium, or demand your homage to the principles of non-resistance. I simply propose that England should offer to enter into an agreement with other countries, France for instance, binding them to refer any dispute that may arise to arbitration.[20]

Cobden was one of the leading voices of the nineteenth century in articulating the pragmatic case for peace and international cooperation.

[17] John Stuart Mill, *Principles of Political Economy, With Some of Their Applications to Social Philosophy*, vol. II (Boston, MA: C. C. Little & James Brown, 1848), 123.
[18] John Morley, *The Life of Richard Cobden*, vol. II (London: Macmillan and Co., 1908), 38–9.
[19] Miles Taylor, "Cobden, Richard (1804–1865)," *Oxford Dictionary of National Biography* (Oxford University Press, 2004). Available online at *Oxford Dictionary of National Biography*, www.oxforddnb.com/view/article/5741 (accessed 15 March 2007).
[20] Morley, *The Life of Richard Cobden*, 9–10.

One of the most articulate and influential expressions of the liberal theory of peace was Norman Angell's *The Great Illusion*, published in 1910 at a time of rapidly expanding commercial interdependence. The strength and well-being of a nation depend not on the size of its army, wrote Angell, but on the productivity of its economy. Great armies are not needed to protect the wealth of the nation. They are a drain on that wealth and endanger social well-being. Transnational financing and industrial development have diminished the importance of national boundaries and changed the meaning of sovereignty. The fundamental illusion of the age, said Angell, is the myth that national power means national wealth, and that the seizure of territory can bring greater economic and political benefit. On the contrary, it is the power of trade and the productivity of economic development that bring true greatness and well-being to nations.[21]

The liberals of the nineteenth and early twentieth centuries made valuable contributions to our understanding of the ways in which democracy and free trade can generate preferences for peace. Their core insight, that the power of trade can be a force for cooperation between nations, was and remains profoundly important. The liberal theorists were overly optimistic, however. They worked from Smith's model of equilibrium and perfect markets and failed to consider the economic and social distortions resulting from such factors as imperialism (Mill was a defender of British rule in India) and the rising power of industrial and financial trusts, which would later contribute to the disaster of 1914. They paid too little attention to militarist tendencies and the weight of the arms manufacturing sector in political affairs. They had no appreciation of the exploitative tendencies within capitalism that were evident even in their lifetimes and that gave rise to widespread social demands for economic justice, voiced by trade unions and the socialist movement, and later by many in the peace movement as well. In their zeal to see natural tendencies toward peace through the evolution of commerce and democracy, they failed to recognize that peace is ultimately a moral imperative that depends on the conscious endeavors of enlightened and empowered citizens.

KANT: THE PHILOSOPHER OF PEACE

Unlike the worldly and politically engaged Cobden, Immanuel Kant was a philosopher who spent his entire life cloistered in academia, reflecting on

---

[21] Norman Angell, *The Great Illusion: A Study of the Relation of Military Power to National Advantage*, 4th edn (New York: G. P. Putnam's Sons, 1913).

the imperatives of human reason and moral behavior. Kant was the quint-
essential rationalist who created a grand edifice of ethical principles entirely
on the basis of reason, without reliance on religious belief or reference to
scripture. His ideas significantly influenced the development of moral and
political philosophy and have had an enduring impact on Western intellectual life ever since. His 1795 volume *Perpetual Peace* remains an unsurpassed
classic in articulating the concepts of liberal peace theory. Kant explained in
great detail the ways in which democracy and liberalism combine to create
the conditions of peace. His theories were amazingly prescient in foretelling
what contemporary analysts call the democratic peace. Kant's ideas remain
vitally important today in outlining the social and political steps that can
reduce the incidence of war.

Kant realized that the prevention of war ultimately must rest on a moral
foundation. He believed that peace had to be continuously created and
protected. There are no guarantees of peace, and many reasons to fear the
enduring inclination toward war. He based his irenic principles on the
famous categorical imperative, to act as if the principle of your behavior
were to become a universal law. Treat others as you would want them to
treat you, always as ends never as means. Only a moral commitment to the
common humanity of all people could assure the vigilance and constant
effort that are needed to prevent war. Kant argued that we must work
unceasingly for peace even if the odds against it seem insurmountable, for
"it is our duty to do so." We must act in accordance with the moral
imperative "even if there is not the slightest theoretical probability of its
realisation, provided that there is no means of demonstrating that it cannot
be realised either." Establishing peace is "the supreme political good." It "is
not just a part of the theory of right within the limits of pure reason, but its
entire ultimate purpose."[22] Achieving this goal requires human agency and
moral commitment: "we must act as if that thing, perpetual peace, existed –
though it may not exist; we must endeavor to make it real."[23] As Michael
Howard observed, the task of preventing war is our "inexorable duty," a
challenge that must be "tackled afresh every day of our lives."[24]

Kant's theory of peace was based on three fundamental principles, which he
called "definitive articles": (1) democratic governance; (2) a federation of nations;
and (3) the "cosmopolitan law" of mutual respect and interdependence. Kant

---

[22] Immanuel Kant, "From *The Metaphysical Elements of Right*," in *International Relations in Political Thought: Texts from the Ancient Greeks to the First World War*, ed. Chris Brown, Terry Nardin, and Nicholas Rengger, 450–5 (Cambridge: Cambridge University Press, 2002), 454–5.
[23] Immanuel Kant, *Perpetual Peace* (New York: Liberal Arts Press, 1957), 57–8.
[24] Howard, *War and the Liberal Conscience*, 135.

emphasized that all three principles were necessary for peace. No single factor alone was sufficient. It is the unique combination of all three – republican representation, international cooperation, and mutual interdependence – that creates the essential foundations for a more peaceful political order among nations.

The first of the definitive articles was the requirement for a republican system of government: the right of citizens to elect their own leaders, and the principle of the separation of powers. Representative government makes peace more likely because it introduces what Kant called "democratic restraint." It creates "hesitation" in political decision making, to replace monarchical caprice. The separation of powers within government adds to this salutary delay, giving others a say in decision making and providing time for reflection and adjustment in the determination of foreign relations. When citizens could select their own leaders and influence their nation's policies, Kant believed, they would naturally choose peace over war. Under such conditions "citizens ... would be very cautious in ... decreeing for themselves all the calamities of war ... and ... a heavy national debt that would embitter peace itself."[25]

The second definitive article was the need for a federation of democratic states. Kant recognized that the anarchy of international relations was a fundamental cause of war. To overcome this condition, nations must forge a community among themselves. Just as individuals within society submit to the rule of law to gain security, so nations must enter into mutual legal arrangements to achieve the benefit of common security. "The distress produced by the constant wars in which the states try to subjugate or engulf each other must finally lead them, even against their will, to enter into a *cosmopolitan* constitution."[26] Kant envisioned the proposed federation as "a pacific union" of liberal republics. It would be an "enduring and gradually expanding *federation* likely to prevent war." The federation would not be a single world government, however. A world superstate, Kant believed, would destroy the civic freedom upon which the development of human potential rested. Rather, a voluntary union of states, a federation of nations working together but retaining their sovereignty, would be the best guarantee of both freedom and peace.

The third article was what Kant called the "cosmopolitan right." He defined this as the "right of a stranger not to be treated with hostility when

[25] Kant, *Perpetual Peace*, 12–13, 19–20.
[26] Immanuel Kant, "From *Essay on Theory and Practice*," in *International Relations in Political Thought*, 428–32, 430.

he arrives on someone else's territory."[27] He linked the cosmopolitan principle to the right of free trade. The universal desire and propensity to engage in trade adds material incentives to the political and moral imperatives for peace. Free trade would have an inevitable pacifying influence on world affairs:

The spirit of commerce, which is incompatible with war, sooner or later gains the upper hand in every state. As the power of money is perhaps the most dependable of all the powers ... states see themselves forced, without any moral urge, to promote honorable peace ... In this manner nature guarantees perpetual peace by the mechanism of human passions ... [but] she does not do so with sufficient certainty ...[28]

Through economic exchange states acquire a self-interest in avoiding policies that disrupt mutually beneficial relationships. Transnational connections and commercial interdependence create incentives for accommodation, cooperation, and the maintenance of stable political relations.

Kant believed that nature helped to promote moral purposes. He perceived patterns in social evolution that created imperatives for cooperation. He acknowledged the aggressive tendencies that are evident among individuals and groups, but he argued that there were also countervailing impulses for cooperation. The very competitive forces that incline communities toward conflict also impel people to band together for mutual support and protection. Kant called this phenomenon "asocial sociability," the impulse that draws humans together in fulfillment of needs for security and material welfare. It is a phenomenon that operates beyond the realm of human agency or free will. It is what nature does "to *compel* us to follow a course which we would not readily adopt by choice."[29] Social evolution naturally generates preferences for mutual aid and cooperation. Modern evolutionary scientists would say that cooperation pays dividends and establishes a foundation for altruistic behavior.

HUMAN NATURE

The theory of democratic liberalism was predicated on an optimistic view of human nature. If liberated from socially imposed constraints, liberals believed, human communities could evolve progressively to create a more peaceful and just political order. Conservative and realist philosophers

---

[27] Immanuel Kant, "Perpetual Peace: A Philosophical Sketch," in *Kant: Political Writings*, 2nd edn, ed. Hans Reiss (New York: Cambridge University Press, 1991), 106.
[28] Kant, *Perpetual Peace*, 32.   [29] Kant, "From *Essay on Theory and Practice*," 429.

countered that human societies are inherently sinful and prone to conflict, that war is unavoidable. As these debates raged into the twentieth century, discoveries in the biological and behavioral sciences began to shed light on the subject. Ethological studies revealed natural tendencies toward both cooperation and competition. Theories of innate aggressiveness dashed the liberal and Marxian dreams of human perfectibility, but evidence of cooperative traits and the existence of nonwarring societies dispelled realist assumptions about the inevitability of war. Science thus revealed a complex and nuanced view of human nature, one that helped to explain the prevalence of war but also the possibilities of peace.

While there is ample evidence of tendencies toward aggressiveness, human nature also includes cooperative traits. Ethologists and anthropologists have discovered cooperative aspects of human behavior that are constant across all cultures: sociability, a concern for kin and family, patterns of hierarchy and rank, and, most importantly, reciprocal altruism. A "readiness to cooperate" seems to be an innate element of human nature, according to Peter Singer. There is now a large scientific literature on this topic.[30] Evidence of cooperative traits has also been found among our nearest animal relatives. Primatologists have discovered that while primates sometimes engage in organized violence akin to war, they are capable of forming coalitions and developing patterns of stable reciprocity. Primates engage in aggressive behavior, but they also exhibit "evolutionarily fruitful" patterns of intelligence and social restraint.[31] Humans and highly evolved animals display a natural tendency toward mutually beneficial social relationships based on generosity, gratitude, and reciprocal obligation. Altruistic traits and generalized forms of reciprocity extend beyond family and kin to others in society. These traits, Robert Wright argued, propel organisms along the "co-evolutionary escalator" and enable them to survive and prosper. As Wright phrased it, "natural selection invented reciprocal altruism" in human and other species as a strategy for self-preservation and reproduction.[32] Singer described cooperation as a strategy for "leaving one's genes in later generations." The formation of "mutually beneficial cooperative relationships" brings biological benefits.[33]

---

[30] Peter Singer, *A Darwinian Left: Politics, Evolution and Cooperation* (New Haven, CT: Yale University Press, 2000), 37, 46–7.

[31] Robert M. Sapolsky, "A Natural History of Peace," *Foreign Affairs* 85, no. 1 (January/February 2006): 109.

[32] Robert Wright, *Nonzero: The Logic of Human Destiny* (New York: Pantheon Books, 2000), 22–3, 294, 324.

[33] Peter Singer, *One World: The Ethics of Globalization* (New Haven, CT: Yale University Press, 2002), 111.

Douglas Fry and other anthropologists have found evidence from ethnographic studies of more than sixty societies that do not wage war. None of these nonwarring societies engages in organized warfare with external social groups. Fry also found evidence of more than eighty societies that are entirely peaceful in their internal relations. The existence of nonwarring societies, however rare, shows that people can live without organized violence. The view that humans are instinctively and unavoidably warlike, wrote Fry, is "simply false."[34] There is no scientific evidence of a biologically inherited tendency toward war.[35]

The evident human tendency to engage in organized violence is not an innate drive, according to biosocial theory, but a learned behavior. Social conditioning and human culture interfere with natural signaling functions that prompt flight in the face of lethal threat. Humans acquire beliefs and assumptions that allow them to override fear and danger, to march willingly into combat. Social learning theory focuses on how violent behavior is assimilated, and how various forms of social and cultural conditioning reinforce aggressiveness. In her famous essay, "Warfare Is only an Invention: Not a Biological Necessity," Margaret Mead traced organized warfare to the influences of culture and conditioning.[36] If war is learned rather than biologically determined, she argued, it can also be unlearned. As Barbara Ehrenreich observed, "the existence of inherited predispositions does not condemn us to enact them."[37] Ralph Waldo Emerson wrote, "It is really a thought that built this portentous war-establishment, and a thought shall also melt it away."[38]

Konrad Lorenz argued that "innate" and "learned" are not mutually exclusive elements in determining behavior. Ritualized behavior and differing response patterns influence how an instinctive impulse is expressed.[39] While our genetic inheritance defines the potential of our behavior, social and cultural interactions determine how that potential is developed and manifest. The degree to which competitive or cooperative tendencies

---

[34] Douglas P. Fry, "Conclusion: Learning from Peaceful Societies," in *Keeping the Peace: Conflict Resolution and Peaceful Societies around the World*, ed. Graham Kemp and Douglas P. Fry (New York: Routledge, 2004), 187–8, 199.

[35] Kaj Björkqvist, "The Inevitability of Conflict but not of Violence: Theoretical Considerations on Conflict and Aggression," in *Cultural Variation in Conflict Resolution: Alternatives to Violence*, ed. Douglas P. Fry and Kaj Björkqvist (Mahwah, NJ: Lawrence Erlbaum, 1997), 34–5.

[36] Margaret Mead, "Warfare Is only an Invention: Not a Biological Necessity," *Asia* 40 (1940): 402–5.

[37] Barbara Ehrenreich, *Blood Rites: Origins and History of the Passions of War* (New York: Metropolitan Books, 1997), 88.

[38] Ralph Waldo Emerson, "War" (1838), *The Works of Ralph Waldo Emerson*, vol. V (New York: Bigelow, Brown and Co., n.d.), 368.

[39] Konrad Lorenz, *On Aggression* (New York: Harcourt, Brace and World, 1966).

predominate is a function of cultural and social factors. Manifestations of aggressive or cooperative behavior are best understood as points along a continuum rather than polar opposites.[40] They arise dynamically in response to differing stimuli. Whether humans behave peacefully or violently depends upon the cultural and social conditions that influence them. The challenge for democratic governance is minimizing the stimuli to violence while reinforcing the conditions that foster cooperation and mutual reciprocity. Human societies are vastly adaptable and are obviously capable of both violent and peaceful behavior. No observer of human history would claim that humans are inherently peaceful, but just as assuredly, science does not prove the inevitability of war or the impossibility of free people choosing peace over war.

FOR DEMOCRATIC CONTROL

Kant's theory of democracy and peace inspired the creation of peace societies and helped to shape their political perspectives. From the initial educational efforts of the early nineteenth century through to the disarmament and antiwar campaigns of the present, peace advocates have consistently pointed to democracy as an antidote to war. The early peace societies of Britain, the United States, and France argued that the spread of democracy would reduce the likelihood of armed conflict. Many of these groups agreed with Bentham's emphasis on the need for public education. They believed that informed voters would choose leaders who promised peace over war and that enlightened public opinion would make military conflict less likely. Citizen groups have struggled constantly to exert democratic control over matters of war and peace, and to overcome the secrecy and layers of executive privilege that limit the "democratic restraint" that Kant envisioned. Political leaders have resisted such efforts and have clung to their war making powers as the prerogative of executive rule. Democracy has often been slowest to penetrate the realm of foreign and military policy. Much of the political struggle on peace issues over the last two centuries can be seen as a continuing and still unfulfilled attempt to assert popular control over the power to wage war.

Peace organizations in the late nineteenth century were among the first to campaign for democratic control over foreign policy. Delegates to the 1878 International Peace Congress in Paris criticized the continuing prerogatives of monarchs in the area of foreign policy as an affront to democracy and an

---

[40] Fry, "Conclusion: Learning from Peaceful Societies," 186.

encroachment on the rights of the people's elected representatives. British Liberal Party leaders argued for democratic control over the Foreign Office and for the creation of a foreign affairs committee in Parliament that would provide greater public oversight of and involvement in the conduct of international diplomacy.[41] In France Radical members of the Chamber of Deputies denounced secret diplomacy as a formula for war and demanded that all international treaties be submitted for parliamentary approval.[42] Some peace activists supported extending the franchise to workers and women as a means of achieving a more peaceful foreign policy and strengthening the democratic preference for peace.

When World War I broke out peace advocates blamed the disaster on unaccountable systems of autocratic political leadership and secret diplomacy. Many in Britain agreed with writer E. D. Morel's diagnosis of the causes of war, which he traced to four major factors: (1) the balance-of-power and alliance system of the leading European states; (2) the practice of secret diplomacy; (3) the accelerating competition in the accumulation of offensive weaponry; and (4) the unwarranted influence exerted on governments by private munitions manufacturers. All of these factors boiled down to one overriding theme – a lack of democratic control over foreign affairs. The solution, Morel and his colleagues argued, was the creation of effective machinery for democratic accountability. The "selfishly bellicose" interests of arms merchants and military officials had to be brought under control.[43] The obvious conclusion was that peace depended upon the spread and strengthening of democracy.

These perspectives were embodied in the Union of Democratic Control (UDC), which was founded in London within hours of Britain's entry into the war. UDC leaders included writers Morel and Norman Angell, Liberal (later Labour) Members of Parliament such as Arthur Ponsonby and Charles P. Trevelyan, and Independent Labour Party Members Ramsay MacDonald and Philip Snowden. These and other Members of Parliament constituted an informal "peace party" of about forty members of the House of Commons.[44] UDC members had been critical of the government's policies leading up to the war, but they chose not to challenge the fighting

---

[41] Marvin Swartz, *The Union of Democratic Control in British Politics during the First World War* (Oxford: Clarendon Press, 1971), 6.

[42] Sandi E. Cooper, *Patriotic Pacifism: Waging War on War in Europe, 1815–1914* (New York: Oxford University Press, 1991), 182.

[43] Martin Ceadel, *Thinking about Peace and War* (Oxford: Oxford University Press, 1987), 118.

[44] Peter Brock and Nigel Young, *Pacifism in the Twentieth Century* (Syracuse, NY: Syracuse University Press, 1999), 24.

once it was underway. They focused instead on analyzing the causes of the conflagration and preventing war in the future. They sought to craft a postwar international security system that would strengthen international cooperation and peace. At the core of this envisioned system was the spread of democratic governance.

The UDC manifesto of November 1914 offered five principles for a "new diplomacy." These were, paraphrasing:

1. No territory should come under the control of any government without the consent of the population of the territory in question.
2. The government of Great Britain should not enter into treaties without the consent of Parliament, which should establish machinery to exert greater control over foreign policy.
3. Great Britain should eschew "balance of power" alliances and instead work with other nations as determined by an international court.
4. As part of the peace settlement, Great Britain should propose drastic reductions in armaments and the nationalization of weapons manufacture.
5. Economic warfare should end when the war ceases, and the British government should promote free trade among all nations by expanding the principle of the "open door."[45]

The priority goal of the UDC was to end the system of secret diplomacy.[46] The UDC remained active into the 1920s and helped to shape the positions of the Labour Party. When the first Labour government took office in 1924, fifteen UDC members entered government, and Ramsay MacDonald and Arthur Ponsonby took charge of British foreign policy. Gradually many of the reforms advocated by the UDC were adopted, and Parliament gained greater say over foreign policy matters – although the British cabinet, like the White House in the United States, continued to exert predominant control over international affairs and to this day retains extraordinary privileges in matters of war and peace.

The struggle to extend democratic control over the decision to wage war continued into the Vietnam era and beyond. In the acrimony and debate over what went wrong in Indochina, members of Congress, foreign policy scholars, and citizen groups focused on flawed decision-making processes that had dragged the country into war. Congressional hearings and the publication of the Pentagon Papers revealed deceit and lawlessness at the

---

[45] Paraphrased from Thomas J. Knock, *To End All Wars: Woodrow Wilson and the Quest for a New World Order* (New York: Oxford University Press, 1992), 37; and Swartz, *The Union of Democratic Control*, 42.
[46] Swartz, *The Union of Democratic Control*, 25.

highest levels of government. Scholars and former officials pointed to the dangers of an "imperial presidency" and the excessive warmaking powers that had accumulated in the hands of an unaccountable "national security state." The resulting backlash against executive war making led to adoption in 1973 of the War Powers Act, which required congressional approval within thirty days of a decision to use force overseas. The Act did not prevent the president from waging aggressive war, however, as the invasion of Iraq illustrated thirty years later. Through official deceit and the manipulation of public opinion, presidents and prime ministers are still able to go to war without democratic constraint.

THE KANTIAN TRIAD

In recent decades empirical studies have confirmed many of the basic tenets of the liberal peace theory. Kant's concepts of democracy, economic interdependence, and international organization as predicates of peace have been tested through modern social science methods and have stood up well. A review of the contemporary evidence shows that Kant was amazingly prescient in identifying the fundamental political and economic conditions of peace.

It is a "striking fact," Bruce Russett observed, that mature democracies have almost never fought each other.[47] Louis Kriesberg described this as "one of the few well-documented empirical findings about the occurrence of war ... democratic dyads are much less likely than nondemocratic dyads to engage in any kind of militarized dispute."[48] Empirical analyses of interstate conflicts provide strong confirmation for this assertion. Russett and his colleagues examined every incident of armed conflict between nations from 1886 to 1992, drawing from the Correlates of War database and other widely accepted sources of empirical evidence. They found that the relationship between democracy and peace was "statistically significant" through the entire period and became stronger after 1945 as the number of democratic states increased.[49] Empirical studies of interstate disputes confirm a strong statistical correlation between democracy and peace and show

---

[47] Bruce Russett, *Grasping the Democratic Peace: Principles for a Post-Cold War World* (Princeton, NJ: Princeton University Press, 1993), 4.

[48] Louis Kriesberg, *Constructive Conflicts: From Escalation to Resolution*, 2nd edn (Lanham, MD: Rowman and Littlefield, 2003), 143.

[49] Bruce Russett and John R. Oneal, *Triangulating Peace: Democracy, Interdependence, and International Organizations* (New York: W. W. Norton & Company, 2001), 113.

that democratic states are unlikely to become involved in war against one another.

The relationship between democracy and peace becomes greater as the depth and maturity of democracy increases. The greater the degree of democracy, the less likely it is that states will go to war against each other. "The more democratic each member of a dyad is," Russett found, "the less likely is conflict between them."[50] The converse of this finding is also true: the more autocratic a state, the greater the likelihood of armed conflict. This finding is highly robust and holds constant across a range of data sets and different independent variables. There is no other aspect of international relations that is more consistently and empirically valid than the relationship between mutual democracy and peaceful political relations.

There are important qualifications to the democratic peace phenomenon, however. Countries making the transition to democracy may actually become more bellicose. Edward Mansfield, Jack Snyder, and other scholars have found that as states make the change from autocracy to democracy they are more war prone than fully democratic states. Newly developing democratic systems tend to be unstable and lack the deeply rooted political institutions and culture of openness that are usually associated with mature democracies. In these settings the democratic peace effect is less evident. States that are only partly democratic are more bellicose than well-established democracies. Democracy is best at preventing conflict when it is complete. "The higher the level of democracy a state achieves," Russett and Oneal concluded, "the more peaceful that state is likely to be."[51]

A major limitation of the democratic peace theory is that it does not address the most common form of armed violence in the world today, intrastate and internal conflict. From Iraq to Sri Lanka through Africa and beyond, the most prevalent and violent forms of armed conflict involve nonstate actors, militias, and para-state forces. Interstate warfare between contending armies is rare among all countries, democratic and nondemocratic alike. A theory of how states relate to one another is of little value in addressing these realities.

Another significant exception to the rule is the pattern of military intervention by major democratic nations against developing nations. While democracies may be less likely to wage war on one another, they show no compunction about using military force against other countries. This is obvious from the pattern of US foreign policy. In recent decades the United States has been one of the most warlike nations on earth,

[50] Russett, *Grasping the Democratic Peace*, 86.   [51] Russett and Oneal, *Triangulating Peace*, 122.

notwithstanding its system of democratic governance. Washington has engaged in covert action to subvert or overthrow democratic governments – as evidenced by the US interventions against Guatemala in 1954 and Chile in 1973. In other instances, such as the Contra war against the Sandinistas of Nicaragua in the 1980s, the United States sponsored and trained paramilitary forces that attacked a revolutionary government that had been confirmed in office through democratic elections. These actions are not counted as uses of military force, since they did not involve combat by regular US armed forces, but they had effects equivalent to those of war. Britain and France have also engaged in military campaigns against developing states in former colonies. The democratic peace turns out to be just that – a peace among mature democratic states. It does not prevent such states from intervening in and invading other, less fully developed countries.

The Kantian theory of peace is also premised on the assumption that expanded free trade reduces the likelihood of war. Classic liberal theory holds that commerce and economic interdependence create the foundations for more peaceful and cooperative relations, while protectionism and autarky lead to greater conflict.[52] Many contemporary political analysts echo this view. Richard Rosecrance argued in *The Rise of the Trading State* that increased trade and commercial interaction reinforce preferences for peace and make war less likely.[53] Lloyd J. Dumas emphasized that equitable and mutually beneficial trade relations among nations can create understanding and interdependence and strengthen the preference for cooperation over conflict.[54] William Domke concluded that nations that were closely connected to the global economy were less likely to go to war.[55]

Empirical studies provide solid evidence that trade between nations tends to increase cooperation and decrease conflict.[56] Edward Mansfield and Brian Pollins found "strong evidence that heightened trade flows inhibit the outbreak of military disputes between members of preferential trade arrangements." Their research showed that "heightened global trade (as a

---

[52] See the discussion in Neil R. Richardson, "International Trade as a Force for Peace," in *Controversies in International Relations Theory: Realism and the Neoliberal Challenge*, ed. Charles W. Kegley, Jr. (New York: St. Martin's Press, 1995), 284–5.

[53] Richard Rosecrance, *The Rise of the Trading State: Commerce and Conquest in the Modern World* (New York: Basic Books, 1986).

[54] Lloyd J. Dumas, "Economics and Alternative Security: Toward a Peacekeeping International Economy," in *Alternative Security: Living without Nuclear Deterrence*, ed. Burns H. Weston, 137–75 (Boulder, CO: Westview Press, 1990), 140–4.

[55] William K. Domke, *War and the Changing Global System* (New Haven, CT: Yale University Press, 1988), 131.

[56] Solomon William Polachek, "Conflict and Trade," *Journal of Conflict Resolution* 24, no. 1 (March 1980): 67; Mansfield and Pollins, "Interdependence and Conflict," 1.

percentage of global output) was inversely related to the frequency of war throughout the international system during the nineteenth and twentieth centuries."[57] According to Russett, "the evidence that trade reduces conflict forms a strong and robust generalization."[58] Kriesberg wrote that "the level of international trade is inversely related to the incidence of wars ... That relationship is quantitatively large and statistically significant."[59] The greater the degree of trade and economic interdependence, the lower the probability of violent conflict. "Both democracy and economically important trade are strong and statistically significant constraints on the use of force," wrote Russett and Oneal. "Kant and the other classical liberals were right: both democracy and trade increase the prospects for peace."[60]

Incorporating trade and economic development factors into democratic peace theory helps to address the problem of intrastate conflict. It is widely recognized that inadequate economic development is a major cause of civil conflict.[61] As noted in the next chapter, scholarly studies have identified links between armed violence and economic deprivation. Societies that lack a diversified economic base and that have large numbers of unemployed young men are prone to military conflict. Economic development, if balanced and equitable, can help to ameliorate these conditions and provide opportunities for those who might otherwise be inclined toward militancy.

As Bentham and other philosophers noted, trade and economic investment depend upon the rule of law and the right to own property. These are conditions that also give rise to democracy.[62] To the extent that they can be nurtured in developing countries, the prospects for economic development improve, and the likelihood of civil conflict diminishes. International development agencies such as the UN Development Programme (UNDP) increasingly recognize that "good governance" is a vital ingredient of sustainable economic development, and is also a formula for reducing violent conflict. Democracy, economic prosperity, and peace are interconnected, as Cobden, Kant, and other philosophers recognized. The prevention of war is not just a

[57] Mansfield and Pollins, "Interdependence and Conflict," 9, 12.
[58] Bruce Russett, "Violence and Disease: Trade as a Suppressor of Conflict when Suppressors Matter," in *Economic Interdependence and International Conflict: New Perspectives on an Enduring Debate*, ed. Edward D. Mansfield and Brian M. Pollins (Ann Arbor, MI: University of Michigan Press, 2003), 159.
[59] Louis Kriesberg, *Constructive Conflicts: From Escalation to Resolution*, 2nd edn (Lanham, MD: Rowman and Littlefield, 2003), 141, 144, 152.
[60] Russett and Oneal, *Triangulating Peace*, 145–6.
[61] Paul Collier et al., *Breaking the Conflict Trap: Civil War and Development Policy* (Washington, DC: World Bank, 2003), 53.
[62] Michael Mandelbaum, *The Ideas That Conquered the World: Peace, Democracy, and Free Markets in the Twenty-First Century* (New York: Public Affairs, 2002), 269–72.

matter of political relations between democratic states. It also requires the rule of law and sustainable economic development.

The third leg of what Russett and Oneal call the Kantian triad is international organization. States that are tied together in mutually agreed legal arrangements are less likely to wage war on one another. Russett and Oneal found solid empirical evidence of a correlation in this regard. Two states that participate jointly in multilateral institutions are significantly less likely to engage in military conflict than states that are not partners to such organizations.[63] The ties that bind in international law and organization help to reduce the incidence of war.

International institutions not only encourage cooperation among member states but help to resolve and prevent conflict in global trouble spots. The *Human Security Report of 2005* documented a significant drop in the number of armed conflicts in the world during the previous decade. The report attributed this development in substantial part to an unprecedented upsurge of international activism by the United Nations and other multilateral organizations.[64] Since the end of the cold war the frequency and scale of UN-led international peacemaking efforts have increased dramatically. UN preventive diplomacy missions expanded sixfold, peacekeeping operations quadrupled, and the use of targeted Security Council sanctions multiplied greatly. During the same period the number of conflicts ending in negotiated settlement rose significantly. A RAND Corporation study found that most UN nation-building missions were successful.[65] Increased activism by international institutions was directly correlated with reduced levels of military conflict.

The three elements of the Kantian triangle correspond to the "definitive articles" of Kant's theory of perpetual peace. The prospects for preventing war are greatest in the presence of all three elements: mutual democracy, economic interdependence, and participation in international organization. The principles of Kantian peace are mutually reinforcing. Democracy both sustains peace and is easier to maintain in a peaceful environment. Mutually beneficial trade relations increase the prospects for peace and are more likely to prosper in peaceful settings. International organizations enhance cooperation and are more effective during peacetime. The reverse of these statements is also true. Wars are more frequent between nondemocratic

---

[63] Russett and Oneal, *Triangulating Peace*, 172.

[64] Human Security Centre, *Human Security Report 2005: War and Peace in the 21st Century* (New York: Oxford University Press, 2005).

[65] James Dobbins *et al.*, *The UN's Role in Nation-Building: From the Congo to Iraq* (Santa Monica, CA: RAND Corporation, 2005), xv–xxxviii.

states and tend to undermine democratic liberties. Armed conflicts occur where trade is infrequent and are likely to discourage further economic interaction and investment. Wars undermine international institutions and make international cooperation more difficult.

The democratic peace phenomenon can be analyzed as a function of political, economic, and social integration. The groundbreaking research of Karl Deutsch and his colleagues developed the concept of a "secure community" – a distinct population or group of nations that does not expect war and therefore does not prepare for it.[66] Such communities develop numerous forms of interaction and mutual benefit that become ubiquitous and institutionalized. As these communities become more dependent on one another, the costs of disrupting mutual interaction rise. Dense networks of social exchange develop and strengthen the integration process, creating incentives to maintain interdependence. These tendencies are most prevalent in nations that are democratic, economically interdependent, and legally and institutionally linked. They serve as the glue that binds communities together in democratic peace.

The European Union is the most obvious manifestation of this process of democratic integration leading to a secure community. Deutsch and his colleagues wrote in the 1950s when the European Coal and Steel Community was being created. They were remarkably prescient in anticipating the continuous integration process that would lead to the European Common Market, the European Community, and ultimately the European Union, which has gone through stages of expansion and which established monetary union in 1999. Through all of these remarkable developments, the underlying process of integration has followed the Kantian path, steadily enlarging democracy, economic interdependence, and international organization. Much has been written about the European Union and the profound transition of the European continent since World War II – from a caldron of horrific industrialized warfare to a community of unprecedented prosperity and peace. This is not the place for a detailed examination of this development, or for an assessment of the many challenges that face contemporary European integration. The European Union is not a United States of Europe, as Victor Hugo and nineteenth-century enthusiasts envisioned it. It is merely a community, a federation of sovereign nations, much as Kant described. It is a region of political and economic cooperation and political integration that is of historic significance to an understanding of the prospects for peace. As Russett and Oneal observed,

---

[66] Russett and Oneal, *Triangulating Peace*, 74–5.

the economic and political transformation of western Europe after World War II was based on interlocking "virtuous circles" that directly and indirectly promoted peaceful relations.[67] The development of European cooperation confirms the core insights of the Kantian model: democracy, economic interdependence, and international legal agreement are the foundations upon which a more peaceful future can be built.

THE INSIGHTS OF FEMINISM

Missing in Kant's theory is a consideration of the empowerment of women as an additional factor that inclines nations toward peace. Empirical evidence suggests that the political, economic, and social empowerment of women is a significant influence in reducing the tendency of governments to utilize military force. Greater gender equality could be considered part of democratization, the first element of the Kantian triad, but it is sufficiently important in its own right and raises such significant questions about the nature of society that it deserves to be considered separately. The Kantian trio should be a quartet.

Many of the early suffragists believed that the empowerment of women would help to put an end to war. In 1908 the German Union for Women's Suffrage argued that the vote for women "encourages peace and harmony between different peoples." The French Union for Women's Suffrage predicted in 1913 that women voters would support social reform, including legislation to prevent wars and encourage international arbitration.[68] Jane Addams considered militarism and feminism polar opposites. She participated in founding the WPP as an expression of what she considered the natural linkage between women's rights and peace. She and other feminist leaders promoted the vote for women as part of the strategy for achieving global peace. Margaret Sanger was a supporter of suffrage, but she campaigned for a more comprehensive form of women's empowerment. Influenced by Emma Goldman, Sanger argued not only for the right to vote but for women's reproductive freedom and economic and social advancement. The franchise was important but not sufficient, she believed. Social transformation and personal liberation were also necessary to improve the lives of women and create the conditions for a more just and peaceful society. Virginia Woolf wrote in *Three Guineas* that the way to

---

[67] *Ibid.*, 24.

[68] Richard J. Evans, *Comrades and Sisters: Feminism, Socialism and Pacifism in Europe, 1870–1945* (New York: St. Martin's Press, 1987), 123.

peace is through the social and economic advancement of women. Education and professional employment would enable women to achieve positions of social influence outside the home, which they would use to cast aside structures of patriarchy and create a more cooperative, peaceful world. Many feminists campaigned for equal education and employment opportunities for women as an integral part of their pacifist commitment.

Modern feminists dismiss the "essentialist" idea that women are inherently more nonviolent and peaceful than men. The association of femininity with peace is a form of biological determinism that has been used historically to reinforce the subordination of women, to deny women political responsibility. Addams and other early feminists also rejected the assumption that a woman is against war "simply and only because she is a woman."[69] It is an obvious fact, Addams admitted, that many women consider war inevitable and even righteous. As scholar Jean Bethke Elshtain noted, women historically have served as vital sources of support for war.[70] Militarism is a social construct that can afflict women as well as men. British pacifists Helena Swanwick and Vera Brittain were critical of women who looked admiringly, even adoringly, upon men in uniform. There is something atavistic in women that leads them to idealize the hero in battle, Swanwick wrote. Swanwick and Brittain urged women to overcome the myths of militarism and stop hiding behind their status as wives. They called for women to adopt positions based on their own thinking rather than that of their husbands.[71]

If women are less likely than men to support war, Woolf argued, it is because of their different life experience and social conditioning. Gender differences on peace issues are not innate but result from law, education, custom, and practice in male-dominated society. War traditionally has been "the man's habit, not the woman's," wrote Woolf.[72] In patriarchal society women have been treated as outsiders and have not been subjected to the same level of military socialization and indoctrination as men. As a result women have less to gain from war and bellicose patriotism. Dorothy Day

---

[69] Jane Addams, excerpt from speech at Carnegie Hall, New York, 9 July 1915. Printed in Cambridge Women's Peace Collective, *My Country is the Whole World: An Anthology of Women's Work on Peace and War* (Boston, MA: Pandora Press, 1984): 86–7.

[70] Jean Bethke Elshtain, *Women and War*, 2nd. edn. (Chicago, IL: University of Chicago Press, 1993).

[71] Helena Swanwick, *The Roots of Peace; A Sequel to Collective Insecurity, Being an Essay on Some of the Uses, Conditions and Limitations of Compulsive Force in the Prevention of War* (London: J. Cape, 1938), 187; Josephine Eglin, "Women Pacifists in Interwar Britain," in *Challenge to Mars: Essays on Pacifism from 1918 to 1945*, ed. Peter Brock and Thomas P. Socknat (Toronto: University of Toronto Press, 1999), 158–9.

[72] Virginia Woolf, *Three Guineas* (New York: Harcourt, Brace & World, 1938), 6.

adopted a more essentialist view when she argued that women think differently than men and are more inclined toward caring and love for others. Men tend to think abstractly and are preoccupied with distant ends, she believed, while women are more rooted in the present and are more focused on practical means of resolving problems. "More than men do, women see things as a whole," Day wrote.[73] Modern feminists argue that mutually exclusive modes of thinking are gendered and are part of the power structure that keeps women subordinated.[74] Feminists seek to transcend these dichotomies and promote gender equality to replace male-dominated hierarchy.

Swanwick argued that the subordination of women and the glorification of war are based on the same principle – the use of force. Militarism is the enthronement of physical force, just as the abuse and domination of women are based partly on physical force. As long as violence remains the preferred means of settling differences, men will continue to dominate women. Brittain made a similar point: "militarism and the oppression of women are both based on force." The women's movement is based on the opposite belief, that reason is "superior to force as a factor in human affairs. That is why the struggle against war, which is the final and most vicious expression of force, is fundamentally inseparable from feminism."[75] Pacifism and feminism are based on the same principle, the elevation of moral force over the use of physical force. Modern writers define feminism as the struggle against patriarchal hierarchies that are at the root of violence and oppression.[76] Feminism rejects the personal violence that subjugates women and the political violence that oppresses society. Feminism seeks to break the social conditioning that sustains violence against women and perpetuates institutionalized warmaking.

EMPOWERING WOMEN

Studies of public opinion provide evidence of a substantial "gender gap" on war and military-related issues, with women consistently showing a greater propensity to support peaceful solutions to international conflict and

[73] Quoted in Jim Forest, *Love Is the Measure: A Biography of Dorothy Day* (New York: Paulist, 1986), 85.
[74] Catia C. Confortini, "Galtung, Violence, and Gender: The Case for a Peace Studies/Feminism Alliance," *Peace & Change* 31, no. 3 (July 2006): 333.
[75] Quoted in Eglin, "Women Pacifists in Interwar Britain," 160.
[76] Berenice A. Carroll, "Feminism and Pacifism: Historical and Theoretical Connections," in *Women and Peace: Theoretical, Historical and Practical Perspectives*, ed. Ruth Roach Pierson (London: Croom Helm, 1987), 19.

greater reluctance to endorse the use of military force. A detailed analysis of empirical data in *International Security* in 2003 revealed a "scholarly consensus that women appear less likely to support policies that involve the use of force." Polling data in the United States and Britain disclose substantial differences in policy preferences between women and men on a range of national security issues. A longitudinal study of responses to foreign policy questions in four surveys from 1975 to 1986 found "significant gender differences." Studies of public opinion during the Gulf crisis in 1990–1 noted that women were far more sensitive – and negative – about the prospects of war-related casualties.[77] These and other findings confirm that women are consistently more likely to support peaceful solutions and less likely to endorse war than men.

Empirical studies of warmaking tendencies among nations show a strong correlation between the empowerment of women and more peaceful foreign policies. In his classic study *Development as Freedom* economist Amartya Sen noted that the political empowerment of women in India is directly related to such variables as a woman's literacy and education, and her ability to find employment and income outside the home.[78] A 2001 study of gender and violence in the *Journal of Conflict Resolution* found that countries in which women are relatively empowered, as measured by education, professional employment, and participation in government, are less likely to use military force in international relations. "States that are characterized by higher levels of gender equality use lower levels of violence during crises than those with lower levels of gender equality," wrote authors Mary Caprioli and Mark Boyer. These findings suggest that "the pursuit of gender equality in societies throughout the world may have positive effects for the lessening of violence." A similar study by Monty Marshall and Donna Ramsey Marshall in 1999 found strong support for the proposition that "gender empowerment is closely associated with a state's willingness to use force: the gender factor is negative and significant in all of the analyses."[79] Studies also show that women are less likely than men to commit violent crime.[80] The higher the female–male ratio in a given population, the lower the murder rate.[81]

[77] Richard C. Eichenberg, "Gender Differences in Public Attitudes toward the Use of Force by the United States, 1990–2003," *International Security* 28, no. 1 (summer 2003): 118–20.

[78] Amartya Sen, *Development as Freedom* (New York: Alfred A. Knopf, 1999), 191.

[79] Monty G. Marshall and Donna Ramsey Marshall, "Gender Empowerment and the Willingness of States to Use Force" (paper presented at the annual meeting of the International Studies Association, Washington, DC, 19 February 1999), 22.

[80] James Gilligan, *Preventing Violence* (New York: Thames & Hudson, 2001), 56.

[81] Sen, *Development as Freedom*, 200.

Perhaps there is something to Woolf's prescription for peace after all. As women are empowered socially, economically, and politically, as they take their rightful place in the councils of government, the tendency to resort to violence and the use of military force as a means of settling differences diminishes. When these trends are combined with the spread of democracy, increasing interdependence, and participation in international organizations, they increase the prospects for peace. The empowerment of women and the rise of gender equality are significant factors in the creation of a more democratic and peaceful society.

12

Social justice

On the left the theory of peace was influenced more by Karl Marx than Adam Smith. Where liberals emphasized free trade and economic interdependence, socialists focused on questions of equality and economic justice. They criticized rather than praised capitalism, exposing the economic motives of imperialism, and the bellicose influence of munitions makers. They agreed that interdependence promoted peace, but they had a very different model of socialist solidarity in mind. Gradually the two movements began to converge, as peace advocates increasingly embraced social justice concerns. In many respects a natural affinity existed between socialism and pacifism. Socialism was quintessentially an international movement, as reflected in the title of its famous anthem. Marx emphasized the transnational character of class society and the need for a global solution to the problems of injustice and war.[1] Peace and justice are inextricably linked, socialists insisted. An end to economic exploitation and imperialism is necessary for genuine peace. Many pacifists agreed with this analysis and incorporated the struggle against inequality into the peace agenda.

There were also sharp differences between socialism and pacifism. Marx opposed capitalist war but favored the class war. Support for armed struggle was a defining feature of socialism in its early years, especially in the communist Third International, and it remains so today among Trotskyists, Maoists, and other communist groups. Most European socialists began to abandon the idea of armed revolution early in the twentieth century, but the continued acceptance of armed struggle by many on the left impeded cooperation between pacifism and socialism. The two movements also differed in their social composition and attitudes toward religion. Peace groups drew their greatest support from the middle classes, particularly educators, professionals, and the clergy. Socialism was a working-class

---

[1] Michael Doyle, *Ways of War and Peace: Realism, Liberalism, and Socialism* (New York: W. W. Norton & Co., 1997), 320, 326.

movement, although some of its leaders were middle class, and it had its strongest ties within trade unions and labor groups. Pacifists were often religiously motivated, while socialists tended to be agnostic or atheist. Some were hostile toward religious institutions, which they criticized for siding with landowners and capitalists rather than peasants and workers.

Pacifists and socialists also had different theories on the causes of war and the ways to achieve peace. Many peace advocates subscribed to the theories of Kant and Cobden, believing that the spread of capitalism and international commerce would bring peace by fostering interdependence, cooperation, and the rule of law. Socialists took the opposite view, that capitalism was the cause of imperialism and war. Marx wrote that the capitalist drive for markets leads to imperial rivalry and greater exploitation of colonized peoples. The resulting increase in social and political tensions leads to conflict and war. The German socialist leader Karl Kautsky said that militarism was intrinsic to the capitalist system.[2] Poverty, inequality, and war were the inevitable consequences of capitalism, early socialists believed.

In this chapter I examine the interaction between socialism and pacifism and the evolution of a "peace with justice" perspective among opponents of war. I trace the relations between the disciples of Kant and the followers of Marx and how the two movements began to converge, driven on the socialist side by the imperatives of creating the broadest possible coalition against war, and on the pacifist side by greater understanding of the economic causes and consequences of militarism. By the early twentieth century the links between economic justice and peace commanded greater attention on both sides. The socialist-influenced theory of scientific pacifism highlighted the economic underpinnings of war and identified social trends toward the evolution of cooperation. During the interwar era and in the decades since, social justice and economic development issues have become a dominant concern among internationalists and peace advocates. A commitment to economic development was incorporated into the Charter of the United Nations, and was embodied in UN programs over the decades that promoted economic growth as a means not only of advancing human welfare but preventing war. The connection between economic development and peace has received even greater attention in recent years, as part of a growing global commitment to the interrelated goals of improving economic well-being and addressing the root causes of terrorism and armed conflict. Economic exploitation and underdevelopment are now widely recognized as causes of war and as

---

[2] Roger Chickering, *Imperial Germany and a World without War: The Peace Movement and German Society, 1892–1914* (Princeton, NJ: Princeton University Press, 1975), 268, 272.

legitimate and necessary concerns for building peace. These ideas are summarized succinctly in the famous expression of Pope Paul VI, "If you want peace, work for justice." Recent empirical analysis has confirmed the importance of sustainable economic development as a strategy for peace.

SOCIALISM AND PACIFISM: EARLY DIFFERENCES

When socialists and pacifists first interacted in the nineteenth century, they often spoke past one another. Even when socialists and peace advocates shared similar perspectives on the permissible use of military force, they had difficulty working together. Organizers of the *Ligue internationale de la paix et de la liberté* shared the view of many early socialists that military force was justified when used in a legitimate struggle of national liberation. As the *Ligue* was formed in 1867 it sought to form a partnership with the First International. The founding congress of the *Ligue* was arranged in Geneva to coincide with a meeting of the First International in Lausanne. Organizers of the *Ligue* presented a resolution at the Lausanne meeting inviting socialists to join the *Ligue* and participate in the emerging new movement for liberty and peace. The socialist delegates listened politely but declined the offer and instead issued a statement identifying the main causes of war as poverty, inequality, and injustice. Marx distrusted peace advocates and urged socialists to stay away. A resolution at the 1868 Brussels meeting of the First International declared that organizations such as the *Ligue de la paix et de la liberté* had no reason to exist. If peace advocates wanted to create a more peaceful world, the socialists argued, they should merge their efforts with the International, which had a more realistic program for achieving peace through revolution and social justice. Mikhail Bakunin declared on behalf of the meeting that peace would not be possible without a radical alteration of the existing economic system and the liberation of the working class.[3]

Marx and other socialists dismissed pacifism as bourgeois sentimentalism. At a socialist conference in Brussels in 1891 the delegates declared that "all efforts to eliminate militarism and institute peace that do not take into consideration the economic causes of the problem are impotent, however noble their motives may be." An international socialist congress in London in 1896 derided Bertha von Suttner's famous novel: "like every other appeal

---

[3] Sandi E. Cooper, *Patriotic Pacifism: Waging War on War in Europe 1815–1914* (New York: Oxford University Press, 1991), 37, 40.

to the humanitarianism of the capitalist class, the cry, 'Down with Weapons' dies fruitlessly out."[4]

These suspicions from the socialists were reciprocated on the pacifist side. Many peace advocates were skeptical of the socialist claim that the abolition of classes and an end to private property would bring peace. Peace advocates tended to be liberals and believed with John Locke that private property and personal liberty were the foundations of social stability and peace. Where socialists placed their faith in the collective, liberal pacifists emphasized the importance of individual freedom. They considered talk of overthrowing capitalism utopian and unrealistic, and a diversion from the necessity of adopting practical measures to reform society and prevent war. They favored more pragmatic, incremental efforts to reduce the threat of war by strengthening international law and creating mechanisms for the arbitration of interstate disputes.

Many moderate peace leaders rejected class analysis altogether. During the International Peace Congress in Paris in 1878, Frédéric Passy and others objected to a proposed resolution that singled out the hardships war imposes on "the most numerous and poorest classes." War is horrendous for all people, Passy emphasized; class divisions are not relevant to the question of peace. The majority at the conference concurred and agreed to remove the reference to class in the resolution. Many peace supporters believed that overcoming war and militarism would help to resolve what they called the "social question." Excessive military spending was the principal factor holding back social and cultural progress.[5] Redirecting expenditures from military to social programs would go a long way toward overcoming poverty and inadequate development. The best way to achieve justice and economic equality, Passy argued, is to work for an end to militarism and the prevention of war.

Outside of Europe the relationship between peace advocacy and socialism was more cordial. In Japan the founding platform of the Social Democratic Party in 1901 called for the "total abolition of armaments as a first step toward the establishment of peace among nations." The platform was written by peace advocate Abe Isoo. In an essay written at the time, Abe compared war to banditry:

We socialists are absolutely opposed to both brigandage and war. As there cannot be "good bandits" so there can never be a just war. We can sympathize with those who have been forced into banditry by the imperfections of the social order . . . but none of these reasons can justify either banditry or war . . . war is a crime against humanity.

[4] Chickering, *Imperial Germany and a World without War*, 261.
[5] Cooper, *Patriotic Pacifism*, 50, 74, 207.

Abe used the analogy of labor relations to explain the need for international law. "We ought to seek a structure of international law which will fulfill among nations the same function that labour arbitration provides within them."[6] In Japan and other countries the socialist movement spoke out vigorously against militarization.

CONVERGENCE

As the dangers of war increased in the years prior to 1914, the socialist and pacifist movements drew closer together. On the pacifist side an increasing number of analysts recognized the economic and social roots of war and the need for a more scientific, less moralistic basis for peace. Within the socialist movement many organizers began to adopt a less rigid and doctrinaire peace strategy. While communist factions associated with Lenin maintained a hardline stance, many socialists and their trade union allies took a more pragmatic approach. The socialist analysis of capitalism and war began to change, and cooperation with peace societies increased. Jean Jaurès of France took the lead in attempting to build as broad a political coalition as possible to prevent the impending doom. He advocated alliances with pacifists and other opponents of war. He and other democratic socialists maintained their hatred of capitalist exploitation, but they rejected armed struggle in favor of a nonviolent strategy for change. They urged workers to refuse to serve in imperialist wars. These positions were officially endorsed in 1906 and 1908 by the socialist labor federation, the *Confédération générale du travail* (CGT). Similar views coalesced around the Socialist Party leadership of Jules Guesde and Paul Lafargue.[7]

All across Europe socialist parties began to cooperate with pacifist groups. In Italy socialist leader Claudio Treves urged radicals and leftists to unite with liberals and republicans in a common struggle to oppose militarism, reduce arms spending, and resist imperialism.[8] In France two-thirds of the socialist members of the Chamber of Deputies belonged to the Interparliamentary Union. In Switzerland the Social Democratic Party agreed en masse to join the International Peace Bureau. In Germany the

---

[6] Quotes from Cyril H. Powles, "Abe Isoo: The Utility Man," in *Pacifism in Japan: The Christian and Socialist Tradition*, ed. Nobuya Bamba and John F. Howes (Vancouver: University of British Columbia Press, 1978), 155–6.

[7] Chickering, *Imperial Germany and a World without War*, 357–8.

[8] Cooper, *Patriotic Pacifism*, 75.

Social Democratic Party promoted international arbitration and supported negotiations to limit naval armaments.[9] A resolution adopted at the 1907 congress of the Second International declared:

pressure by the proletariat could achieve the blessings of international disarmament through serious use of courts of arbitration instead of the pitiful machinations of governments. This would make it possible to use the enormous expenditure of money and strength which is swallowed by military armaments and war for cultural purposes.

The resolution also called for a general strike of workers in the event of war.[10]

With the change in socialist politics came a change in analysis. Kautsky and other socialist leaders adopted a more nuanced understanding of the causes of war. They joined Jaurès in developing a centrist position that maintained a fierce opposition to imperialism but that focused attention on the immediate struggle against war. In 1911 Kautsky offered a new theory of imperialism that anticipated the analysis of Joseph Schumpeter.[11] Capitalism can indeed lead to imperialism and war, Kautsky wrote, but its development can also move in the opposite direction, toward greater international cooperation and interdependence. Militarism does not grow inevitably out of capitalism. It is the result of specific political decisions made by powerful military, bureaucratic, and financial elites. War is a policy, not an inevitability.[12] If war is a political choice it can be countered through political action. Kautsky's new analysis moved him closer to the position of Eduard Bernstein, who argued for democratic socialism based on peace, freedom, and free trade. To reflect this new understanding, the Social Democrats replaced the previous slogan, "imperialism or socialism," with "world war or disarmament."[13] The socialists now accepted many of the tenets of pacifism and were actively engaged in efforts to prevent war and promote disarmament.

In the years before the war socialist parties and their trade union allies sponsored mass rallies for peace and international solidarity, vastly swelling the ranks of the peace movement and bringing new social relevance to the struggle against militarism. Jaurès declared at a mass rally in Brussels that the proletarian masses "collectively love peace and abhor war." During the

[9] Chickering, *Imperial Germany and a World without War*, 273.
[10] Cooper, *Patriotic Pacifism*, 77, 210.
[11] Chickering, *Imperial Germany and a World without War*, 273, 276–7.
[12] Doyle, *Ways of War and Peace*, 346.
[13] Chickering, *Imperial Germany and a World without War*, 274.

first Balkan War socialist parties in Europe sponsored a series of impressive mass rallies for peace, including a demonstration in Berlin in October 1912 attended by more than 250,000 people. The meeting of the Socialist International at Basel later that year described the working class as "the herald of world peace."[14] Yet the socialists combined their internationalism with strong nationalist sentiment. In each country socialist leaders supported the right of their nation to defend itself against attack. When the guns of August began to fire most socialists closed ranks behind their national colors and marched off to battle.

Only in the United States, still distant from the struggles of Europe, did the Socialist Party remain aloof from the war. When Congress approved Wilson's call for war in April 1917, the Socialist Party meeting in St. Louis the next day adopted a strongly worded resolution amidst turbulent debate condemning the declaration of war as "a crime against the people of the United States." In the following months the party continued to campaign against the war and the military draft, drawing large crowds at antiwar rallies. Congress responded by passing the Espionage Act, outlawing interference with military conscription. Eugene Debs and other party leaders continued to speak out, for which they were arrested and imprisoned. At his trial Debs told the jury:

I have been accused of obstructing the war. I admit it . . . I abhor war . . . I have sympathy with the suffering, struggling people everywhere. It does not make any difference under what flag they were born, or where they live . . . [15]

Debs ran for president as the Socialist Party candidate in 1920 and received more than a million votes while in prison.[16]

THE LENINIST CRITIQUE

Lenin held to a hardline view and sharply differentiated the communist position from pacifism. Communists agree with pacifists in condemning the brutality of war, he wrote, but their attitude is fundamentally different:

We differ . . . in that we understand the inevitable connection between wars and the class struggle within a country; we understand that wars cannot be abolished unless classes are abolished and socialism is created; we also differ in that we regard civil

---

[14] Michael Howard, *War and the Liberal Conscience* (New Brunswick, NJ: Rutgers University Press, 1989), 67.

[15] Quoted in Howard Zinn, *A People's History of the United States 1492–Present* (New York: HarperCollins Publishers, 2005), 367–8.

[16] Charles Chatfield, *The American Peace Movement: Ideals and Activism* (New York: Twayne Publishers, 1992), 44.

wars, i.e., wars waged by an oppressed class against the oppressor class, by slaves against slaveholders . . . as fully legitimate, progressive and necessary.[17]

In *Imperialism: The Highest Stage of Capitalism*, Lenin developed a comprehensive if not always coherent theory of the imperialist nature of capitalism. He borrowed heavily from J. A. Hobson, whose *Imperialism: A Study* developed the main elements in Lenin's thesis.[18] "Imperialist wars are absolutely inevitable under such a [capitalist] economic system," Lenin wrote. With Marx he argued that the internal contradictions of capitalism drive the system toward fierce competition for foreign markets and that the resulting military confrontation among rivals creates war. He also argued, as Marx did, that imperialism and war provide a safety valve for relieving social pressures within capitalist countries. Through war and xenophobic campaigns against external foes, political leaders can divert public attention away from domestic social crises toward supposed threats abroad. Lenin defined this policy as "social chauvinism."[19]

Rosa Luxemburg and other left-wing socialists in Germany embraced the Leninist analysis. They believed that imperialism and militarism were intrinsic to capitalism, and manifestations of inherent contradictions within the system. As these internal contradictions deepen, they believed, war becomes inevitable. Luxemburg, Lenin, and other communists rejected any prospect of accommodation or cooperation with capitalism. The way to peace, they believed, was to hasten the demise of the hated system. They considered the pacifist call for arbitration and disarmament naïve and even counterproductive. The problem of war could only be solved through socialist revolution. Luxemburg was critical of what she called the "bourgeois friends of peace." Pacifists believe that world peace and disarmament can be realized within the framework of the present system, she wrote, "whereas we . . . are convinced that militarism can only be abolished from the world with the destruction of the capitalist class state."[20] Leon Trotsky was contemptuous of "flabby pacifism," which he said was characterized by "temporizing, passivity, and the absence of the will to struggle." Trotsky was vicious in his attacks against the noncommunist left and the peace movement. He condemned the disarmament campaigns of the 1930s as "more dangerous than all the explosives and asphyxiating gases. Melinite and

---

[17] V. I. Lenin, "The Principles of Socialism and the War of 1914–1915," *Collected Works*, vol. XXI (London: Lawrence & Wishart, 1964), 299.

[18] J. A. Hobson, *Imperialism: A Study* (Ann Arbor, MI: University of Michigan Press, 1965).

[19] Quoted in Doyle, *Ways of War and Peace*, 349, 352.

[20] Rosa Luxemburg, "Peace Utopias," in *Rosa Luxemburg Speaks* (New York: Pathfinder Press, 1970), 251.

yperite can do their work only because the masses of people are poisoned in peacetime by the fumes of pacifism."[21] Trotsky's venom reflected the sectarianism that was rife within the left in those years.

Notwithstanding the vitriol of Trotsky the socialist critique of pacifism had some merit. Peace cannot be realized simply through moral appeals or rational argument. The material and political interests of ruling classes must be addressed and challenged if war is to be prevented. The socialist critique also raised sharply the perennial question of just war. Wars for the liberation of oppressed people are appropriate and necessary, Marx and Lenin argued. Marx considered the US Civil War a noble struggle that freed the slaves and elevated northern industrialism over southern feudalism. In the twentieth century communists fought to defend the Spanish republic in the 1930s. Communists took the leading role in national liberation struggles against imperialism in China, Vietnam, and other countries. Pacifists were often torn in these struggles between sympathy for the cause of national liberation and revulsion at the brutal methods employed on its behalf. In most cases pacifism had little to contribute toward achieving justice in national liberation struggles.

The Leninist critique was fundamentally flawed, however. While some capitalist societies do indeed have militarist tendencies communist governments proved to be equally or even more militaristic. The Soviet Union did not engage in war and military intervention as frequently as the United States during the cold war era, but its economic system was more militarized than that of the USA (more than 15 percent of its gross domestic product devoted to military spending, compared to approximately 7 percent for the USA during the 1980s).[22] Capitalist countries are not inevitably bellicose. Many countries have evolved toward social democracy and have become more peaceful and less militaristic in their relations with other countries, just as Kant and Cobden predicted. The Marxist-Leninist obsession with class struggle also proved to be profoundly mistaken. While class analysis is a useful tool for understanding power relationships and political dynamics within society, the communist concepts of proletarian revolution and

---

[21] Leon Trotsky, *Whither France?* (New York: Pioneer Publishers, 1936), 25; and "Declaration to the Antiwar Congress at Amsterdam (25 July 1932)," *Writings of Leon Trotsky [1932]* (New York: Pathfinder Press, 1973), 150, 151–2.

[22] Global Security, "Russian Military Budget," 22 April 2006. Available online at *Global Security*, www.globalsecurity.org/military/world/russia/mo-budget.htm (accessed 21 March 2007); Congressional Budget Office, "NATO Burdensharing After Enlargement," August 2001. Available online at Congressional Budget Office, www.cbo.gov/ftpdocs/29xx/doc2976/NATO.pdf (accessed 21 March 2007).

classless society were abstractions with no relation to the real world. They became shibboleths that were used to justify the most grotesque brutalities.

SCIENTIFIC PACIFISM

Socialism had a significant influence in deepening the pacifist analysis of the causes of war and peace, as reflected in the school of thought known as scientific pacifism. One of the chief proponents of this theory was Alfred Fried, recipient of the Nobel Peace Prize in 1911, a colleague of Bertha von Suttner, and a leading figure in the German peace movement in the late nineteenth and early twentieth centuries. Scientific pacifism borrowed a great deal from Marxism, including the pretension of being "scientific" and an overly determinist perspective. It also incorporated the materialist mode of analysis, which emphasized the role of powerful vested interests in determining the course of history. Political behavior is shaped primarily by social and economic forces, Marx wrote and Fried agreed.[23] The causes of war are to be found in the economic self-interest and dominant political influence of giant industries and government bureaucracies. Fried and the scientific pacifists dismissed as pure sentimentalism the pacifist belief that moral enlightenment and education would be sufficient to tame the scourge of war. They emphasized the primacy of material interests and the importance of addressing the economic and political roots of war. The path to peace was not to be found in morality or religion, they argued, but in understanding and harnessing the natural forces shaping the development of society. They emphasized the role of industry and technology as material forces shaping the nature of imperialism and war and warned against the mass devastation that could result from industrialized warfare.

The scientific pacifists produced a series of studies at the turn of the century which showed that war was becoming so destructive and costly that it could no longer serve any constructive purpose. One of the most influential of these works was Ivan Bloch's 1899 study, *The Future of War in its Technical, Economic, and Political Relations*, which predicted that future wars would entail the massive slaughter of combatants on an unprecedented scale. The lethal effects of machine-gun fire and long-range artillery, Bloch wrote, would give decisive advantages to the defense and make infantry charges suicidal. Wars of the future would become exhausting stalemates in which the contending armies would bleed themselves to death. The sides in a future European war would hunker down in opposing trenches. In such a

[23] Chickering, *Imperial Germany and a World without War*, 95–6.

battle, "everybody will be entrenched," he wrote: "the spade will be as indispensable to a soldier as his rifle."[24] Bloch also examined the implications of industrial war for society. The mobilization of mass armies and the enormous financial costs of war would impose severe social and economic burdens, he warned, and would lead to economic ruin and social chaos. The destructiveness of mass industrial war would unleash the specter of revolution and give credence to socialist and anarchist appeals.

Bloch was remarkably prescient in anticipating the horrors of World War I and its aftermath. He anticipated precisely the lethal effects of machine-gun fire and artillery against massed infantry, unlike many of the generals of the day, and correctly predicted trench warfare. He also anticipated the economic and social consequences of world war, which sparked revolution and social chaos in Russia, Germany, Hungary, and beyond. Bloch deserves to be acknowledged more widely for his astute analysis of the costs and consequences of war. Although air power, precision bombing, and other technologies of destruction have further revolutionized the nature of warfare, Bloch's underlying thesis that war has become too costly remains relevant. Among contemporary analysts John Mueller is the most significant in emphasizing the destructive consequences of technological warfare. In *Retreat From Doomsday: The Obsolescence of Major War*, Mueller argued that the development of military technology, especially nuclear weapons, has made large-scale war virtually impossible.[25]

PEACE THROUGH ECONOMIC JUSTICE

In the years after World War I criticisms of capitalism and support for socialist alternatives increased. Faith in the peacemaking potential of capitalism largely disappeared. The spread of capitalism had led not to cooperation, as Kant and Mill assumed, but to mounting competition and war, as predicted by Marx and Lenin. Socialists helped to sharpen this critique by linking capitalism to imperialism, and to the resulting inequalities and denial of national self-determination that they considered root causes of war. Concerns about injustice and a lack of self-determination were intensified by the unequal terms of the Versailles Treaty, which rewarded the major imperial powers and exacerbated international inequalities. Faith in free trade and capitalism faded further during the Great Depression. Few

---

[24] Quoted in Cooper, *Patriotic Pacifism*, 147.
[25] John E. Muller, *Retreat from Doomsday: The Obsolescence of Major War* (New York: Basic Books, 1989).

expected progress from a system of free market commerce that had delivered neither peace nor prosperity. For several decades the liberal economic theories of the Enlightenment were largely disregarded. It was only in the years after World War II, and especially in the latter decades of the twentieth century, that Kantian ideas began to reappear, framed now as theories of economic interdependence and market-based cooperation.

In the interwar era demands for economic and political equality became essential elements of the peace agenda. Peace advocates developed what Cecelia Lynch termed "an overarching norm of equality of status."[26] The principle of universal participation emerged to embody the goals of economic development and political self-determination for colonized peoples and smaller nations. Peace movement support for the League of Nations rested in part on a hope that the League would help to address international injustices, particularly the need for self-determination and greater social and economic equality. In France the APD advocated a strategy of "economic peace" through the lowering of tariff barriers and the creation of a European customs union that would facilitate cooperative economic development.[27] Radical pacifists and those on the left adopted a "social change" perspective emphasizing the economic roots of war and defining peace as the "overthrow of privilege."[28] The prevention of war requires a restructuring of social relations, they argued, to ameliorate political and economic disparities within and across nations.

This shift toward greater recognition of social justice as a requirement for peace marked a significant conceptual evolution for the peace movement. Earlier theories saw the path to peace in moral and religious enlightenment, in the spread of free trade, in the development of international law, and in more democratic governance within nations. To these concepts was now added a broader understanding of how strivings for participation and equality of status also relate to peace. This more nuanced and holistic justice theory became the dominant outlook through the twentieth century. It remains a primary conceptual paradigm today, with ever more sophisticated and empirically based knowledge now available to determine how questions of economic development and social justice influence the prospects for peace.

Social justice and environmentalism have also converged, according to Paul Hawken. Environmental exploitation and resource disputes inevitably

---

[26] Cecelia Lynch, *Beyond Appeasement: Interpreting Interwar Peace Movements in World Politics* (Ithaca, NY: Cornell University Press, 1999), 58, 65.

[27] Norman Ingram, *The Politics of Dissent: Pacifism in France 1919–1939* (Oxford: Clarendon Press, 1991), 54.

[28] Chatfield, *The American Peace Movement*, 63; Charles DeBenedetti, *The Peace Reform in American History* (Bloomington, IN: Indiana University Press, 1980), 122.

have social dimensions and can cause conflict. Powerful interests often locate polluting industries and appropriate resources in communities with the least power to stop them. Indigenous and low income people suffer most. Early conservationism did not address questions of equity, but with the rise of modern environmentalism, often associated with publication of Rachel Carson's *Silent Spring*, ecology blended with human rights. The green movement discovered that to protect the environment, it had to confront power, corruption, and mendacity in the corridors of government and business. Many recognized, as Hawken argued, that "an environmental movement had to be an environmental *justice* movement," which was "de facto a *social* justice movement."[29]

The concern for economic justice as a means of preventing war continued after World War II with the founding of the United Nations. Article 1 of the Charter linked the goal of achieving peace and security to "solving international problems of an economic, social, cultural, or humanitarian character." The Charter devoted two chapters to establishing mechanisms and procedures for advancing economic and social justice. Article 55 makes these connections explicit:

With a view to the creation of conditions of stability and well-being which are necessary for peaceful and friendly relations among nations based on respect for the principle of equal rights and the self-determination of peoples, the United Nations shall promote: a) higher standards of living, full employment, and conditions of economic and social progress and development; b) solutions of international economic, social, health, and related problems; and international cultural and educational cooperation.

The Covenant of the League of Nations had not explicitly emphasized international economic cooperation and development, although the League developed machinery and had some success in furthering economic and social welfare. This experience influenced the architects of the United Nations system and reinforced the commitment of political leaders and nongovernmental activists alike to promote economic development and social welfare as means of advancing international peace and security.

The economic development policies of the United Nations represent a curious blend of capitalist and socialist principles. The Bretton Woods financial institutions were intended not only to assist reconstruction and development but to bolster free-market economies. The Soviet Union was understandably skeptical of mechanisms that were designed in part to

---

[29] Paul Hawken, *Blessed Unrest: How the Largest Movement in the World Came into Being and Why No One Saw it Coming* (New York: Viking Penguin, 2007), 58–9.

undermine the validity of socialist economic principles. On the other hand, the promotion of active governmental intervention to encourage employment and economic development contradicted *laissez-faire* economic doctrine. UN economic and social policy generally followed the premises of the New Deal and the broader principles of social democracy.[30] The United Nations devoted a substantial effort to encouraging economic development, principally through the United Nations Conference on Trade and Development (UNCTAD) and the UNDP. The United Nations plays a valuable role in collecting and disseminating information on development-related issues. Most actual overseas development assistance is delivered bilaterally or through multilateral institutions such as the World Bank and the International Monetary Fund.

THE DEVELOPMENT–PEACE NEXUS

Development assistance programs in many countries are justified as a means of overcoming the conditions that give rise to armed violence and terrorism. At the international conference on poverty reduction in Monterrey, Mexico in 2002, President Bush said "we fight against poverty because hope is an answer to terror."[31] At the G-8 summit in Scotland in July 2005 British Prime Minister Tony Blair traced the roots of terrorism to extremism and "acute and appalling forms of poverty."[32] There is considerable empirical evidence of a link between armed conflict and inadequate economic development. The causes of war can be traced to social and economic conditions that produce frustration and humiliation among economically disadvantaged social groups. Studies of war from the 1960s through the 1980s identified relative economic deprivation as a major factor prompting armed revolt. The research of Ted Robert Gurr and his colleagues found that anger and resentment over a lack of economic opportunity were principal sources of mass mobilization in virtually every case of armed rebellion.[33] More recent studies of civil wars in the 1980s and 1990s confirm

---

[30] Leland M. Goodrich, *The United Nations* (New York: Thomas Y. Crowell, 1959), 263, 267.

[31] George W. Bush, "President Outlines US Plan to Help World's Poor" (remarks, United Nations Financing for Development Conference, Monterrey, Mexico, 22 March 2002). Available online at the White House, www.whitehouse.gov/news/releases/2002/03/print/20020322-1.html (accessed 21 March 2007).

[32] "Blair: Poverty, Extremism Cause Terrorism," *USA Today*, 9 July 2005. Available online at USA Today, www.usatoday.com/news/world/2005-07-09-tony-roots_x.htm (accessed 21 March 2007).

[33] Jack A. Goldstone, Ted Robert Gurr, and Farrokh Moshiri, eds., *Revolutions of the Late Twentieth Century* (Boulder, CO: Westview Press, 1991).

"a positive correlation between economic decline, high levels of poverty and unemployment, and the incidence of armed conflict."[34]

The relationship between war and economic injustice is complex and indirect, however. The studies that document a relationship between war and a lack of economic opportunity are careful to emphasize that there is no direct causal link between poverty and armed violence. Impoverished and starving populations often lack the energy and resources to organize violent uprisings.[35] Nor is there robust evidence of a direct correlation between socioeconomic inequality and the outbreak of war.[36] Once a conflict is underway, however, it is likely to last longer when incomes are unequal.[37] The presence of lucrative (and lootable) natural resources also contributes to armed conflict. The "greed theory" holds that struggles over the control of commodity resources fuel armed conflict.[38] Statistical analyses show that dependency on primary commodity exports is a significant risk factor for civil war.[39] Commodity dependence is itself a function of inadequate development, and thus another link between economic deprivation and war.

It is not poverty *per se* but a general lack of economic development that seems to be most strongly associated with armed conflict. Studies by Paul Collier and his colleagues at the World Bank found that civil conflict is most likely to occur in poor and underdeveloped countries, where large numbers of young men lack economic prospects. Collier and his team showed that civil conflict is heavily concentrated in the poorest countries. They concluded, "the key root cause of conflict is the failure of economic development."[40] Countries that have low, stagnant, and unequally distributed per capita income and that are dependent on primary commodity exports face the highest risk of prolonged conflict. Empirical analyses by scholars at the University of Maryland's Center for International Development and Conflict Management similarly found that "outbreaks of major collective political violence are strongly associated with various measures of poverty,

[34] Karen Ballentine, "Beyond Greed and Grievance: Reconsidering the Economic Dynamics of Armed Conflict," in *The Political Economy of Armed Conflict: Beyond Greed and Grievance*, ed. Karen Ballentine and Jake Sherman (Boulder, CO: Lynne Rienner Publishers, 2003), 259–83.

[35] Seyom Brown, *The Causes and Prevention of War*, 2nd edn (New York: St. Martin's Press, 1994), 34.

[36] Karen Ballentine and Jake Sherman, "Introduction," in *The Political Economy of Armed Conflict: Beyond Greed and Grievance*, ed. Karen Ballentine and Jake Sherman (Boulder, CO: Lynne Rienner Publishers, 2003), 1–15.

[37] Paul Collier et al., *Breaking the Conflict Trap: Civil War and Development Policy* (Washington, DC: World Bank, 2003), 66.

[38] Ballentine and Sherman, "Introduction," 1–15.   [39] Collier et al., *Breaking the Conflict Trap*, 75–9.

[40] *Ibid.*, 53.

underdevelopment, and maldistribution of resources."[41] Other factors that increase the risk of armed violence are inadequate governance and weak regimes, conditions that are compounded by a lack of economic development.

Poverty and a lack of opportunity are likely to be most disruptive when communities experience a decline in social and economic status, when they feel relatively disadvantaged compared to what they possessed previously or expect to gain in the future. It is not poverty *per se* but the experience of relative deprivation that seems to be most directly associated with violent conflict. Social groups are most susceptible to being mobilized for armed rebellion, according to Gurr, when they perceive that an established regime is unjustly depriving them of benefits enjoyed by other groups.[42] Violent discontent tends to be highest when people experience a discrepancy between what they have and what they feel entitled to, or if a period of improving conditions is interrupted or reversed. These factors help to explain the rise of violence and terrorism in societies where substantial numbers of young men lack opportunities for education and gainful employment.

DEVELOPMENT FOR WHOM?

There is widespread agreement that promoting equitable and sustainable economic development is an effective strategy for peace. Raising economic growth may be the single most important step that can be taken to reduce the incidence of global conflict.[43] How to achieve the desired development, however, remains a huge question. The conventional wisdom in Washington and other capitals is that large-scale development aid and market liberalization are the most effective means of achieving economic development and creating conditions conducive to democracy and peace. This was not always the consensus, however. In the 1970s developing countries proposed a very different strategy for promoting development. They called for a New International Economic Order (NIEO). The principles of the NIEO included the right of developing countries to regulate and control the activities of multinational corporations operating within their territory, to nationalize and expropriate foreign property, to establish commodity cartels (OPEC was just being created), and to obtain fairer and more equitable

[41] Monty G. Marshall, "Global Terrorism: An Overview and Analysis," in *Peace and Conflict 2005: A Global Survey of Armed Conflicts, Self-Determination Movements, and Democracy*, ed. Monty G. Marshall and Ted Robert Gurr (College Park, MD: University of Maryland Center for International Development and Conflict Management, 2005), 68.

[42] Ted Robert Gurr, *Why Men Rebel* (Princeton, NJ: Princeton University Press, 1970).

[43] Collier *et al.*, *Breaking the Conflict Trap*, 135.

terms of trade. This was a bold attempt by third world nations and their supporters to overcome the gross disparities in wealth and income that condemn much of the global south to poverty and frequent armed conflict. Socialist groups and trade unions supported the NIEO, as did a number of peace and justice organizations in the United States and around the world. The UN General Assembly endorsed the concept in 1974. Industrialized nations strongly resisted the effort, however, and prevented any substantive action toward realizing NIEO demands.

Instead, conservative political leaders in Washington and London in the 1980s pushed through policies of privatization, reduced public services, and the loosening of market regulation. This so-called "Washington consensus" enormously benefited major corporations and their investors, but as Joseph Stiglitz observed, it had many negative side effects on the supposed bene-ficiaries in the developing world – fostering corruption, undermining local economies, exacerbating inequalities, and exposing weak economies to destabilizing financial shocks.[44] These policies also accelerated the destruc-tion of the environment and further undermined the livelihood of indigen-ous populations. China and India are sometimes cited as examples of rapid development through market liberalization, but their economic strategies selectively opened some markets but maintained protection for others. Recent studies suggest that the presumed benefits of trade liberalization for development have been overstated.[45] The UNDP report for 2005 stated that "the evidence to support the proposition that import liberalization is automatically good for growth is weak."[46] The supposed benefit of large-scale development assistance is also questionable. Former World Bank economist William Easterly calculated that rich countries spent $568 billion (in 2005 dollars) to end poverty in Africa between 1960 and 2003, while the number of poor people on the continent steadily increased, as did the number of armed conflicts.[47]

In the 1990s the rise of corporate globalization prompted a countervailing global justice movement to resist unjust trade and investment policies. The struggle against corporate globalization burst dramatically onto the world

[44] Joseph E. Stiglitz, *Globalization and its Discontents* (New York: W. W. Norton, 2002).

[45] Jackie Smith, "Economic Globalization and Strategic Peace Building" (paper prepared for the Joan B. Kroc Institute Conference on Strategic Peacebuilding, University of Notre Dame, 6–7 November 2006).

[46] UNDP, *Human Development Report 2005: International Cooperation at a Crossroads* (New York: United Nations Development Programme, 2005), 119.

[47] William Easterly, "Tone Deaf on Africa," *New York Times*, 3 July 2005; cited in Robin Broad and John Cavanagh, "The Hijacking of the Development Debate: How Friedman and Sachs Got it Wrong," *World Policy Journal* 23, no. 2 (summer 2006): 25.

political stage with major protests and urban lockdowns in Seattle in November 1999 and in Washington, Prague, Quebec, Genoa, and other cities in the following years. The "alter-globalization" movement, as some have called it, urged fair and balanced trade and environmentally sustainable and culturally sensitive forms of economic development. "Fair trade, not just free trade," said John Sweeney, head of the American Federation of Labor–Congress of Industrial Organizations, at the Seattle protests.

The global justice movement advocated a new form of development incorporating broader measures of well-being for individuals and communities, including greater social and economic equality, human rights, and opportunities for political participation. They demanded unconditional debt relief for developing countries. They emphasized the principle of subsidiarity and the need for community-based development and small-scale micro-credit programs (such as those that won the Nobel Peace Prize for Mohammad Yunus and Grameen Bank in 2006). Also on the alter-development agenda were reforms in governance, especially greater accountability in the security sector, and the redirection of government resources from military to civilian priorities.

The global justice movement served as an important base of support for the worldwide campaign against war in Iraq. Many of those who campaigned against corporate domination were shocked and outraged by the US-led military campaign against Iraq. They quickly drew connections between the US-led war and Western-oriented globalization, recognizing as one activist leader put it that "militarization is just the other arm of the corporate agenda."[48] Many activists suspected, as events later proved, that a US takeover of Baghdad would lead to corporate profiteering and the attempted privatization of Iraq's economy. The war was seen as a blatant attempt to control Iraq's oil reserves. As Michael Klare argued, oil was not the only factor motivating the US invasion, but guaranteeing US and Western access to the region's petroleum wealth was and still is a strategic objective of US national policy.[49] Corporate interests and petroleum dependency are major factors driving US militarization. The global justice and antiwar movements thus have common ground in opposing the US military and corporate agenda in the Middle East and Gulf region.

The challenge of promoting social justice and economic development as a strategy for peace has proven to be enormously complex and controversial.

[48] Leslie Cagan, interview by the author, 26 August 2003.
[49] Michael T. Klare, *Blood and Oil: The Dangers and Consequences of America's Growing Petroleum Dependency* (New York: Metropolitan Books, 2004), 98–102.

Socialists were the first to advance economic development and equality as a path to peace, but the strategies for development most recently adopted by political leaders have followed the principles of free trade liberalism. The meager economic results and often harmful social consequences of the dominant aid and trade strategies have prompted a new debate about globalization and the principles of achieving economic development. The debate is raising anew old questions about the nature of capitalism. The presumed consensus in favor of privatization and market liberalization has been challenged by a growing global justice movement and by renewed demands for greater economic and political equality. This debate is framed primarily in terms of economic and social development, but it has direct bearing on the challenge of preventing war. Its outcome may well determine the long-term prospects for peace.

13

Responsibility to protect

Peace movements sometimes fail to address the plight of those suffering repression and dictatorship. During the cold war human rights campaigners in the East were often skeptical and even resentful of Western peace movements for overlooking the brutal realities of Soviet totalitarianism. Without guarantees of political freedom, they argued, peace is impossible. For many in the East the very word peace was tainted. The Kremlin's propagandistic manipulation of the term and its creation of communist front peace councils gave the word a foul connotation. The concept came to mean not the peace of a free people, but the enforced order of a police state, the peace of the grave. When Václav Havel, the playwright and future Czech president, was invited by Western activists to attend an international disarmament conference in 1985, he declined. He explained his reticence by emphasizing that the danger of war was caused not by weapons, but by the underlying political tensions and mistrust that arose from the suppression of freedom:

Without internal peace . . . there can be no guarantee of external peace. A state that ignores the will and the rights of its citizens can offer no guarantee that it will respect the will and the rights of other peoples, nations, and states . . . respect for human rights is the fundamental condition and the sole, genuine guarantee of true peace.[1]

Peace and freedom are indivisible, Havel argued. "Lasting peace and disarmament can only be the work of free people."[2] The defense of human rights must be at the core of the peace movement's agenda.

Some activists in the West were reluctant to emphasize human rights abuse in the East for fear that this would reinforce the anticommunist

---

[1] Václav Havel, "Anatomy of a Reticence," in *Open Letters: Selected Writings, 1965–90*, ed. Paul Wilson, 291–322 (New York: Vintage Books, 1992), 314–15.
[2] Václav Havel, "Peace: The View from Prague," *New York Review of Books* 32, no. 18 (21 November 1985): 30.

ideology that fueled militarism in the West, and that gave impetus to the
nuclear weapons build-up. Peace advocates knew the grim history of communist rule and sympathized with the human rights cause in Poland,
Czechoslovakia, and other countries, but they did not believe that the
West's military and nuclear strategies were an appropriate means of advancing freedom. Many viewed NATO as an instrument of US military
hegemony and nuclear brinksmanship rather than an alliance to defend
democracy. They were skeptical of the West's claims to be a bastion of
freedom, pointing to pervasive racial inequality within the USA, and
Washington's embrace of authoritarian regimes around the world in the
name of anticommunism. They condemned and opposed wars of intervention that denied the right of self-determination in Algeria, Vietnam, and
beyond. Activists found it hard to believe the claim of Western nations to be
defending freedom. Peace advocates were even more skeptical in 2003 when
the Bush administration attempted to justify the war in Iraq as a struggle
for democracy. Many acknowledged the brutality of Saddam Hussein's
"Republic of Fear," as Kanan Makiya labeled it, but they insisted that
armed regime change and military occupation were not the way to promote
democracy and human rights.

In this chapter I explore these and other aspects of the debate about peace
and freedom. I review efforts at the end of the cold war to bridge the East–
West divide on human rights. Examining the Iraq war debate, I critique
both the Bush administration's claim of a humanitarian case for war and the
peace movement's failure to give greater attention to human rights concerns. A different kind of human rights challenge emerged in the wake of
genocidal killings and human rights violations in Bosnia, Rwanda, Kosovo,
and Darfur. In these crises peace advocates found themselves caught
between the choice of pacifist inaction and the responsibility to protect.
When the victims of tyranny and abuse cry out for help, at times urging
military intervention to overthrow a tormenting dictatorship or stop genocide, how should peace advocates respond? Is it morally defensible to stand
aside when innocent populations are murdered wantonly and a minimum
application of force could stop the killing? Out of this debate emerged a new
emphasis on the protection of civilians and a new realization of the links
between peace and the defense of human rights and freedom.

BRIDGING THE COLD WAR DIVIDE

During the cold war citizens were free to demonstrate against war and
nuclear weapons in London and New York but not in Warsaw and

Moscow. This perverse disparity was sometimes used against Western peace movements, as if the suppression of free speech in the East made the exercise of that right in the West less worthy. A few Western pacifists attempted to speak out against nuclear weapons in the Soviet Union. One attempt was the 1961 San Francisco to Moscow Walk for Peace, in which thirty-one US marchers sponsored by the Committee for Nonviolent Action (CNVA) entered the Soviet Union (with Moscow's approval). They held demonstrations at two Soviet military installations and addressed large Soviet audiences as part of their protest against nuclear weapons.[3] These were isolated and ineffectual efforts, however, which had little influence in either East or West. For the people of the East the hope for peace was secondary to the struggle for freedom. Courageous activists in Poland, Czechoslovakia, and other Eastern countries attempted to organize for justice and democracy, only to face repression at home and silence from abroad. The two movements – peace in the West, human rights in the East – spoke past one another and failed to connect.

The divide between peace and human rights began to narrow in the 1970s and 1980s. The period of détente and West German *Ostpolitik* that followed the signing of the SALT in 1972 created new political openings in Europe. The conclusion of the Helsinki Accords in 1975 was an important turning point in East–West relations. It froze existing political realities in the center of Europe, but it also enshrined principles of human rights throughout the continent. It extended to the East at least theoretically the Western claim of an inalienable right to freedom and democracy. The European diplomats who forged the agreement hoped that Soviet acceptance of these principles would pave the way for a gradual normalization of relations and a reduction of cold war tensions. It was in the aftermath of this historic agreement that Havel and other activists in Czechoslovakia sought to test the limits of the supposed new freedoms. In January 1977 they launched the Charter 77 campaign, petitioning communist officials for political rights, only to be met with repression and jailings. The stirrings for freedom continued to spread, however. The rise of Solidarity in Poland and peace and human rights movements in East Germany and beyond were signs of a new political wind beginning to blow through the ossified political structures of "real existing socialism."

In the West as well new political trends were developing. The nuclear freeze campaign in the USA and the nuclear disarmament movements

---

[3] Lawrence S. Wittner, *Resisting the Bomb: A History of the World Nuclear Disarmament Movement, 1954–1970*, vol. II of *The Struggle against the Bomb* (Stanford, CA: Stanford University Press, 1997), 285–6.

of western Europe directed their political demands to Moscow as well as Washington, flatly rejecting any Soviet pretense of peaceful intentions. Western activists also began to pay attention to the freedom movements in the East. Activists in Britain, the USA, West Germany, and other countries took the lead in opening channels of communication and mutual support. Mary Kaldor and other scholar/activists in Britain began to reach out to human rights activists in the East. The Green Party in West Germany and the Campaign for Peace and Democracy in the United States also participated in these efforts to build bridges between East and West. This unofficial dialogue was a modest attempt to erode the cold war ideological divide and encourage democratization. Kaldor called the process "détente from below" and credited it with strengthening the disarmament movement. "It established the integrity of large parts of the peace movement. It made it impossible to marginalize the peace movement, as had been done in the past, with the charge that peace advocates were agents of the Kremlin."[4]

One of the key groups in this East–West interaction was European Nuclear Disarmament (END), in which Kaldor played an important role. Founded by the eminent British historian, E. P. Thompson, END condemned the entire cold war system of competing blocs. Thompson and his colleagues met with and expressed public support for leading dissidents in Poland, East Germany, and Czechoslovakia. The END program called for greater human rights and freedom in the East, and more peaceful policies in the West. Democracy and disarmament were inextricably linked and must be achieved together, they asserted. Both were necessary for genuine peace. The philosophy of END was thus fully in accord with the views of many dissidents in the East. While Havel kept his distance from Western peace activists, others in the East were directly involved. Jiri Dienstbier, who later became the first foreign minister of post-Soviet Czechoslovakia, cooperated with Thompson in co-editing a volume of essays on the politics of peace. Jacek Kuron, who became minister of labor in the first Solidarity government of Poland, shared the platform with Thompson at the END convention in 1988.

Kaldor wrote that these cooperative efforts "helped to encourage and provide support for new peace and human rights groups that emerged during the 1980s all over Eastern Europe, groups that played a key role in the revolutions of 1989." By insisting upon the linkage between peace and human rights, and mounting campaigns criticizing both Soviet and Western military policies, Western peace movements encouraged the

---

[4] Mary Kaldor, "Taking the Democratic Way," *The Nation* 252, no. 15 (22 April 1991): 518.

process of political realignment that broke the grip of the cold war. The disarmament movements of the West and the human rights movements of the East reinforced one another. At the beginning of the decade millions of people marched in the West to oppose the deployment of new nuclear weapons and the further militarization of the European continent. At the end of the decade, equal numbers marched for freedom in Poland, East Germany, Czechoslovakia, and other east European countries, mounting a "velvet revolution" that brought down decades of communist dictatorship. Together the two movements changed the course of history. Again Kaldor:

The cold war was ended by a wave of popular movements in the East and West that ... discredited the cold war idea. It was the Eastern European democracy movements, not Western governments, that brought about the final collapse of Communism. And it was the Western European peace movements that first challenged the status quo in Europe.[5]

The linkage of peace and freedom proved to be of decisive importance in ending the militarized stand-off in Europe.

WAR FOR DEMOCRACY?

The US and British governments claimed in 2003 and afterwards that the invasion of Iraq was a justifiable act to free the Iraqi people from the tyranny of Saddam Hussein and to spread freedom and democracy in the region. The US military dubbed its invasion Operation Iraqi Freedom. This emphasis on freedom was largely an *ex post facto* justification, which rose to the fore only after prior explanations for war proved groundless. Claims about weapons of mass destruction and a supposed link to Al Qaida were proven false, and were challenged by independent analysts prior to the invasion.[6] When the postwar search for prohibited weapons came up empty

---

[5] *Ibid.*, 518.
[6] Among the many articles and reports disputing the stated case for war were Joseph Cirincione *et al.*, *WMD in Iraq: Evidence and Implications* (Washington, DC: Carnegie Endowment for International Peace, January 2004). Available online at the Carnegie Endowment for International Peace, www. carnegieendowment.org/publications/index.cfm?fa=view&id=1435 (accessed 19 June 2007); David Cortright and George A. Lopez, "Disarming Iraq: Nonmilitary Strategies and Options," *Arms Control Today* 32, no. 7 (September 2002): 3–7; and David Cortright, Alistair Millar, and George A. Lopez, *Sanctions, Inspections, and Containment: Viable Policy Options in Iraq*, Policy Brief F3 (Goshen, IN: Fourth Freedom Forum, June 2002). Available online at the Fourth Freedom Forum, www. fourthfreedom.org/Applications/cms.php?page_id=14 (accessed 19 June 2007). See also the following joint policy reports of the Fourth Freedom Forum and the Joan B. Kroc Institute for International Peace Studies at the University of Notre Dame, all available online at the Fourth Freedom Forum, www.fourthfreedom.org: *Winning Without War: Sensible Security Options for Dealing With Iraq*,

handed,[7] the Bush and Blair governments focused increasingly on the claimed benefit of promoting Iraqi democracy and freedom. A White House statement in December 2005 asserted that "the Iraqi people have built momentum for freedom and democracy" and their example "will inspire reformers across the Middle East."[8]

It would be easy to dismiss such claims because of their obvious political motivation, but it is important to address them because of the precedent Washington and London established and the prospect that similar justifications for war will be offered in the future. The case presented was an argument for humanitarian intervention. Because of the brutality and tyranny of Saddam Hussein's rule, defenders of the war claimed, the freedom and human rights of the Iraqi people could be secured only through armed regime change. The Iraqi people had suffered grievously under the dictator and had to be saved by military intervention. These arguments had a surface appeal. Many Iraqis, especially Shia in the south and Kurds in the north, were murdered and cruelly oppressed by the Baathist regime. Kurds generally welcomed the invasion and referred to the US takeover not as occupation but as liberation. No one doubted that Iraq would be better off without the dictatorial rule of Saddam Hussein. The existence of a tyrannical government is not in itself a *casus belli*, however. To justify military action it is also necessary to demonstrate that the regime in question poses an imminent and grave threat of mass slaughter. In the case of Saddam Hussein's Iraq in 2003, this was not the case.

Human Rights Watch addressed these questions in its 2004 annual report. Unusually among human rights groups, Human Rights Watch has a policy of supporting the use of force when it is imperative to stop genocide or other systematic slaughter. In a lead essay for the 2004 report executive director Ken Roth acknowledged the legitimacy of the concern for freedom and democracy in Iraq but rejected the human rights argument for war. Humanitarian intervention is permissible only in situations that

Policy Brief F5 (Goshen, IN: Fourth Freedom Forum, October 2002; *The Progress of UN Disarmament in Iraq: An Assessment Report*, Policy Brief F7 (Goshen, IN: Fourth Freedom Forum, January 2003); *Contested Case: Do the Facts Justify the Case for War in Iraq?*, Policy Brief F8 (Goshen, IN: Fourth Freedom Forum, February 2003); and *Grading Iraqi Compliance*, Policy Brief F10 (Goshen, IN: Fourth Freedom Forum, March 2003).

[7] See the reports of the Iraq Survey Group, which involved more than 1,400 investigators and cost more than $100 million per month. Iraq Survey Group, *Comprehensive Report of the Special Advisor to the DCI on Iraq's WMD* (30 September 2004). Available online at the Central Intelligence Agency, www.cia.gov/library/reports/general-reports-1/iraq_wmd_2004/index.html (accessed 19 June 2007).

[8] The White House, President George W. Bush, "Fact Sheet: Democracy in Iraq," 12 December 2005. Available online at The White House, www.whitehouse.gov/news/releases/2005/12/20051212-1.html (accessed 19 June 2007).

involve mass killing. A serious case for humanitarian intervention on behalf of the Iraqi people could have been and was made by some human rights advocates when the regime's infamous Anfal campaign in the late 1980s left more than 100,000 Iraqi Kurds dead from the use of chemical weapons, mass executions, and systematic ethnic cleansing.[9] A legitimate case for intervention, or at least for support of Iraqi rebellion, also existed in 1991, when Shiite and Kurdish populations revolted against the Baghdad regime at the end of the Gulf War, partly in response to the urging of the first President Bush. In 2002–3, however, there was no evidence of mass killing or wholesale ethnic cleansing. Saddam Hussein's government was indeed a totalitarian dictatorship, but in the years preceding the US invasion it did not engage in mass repression against its own citizens. Nor did it commit or threaten aggression against its neighbors. There was no large-scale, imminent threat of violence or genocidal action by the government against its citizens or neighboring countries that would have been sufficient to justify the drastic action of unprovoked military intervention.

The promotion of democracy is an appropriate strategy for building the long-term foundations of peace, but it does not justify war and military invasion. There is no accepted political or ethical principle that allows for armed intervention to change the form of government of another state. International law does not authorize military action to make a country more democratic or representative. Invading another country without provocation is an act of aggression and is a clear violation of international law. "Any use of force or imminent threat of force by one state against the political sovereignty or territorial integrity of another," wrote Michael Walzer, "constitutes aggression and is a criminal act."[10] The UN Charter grants the right of self-defense but expressly forbids the use of military force against other nations without the explicit approval of the Security Council. The Bush and Blair governments attempted to skirt these principles by claiming that Iraq was in material breach of Security Council resolutions dating from 1991, which had authorized "all necessary means" to enforce disarmament and compliance with UN mandates. When this issue was presented to the council by the USA and Britain in February and March 2003, however, the majority on the Council rejected the proposal to take enforcement action.

[9] Human Rights Watch, *World Report 2004: Human Rights and Armed Conflict* (New York: Human Rights Watch, 2004), 18, 21.

[10] Michael Walzer, *Just and Unjust Wars: A Moral Argument with Historical Illustrations* (New York: Basic Books, 1992), 62.

The question of agency also enters into this debate. By what right did the United States presume to exercise jurisdiction over Iraqi affairs? The responsibility for assuring compliance with UN mandates belonged to the Security Council, not the United States or any individual nation. The United States itself had fully supported and in some cases written the resolutions giving this authority to the United Nations, beginning in 1990 and continuing right up to the months before the invasion. Critics in the peace movement also questioned how the USA could claim to be concerned with protecting the Iraqi people when it had imposed draconian economic sanctions that caused massive civilian suffering and hundreds of thousands of preventable deaths during the 1990s.[11]

OPPOSING WAR, ADVANCING FREEDOM

The hypocrisy of governments on the question of human rights does not obviate the responsibility of antiwar movements to support democracy and freedom as essential elements of peace. This is a matter of both principle and political tactics. Peace movements are more credible when they address the human rights abuses of oppressive regimes. The challenge is to oppose unprovoked military intervention while simultaneously condemning repression and supporting indigenous efforts to create democratic alternatives. In 2003 Jim Wallis urged opponents of war to take a tough stance against the crimes of Saddam Hussein. It was not enough simply to point to US and British complicity in previously supporting the Iraqi dictator. Peace advocates needed to take a clear and unequivocal stand against tyranny. To address this concern, Wallis and other religious leaders published a six-point plan as an alternative to war in all the major British daily newspapers on the eve of the parliamentary debate authorizing war. The six-point plan expressed support for the goal of a democratic Iraq, and it urged the indictment of Saddam Hussein for crimes against humanity. A war crimes indictment, the statement read, would further isolate the Iraqi dictator and could set in motion internal and external forces that might remove him from power and foster Iraqi democracy. Wallis and his colleagues were in

---

[11] For scientific assessments of the rise in preventable deaths in Iraq during the 1990s, see Richard Garfield, *Morbidity and Mortality among Iraqi Children from 1990 to 1998: Assessing the Impact of Economic Sanctions*, Occasional Paper Series 16:OP:3 (Goshen, IN: Joan B. Kroc Institute for International Peace Studies at the University of Notre Dame and the Fourth Freedom Forum, March 1999), available online at the Fourth Freedom Forum, www.fourthfreedom.org (accessed 19 June 2007); and Mohamed M. Ali and Iqbal H. Shah, "Sanctions and Childhood Mortality in Iraq," *The Lancet* 355 (May 2000): 1851–7.

effect agreeing with the need for regime change in Baghdad, while preserving UN jurisdiction and remaining true to their nonviolent witness in opposing a unilateral US military invasion. They argued that legal, multilateral, nonmilitary means were available for countering Saddam Hussein.

Supporting the goal of Iraqi freedom prior to the war might have prepared the antiwar movement better for addressing the challenges of the postwar occupation, when the need to protect Iraqi freedom became a justification for maintaining the presence of foreign troops. In the USA many who had opposed the initial invasion found themselves uncertain about how to end the occupation. The Bush administration never should have invaded Iraq, many agreed, but once the deed was done, the USA had a responsibility under international law to provide security and humanitarian assistance for the Iraqi population. To withdraw US military forces precipitously, many cautioned, could cause even greater chaos and violence. Others argued that the US occupation was the principal cause of the insurgency and violence, and that the Iraqis could not be genuinely free under the boot of foreign occupation. The best way to help Iraq, they argued, was to develop a responsible US exit strategy, one which combined the withdrawal of US military forces with increased international support for Iraqi sovereignty and stability. The question of Iraqi freedom, and how best to achieve it in the aftermath of war and occupation, thus came back to haunt peace advocates, as it did the US and British governments.

HUMAN RIGHTS AND SECURITY

Within the peace movement a kind of implicit pacifism exists. It is assumed by many peace activists that the use of military force is never justified, that conflict resolution techniques and nonviolent methods are sufficient to prevent armed violence. Some hold these beliefs absolutely, others only to a degree, but among all there is a strong presumption against the use of force, as also exists in ethical doctrine. These beliefs reflect strong moral and religious objections to war. They are a reaction to the unjust and illegal wars of intervention which peace activists have opposed in Vietnam, central America, and Iraq. They are a proper caution against the policies of bellicose nations that seek to disguise military aggression behind the rhetoric of support for democracy or humanitarian intervention. But what about genuine humanitarian crises such as in Bosnia, Rwanda, and Darfur, where civilian populations have faced genocide and extreme human rights abuse? What happens when nonmilitary preventive measures fail to stop the outbreak of mass murder? Is there a moral right and political obligation under such circumstances to intervene militarily to protect the innocent?

The concern about these issues reflects the growing importance of human rights, and the broader concept of human security, in the contemporary debate about war and peace. The term "human security" has evolved in recent decades in response to dissatisfaction with the traditional realist security paradigm, which focuses on the role of the state and has little to say about the rise of intrastate conflict. As "new wars" of civil and ethnic violence replaced industrialized warfare between states, narrow concepts of national security became less relevant. The roots of the human security concept can be traced back to the 1982 *Common Security* report of the Palme Commission and other earlier studies of development, global governance, and human rights. Pioneering work during the 1990s by Mahbub ul Haq, economist at the UNDP, and Lloyd Axworthy, the foreign minister of Canada, reexamined the security paradigm to ask the questions "security for whom?" and "security from what threats, and by what means?" Axworthy and other advocates of the new paradigm urged a greater focus on the defense of individuals and communities. They called for broadening the concept of security to include not only protection from state aggression but guarantees of human rights and defenses against civil conflict, economic privation, and preventable disease. They urged the use of cooperative methods and the recognition of development and human rights as fundamental ingredients of security.[12] Many advocates of social justice embraced the human security concept and integrated it into their proposals for more holistic economic development strategies.

The concept of human rights has a long heritage in human history dating back at least to ancient Mesopotamia and the Code of Hammurabi and encompassing the Magna Carta, the American and French revolutions and countless other expressions of the fundamental right of people to political and civil liberties. Movements against slavery, for worker rights, to protect indigenous people, to gain voting rights for women and racial minorities – all can be counted broadly as human rights struggles. Guarantees of human freedom were incorporated into the UN Charter and the Universal Declaration of Human Rights in 1948. Amnesty International evolved in the 1960s as the first major human rights organization. Andrei Sakharov and others formed the Moscow Human Rights Committee in 1970, for which he received the Nobel Peace Prize. Helsinki Watch was born in 1978 and later merged with other watch groups to form Human Rights Watch. These

---

[12] Lloyd Axworthy, *Navigating a New World: Canada's Global Future* (Toronto: Vintage Canada, 2004).

were but a few of the many manifestations of a deeply rooted and steadily expanding commitment of people throughout the world to the defense of human rights and freedom. The gradual emergence of universal principles of human rights and the accompanying worldwide movement to advocate and protect such rights have had a major influence in shaping thinking about the permissible behavior of states. The result is a new sense of global responsibility to protect those who are victimized by human rights abuse. Despotic rulers who cause massive suffering to their own citizens can no longer hide behind the mask of absolute sovereignty. A new norm of human rights accountability has emerged to protect the victims of abuse and guarantee fundamental freedoms. This growing recognition of the primacy of human rights is embodied in the principle of human security.

Numerous advances have been achieved in establishing human rights and humanitarian law – UN conventions and covenants on the rights of women and children, and for the protection of civil, political, socio-economic, and cultural rights; national laws in many countries prohibiting human rights abuse; the various UN tribunals dealing with crimes against humanity; and the creation of a permanent International Criminal Court. The UN Convention on the Prevention and Punishment of the Crime of Genocide defined genocide as a crime against humanity, even if committed in peacetime, and created a presumption in favor of Security Council action to protect the victims of such crimes. These and other advances in international law strengthened the foundation for defending human rights.

DEBATING KOSOVO

In May 1999 nearly 10,000 peace advocates from around the world gathered in Holland for the Hague Appeal for Peace, one of the largest citizen peace conferences in history. Convened a hundred years after the Hague Peace Conference organized by Tsar Nicholas II of Russia, the 1999 Hague Appeal was intended to launch a new era of citizen-initiated peacemaking. As preparations for the conference took place, however, NATO forces launched a bombing campaign against Serbia to force its withdrawal from Kosovo. While the official conference proceedings unfolded in the main auditorium of the Hague convention center, hundreds of activists gathered in basement conference rooms for impromptu sessions to debate the pros and cons of NATO intervention. It was a heated discussion in which colleagues who had worked together for disarmament in the 1980s found themselves on opposite sides of the question of intervention in Kosovo. Some activists expressed sympathy for the plight of the Kosovar people and defended the right of humanitarian intervention to provide protection from Serbian oppression. Others granted the principle of intervention to protect the innocent, but questioned the legitimacy and legality of the NATO military action and demanded more rigorous legal and moral standards to guide such intervention in the future. The debate was a defining moment for many activists, and it sparked an intensive discussion within peace and human rights communities on the principles and standards of humanitarian intervention.

For nearly a decade in the 1990s the Kosovar liberation movement had been led by Ibrahim Rugova on a nonviolent basis, in a classic illustration of the power of boycotts and the creation of alternative institutions to undermine the political legitimacy of repressive authority.[13] The Kosovar nonviolence movement failed to attract external support, however, and in 1997 gave way to armed resistance led by the Kosovo Liberation Army (KLA). As the Milosevic regime intensified its repression in response to armed attacks, the United States and other NATO governments increased the pressure on the Belgrade regime and began to threaten military intervention. Following negotiations at Rambouillet, France in 1999, the United States and its NATO partners issued an ultimatum to the Belgrade government demanding among other things that NATO forces be given complete freedom to operate throughout Serbian territory. When the Belgrade government refused NATO began its bombing campaign and in June 1999 established a military protectorate over the Kosovo region.

The legitimacy of the NATO intervention was complicated by several factors. The military action was intended to save lives and prevent civilian suffering, but it prompted Serbian forces to intensify their attacks on civilians and led to a massive forced migration of approximately 1.4 million people, some two-thirds of the Kosovar population. In the year before the NATO operation approximately 1,000 civilians were killed in Kosovo, but during the two-and-half-month war an estimated 10,000 died, including 500 Serbian civilians killed in the NATO bombing.[14] The intervention lacked authorization from the UN Security Council. The majority of Council members were willing to authorize the use of force, but Russia blocked Security Council action. Critics questioned the legitimacy of a NATO military intervention conducted outside the alliance's defined

---

[13] See the detailed study by Howard Clark, *Civil Resistance in Kosovo* (Sterling, VA: Pluto Press, 2000).

[14] Independent International Commission on Kosovo, *The Kosovo Report: Conflict, International Response, Lessons Learned* (Oxford: Oxford University Press, 2000), 1–2. Citations are taken from the online version, available at Relief Web, www.reliefweb.int/library/documents/thekosovoreport. htm (accessed 19 June 2007).

region. Alternative means of addressing the crisis were not given a chance to work, some contended. The October 1998 Holbrooke–Milosevic agreement led to the partial withdrawal of Serbian forces and the introduction of more than a thousand unarmed international monitors. For a brief time this helped to reduce the level of violence. When fighting intensified again, however, the monitors were withdrawn. KLA units launched military attacks and took up positions vacated by Serbian forces, a development which UN Secretary-General Kofi Annan called "disturbing."[15] The conditions on the ground in Kosovo were complex and ambiguous. For many they lacked the degree of moral clarity that is required before the resort to military force can be justified.

Following the war an independent commission on Kosovo was convened at the initiative of Swedish Prime Minister Göran Persson to assess the moral and legal implications of the NATO intervention. The commission's report, released in October 2000, concluded that the NATO action was legitimate and morally justified. The report did not shy away from the ambiguities of the Kosovo experience, however. The NATO bombing campaign was both a success and a failure, the commission argued. NATO action forced the Serbian army to withdraw, but it did not prevent further ethnic cleansing and repression. The commission concluded that the NATO intervention was "illegal because it did not receive prior approval from the UN Security Council." The intervention was nonetheless justified, in its view, because diplomatic avenues were exhausted and "the intervention had the effect of liberating the majority population of Kosovo from a long period of oppression under Serbian rule." The commission found a troubling "gap between legality and legitimacy" in circumstances of humanitarian intervention.[16] It called for the creation of a new political framework that would make future humanitarian interventions both legal and legitimate.

The Kosovo commission defined three "threshold principles" to guide any consideration of the use of force to protect the innocent. Intervention should occur only in instances of significant civilian suffering caused by severe human rights violations or the breakdown of government authority. The goal of intervention should be limited to the protection of civilians, and military action must have a reasonable chance of ending the humanitarian catastrophe. The commission also outlined a series of contextual principles for judging whether a particular use of force was justifiable. It recommended further efforts to refine international principles for the protection of

---

[15] *Ibid.*, 20.   [16] *Ibid.*, 2, 3, 36.

civilians in humanitarian emergencies. "The time is now ripe," the report argued, "for the presentation of a principled framework for humanitarian intervention."[17]

THE RESPONSIBILITY TO PROTECT

The Kosovo report led directly to the creation of the International Commission on Intervention and State Sovereignty, which became known as the Responsibility to Protect (R2P) commission, after the title of its report, which was released in December 2001. The commission addressed the failure of the international community to protect civilians not only in Kosovo but in Somalia, Rwanda, Bosnia, Sudan, and other humanitarian crises. In 1999 and 2000 UN Secretary-General Kofi Annan challenged world leaders to develop principles for addressing such tragedies. The international community must develop means, he pleaded, for responding to "gross and systematic violations of human rights that affect every precept of our common humanity."[18] In many of these settings the modest application of military force could save many lives. A few months after the 1994 genocide in Rwanda, the commander of UN peacekeeping forces there, Canadian Major General Roméo Dallaire, stated: "I came to the United Nations from commanding a mechanized brigade group of 5,000 soldiers. If I had had that brigade group in Rwanda, there would be hundreds of thousands of lives spared today."[19] Developing legally acceptable principles for the limited use of force to save innocent lives is an urgent moral and political priority, government leaders and civil society activists alike agreed. The government of Canada responded to this challenge by agreeing to fund the commission, selecting as its co-chairs former Australian Foreign Minister Gareth Evans and former Algerian ambassador and special UN adviser Mohamed Sahnoun. The new commission was launched by Canadian Foreign Minister Lloyd Axworthy at the UN Millennium Assembly in September 2000.

The R2P commission touched a sensitive nerve in international politics and attracted widespread attention and support. Unlike other commission reports, which often fall on deaf ears, the R2P study created an immediate

---

[17] *Ibid.*, 3.
[18] Quoted in International Commission on Intervention and State Sovereignty, *The Responsibility to Protect* (Ottawa: International Development Research Centre, December 2001), vii.
[19] See Scott R. Feil, *Could 5,000 Peacekeepers Have Saved 500,000 Rwandans? Early Intervention Reconsidered*, ISD Report (Georgetown University, School of Foreign Service, Institute for the Study of Diplomacy) III, no. 2 (April 1997).

sensation. It did so in large part because it introduced a new way of conceptualizing the question of humanitarian intervention. The previous emphasis on "intervention" generated concern and opposition from peace advocates who opposed military interventions such as Vietnam that were sometimes falsely justified on humanitarian grounds. The prospect of additional military intervention also raised the hackles of postcolonial states, which were understandably suspicious of proposals from Western states to intervene in the affairs of other nations. The new phrase "responsibility to protect" helped to reframe the debate. The issue was no longer intervention but protection. The emphasis shifted from a discussion about abstract principles of state sovereignty to an assessment of concrete ways to protect suffering civilians.

The R2P report provided a rigorous set of principles for determining when and how military intervention would be appropriate to defend innocent life and prevent humanitarian disaster. The commission acknowledged the importance of the principle of state sovereignty, forged at the Treaty of Westphalia in 1648, as an essential protection against the threat of external attack. It recognized that the UN Charter guaranteed the sovereign equality of states and established a code of nonintervention. A sovereign state is entitled to exercise exclusive jurisdiction within its borders, and other states have a corresponding duty to refrain from interfering in the internal affairs of that state. The principle of sovereignty does not allow a state to do whatever it wants to its own people, however. According to the commission, sovereignty implies a dual responsibility: externally to respect the sovereignty of other states, and internally to respect the dignity and basic rights of its own citizens. "In international human rights covenants, in UN practice, and in state practice itself, sovereignty is now understood as embracing this dual responsibility."[20] When this internal responsibility is neglected, the principle of nonintervention yields to the responsibility to protect.

The protections provided by state sovereignty can be superseded only in the most exceptional and extraordinary circumstances, according to the commission. The exceptional circumstances are cases of violence which genuinely "shock the conscience" or pose a clear and present danger to international security – when serious and irreparable harm is occurring or is imminent, and the state in question is unable or unwilling to end the harm, or is itself the perpetrator. The commission defined the "just cause threshold" as actual or anticipated harm involving large-scale loss of life caused by

---

[20] International Commission, *The Responsibility to Protect*, 8, para. 1.35.

deliberate state action or neglect; and large-scale ethnic cleansing caused by killings, forced expulsion, acts of terror, or rape.[21] Only when there is serious and irreparable harm to large numbers of people is humanitarian military intervention justified.

The question of right authority – who can authorize a military intervention – was considered of such critical importance that the commission devoted an entire chapter to the subject. Under Article 24 of the UN Charter the responsibility for maintaining international security and peace rests squarely with the UN Security Council. Chapter VII of the charter permits the Council to employ coercive measures and even the use of military force to address threats to the peace. "There is no better or more appropriate body than the United Nations Security Council to authorize military intervention for human protection purposes," said the commission.[22] The legitimacy of the Security Council is weakened, however, by the veto power of the permanent five and the Council's narrow representation, which has excluded major countries in Africa, Asia, and Latin America from permanent membership. The Council is unable to act when permanent members invoke their veto power to block interventions that others see as legitimate, as was the case in Kosovo. Until the Security Council is reformed and its composition broadened to more accurately represent the world community, its credibility and authority on controversial matters of humanitarian intervention will be constrained.

If the Security Council fails to act, alternative options are available, according to the commission. One option is to seek UN General Assembly authorization in an emergency special session under the "Uniting for Peace" procedures developed in 1950 to address the Korean War crisis. Another option would be for a regional or subregional organization to take collective action within its region, provided that organization seeks subsequent authorization from the Security Council. The ultimate responsibility to use force for humanitarian protection rests with the Security Council, however. The unwillingness of states to work through the Council weakens the overall stature and credibility of the UN, the commission observed, and makes it easier for major states to intervene unilaterally, often for self-interested rather than humanitarian purposes.

The recommendations of the R2P commission were echoed in the December 2004 report of the Secretary-General's High-level Panel on Threats, Challenges and Change.

[21] *Ibid.*, xii.   [22] *Ibid.*

The issue is not the 'right to intervene' of any State but the 'responsibility to protect' of *every* State when it comes to people suffering from avoidable catastrophe – mass murder and rape, ethnic cleansing by forcible expulsion and terror, and deliberate starvation and exposure to disease.

If sovereign governments fail to protect their citizens from avoidable disasters, or if they cause such disasters, other nations have the responsibility to step in and provide protection. The panel endorsed the emerging norm of

collective international responsibility to protect, exercisable by the Security Council authorizing military intervention as a last resort, in the event of genocide and other large-scale killing, ethnic cleansing or serious violations of international humanitarian law which sovereign Governments have proved powerless or unwilling to prevent.[23]

The primary emphasis should be avoiding violence through diplomatic efforts, peace missions, and policing, the panel argued, but when preventive efforts fail force should be used as the last resort to protect the innocent.

At the UN World Summit in September 2005 international leaders formally endorsed the R2P doctrine. They declared that the international community, acting through the Security Council, is "prepared to take collective action, in a timely and decisive manner" when states "manifestly fail to protect their populations from genocide, war crimes, ethnic cleansing and crimes against humanity."[24] This development was welcomed by human rights and peace groups as one of the most significant achievements of the summit. For the first time in history world leaders pledged to protect civilian populations threatened by genocide or similar large-scale atrocities. In February 2006 the World Council of Churches (WCC), meeting in Porto Alegre, Brazil, issued a statement declaring "support of the emerging international norm of the responsibility to protect." The WCC statement noted "the essential role of preventive efforts" but declared that "protection becomes necessary when prevention has failed." The WCC statement explicitly addressed the pacifist presumption against the use of force:

The fellowship of churches is not prepared to say that it is never appropriate or never necessary to resort to the use of force for the protection of the vulnerable. This refusal in principle to preclude the use of force is not based on a naïve belief that force can be relied on to solve intractable problems. Rather, it is based on the

---

[23] United Nations General Assembly, *A More Secure World: Our Shared Responsibility, Report of the High-level Panel on Threats, Challenges and Change*, A/59/565, New York, 29 November 2004, paras. 201 and 203.

[24] United Nations General Assembly, *World Summit Outcome*, A/60/L.1, New York, 15 September 2005, para. 139.

certain knowledge that the objective must be the welfare of people, especially those in situations of extreme vulnerability and who are utterly abandoned to the whims and prerogatives of their tormentors. It is a tragic reality that civilians, especially women and children, are the primary victims in situations of extreme insecurity and war.[25]

In April 2006 the Security Council reiterated the international commitment to protect civilians by adopting resolution 1674, affirming the principles approved at the 2005 world summit and urging states to act on their behalf. Human rights and internationalist groups referred to the resolution and the world summit declaration to encourage states to take greater action to protect civilians victimized by genocide in Darfur.

PEACE OPERATIONS

Until recently UN peace operations were carried out under Chapter VI of the UN Charter and were limited to traditional blue helmet peacekeeping missions in which troops usually deploy in an impartial manner after a ceasefire and refrain from combat. Peacekeeping missions have been extremely valuable in numerous settings around the world (for which the United Nations received the Nobel Peace Prize in 1988), helping to monitor peace settlements, assure the delivery of humanitarian assistance, protect development and election workers, verify disarmament arrangements, and assist with post-conflict demobilization and military training. Since the early 1990s the UN Security Council has mounted dozens of peacekeeping operations. As of early 2007 there were approximately 80,000 uniformed peacekeepers deployed in sixteen missions.[26]

Notwithstanding their many achievements UN peacekeeping missions often have failed to keep the peace. This was most tragically illustrated in Rwanda, when UN peacekeepers withdrew during the height of the genocide, and at Srebrenica when they stood aside as thousands of Bosnians were massacred. In 2000 Secretary-General Kofi Annan convened a Panel on United Nations Peace Operations, chaired by former Algerian Foreign Minister Lakhdar Brahimi, which identified significant shortcomings in

---

[25] World Council of Churches, *Report from the Public Issues Committee of the World Council of Churches*, adopted at the 9th Assembly, February 2006, section 2, para. 12. Available online at the World Council of Churches, www.wcc-assembly.info/index.php?id=2152&MP=1507-1514 (accessed 19 June 2007).

[26] United Nations Peacekeeping, *United Nations Peacekeeping Operations Year in Review 2006*, 31 December 2006. Available online at United Nations Peacekeeping, www.un.org/Depts/dpko/dpko/pub/year_review06/PKmissions.pdf (accessed 19 June 2007).

traditional peacekeeping missions. The use of consent-based, impartial forces is not appropriate in every setting, the panel noted. This is especially true in situations where conflict has not been completely settled and the contending parties are still engaged in armed hostilities. As the Brahimi report argued, impartiality in the face of continuing abuses and violations of a peace agreement "can in the best case result in ineffectiveness and in the worst may amount to complicity with evil."[27] The traditional reluctance to distinguish victim from aggressor has failed to prevent genocide and has undermined the credibility of the United Nations. To overcome these problems the Brahimi report recommended that the United Nations establish more robust peace operations that could, where necessary, confront and defeat forces that continue to perpetrate mass violence and human rights abuse. These would be Chapter VII operations, which allow peacekeepers to use force not only for self-defense but to protect civilians and enforce a peace settlement. Examples of such operations include the NATO interventions in Bosnia and Kosovo, the Australian-led military operation in East Timor, and the military interventions by the Economic Community of West African States (ECOWAS) in Sierra Leone and Liberia.

The UN Charter gives the Security Council primary responsibility for preserving international peace and security, but Chapter VIII of the Charter also recognizes and encourages the peacemaking role of regional and sub-regional organizations. Regional organizations such as the African Union (AU) have played an increasingly important role in attempting to address security and humanitarian emergencies. African states have suffered most from civil conflict in recent decades, and they have been increasingly active in peacekeeping missions designed to protect civilians and prevent genocide. The AU and subregional organizations such as ECOWAS and the South African Development Community (SADC) have established programs for responding to civil violence, genocide, and ethnic cleansing. The Peace and Security Council of the AU has been legally empowered by its member states to implement the "responsibility to protect" doctrine, making the AU the first regional body to recognize explicitly the right to humanitarian intervention.[28] These African organizations suffer from

---

[27] United Nations General Assembly Security Council, *Report of the Panel on United Nations Peace Operations*, A/55/305-S/2000/809, New York, 21 August 2000, Executive Summary, ix.

[28] Centre for Conflict Resolution, "Building an African Union for the 21st Century: Relations with Regional Economic Communities (RECS), NEPAD and Civil Society," policy seminar report, Cape Town, South Africa (20–22 August 2005), 20. Available online at the Centre for Conflict Resolution, www.ccr.uct.ac.za/fileadmin/template/ccr/pdf/hivinvite/Policy06/BuildAU.pdf (accessed 19 June 2007). See also Kristiana Powell and Stephen Baranyi, "Delivering on the Responsibility to Protect

inadequate resources and institutional capacity, however, which has limited their contribution to the maintenance of peace.

If UN and regional peace operations are to involve the use of coercive force, issues of legitimacy and political authority become all the more important. Action to protect the innocent must be morally and politically legitimate, and fully compliant with international law. Like the Kosovo and R2P commissions, the Secretary-General's High-level Panel devoted considerable attention to these questions. It concluded that the Security Council, for all of its limitations, remained the sole legitimate international body to authorize the use of force to protect the peace. The panel suggested a series of guidelines to assist the Security Council in deciding when military force could be used. The panel's criteria for intervention closely paralleled those of the earlier commissions and fit well with the criteria of just war doctrine:

Seriousness of threat. Is the threatened harm to State or human security of a kind, and sufficiently clear and serious, to justify prima facie the use of military force? In the case of internal threats, does it involve genocide and other large-scale killing, ethnic cleansing or serious violations of international humanitarian law, actual or imminently apprehended?

Proper purpose. Is it clear that the primary purpose of the proposed military action is to halt or avert the threat in question, whatever other purposes or motives may be involved?

Last resort. Has every non-military option for meeting the threat in question been explored, with reasonable grounds for believing that other measures will not succeed?

Proportional means. Are the scale, duration and intensity of the proposed military action the minimum necessary to meet the threat in question?

Balance of consequences. Is there a reasonable chance of the military action being successful in meeting the threat in question, with the consequences of action not likely to be worse than the consequences of inaction?[29]

These principles provide a set of now widely accepted guidelines that allow for the strictly conditioned and limited use of force under legal auspices to achieve justice. They represent a major advance in bridging the gap between pacifism and the principle of just war.

---

in Africa," North–South Institute Policy Brief (October 2005). Available online at the North–South Institute, www.nsi-ins.ca/english/pdf/responsibility_protect_africa.pdf (accessed 19 June 2007), and Stephanie Hanson, "The AU's Responsibility to Protect," Council on Foreign Relations, 6 October 2006. Available online at the Council on Foreign Relations, www.cfr.org/publication/11621/aus_responsibility_to_protect.html (accessed 19 June 2007).

[29] United Nations General Assembly, *A More Secure World*, 85–6.

THE CHALLENGE IN DARFUR

The crisis in Darfur has tested whether nations are serious about or capable of applying responsibility to protect principles. The results so far have not been encouraging. The violence in this semi-arid region of western Sudan began in early 2003 as a guerilla war and greatly intensified when the Khartoum government responded by bombing villages and mobilizing proxy militias known as the Janjaweed. The conflict defied mediation and became more complex by 2007 as rebel groups splintered. The estimated death toll reached more than 200,000, with almost 3 million people displaced.[30] The fighting and suffering overlapped with conflict in neighboring Chad, threatening a regional crisis.

In September 2004 US Secretary of State Colin Powell declared to the Senate that "genocide has been committed in Darfur."[31] This was a dramatic statement that should have triggered concerted action, but the United States and other governments did little to halt the killing. The United Nations and African states made several half-hearted attempts to stem the violence. In April 2004 the AU established the Africa Mission in Sudan (AMIS), deploying approximately 7,000 peacekeepers to monitor the conflict and provide humanitarian assistance. That under-staffed force was attacked by rebel groups in September 2007 and suffered casualties and the theft of equipment. The UN Security Council imposed an arms embargo and limited economic sanctions against Sudanese leaders but these had little effect. In August 2006 the Council authorized the deployment of 20,000 UN peacekeepers, contingent on the consent of the Khartoum government, although the fate of that force remained uncertain.

While governments equivocated civil society organizations around the world mounted a major campaign to urge protective action. In 2004 the Save Darfur Coalition was launched in the United States, bringing together hundreds of faith-based, advocacy and humanitarian groups. In 2006 the coalition organized a "Million Voices for Darfur" campaign urging the White House to take action to stop the killing. In April 2006 a "Rally to Stop Genocide" in Washington, DC attracted nearly 50,000 people. It was, wrote former White House Africa specialist John Prendergast, "the most

---

[30] Lee Feinstein, "Darfur and Beyond: What is Needed to Prevent Mass Atrocities," Council on Foreign Relations, CSR no. 22 (January 2007), 39. Available online at the Council on Foreign Relations, www.cfr.org/content/publications/attachments/DarfurCSR22.pdf (accessed 19 June 2007).

[31] BBC News, "Powell Declares Genocide in Sudan" (9 September 2004). Available online at BBC News, http://news.bbc.co.uk/2/hi/africa/3641820.stm (accessed 19 June 2007).

energetic campaign by US citizens on an African issue since the anti-apartheid struggle in South Africa."[32]

Governments were unwilling to intervene in Darfur for a variety of reasons. The United States was consumed by the burdens of occupying Iraq and reluctant to apply pressure on Khartoum for fear of disrupting the 2005 peace agreement in southern Sudan. Washington also did not wish to jeopardize Khartoum's assistance in counterterrorism efforts. China and other nations were concerned about protecting their economic interests in Sudan's oil resources. Differences also existed over what should be done. Former Clinton administration officials Susan Rice and Anthony Lake advocated a Kosovo-style bombing campaign, but at the United Nations and in many other countries, leaders cautioned against Western intervention and emphasized the need for an African solution.[33] Activists within the Save Darfur Coalition argued for coercive measures against Sudan, including the enforcement of a no-fly zone. Prendergast proposed greater peacemaking efforts, planning for nonconsensual force deployment to protect civilians, and more effective punitive sanctions and international criminal indictments against Sudanese officials.[34] Africa scholar Mahmood Mamdani cautioned against one-sided perspectives that ignored the crimes of the Darfur rebel groups and urged a more evenhanded approach that would strengthen groups on both sides of the conflict which supported a political settlement.[35] The Darfur case illustrates the challenges and ambiguities of attempting to apply responsibility to protect principles. International action to prevent armed conflict depends not only on agreed principles of protection and effective peacemaking mechanisms, but on international consensus about the nature of the conflict and the necessity of concerted action.

The acceptance of the responsibility to protect as a principle of peace does not mean that the use of military force is a preferred or normal response to human rights abuse and threats to human security. The presumption against violence remains an essential element of both pacifist and just war theory. Václav Havel never suggested and would not have imagined that external military intervention was the solution to the lack of freedom in

---

[32] John Prendergast, "So How Come we Haven't Stopped it?," *Washington Post*, 19 November 2006.

[33] Susan E. Rice *et al.*, "We Saved Europeans: Why Not Africans?," *Washington Post*, 2 October 2006.

[34] John Prendergast, *The Answer to Darfur: How to Resolve the World's Hottest War*, International Crisis Group, Strategy Paper 1, March 2007. Available online at Enough Project, http://enoughproject.org/reports/pdf/answer_to_darfur.pdf (accessed 19 June 2007).

[35] Mahmood Mamdani, "The Politics of Naming: Genocide, Civil War, Insurgency," *London Review of Books* 29, no. 5 (8 March 2007).

Eastern Europe. There are many forms of intervention short of military action that can be effective in defending human rights and upholding justice. In the case of Kosovo, active support for the nonviolent resistance movement led by Rugova during the 1990s might have helped to advance justice without causing further armed violence and ethnic cleansing. The presence of international observers in Kosovo helped to reduce the level of violence and could have been maintained and expanded to protect against repression. The Responsibility to Protect is not solely a military concept but embodies a wide range of actions that can be taken by governments and civil society actors to protect the innocent from violence and transform conditions of extreme human rights abuse and injustice.

The principal imperative is to intercede on behalf of the victims of violence, to recognize, as Michael Walzer wrote, that inaction in the face of genocide and mass suffering is morally unacceptable.[36] Action can take the form of military intervention by regional alliances or UN peacekeepers, or it can include nonmilitary measures such as international monitoring, humanitarian assistance, targeted economic sanctions, and support for human rights and democracy movements. Civil society groups increasingly play an important role in protecting the vulnerable, not merely as a voice of conscience in calling attention to abuses, but by volunteering to serve in violence-prone settings around the world, and in some circumstances by providing direct protection and accompaniment for the victims of abuse. Peace and human rights advocates are often on the front lines in regions of conflict helping to protect those in need. All of these responses, from humanitarian service to the limited use of military force, fit within the rubric of the responsibility to protect. They embody a new, more realistic form of pacifism that incorporates the defense of human rights into a more holistic concept of peace and human security.

---

[36] Walzer, *Just and Unjust Wars*, 107–8; and Michael Walzer, *Arguing about War* (New Haven, CT: Yale University Press, 2004), 74.

14

A moral equivalent

The theory of democratic peace was based on the assumption that mass public opinion would be a force for moderation. The citizens of a free country, if given the chance to determine national policy, would naturally prefer peace over war. History quickly disproved that belief. As nations became more democratic they did not necessarily become more peaceful. Democratic states developed peaceful relations with one another, but they showed a very different, more bellicose face toward less democratic countries. The assumption that free people would naturally reject war was sadly mistaken. Support for war was no less virulent among the so-called industrious classes than among kings and nobles. The socialist creed of labor internationalism proved to be just as illusory. Most of those who cheered the call to solidarity of Jaurès in 1912 enthusiastically marched off to kill their fellow workers in 1914.

In the nineteenth and twentieth centuries the rise of democracy was linked to nationalism and the demand for self-determination. As ethnic and linguistic communities rebelled against colonialism and external control, they identified themselves as nations. They were no longer willing to accept constraints that suppressed their economic, cultural, and political rights. The demand for self-rule inevitably challenged the existing political order and often led to armed conflict. Many of the most ardent advocates of peace in nineteenth-century Europe were supporters of national liberation. They strongly sympathized with the democratic movements struggling against the Hapsburg, Ottoman, and Russian empires. The *Ligue internationale de la paix et de la liberté* was the embodiment of this sentiment. *Ligue* supporter Giuseppe Mazzini asserted that wars of liberation were necessary for "the noble intention of restoring Truth and Justice, and of arresting Tyranny in her inhuman career, of rendering the Nations free and happy."[1] Mazzini

[1] Michael Howard, *War and the Liberal Conscience* (New Brunswick: Rutgers University Press, 1989), 50–1.

and other nationalists believed that nations would have to "fight themselves into existence," to use Michael Howard's phrase.[2] Once nations such as Italy were liberated and consolidated military conflict would diminish.

The belief that national liberation would lead to peace proved to be a chimera. In many places nationalism degenerated into jingoism. The unification of Germany under Prussian militarism undermined the dreams of liberals and republicans. The aggressive new nationalism that emerged under Bismarck's direction, backed by Europe's strongest army, differed drastically from Mazzini's vision of a generous, liberal nationalism. The philosophers and idealists who originally articulated the noble aspirations of free people living in peace were replaced by nationalist military leaders who twisted patriotic virtues into a justification for war and conquest. By the early twentieth century a new, aggressive form of nationalism had taken hold in Europe. It was a "street" nationalism, a passion of the mob. It extolled violence and war as legitimate means to build and defend the nation.[3] As Howard wrote, "Hegel was mutating into Hitler; Mazzini into Mussolini."[4] Rather than a guarantee of peace, nationalism became a cause of war.

In this chapter I probe the passions of nationalism, especially the social and psychological dimensions, and review how advocates of justice and peace have sought to find alternative channels of social mobilization. I attempt to distinguish nationalism, which connotes militarism and xenophobia, from patriotism, which implies sacrifice for others. "Nationalism is not to be confused with patriotism," wrote George Orwell. The former is inseparable from the desire for power, while the latter means devotion to a particular place or way of life. The first is inherently expansionist, while the latter is merely defensive and does not seek to force itself on other people.[5] In the pacifist interpretation patriotism includes internationalism, or "cosmopolitanism" to use Mary Kaldor's term.

The susceptibility of the masses to belligerent nationalism became all too obvious during the twentieth century, shattering the optimistic assumptions of liberalism and socialism. Among those who sought to understand the collective madness of war were Albert Einstein and Sigmund Freud,

---

[2] Michael Howard, *The Invention of Peace and the Reinvention of War* (London: Profile Books, 2002), 45.
[3] Sandi E. Cooper, *Patriotic Pacifism: Waging War in Europe, 1815–1914* (New York: Oxford University Press, 1991), 45, 162.
[4] Howard, *The Invention of Peace*, 55.
[5] George Orwell, "Notes on Nationalism," May 1945, *The Complete Works of George Orwell*. Available online at George-Orwell, www.george-orwell.org/Notes_on_Nationalism/0.html (accessed 12 April 2007).

whose 1932 dialogue on the subject explored ways of controlling bellicose impulses or channeling them into constructive purposes. Perhaps the most famous exploration of these themes was that of William James, who advocated harnessing the universal desire for belonging and service into a force for the common good. Gandhi proposed the creation of a nonviolent army that would perform patriotic service for the nation, a concept that Abdul Ghaffar Khan brilliantly implemented during the freedom struggle against British colonialism. In recent decades pacifist groups have attempted to apply this model on a small scale in various nonviolent peacemaking initiatives and international conciliation programs. Some peace researchers have proposed transforming the nature of military service itself, by incorporating principles of civilian protection and humanitarian service into a new type of human security force. Activist leaders in the United States have also sought to redefine the meaning of patriotism to include an active commitment to peace and social justice. In all of these ways peace advocates have sought to transcend the constraints of narrow nationalism through a new form of patriotic pacifism.

THE BELLIGERENCE OF THE MASSES

The mass psychology of war was evident during the time of Napoleon. War developed on the largest scale ever seen, as hundreds of thousands of conscripts spread the creed of revolution by force of arms. The Napoleonic era transformed a republic based on values of liberty and civic virtue into a regime of terror and militarism. It paved the way for the nationalist movements that swept through Europe and much of the world in subsequent decades. It also sparked a Counter-Enlightenment that emphasized the virtues of nation and the nobility of the *Volk* against the principles of Napoleonic universalism. Militant nationalism spawned movements appealing to sentiment rather than the claims of reason. The roots of twentieth-century fascism, Howard wrote, could be found "deep in the soil of the Counter-Enlightenment; the belief in the community or *Volk* as against the individual, in intuition and emotion as against reason, in nationalism as against internationalism, and in will and action as against reasoned discussion and peaceful co-operation."[6] The liberal theory of peace failed to anticipate the horrors of totalitarianism and the ways in which masses of people could be aroused and disciplined by ideology. The

[6] Howard, *The Invention of Peace*, 67.

age of reason had led not to perpetual peace but to an era of collective madness.

Max Weber was deeply skeptical of the supposed pacific impulses of the masses. He argued that the citizens of the emerging democracies and industrial states could be easily swayed by appeals to patriotism and class interest. Weber noted that war and military service could provide opportunities for advancement that were not available in ordinary society, either in the factory or on the farm. Through war newly emergent sectors of society could strive for status and recognition. They could establish their identity in societies where the warrior ethos inherited from previous eras was still dominant. For the politically aggressive war was an avenue to advancement and radical transformation. Lenin recognized that the chaos of war could provide fertile ground for political revolution, and that insurrection could arise from the smoke of battle. War and militarism also had a gender dimension. They offered a venue for men to prove their masculinity, to assert their virility in societies where traditional male social roles were changing. All of these factors combined to make war attractive to the masses in ways that the earlier theorists of peace and democracy never imagined.

J. Glenn Gray analyzed the hypnotic appeal of war in his masterful study, *The Warriors*, drawing from his own experiences as a soldier during World War II. War binds humans together in a unique experience of mutuality, Gray observed. "Many veterans who are honest with themselves will admit . . . that the experience of communal effort in battle . . . has been a high point in their lives."[7] War is a "potent and often lethal addiction," wrote war correspondent Chris Hedges, "an enticing elixir." It is a force that gives meaning, an experience that overshadows the "shallowness and vapidness" of ordinary life.[8] The trauma of war, like that of natural disaster, mobilizes people toward solidarity and interdependence. It is a kind of ecstasy, wrote Gray, an experience that transcends the limits of self and forges intense feelings of belonging and community. Ralph Waldo Emerson observed that war "educates the senses, calls into action the will, perfects the physical constitution . . . endures no counterfeit, [and] shakes the whole society."[9] War and nationalism call forth the deepest impulses of self-sacrifice and commitment to others. They also unleash sinister forces of

---

[7] J. Glenn Gray, *The Warriors: Reflections on Men in Battle* (New York: Harper & Row, 1959), 44–5.

[8] Chris Hedges, *War is a Force that Gives us Meaning* (New York: Public Affairs, 2002), 3.

[9] Ralph Waldo Emerson, "War" (1838) *The Works of Ralph Waldo Emerson*, vol. V (New York: Bigelow, Brown and Co., n.d.), 360, 374.

violence and madness, of course, but it is the spirit of collectivity and solidarity that best explains the mystical appeal of war, and which theorists of peace have too often overlooked.

PEACE AND ITS DISCONTENTS: THE EINSTEIN–FREUD DIALOGUE

Albert Einstein was deeply troubled by the irrationality of the masses and the "collective psychosis" that can lure people into "a lust for hatred and destruction." In 1932, acting under the auspices of the League of Nations and the International Institute of Intellectual Cooperation, he wrote a famous open letter to Sigmund Freud asking the great psychoanalyst's advice on the challenge of "delivering mankind from the menace of war." Describing himself as "one immune from nationalist bias," Einstein asked Freud to explain the psychology of the masses and the emotional appeal of war. He also asked Freud's opinion on his proposed solution: "the setting up, by international consent, of a legislative and judicial body to settle every conflict arising between nations."[10]

Einstein opined that war was caused by the unwarranted influence of ruling classes who regarded war "simply as an occasion to advance their personal interests and enlarge their personal authority." The corrupt power of capitalist elites was obvious to Einstein, which was why he considered himself a socialist. The more troubling question was how this small clique could bend the will of the masses to support war and military aggression. Part of the answer, Einstein noted, was that the ruling classes have at their disposal the press, the schools, and even the churches, which they use to "organize and sway the emotions of the masses." But why are these efforts successful "in rousing men to such wild enthusiasm, even to sacrifice their lives?" Deeper psychological factors must be at work, which paralyze rational thought. These destructive passions are latent in normal times, but they can be aroused by the call to arms into a force of collective madness. Is it possible to control the mental evolution of humans, Einstein asked, to inoculate humans against this psychosis of fear and destructiveness? Is it possible to control aggressive instincts in order to prevent international war?

Freud replied by declaring himself to be a pacifist who shared Einstein's revulsion against war. "Pacifists we are, since our organic nature wills us thus

---

[10] All citations from correspondence in Albert Einstein, *Einstein on Peace* (New York: Simon and Schuster, 1960), 189–202.

to be," he wrote. The cultural development of humankind is an organic process leading gradually to a strengthening of the intellect, he argued.

War runs most emphatically counter to the psychic disposition imposed on us by the growth of culture; we are therefore bound to resent war, to find it utterly intolerable. With pacifists like us it is not merely an intellectual and affective repulsion, but a constitutional intolerance, an idiosyncrasy in its most drastic form.

Freud agreed with Einstein's proposal for a supranational authority among nations. The solution to war was the establishment of "a central control which shall have the last word in every conflict of interests. For this, two things are needed: first, the creation of such a supreme court of judicature; secondly, its investment with adequate executive force." The creation of international organization was not enough, however. It was also necessary, Freud wrote, to probe the psychological roots of war and to understand the power of the destructive impulses in human nature. During war the release of destructive impulses is linked to higher ideals of patriotism and service to others. The goal of serving the nation and the community justifies war and helps to unleash the basest instincts.

"There is no likelihood of our being able to suppress humanity's aggressive tendencies," Freud concluded. The vast majority of people allow rulers to make decisions for them to which they "usually bow without demur." The need is for a community where people subordinate their instinctive life to the dictates of reason. Such a hope is "utterly utopian" under current conditions, however, in part because politicians and religious leaders discourage freedom of thought. Pacifists should attempt "to divert [the aggressive impulse] into a channel other than that of warfare." An "indirect method of eliminating war" is to emphasize love as a counter agent to the destructive instinct. All that produces ties of solidarity and sentiment between people "must serve us as war's antidote," Freud wrote. This can occur through increased service to others and through greater identification with fellow human beings.

NONMILITARY SERVICE

The philosopher William James addressed the lure of war, and the need for an alternative, in his famous essay "The Moral Equivalent of War." James was a self-described pacifist who believed devoutly "in the reign of peace and in the gradual advent of some sort of socialistic equilibrium." He condemned war as an absurd monstrosity. He looked forward to "a future when acts of war shall be formally outlawed as between civilized peoples." He was

a fierce opponent of the US war against the Philippines and for a time served
as vice-president of the American Anti-Imperialist League.[11]

Despite his passion for peace, or perhaps because of it, James lamented
the failure of peace advocates to make progress in reducing the influence of
militarism. It is "desperately hard" to bring the peace party and the war
party together, he wrote. "I believe that the difficulty is due to certain
deficiencies in the program of pacifism." The proponents of peace have not
paid sufficient attention, he declared, to the underlying psychological and
emotional factors that sustain the culture of war. The war against war
requires a deeper understanding of these motivational factors and the
development of compelling alternatives.

The militaristic spirit will not be moved by concerns about war's horrors
and economic costs. "The horror makes the thrill," James wrote, and when
supreme sacrifice is at stake "talk of expense seems ignominious." Social
support for the war system is rooted in the traditions of heroism that have
been handed down from earlier generations. "We inherit the warlike type,"
James wrote. The pageantry and glory of national honor have evolved from
the history of war. "Our ancestors have bred pugnacity into our bone and
marrow, and thousands of years of peace won't breed it out of us." The
memories and legends of past US wars "are the most ideal part of what we
now own together, a sacred spiritual possession worth more than all the
blood poured out." To its apologists, war is a "kind of sacrament," a ritual of
national sacrifice that is to be honored and preserved. It is the very
embodiment of national identity.

War also appeals to the desire for sacrifice, James observed. It brings out
higher ideals of service and social discipline. War is the strong life. "It is
life *in extremis*," the essence of what Theodore Roosevelt extolled as "the
strenuous life." The advocates of war point to the great virtues of the martial
spirit – fidelity, cohesiveness, tenacity, heroism, discipline, physical fitness.
These virtues also exist in other social pursuits, but they are called forth
most intensely in war and military service. The noble "ideals of hardihood"
should be preserved, James believed, and channeled into service on behalf of
enduring peace. To date only war has had the ability to discipline and
inspire a whole community. Until an equivalent discipline is arranged,
James wrote, "war must have its way." The virtues of sacrifice and discipline
must be developed in civilian life if the appeal of war is to be overcome.

---

[11] All citations from William James, "The Moral Equivalent of War," in *William James: The Essential
Writings*, ed. Bruce W. Wilshire (New York: Harper Torchbooks, 1971), 349–59.

Sacrifice and hardship acquire dignity when they are rendered in the service of the collective. "No collectivity is like an army," James wrote, "for nourishing such pride." The challenge is to develop a moral equivalent for civilian society that can tap into the universal desire to serve and the need to belong to a larger community. Patriotic pride and military ambition are the first form of this desire, but there is "no reason for supposing them to be its last form." It should be possible, he wrote, to develop feelings of "civic passion," to defend and advance the interests of the community without resort to military violence. Many have acknowledged and seconded James's call for a moral equivalent to the heroism of war. It seems that a spirit of war is needed to overcome the reality of war. Martin Luther King, Jr. said that the advocates of peace must develop the same sense of bravery, discipline, and self-sacrifice as the practitioners of war. It is not enough to oppose violence, he said, it is also necessary to love peace and sacrifice for it.

To instill a sense of nonmilitary patriotism James advocated a system of national service, a conscription of the whole youthful population for what he described as a campaign against Nature. James did not intend this as a war to subdue the environment but rather as a campaign against social injustice. He proposed a program requiring the sons of the privileged classes ("our gilded youths") to work for a period of time in mines, railroads, fishing fleets, and other "sour and hard foundations" of economic life. He believed that this experience would knock the childishness out of youth and give them "healthier sympathies and soberer ideas." It would also preserve the "manly" traits of military service without war and instill necessary virtues of toughness and discipline into society.

James's proposal was never implemented, of course, and his male exclusivist language reflected gender biases that have long since been discredited, but the concept of public sacrifice to serve the national interest has endured. The Civilian Conservation Corps (CCC) of the 1930s was a fairly close approximation of James's idea, with an emphasis on forestry and environmental conservation. The program was pronounced as a "moral equivalent of war," and Franklin Roosevelt described it as a "war" against the Depression. The CCC was modeled on military life, replete with military barracks and camp discipline enforced by military officers.[12] The influence of James's concept can also be seen in the development of the Peace Corps, AmeriCorps, and other programs of voluntary national service. Proposals for comprehensive national service have surfaced periodically in the United

---

[12] "Civilian Conservation Corps (Ccc)," available online at Bookrags, www.bookrags.com/history/americanhistory/civilian-conservation-corps-ccc-aaw-03.html (accessed 12 April 2007).

States, but these plans have been offered as complements to rather than substitutes for military service. They have been opposed both by conservatives who reject greater government interference in society, and by peace advocates who fear they will lead to greater militarization. In Germany and other European countries where conscientious objection has become widespread, alternative civilian service has become a common experience for large numbers of young people. A year of low paid work as a hospital orderly or forest conservationist may not be the kind of strenuous duty that James had in mind, but the programs are an alternative to military service and are to some degree its moral equivalent.

NONVIOLENT WARRIORS

On a number of occasions Gandhi proposed the concept of a *Shanti Sena*, or peace army, as an equivalent to traditional military service. The idea was to enlist volunteers who would undergo training in nonviolent action methods and be available to prevent violence and support campaigns for economic and social justice. Gandhi was inspired in this vision by the example of the *Khudai Khidmatgars*, the "Servants of God." Founded in 1929 among the Pathan (or Pashtun) tribal communities of the North-West Territories in present day Pakistan, the *Khudai Khidmatgars* became the first organized nonviolent army in history. They were created and led by Adbul Ghaffar Khan, also known as Badshah Khan, who became a close ally of Gandhi in the freedom struggle against British colonialism and was a devoted follower of the nonviolent method. Khan organized the proud, independent-minded Pathan people to participate in a liberation army on the basis of an oath that pledged recruits to refrain from violence, treat others with respect, live a simple life, and serve the community. Members of the *Khudai Khidmatgar* learned basic army discipline, including marching drill and calisthenics. They had their own flag, badges, military hierarchy of ranks, even a bagpipe corps – everything except weapons.[13]

Khan brilliantly molded the fighting spirit and willingness to sacrifice of the Pathans into an effective force for nonviolent revolution. The Pathans knew how to fight, but they were also disciplined and imbued with a spirit of honor and service. The *Khudai Khidmatgars* played a critical role in the struggle for freedom, leading demonstrations, pickets, boycotts, and mass noncooperation campaigns, while also participating in Gandhi's

[13] Eknath Easwaran, *A Man to Match his Mountains: Badshahkhan, Nonviolent Soldier of Islam* (Petaluma, CA: Nilgiri Press, 1984) 111–13, 121–8, 168–9.

"constructive program" to promote economic self-reliance and social development in the villages. The *Khudai Khidmatgars* were warriors in every sense. They were prepared to die in the struggle against British imperialism, and many did. An estimated 200 unarmed *Khudai Khidmatgars* were killed by British forces at the infamous Kissa Khani Bazaar massacre in Peshawar in April 1930.[14] Some Pathans used violence in resisting the British, but the *Khudai Khidmatgars* generally maintained nonviolent discipline, even when they were brutally mistreated by the British.[15] They were prepared to die for their cause but not to kill for it. Gandhi always said that nonviolence was for the strong and courageous. The *Khudai Khidmatgars* proved that. They exemplified the disciplined bravery that is necessary for nonviolent action, and that Gandhi proposed as the basis for a peace army.

After India became independent a number of Gandhi's followers attempted to institutionalize the peace army concept. In 1957 his disciple Vinoba Bhave established a *Shanti Sena* organization and recruited volunteers for the challenge of combating communal violence. Under the leadership of Narayan Desai, son of Gandhi's secretary Mahadev Desai, the *Shanti Sena* grew to a membership of about 6,000 by the mid-1960s. When incidents of communal violence occurred, male and female *sainiks* would arrive in their distinctive uniforms of white khadi and saffron scarves to hear grievances, counteract rumors, serve as intermediaries between contending parties, and station themselves at trouble spots to calm communal violence. A notable success occurred in Calcutta in 1964 when the *sainiks* organized a silent procession of 3,000 people through riot-torn streets that helped to defuse tensions. The *Shanti Sena* declined in the late 1970s when political differences split the organization.[16]

In recent years pacifists in the United States and other countries have developed similar, though more modest, attempts to develop nonviolent peace forces. These efforts emerged in the early 1980s as part of the struggle for peace and justice in Central America. The international reaction to the intense violence in the region, much of it sponsored by the United States, led to the creation of an unprecedented international solidarity movement. Two of the organizations that developed out of that movement were Peace Brigades International (PBI), founded in 1981 at an international conference

[14] Mukulika Banerjee, *The Pathan Unarmed: Opposition & Memory in the North West Frontier* (Karachi: Oxford University Press, 2000), 57.

[15] Mohammad Raqib, "The Muslim Pashtun Movement of the North-West Frontier of India: 1930–1934," in *Waging Nonviolent Struggle: 20th Century Practice and 21st Century Promise*, ed. Gene Sharp (Boston, MA: Extending Horizons Books, 2005), 128–31.

[16] David Hardiman, *Gandhi in His Time and Ours* (New Delhi: Pauls Press, 2003), 192, 195.

in Canada, and Witness for Peace, founded by US activists two years later. PBI was created to provide trained volunteers in conflict zones to monitor ceasefires, offer mediation services, and perform tasks of reconstruction and reconciliation. The first PBI team was deployed in Guatemala in 1983, with later teams serving in El Salvador, Sri Lanka, Colombia, and Haiti. Witness for Peace was initiated by US activists who were moved by what they learned during a fact-finding mission to Nicaragua and decided to organize a campaign of protective accompaniment for people victimized by the violence there. The organization eventually sent thousands of Americans on short-term visits to Nicaragua. It also sponsored significant programs of public education and lobbying among citizens in the United States and officials in Washington.[17] In 1987 Witness for Peace member Ben Linder was killed in an attack by Contra forces while working on a rural electrification project.

Christian Peacemaker Teams (CPT) emerged in 1984 at the initiative of Mennonites, Brethren, and Quakers, with broad ecumenical participation. The creation of CPT was inspired by an address to the 1984 Mennonite World Conference from Ronald Sider, Canadian-born Christian activist and leader of Evangelicals for Social Action. Sider challenged his listeners to show the same level of courage in working for peace as soldiers display in their willingness to die in battle. Do those who claim to follow Jesus's message of love and nonviolence have as much faith as those who risk their lives in war? Sider envisioned a nonviolent peacekeeping force of 100,000 Christians, trained and ready to be deployed to conflict zones around the world.[18] The founders of CPT sought consciously to emulate the spirit of disciplined self-sacrifice that is characteristic of armies facing battle. CPT has utilized methods of nonviolent intervention, sometimes risking injury and death, in attempts to prevent and transform armed conflict. CPT volunteers attempt to "get in the way" when acts of abuse and injustice are occurring. They serve as public witnesses and attempt to report human rights violations to the world press. CPT volunteers have been deployed in Gaza and the West Bank, Chechnya, Haiti, Bosnia, Colombia, Iraq, in Arizona along the US border with Mexico, and in native first American communities in the United States and Canada. CPT came to world

---

[17] Liam Mahony and Luis Enrique Eguren, *Unarmed Bodyguards: International Accompaniment for the Protection of Human Rights* (West Hartford, CT: Kumarian Press, 1997), 3–5.

[18] Joseph S. Miller, "A History of the Mennonite Conciliation Service, International Conciliation Service, and Christian Peacemaker Teams," in *From the Ground Up: Mennonite Contributions to International Peacebuilding*, ed. Cynthia Sampson and John Paul Lederach (New York: Oxford University Press, 2000), 25.

attention tragically in 2005 when four of its volunteers were kidnapped in Iraq and one, Tom Fox, was later found dead.

Volunteers for the International Solidarity Movement (ISM) also suffered casualties while performing solidarity work. ISM was founded in 2001 to engage in nonviolent resistance to the Israeli occupation of Palestinian territories. The group's goals include protecting Palestinians from repression and home demolitions, publicizing the brutality of the occupation, and organizing divestment campaigns to apply economic pressure on Israel. In March 2003 ISM volunteer Rachel Corrie was killed while attempting to obstruct an Israeli bulldozer in Rafah near the Egyptian border. In April 2003 ISM member Thomas Hurndall was fatally shot by an Israeli soldier during a protest at a roadblock in the Gaza Strip.

Many other solidarity movements and peace witness programs have been established in countries around the world. Nonviolent Peaceforce was formed in 1999 at the Hague Appeal for Peace in the Netherlands. It seeks consciously to emulate the Gandhian "peace army" by creating teams of trained nonviolent activists willing to intervene in armed conflicts to protect human rights, deter violence, and facilitate peacemaking efforts. Initial deployments sent trained nonviolent peacemakers to Sri Lanka and the Philippines. The group is supported by dozens of organizations from Africa, Asia, Europe, and North America. Such programs testify to the extraordinary commitment to service and solidarity that some peace activists around the world have been willing to make. These programs have made a significant difference in the lives of the volunteers and those they serve. Although the scale of these programs is relatively small (a few thousand volunteers in total) they represent a significant attempt to prevent and transform armed conflict. They are fashioning a new spirit of heroism, sacrifice and service as a moral alternative to war.

TRANSFORMING CONFLICT

The commitment to conflict mediation and conciliation is another form of service to peace. As "new wars" of intrastate ethnic and civil strife have become more prevalent in recent decades, supporters of peace have responded by creating and participating in a wide array of international conciliation services. Global mediators have sought not only to prevent war but to act in the midst of war to mitigate its impacts. These emerging conflict transformation programs offer peacemakers a way of responding concretely to the most common forms of armed violence in the world.

Mennonites and Quakers played a leading role in the development of conflict resolution and mediation programs during the 1960s and 1970s. For some religiously motivated pacifists, conciliation programs offered a middle ground between political activism and quietism. Mediation services were seen as being less radical and more socially acceptable than antiwar resistance.[19] Programs for preventing and resolving conflict had appeal across the political spectrum. They gave peace advocates a way of working with all parties, including the military, to reduce the likelihood and severity of war. By entering conflict zones to facilitate peace settlements and end military hostilities, conciliators earned respect for themselves and respectability for the cause of conflict resolution.

As the field of conflict mediation expanded in the late 1960s, however, practitioners and researchers faced sharp challenges over questions of social justice. The pages of the *Journal of Peace Research* and other publications reverberated with debate about the structural roots of conflict and the limitations of third-party mediation. This discussion paralleled debates during earlier historical periods, when democratic nationalists and socialists questioned whether peace was possible without fundamental changes in political and economic relationships. The critics of conflict resolution questioned whether narrowly focused conciliation was legitimate if it papered over structural injustices. Mediation programs too often play into the hands of the powerful, the critics charged, consigning the weak and marginalized to continued subjugation, and perpetuating conditions that cause violence. How can one adopt a stance of neutrality, they asked, in the face of glaring injustices and inequality? The problem in most conflict situations is not poor communication between the parties but fundamental imbalances of power. In these settings conflict resolution may merely reinforce a master–slave relationship that perpetuates injustice.[20]

In response to these criticisms, and based on field experience in numerous trouble spots around the world, mediators developed a new paradigm of conflict transformation, which emphasized the importance of structural issues to the practice of peacemaking. John Paul Lederach encouraged the development of an elicitive method that gives voice to those who have been victimized by violence and oppression.[21] He called for "a holistic response to human conflict," one that "addresses the immediate human suffering, the

---

[19] *Ibid.*, 11.
[20] C. H. Mike Yarrow, *Quaker Experiences in International Conciliation* (New Haven, CT: Yale University Press, 1978), 285–7.
[21] John Paul Lederach, *Preparing for Peace: Conflict Transformation across Cultures* (Syracuse, NY: Syracuse University Press, 1995).

root problems engendering the destructive cycle of violence, and the creation of space where problems can be seriously dealt with in a way that respects human life." Conciliation efforts must address the underlying grievances, power relationships, and social and cultural patterns that cause and sustain armed conflict. The goal is to "create a new and hopefully transforming space," to help people in the midst of conflict "act as transforming agents within their own context" – to empower those affected by conflict to achieve greater equality and justice.[22]

Conflict transformation goes beyond the resolution of differences. At the personal level it seeks to minimize the destructive effects of violent conflict upon the individuals involved. At the relational level it seeks to improve communication and mutual understanding among contesting communities. At a structural level it seeks to understand the underlying causes of violent conflict and fosters nonviolent strategies for meeting human needs and maximizing the participation of the marginalized. Culturally, transformation seeks to create new patterns of understanding and interaction that go beyond violence and promote constructive cooperation. This integrated framework of transformation seeks not merely to end violent conflict, but to build new relationships and patterns of social interaction that create the basis for sustainable peace.[23] The thousands of mediators who bring this practice of transformation to the front lines of conflict around the world provide a unique service against war and armed violence.

HUMAN SECURITY SERVICE

It will never be possible for peace organizations or civilian agencies to replace military service completely. It may not be necessary. Military service itself is beginning to evolve in new directions. In many countries, especially the mature democracies that are at peace with one another, armed forces increasingly have assumed constabulary and peacekeeping missions and are unlikely to be involved in aggressive war. William James was writing at a time when armed forces were used exclusively for imperial adventures and war against other nations. The waning of interstate war seems to be changing this. Today the mission of the armed forces in many countries has shifted toward civic action and policing duties. Armed forces are used increasingly in peacekeeping or multilateral peace enforcement missions.

---

[22] Quoted in Miller, "A History of the Mennonite Conciliation Service," 24.
[23] John Paul Lederach, *Building Peace: Sustainable Reconciliation in Divided Societies* (Washington, DC: United States Institute of Peace Press, 1997), 82–3.

In many countries the only opportunities for overseas deployment are in multilateral missions that often resemble civilian policing more than military combat. This is not to suggest that uses of the military for aggressive war and military combat are a thing of the past. Far from it, especially for the United States and Great Britain, where the armed forces are deployed in wars of military intervention and occupation. Even in the United States, however, the military mission has started to change. Military deployments in Bosnia, Kosovo, and Afghanistan have involved US and NATO units in civil policing functions and peacebuilding efforts to an unprecedented degree.

To encourage this trend peace researchers and human rights advocates in Europe have developed the concept of "human security operations." These would be missions, in keeping with the definition of human security, to provide protection for individuals and communities as well as governments. They would embody "responsibility to protect" principles by placing military forces alongside civilian specialists in multifaceted operations that address all aspects of conflict, military and civilian. These ideas were developed in the *Barcelona Report*, which was written by a team of international peace and security specialists, convened by Mary Kaldor, and presented to European Union foreign policy chief Javier Solana in September 2004.[24] As the report noted, security threats today have become much more complex and diverse. They involve not only armed aggression but gross violations of human rights, rampant lawlessness, and terrorism. Against many of these threats the traditional reliance on combat forces with heavy firepower and technology is not appropriate. When civilians are targeted with impunity, as is often the case in ethnic conflicts and terrorist campaigns, the role of security forces is not to cause further destruction but to protect people and minimize casualties. The function of security forces in these settings is more akin to the role of civilian policing than military combat.

The *Barcelona Report* proposed the creation of a Human Security Response Force, as a cornerstone of the European Security Strategy approved by the Council of Europe in December 2003. In adopting a distinctive EU strategy European leaders expressed a desire to make a greater contribution to international security, but with an emphasis on preventive

---

[24] *A Human Security Doctrine for Europe: The Barcelona Report of the Study Group on Europe's Security Capabilities*, presented to the EU High Representative for Common Foreign and Security Policy, Javier Solana, Barcelona, 15 September 2004. Available online at the London School of Economics and Political Science, www.lse.ac.uk/Depts/global/Publications/HumanSecurityDoctrine.pdf (accessed 12 April 2007).

action and multilateralism. The *Barcelona Report* called for a new security doctrine based on the primacy of human rights, clear political authority, multilateralism, a bottom-up approach, regional focus, adherence to the rule of law, and appropriate use of force. The report proposed the creation of a security force of 15,000 men and women, at least one-third of them civilian police officers, human rights monitors, humanitarian aid workers, development assistance specialists, and others who would help to build and support civil society. Traditional security operations, both military and police, would be coordinated with civilian peace-building efforts, to address not only the immediate problem of preventing armed violence but the deeper challenge of creating conditions for justice and lasting peace.

This kind of thinking is very new and has not yet won official acceptance by government officials. It requires a leap of imagination and a broadening of loyalties far beyond the limits of traditional patriotism. The proposed human security force would serve a community of nations rather than any single state. This is an enormous challenge even for the most enlightened internationalist. It would mean transcending the social and psychological impulses that motivate people to sacrifice for the nation and creating a new sense of belonging and service to the broader human community. It is doubtful whether such a radical transformation in culture and conscious-ness can be achieved in the foreseeable future, but realities on the ground are beginning to move in this direction. In many conflict settings soldiers are serving alongside humanitarian workers, representatives of international institutions, and civil society workers in combined efforts to halt and prevent armed conflict and protect innocent victims.

As armed forces develop these new forms of human security service, they may themselves become a moral equivalent of war. The time may come, and may already be here in a few countries, when military duty means service not only to the nation but to the broader international and human com-munity. The rigor and discipline of military life will be for the purpose of peacekeeping and the prevention of war, not aggressive combat. This could be a form of sacrifice and heroism on behalf of the broader community that would satisfy the yearning for meaning, and perhaps begin to supersede the appeal of war.

PATRIOTIC PACIFISM

Though rarely recognized as such, the struggle against war is seen by many as a form of service to nation. Working for peace is itself a moral equivalent of war, a commitment to sacrifice and serve the common good. In Germany during the 1920s some pacifists advocated war resistance as a form of "new heroism," not as treason but as an attempt to rescue the country from militarism.[25] In the United States peace activists often carry placards reading "peace is patriotic." This is an assertion by opponents of war that they love their country as much as anyone else. Their patriotic service takes a different form, however. They express their devotion by volunteering their time and energy, often in the face of misunderstanding and rebuke, to prevent wars that harm and dishonor the nation. The patriotism of the peace movement incorporates the spirit of internationalism and recognizes the essential interdependence of nations. In the 1930s some opponents of war supported the nationalist America First Committee and were isolationists, but most peace advocates then and since have maintained an internationalist perspective. They emphasize that the security of one is dependent upon the security of all, as expressed in the principle of common security, and that the interest of the nation is best served through cooperation with others.

Peace movements in the United States have become increasingly effective in emphasizing the patriotic dimensions of their opposition to war. This was not always the case. As Larry Wittner and other historians noted, the advocates of disarmament during the cold war were often dismissed as unpatriotic and even subversive. During the Vietnam War media coverage sometimes portrayed antiwar activists and radicals as anti-US extremists. These misperceptions were less prevalent during the Iraq War debate. Opponents of the US invasion of Iraq were able to parry such charges by framing antiwar sentiment in a patriotic context. The Win Without War coalition, one of the main antiwar coalitions in the United States, specifically and consciously positioned itself as a mainstream movement. Its press releases and newspaper ads featured a US flag, and its mission statement began with "We are patriotic Americans . . ." By framing its message in this manner, Win Without War sought to appropriate the symbolism of the flag and inoculate itself against charges of anti-Americanism. The coalition endorsed UN inspections as a means of disarming Iraq. It expressed full support for international efforts to combat terrorism, although it was careful to avoid any specific reference to the Bush administration's so-called "war on terror," so as not to reinforce the militarized metaphor and bellicose policies of the administration. Through the framing and the delivery of

---

[25] Guido Grünewald, "War Resisters in Weimar Germany," in *Challenge to Mars: Essays on Pacifism from 1918 to 1945*, ed. Peter Brock and Thomas P. Socknat (Toronto: University of Toronto Press, 1999), 76.

patriotic messages, the coalition sought to reach the political mainstream and more effectively contest the Bush administration's case for war.

During the Iraq war most antiwar groups in the United States adopted a "support the troops" position, even as they sharply criticized the policies that sent those troops into dubious battle. This was another improvement over previous antiwar movements, when activists were misperceived as being hostile toward members of the military. During the Vietnam era it was claimed that veterans and soldiers were spat upon by antiwar demonstrators. Later research showed this to be a myth.[26] During the Iraq debate, antiwar activists were careful to avoid such distortions by allying themselves with veterans groups and military family members and by consistently supporting efforts to provide benefits for members of the military and their families. Peace activists coopted the "support the troops" slogan, which in the past had been used to justify war, and even tried to turn it to their advantage by arguing that the best way to support the troops was to bring them home from an unjust war.

Not all peace advocates support the use of patriotic symbols and language, however. Some activists, especially absolute pacifists, are uncomfortable with this approach. They associate the flag and patriotic messages with militarism and jingoism. Governments and pro-war groups have indeed manipulated patriotic language and appropriated the meaning of the flag to advance militaristic purposes. The historic derivation of national flags is rooted in the experience of war. They were an emblem of battle, a guide to combatants through the smoke and chaos of combat. But the flag is also seen by many as a symbol of common sacrifice and suffering for the protection of the greater good. Many peace activists seek to contest the militarized meaning of the flag. They attempt to associate the flag with positive achievement, such as the advance of civil and human rights, or the successful struggle to win the vote for women. These attempts to interpret and recapture patriotic symbols and messages are an important part of the struggle for peace.

Peace and justice leaders seek to make the distinction between patriotism and nationalism. Patriotism implies values of sacrifice, duty, honor, selflessness, and generosity toward others – all the positive virtues that William James identified. Nationalism, by contrast, evokes images of domination, militarism, and xenophobia. The challenge for peace advocates is to

---

[26] See Jerry Lembcke, *The Spitting Image: Myth, Memory, and the Legacy of Vietnam* (New York: New York University Press, 1998); and H. Bruce Franklin, *Vietnam and Other American Fantasies* (Amherst, MA: University of Massachusetts Press, 2000), 62.

emphasize the former over the latter. Howard Zinn said that it was necessary to redefine patriotism as "loyalty to the principles of democracy," to "expand it beyond that narrow nationalism that has caused so much death and suffering."[27] For Americans "true patriotism lies in supporting the values the country is supposed to cherish: equality, life, liberty, the pursuit of happiness."[28] Patriotism differentiates between loyalty to country and support for specific policies. Some of the greatest and most eloquent peace advocates in US history have been passionately patriotic. Martin Luther King, Jr. spoke often of the greatness of the USA and the grandeur of the American dream. He extolled the Constitution of the United States as a marvelous foundation upon which to build a just society. His objection to the Vietnam War was rooted in a desire to return the country to the noble principles which made it great. "I oppose the war in Vietnam because I love America," he declared in his famous April 1967 sermon on the war. He wanted the United States to stand as a moral example to the world. "I speak out against this war because I am disappointed with America. There can be no great disappointment where there is no great love."[29] Rev. William Sloane Coffin, Jr. also spoke of his patriotic passion. Like King he wanted to see his country live up to its ideals. "The real patriots in every country are those who carry on a lover's quarrel with their country."[30] The true patriot, Coffin said, is one who takes risks to speak for truth, who is not complacent in the face of unjust war but is prepared to act and sacrifice for peace. "The cause of peace is not the cause of cowardice," wrote Emerson. If peace is to be achieved it must be the work of the brave, who "have come up to the same height as the hero" but have gone a step beyond and will not seek to take another person's life.[31]

---

[27] Howard Zinn, "Patriotism and the Fourth of July," 4 July 2006. Available online at AlterNet, www.alternet.org/story/38463 (accessed 12 April 2007).

[28] Howard Zinn, *A Power Governments Cannot Suppress* (San Francisco, CA: City Lights Books, 2007), 112.

[29] Martin Luther King, Jr., "Why I am Opposed to the War in Vietnam" (sermon, Ebenezar Baptist Church, Atlanta, GA, 16 April 1967).

[30] William Sloan Coffin, Jr., quoted in "Interview With John Snow; Cosby's Controversial Comments," *CNN Newsnight with Aaron Brown*, 2 July 2004, transcript 070200CN.V84.

[31] Emerson, "War," 374–5.

15

Realizing disarmament

The 1990s were a heady decade for disarmament. As Jonathan Schell wrote, the wishes of antinuclear activists "were more than granted: nuclear arsenals were not merely frozen, they were reduced." In Europe the INF treaty eliminated an entire class of nuclear missiles on the continent. Congress forced an end to US nuclear testing in 1992. The first and second Strategic Arms Reduction Treaties (START) cut US and Russian arsenals by two-thirds. For the first time since the beginning of the atomic age strategic analysts began to contemplate seriously the prospect of completely eliminating nuclear weapons. With the fall of the Soviet Union, Schell observed, the previous barrier of implausibility fell. Gone was the implacable hostility toward a totalitarian empire. Gone were the obstacles to inspection which had been considered the principal impediment to disarmament. It was now "entirely reasonable to believe that the goal [of disarmament] could be reached." Prestigious international commissions developed detailed blueprints for moving toward zero nuclear weapons. Retired military officers, led by General George Lee Butler, the former head of US Strategic Command, spoke vocally of the desirability of nuclear abolition. The dawn of a new era seemed in sight as disarmament activists around the world formed a new movement for nuclear abolition.

In Washington and other capitals, however, government leaders failed to take advantage of the favorable climate for disarmament, which as a result was all too brief. The vested interests of the nuclear and military lobbies reasserted themselves, reinforcing the realist assumptions of the cold war paradigm that still dominated strategic thinking. Unwilling to give up atomic weapons or allow the nuclear infrastructure to atrophy, military planners developed new missions and capabilities that gave these weapons a life beyond the cold war. Thus began what Schell termed the "second nuclear era."[1] In Russia the

---

[1] Jonathan Schell, *The Gift of Time: The Case for Abolishing Nuclear Weapons Now* (New York: Metropolitan Books, 1998), 7, 10, 17.

production of nuclear missiles resumed as the Kremlin sought to modernize and replace decaying cold war systems. In the United States policy makers developed a new doctrine of counter-proliferation that called for the possible use of nuclear weapons against governments and nonstate actors seeking to develop mass destruction capability.[2] Nuclear weapons were to be used not merely to deter but to strike first against weapons of mass destruction threats.

Nuclear weapons also spread to other actors. The Nuclear Non-Proliferation Treaty (NPT) helped to slow but was unable to prevent the spread of nuclear weapons. Israel refused to sign the treaty and developed substantial nuclear capabilities. India and Pakistan demonstrated their nuclear credentials in 1998. Iraq, UN inspectors discovered in 1991, was only a year or two from nuclear weapons capability. North Korea conducted a nuclear weapons test in 2006. Iran made steady progress toward nuclear weapons capability, prompting rising international concerns. Looming over all of these developments was the possibility that Osama bin Laden and the Al Qaida terrorist network might acquire such weapons. Documents found in Afghanistan after the US invasion revealed bin Laden's desire to obtain weapons of mass destruction.[3] International Atomic Energy Agency Chief Mohamed ElBaradei told Norwegian television in 2005 that Al Qaida was actively seeking to acquire a nuclear weapon.[4]

These increasing dangers prompted former US Secretary of Defense William Perry to state in 2004, "I have never been as worried as I am now that a nuclear bomb will be detonated in an American city. I fear that we are racing towards an unprecedented catastrophe."[5] The risk of an actual nuclear explosion is arguably greater now than during the cold war, and is likely to grow in the years ahead.

The USA responded to the new nuclear danger by increasing counter-proliferation pressures on selected countries, members of what George W. Bush termed the "axis of evil." The "deadly nexus" of terrorism and proliferation was used to justify the administration's new national security

---

[2] United States Joint Chiefs of Staff, *Doctrine for Joint Theater Nuclear Operations*, Joint Pub 3-12.1, 9 February 1996, III-6 and III-7. Available online at The Nuclear Information Project, www.nukestrat. com/us/jcs/JCS_JP3-12-1_96.pdf (accessed 30 March 2007).

[3] David Albright, "Al Qaeda's Nuclear Program: Through the Window of Seized Documents," *Policy Forum Online* 47 (Nautilus Institute, 6 November 2002). Available online at the Nautilus Institute, www.nautilus.org/archives/fora/Special-Policy-Forum/47_Albright.html (accessed 30 March 2007).

[4] "Al-Qaida sought nuke, IAEA chief says," *Reuters*, 10 April 2005.

[5] William J. Perry (keynote address of the former Secretary of Defense at the conference, Post–Cold War U.S. Nuclear Strategy: A Search for Technical and Policy Common Ground, Committee on International Security and Arms Control, National Academy of Sciences, Washington, DC, 11 August 2004). Available online at The National Academies, www7.nationalacademies.org/cisac/ Perry_Presentation.pdf (accessed 30 March 2007).

doctrine of unilateralism and preventive war, announced in 2002.[6] This led directly to the US invasion of Iraq, which Jonathan Schell ironically termed "war for disarmament." The attack on Iraq seemed only to harden the nuclear ambitions of North Korea and Iran and contributed to regional and global insecurities, exacerbating the very conditions that often impel countries to seek greater military capability.

In this chapter I examine the nuclear paradox of the modern era: the unprecedented opportunity for achieving disarmament and the continuing political obstacles that stand in the way of this goal. I review the disarmament bargain at the heart of the NPT, the pledge by nuclear weapons states to eliminate their arsenals in exchange for the agreement of all other nations not to acquire such weapons. The chapter reviews the most authoritative international blueprints for reducing and eliminating nuclear weapons, the reports of the Canberra Commission in 1996 and the Blix Commission in 2006. The chapter concludes by probing the political requirements for disarmament, returning to Hans Morgenthau's famous observation that the reduction of weapons is contingent upon the reduction of political animosities. Realizing disarmament will require the building of more reliable structures of peace and international cooperation.

FROM NONPROLIFERATION TO DISARMAMENT

Peace advocates have long insisted that nonproliferation must be universal. The NPT was conceived as a grand bargain in which the five acknowledged nuclear weapons states agreed under Article VI to disarm, in exchange for a pledge from all other countries not to develop such weapons. During the 1995 and 2000 NPT conferences, the United States and the other nuclear states pledged to achieve nuclear disarmament. In 1995, as a condition for achieving the indefinite extension of the treaty, the nuclear states promised the "determined pursuit by the nuclear-weapon States of systematic and progressive efforts to reduce nuclear weapons globally, with the ultimate goal of eliminating those weapons."[7] At the NPT review conference in 2000 the United States and the other states reiterated these pledges, agreeing to "practical steps" for the implementation of Article VI, including an "unequivocal undertaking by the nuclear-weapon States to accomplish the total

---

[6] George W. Bush, *The National Security Strategy of the United States of America*, September 2002. Available online at the White House, www.whitehouse.gov/nsc/nss.pdf (accessed 30 March 2007).

[7] "Resolutions Adopted at the NPT Extension Conference," *Arms Control Today* 25, no. 5 (June 1995): 30.

elimination of their nuclear arsenals."[8] The United States refused to fulfill these pledges, however, and at the 2005 NPT conference blocked attempts to renew the disarmament commitments made in previous conferences.

Officials in the United States and other nuclear states dismiss nuclear abolition as a dangerous chimera, but technological progress and conceptual advances in international security have made disarmament a realistic possibility. Improvements in the physical sciences have enormously expanded the possibilities for monitoring and verifying weapons reduction and elimination. This has increased the ability of governments to have political confidence in the viability of disarmament. The intrusive on-site inspection mechanisms applied by UN officials in Iraq were highly effective in assuring the elimination of Saddam Hussein's clandestine weapons programs. The UN experience in Iraq demonstrated the viability of international monitoring as a tool of disarmament. Through hundreds of on-site visits over the course of more than a decade UN weapons officials identified and assured the dismantling of Iraq's nuclear, chemical, and biological weapons and the long-range ballistic missiles intended to deliver them. The success of weapons dismantling in Iraq confirmed that intrusive inspection is a viable means of assuring disarmament. If disarmament could succeed in the difficult circumstances of a totalitarian regime reluctant to accept and determined to obstruct external monitoring, a more cooperative and consensual disarmament process certainly should be workable. The effectiveness of the UN weapons mission in Iraq indicated that the challenge of disarmament was not technical but political. The means are available. The problem lies in mustering the political will to accept those means.

Throughout the nuclear age prestigious governmental commissions developed detailed proposals for disarmament. One of the first and most influential of these was the Commission on Disarmament and Security Issues, chaired by Swedish Prime Minister Olof Palme. The commission's 1982 report, *Common Security: A Blueprint for Survival*, elaborated the links between development and disarmament, crafted a new framework for conceptualizing international security, and offered strategies for reversing the nuclear arms race through East–West arms control negotiations. Most observers credited the commission report with helping to reframe the

---

[8] For a complete text of the NPT and the 1995, 2000, and 2005 review documents see the United Nations, *Weapons of Mass Destruction*, "Treaty on the Non-Proliferation of Nuclear Weapons (NPT)." Available online at the United Nations Peace and Security Through Disarmament, disarmament2.un. org/wmd/npt/index.html (accessed 30 March 2007).

discourse on international security issues, through its emphasis on mutual vulnerability and the need for cooperative solutions to global challenges. The concept of common security captured a fundamental truth of international politics, that the security of one nation cannot be gained at the expense of others. In an increasingly interdependent world, security is indivisible and depends upon cooperation. The *Common Security* report established a normative principle for state behavior and became a rallying cry for civil society advocates.

The Palme Commission had a significant impact on Mikhail Gorbachev's "new thinking" in international affairs. Gorbachev personally acknowledged his debt to Palme in his book *Perestroika*: "The idea of 'security for all,' which was put forward by ... the International Palme Commission, has many points of similarity with our concept of comprehensive security."[9] When Gorbachev gave a memorial lecture in Sweden following Palme's assassination, he shared his admiration for Palme with one of the commission's staff members, emphasizing how much the report had influenced his thinking.[10] Gorbachev and his top aides were strongly attracted to Palme's ideas and relied on the *Common Security* report as they fashioned their revolutionary new approach to international security.[11]

THE CANBERRA COMMISSION

The most authoritative and detailed report on how to end the danger of nuclear weapons was issued by the Canberra Commission in 1996, at a moment of unprecedented opportunity for nuclear arms reduction. It came in the wake of a parade of international arms control agreements, including the INF Treaty (1987), the Conventional Forces in Europe (CFE) Treaty (1990), START I and II (1991 and 1993), the Chemical Weapons Convention (CWC, 1993), the indefinite extension of the NPT (1995), and the Comprehensive Test Ban Treaty (CTBT, 1996). In this hopeful atmosphere of accelerating denuclearization, Australia's Prime Minister Paul Keating

---

[9] Mikhail Gorbachev, *Perestroika: New Thinking for Our Country and the World* (New York: Harper and Row, 1987), 207.

[10] Emma Rothschild, interview by the author, 29 July 2004.

[11] A sampling of the many analysts making this point includes Thomas Risse-Kappen, "Ideas Do Not Float Freely: Transnational Coalitions, Domestic Structures, and the End of the Cold War," *International Organization* 48, no. 2 (spring 1994); Ken Booth, "Steps Towards Stable Peace in Europe: A Theory and Practice of Coexistence," *International Affairs* (Royal Institute of International Affairs) 66, no. 1 (January 1990); Thomas Risse-Kappen, "Did 'Peace Through Strength' End the Cold War? Lessons from INF," *International Security* 16, no. 1 (summer 1991); and John Tirman, "How We Ended the Cold War," *The Nation* 269, no. 14 (1 November 1999).

and Foreign Minister Gareth Evans established an independent international commission to explore the prospect of reducing nuclear weapons to zero.

The creation of the Canberra Commission was motivated in part by the political reaction within Australia to the resumption of French nuclear testing in the South Pacific. The French tests that began in June 1995 sparked worldwide protests, including boycotts of French wine. The reaction in the Asia–Pacific region was especially sharp, and Australia's Labor government joined with other nations to apply diplomatic and moral pressure on France. Keating and Evans framed their opposition in the context of a broader argument against nuclear weapons in general.[12] They responded to mounting antinuclear pressures in Australia and around the world by creating a commission to advocate nuclear weapons elimination. Evans was already skeptical of nuclear weapons, and he and other officials used the public reaction to renewed testing to make the case for a nuclear weapons free world.[13]

The seventeen members of the Canberra Commission were drawn mostly from the five nuclear weapons states and included several former senior commanders and defense officials. Among the major players were General George Lee Butler, former commander-in-chief of US Strategic Command; retired field marshal Michael Carver, former chief of the British General Staff; Robert McNamara, former US secretary of defense; and Michel Rocard, former prime minister of France. The commission also included long-time advocates of disarmament, such as Nobel Peace Prize winner Joseph Rotblatt and former Swedish disarmament ambassador Maj Britt Theorin. Butler played a crucial role in building consensus within the commission and was the major voice for several years afterward in carrying the commission's message to the public. Butler had supported nuclear reductions as senior nuclear commander and adviser to the first Bush administration but he came to the commission as a skeptic of abolition. The depth and seriousness of the commission's deliberations were a transformative experience that allowed him to see the merit of a nuclear reduction process that would lead to zero.[14] Carver experienced a similar conversion. His discussions with fellow commissioners convinced him that abolition was feasible, and that the absence of tension between the superpowers created a historic opportunity to strive for a nuclear weapons

---

[12] Marianne Hanson and Carl Ungerer, "The Canberra Commission: Paths Followed, Paths Ahead," *Australian Journal of International Affairs* 53, no. 1 (1999): 7.
[13] Marianne Hanson and Carl J. Ungerer, "Promoting an Agenda for Nuclear Weapons Elimination: The Canberra Commission and Dilemmas of Disarmament," *Australian Journal of Politics and History* 44, no. 4 (1998): 539.
[14] George Lee Butler, interview by the author, 10 August 2004.

free future.[15] Rocard too was persuaded by the commission process to endorse the final report. The political views of the commissioners varied widely, but in the end this eminent group of former policy makers from diverse backgrounds agreed on a concrete plan for a step-by-step process of reducing and eliminating nuclear weapons.

The Canberra Commission report concluded that "immediate and determined efforts need to be made to rid the world of nuclear weapons and the threat they pose to it." The proposition that nuclear weapons could be retained in perpetuity and never be used, accidentally or by design, "defies credibility." Reflecting the military experience of its authors, the report emphasized that nuclear weapons are too destructive and indiscriminate to achieve military objectives on the battlefield. The possession of nuclear weapons has not prevented wars involving the major powers. The only legitimate purpose of nuclear weapons is to deter their use by others. If nations agreed to their elimination, there would be no need for such weapons. The commission report emphasized both the opportunity created by the end of the cold war and the urgency of addressing the growing threat of possible acquisition of nuclear weapons by terrorists. It emphasized that the elimination of nuclear weapons must be a global endeavor involving all states. This should proceed in a series of stages involving phased verifiable reductions that would allow states to satisfy themselves each step along the way that further movement toward elimination could be made safely and securely. The necessary first step was for the five nuclear weapons states to "commit themselves unequivocally to the elimination of nuclear weapons and agree to start work immediately on the practical steps and negotiations required for its achievement." The commission recommended the following specific steps:

• taking nuclear weapons off alert;
• removing warheads from delivery vehicles;
• ending deployment of nonstrategic weapons;
• ending nuclear testing;
• negotiating further US-Russian reductions;
• establishing no-first-use policies;
• preventing horizontal proliferation;
• strengthening verification arrangements;
• halting the production of fissile material.[16]

---

[15] Michael Carver, "A Nuclear (Elimination) Exchange," *Royal United Services Institute Journal* 141, no. 5 (1996): 51–4.

[16] All text citations from Canberra Commission on the Elimination of Nuclear Weapons, Australia, Department of Foreign Affairs and Trade, *Report of the Canberra Commission on the Elimination of Nuclear Weapons* (Canberra: Department of Foreign Affairs and Trade, 1996), 9–12.

SPARKING THE DEBATE

Although the United States, Russia, and the other nuclear weapons states were indifferent to the Canberra Commission's report, many other countries supported its recommendations. Several so-called middle powers joined together to form the New Agenda Coalition to press for greater progress toward disarmament. In June 1998 the foreign ministers of Brazil, Egypt, Ireland, Mexico, New Zealand, Slovenia, South Africa, and Sweden issued a statement declaring their full support for the conclusions of the Canberra Commission and calling upon the governments of each of the nuclear-weapons states and the three nuclear-weapons-capable states (Israel, India, Pakistan) to develop plans for nuclear abolition. Slovenia later withdrew from the coalition, but the other states continued to work together in promoting the recommendations of the Canberra Commission. The New Agenda Coalition states, supported by a coalition of disarmament activists, played a key role in the 2000 NPT review conference. They succeeded in gaining agreement in the final conference declaration on language calling for concrete steps toward the elimination of nuclear weapons.

The Canberra Commission report generated considerable enthusiasm among nongovernmental groups, nuclear policy experts, and think tanks. It was a major morale builder and source of encouragement for advocates of nuclear arms restraint. The report sparked efforts to push the question of nuclear disarmament onto the international policy agenda and became the inspiration for a growing worldwide movement for nuclear weapons abolition. For a brief time the movement showed promise of being able to mobilize public awareness and support, but it was cut short by the terrorist attacks of September 2001 and the deterioration of international relations following the US invasion and occupation of Iraq.

The Canberra Commission report prompted a number of follow-up efforts to examine and promote plans for the elimination of nuclear weapons. The recommendations of the Canberra Commission were incorporated into two major studies that were released in 1997. The Stimson Center in Washington, DC produced a report, *An American Legacy: Building a Nuclear-Free World*,[17] and the Committee on International Security and Arms Control of the National Academy of Sciences released the study, *The Future of US Nuclear Weapons Policy*. Both acknowledged the work of the Canberra Commission and adopted many of its proposals. In 1998 the

---

[17] Steering Committee Project on Eliminating Weapons of Mass Destruction, *An American Legacy: Building a Nuclear-Weapon Free World*, Report no. 22 (Washington, DC: Stimson Center, 1997).

Japan Institute of International Affairs, the Hiroshima Peace Institute, and the Japanese government created the Tokyo Forum on Nuclear Non-proliferation and Disarmament, which released a report the following year that reiterated many of the recommendations of the Canberra Commission.

In December 1996 George Lee Butler joined with retired general and former NATO commander Andrew Goodpaster to release a statement urging the United States and Russia to move toward "the complete elimination of nuclear weapons from all nations."[18] The Butler–Goodpaster appeal was followed the next day by the release of a *Statement on Nuclear Weapons by International Generals and Admirals*, which was signed by sixty retired generals and admirals from seventeen countries. The generals' and admirals' statement declared support for the "principle of continuous, complete and irrevocable elimination of nuclear weapons."[19] For the next several years Butler devoted himself to public education and advocacy on behalf of nuclear arms reduction and elimination. He gave numerous presentations before prestigious audiences throughout the world and met with government officials of the nuclear weapons states and many other countries to argue the case for nuclear disarmament. In nearly every presentation, Butler mentioned the Canberra Commission report and extolled its recommendations for reducing and eliminating nuclear weapons.

"WEAPONS OF TERROR"

In 2003, in the wake of intensive international attention to disarmament issues in Iraq, Swedish Foreign Minister Anna Lindh took the initiative to create a new international commission to focus on the broader problem of disarmament. The original idea of the commission came from Jayantha Dhanapala, then UN Under-Secretary General for Disarmament. Lindh was subsequently murdered, like Palme the victim of assassination, but Swedish Prime Minister Göran Persson and Foreign Minister Laila Freivalds carried on the project. The Commission on Weapons of Mass Destruction, as it was called, was chaired by Hans Blix, the former head of the International Atomic Energy Agency and former chief of the UN disarmament mission in Iraq. Its June 2006 report, *Weapons of Terror*, addressed all forms of deadly weapons and examined the danger posed by potential terrorist acquisition of such weapons. The Blix report proposed a world

---

[18] Tim Weiner, "Rejection of 'Star Wars' Not Political, Inquiry Says," *New York Times*, 5 December 1996.
[19] Nuclear Age Peace Foundation, "Statement on Nuclear Weapons by International Generals and Admirals," 5 December 1996. Available online at Nuclear Files, www.nuclearfiles.org/menu/key-issues/ethics/issues/military/statement-by-international-generals.htm (accessed 30 March 2007).

summit at the United Nations in New York to provide global leadership for efforts to eliminate weapons of mass destruction. In releasing the report Blix made a special point of emphasizing that policies of unilateralism and military action had failed to stem the dangers of terrorism and weapons proliferation. He called for a renewed emphasis on international cooperation in reducing these threats.

The Blix Commission issued sixty recommendations for preventing nuclear proliferation, reducing the threat from existing weapons, controlling biological and chemical weapons and toxins, limiting weapons delivery systems, preventing the weaponization of space, and strengthening the disarmament verification and enforcement role of the United Nations. The commission called on states to start preparing for a process of outlawing nuclear weapons. It urged the existing nuclear weapons states to fulfill their NPT commitments to implement disarmament in conformity with principles of verification, irreversibility, and transparency. In a veiled reference to the United States the report urged states to abide by the UN Charter prohibition on the threat or use of force except in self-defense or as authorized by the Security Council. It called for a verified ban on the production of fissile materials and urged states to ratify the CTBT. The commission called for a new strategic nuclear weapons reduction agreement between Russia and the United States, specifically proposing a further 50 percent cut in weapons levels and the dismantlement of warheads withdrawn under the 2002 Strategic Offensive Reductions Treaty (SORT).[20]

The *Weapons of Terror* report also offered proposals for dealing with nuclear proliferation challenges in Iran and North Korea and addressing the threat posed by global terrorist networks. To induce Iran to suspend its uranium enrichment program it called for security assurances that would take into account Iran's perception of threats. It urged the renunciation of regime change as a goal of policy. It proposed a freeze on the production of fissile materials in the region, including by nuclear-armed Israel, as a step toward the creation of a regional zone free of weapons of mass destruction. To induce North Korea to dismantle its nuclear weapons program, it called for similar security assurances to the Pyongyang government. It urged the reinstatement of the previous commitment to ban the production of fissile materials by both North and South Korea as a step toward making the

---

[20] All citations of text from Weapons of Mass Destruction Commission, final report, *Weapons of Terror: Freeing the World of Nuclear, Biological, and Chemical Arms* (Stockholm, Sweden, 1 June 2006), 18, 25, 56–7, 64–5, 67–72, 83–7, 93, 105–8, 167–6. Available online at the Weapons of Mass Destruction Commission, www.wmdcommission.org/files/Weapons_of_Terror.pdf (accessed 30 March 2007).

Korean peninsula a zone free of weapons of mass destruction. To prevent terrorists from gaining access to nuclear weapons or materials, the commission called for an effective worldwide accounting and control of weapons and weapons-related materials. It urged greater compliance with United Nations conventions and Security Council Resolution 1540 (2005) to prevent terrorists from acquiring deadly weapons.

WHAT IS ZERO?

The goal of abolishing nuclear weapons faces unavoidable technical and political uncertainties. It is an obvious fact that nuclear weapons cannot be uninvented. The materials, technologies, and scientific knowhow to make nuclear weapons will remain a permanent fixture of the human experience. Even after the weapons themselves have been abolished, the scientific knowledge and equipment necessary for their creation will remain. The risk that rogue actors might seek to "break out" and redevelop nuclear weapons can never be eliminated. Permanent vigilance is the price humankind must pay for having developed these weapons.

Because of this reality, the 1997 National Academy of Sciences report, *The Future of US Nuclear Weapons*, recommended the use of the term "prohibit" rather than "abolish." The term prohibit is better than abolish because it does not create the false impression that nuclear weapons can be eliminated absolutely. The report called for consideration of a global prohibition of nuclear weapons, and emphasized the need for realism in assessing the challenges of disarmament.[21] A prohibition agreement implies a legal commitment and an enforcement duty. Such an agreement would explicitly outlaw the possession and use of nuclear weapons. It would universalize the denuclearization process and create an obligation on all states, nuclear and nonnuclear alike, to renounce reliance on nuclear weapons. It would signify the determination of nations to break their dependence on nuclear weapons without qualification or reservation, and to rely entirely on other means for achieving security.

In *The Gift of Time* Jonathan Schell distinguished between technical zero and political zero. At a technical level, the capability to develop nuclear weapons will always exist, but latent potential is very different from actual nuclear capability. As Schell wrote, "it is unquestionably possible, through technical means, to turn something that is a nuclear weapon

---

[21] National Academy of Sciences (US), Committee on International Security and Arms Control, *The Future of US Nuclear Weapons Policy* (Washington, DC: National Academy Press, 1997), 8–10.

into a collection of materials that plainly is not."[22] It is technically feasible to dismantle nuclear weapons and to establish systems of scientific monitoring, verification, and control to reach a point of zero nuclear weapons.

The greater challenge is reaching political zero, that stage of political relations where nations have no desire or need to possess such weapons. Schell defined political zero as the "complete disavowal by political authorities of the intention to use nuclear weapons, in any circumstances." The United States and Britain have nuclear weapons but would never think of using them against each other "because their confidence in their political zero is so strong." When political animosity is low, so is the motivation to develop nuclear weapons. Cooperative political relations and mutual democracy are the greatest assurance of security and the best guarantee against war and weapons proliferation. The development and strengthening of cooperative political relationships can help to create the mutual political confidence, the political zero, that would allow nations to end their reliance on nuclear weapons.

The process of disarmament cannot be separated from the requirement for strengthened systems of international cooperation and conflict resolution. The legal prohibition against nuclear weapons must be backed up by effective enforcement mechanisms and a sustained commitment to nonviolent dispute resolution. This will require the creation of more reliable and effective international security mechanisms, and greater efforts to prevent and resolve conflicts before they degenerate into war. The general history of collective security efforts through the United Nations and the earlier League of Nations is not a hopeful one, but there are many examples of successful cooperative action. There is no shortage of lessons that can be gleaned from experience to enhance cooperative security. The 1997 report of the Carnegie Commission on Preventing Deadly Conflict contained an array of proposals, examples, and recommended policies for reducing the frequency and intensity of armed violence. Knowledge of what causes conflict and how it can be prevented has increased enormously in recent decades. It is now possible, if the political will exists, to prevent and resolve most conflicts before they reach the stage of war. It is only through such measures to strengthen international cooperation and resolve armed conflict that nuclear disarmament can succeed in lifting the threat of mass annihilation that still clouds the human future.

As Michael Howard noted, a disarmed world will not automatically be more peaceful. Nations will still be vulnerable to the underlying historical

---

[22] Schell, *The Gift of Time*, 218.

forces and security dilemmas that contribute to armed conflict.[23] Even the most successful disarmament process cannot guarantee security if the political relations among nations are confrontational rather than cooperative. Morgenthau was right to emphasize the primacy of settling political differences as the precondition for disarmament. Bertha von Suttner and nineteenth-century peace advocates were right to link disarmament to the creation of a more secure international order based on the rule of law and the resolution of interstate conflict. Disarmament is a dynamic process, not an absolute end state. It is an essential part of the strategy for peace, but it must be accompanied by a wide range of other peacemaking measures. To achieve lasting disarmament it is necessary to prevent war itself. Nuclear pacifism leads unavoidably to general pacifism, to a rejection of war and a commitment to enhancing cooperative security and building structures of peace.

[23] Michael Howard, "Problems of a Disarmed World," in *Studies in War and Peace* (New York: Viking Press, 1971), 224–34.

16

Realistic pacifism

After a long journey of inquiry into the history of movements and ideas for peace, we return again to the concept of pacifism, to consider its meaning and implications. In the nuclear realm pacifism is absolute, rejecting any use of weapons that are grossly destructive and inherently indiscriminate. In other dimensions of conflict, however, pacifism is conditional and pragmatic. It is predicated on a presumption against armed violence, but it acknowledges that the use of force, constrained by rigorous ethical standards, may be necessary at times for self-defense and the protection of the innocent. When understood in this "realistic" context, as Martin Luther King, Jr. phrased it, pacifism is not a term of opprobrium, after all. It is a word to describe movements, ideas, and practices for preventing war and building peace, just as intended by those who originally coined the term. It is part of a tradition dating back hundreds of years and originating in religious and philosophical principles that have evolved over thousands of years. This is not to deny the occasional inconsistencies of pacifism and the peace movement more broadly – a persistent naïveté, a tendency toward utopianism (perhaps evident in this volume), an inadequate grasp of the unavoidable dilemmas of security, an unwillingness to accept the inherent egoism of human communities – but these limitations do not detract from the status of pacifism as a legitimate social movement and scholarly discipline.

I am not suggesting that the term should be resurrected. The meaning of pacifism has been distorted beyond the point where it can be restored to the original intent. It is best to set the term aside and to describe the practice and theory of peace in the context of more contemporary terms, such as peace-building and peacemaking. These latter terms are admittedly vague and imprecise, but they have the merit of suggesting contingency and agency. They acknowledge that peace is not yet fully realized, and may never be, and that the prevention of war depends on active human endeavor. They embody Kant's moral imperative to work for peace, even when it may seem unachievable, as the ultimate human right, the "supreme political good."

THEORY

After the bitter lessons of the twentieth century peace advocates have become more realistic and, it is hoped, wiser. They have learned that they cannot be indifferent to the sufferings and needs of those who are victimized by repression, or ignore the necessary connections between peace and broader issues of democracy, social justice, and human rights. To be sure some peace advocates remain narrowly focused on the absence of war rather than the presence of justice, but most recognize that justice and peace are inextricably linked. Peace advocates are urgently concerned about the plight of those who suffer oppression at the hands of repressive regimes or armed factions. They are strong advocates for the United Nations, while remaining critical of its many shortcomings, and support the strengthening of international law and multilateral institutions. They are patriots who love their nation, although often critically, but their loyalties stretch beyond national boundaries to embrace solidarity with people in other countries and cultures.

Peace activists and scholars today have access to a much wider array of historical experience and empirical evidence in attempting to understand the causes of war and the conditions of peace. History and the findings of social science have verified many of the moral and humanist principles that motivated peace advocacy in the nineteenth and early twentieth centuries. We know that imperialism and unrestrained arms competition contribute to war, that isolationism and neutrality in an interdependent world are illusions, and that international law and institutions can help to prevent and restrain war. We have evidence to confirm the theory of the "Kantian triad" – democratic states tend not to wage war on one another, economic interdependence fosters cooperation, and mutual participation in international institutions encourages peace. We know that societies in which women are empowered politically and socially are less likely to use military force to solve international problems, and that promoting balanced and sustainable development is an effective strategy for preventing war and terrorism. We know that unresolved political grievances can turn violent, and that greater efforts are needed to address legitimate demands for justice and self-determination.

These proven correlates of peace correspond to the principles promoted by pacifists and internationalists over the centuries. Religious teachers, philosophers, moral reformers, liberals, democratic nationalists, socialists, feminists – all have contributed to the deepening body of peacemaking knowledge and practice. Theory and empirical research have come together to establish the outlines of the modern peace agenda, to create a greater understanding of the policies and conditions that can lead to a more secure, less violent world.

The prevalence of war can be reduced by promoting democracy, economic interdependence, international organization, gender equality, equitable economic development, and the resolution of political grievances.

PRACTICE

Along with more complete and empirically based theories of peace, we also have more sophisticated and proven techniques of peace building. Practical methods are now available in every field of conflict – from the realm of civil strife to the problem of nuclear proliferation – for reducing the likelihood of armed violence. As Charles Chatfield observed, virtually every existing means of preventing and constraining war originated with the peace movement. International law, arbitration and mediation, the creation of international organizations, disarmament, decolonization, economic development, democratization, human rights, the protection of civilians – all were proposed by peace advocates well before they were adopted by governments.[1]

Peacemaking and conflict transformation efforts have multiplied in recent decades. According to the *Human Security Report* of 2005, the increase of international peacemaking efforts since the 1990s has led to a 40 percent reduction in the number of armed conflicts in the world. The United Nations and other international institutions have promoted economic development, mediated conflicts, monitored human rights, organized democratic elections, ameliorated humanitarian emergencies, deployed peacekeepers, established international criminal tribunals, imposed economic sanctions, and organized post-conflict peace-building missions. Governments and regional organizations have devoted greater attention to economic development, conflict prevention, and international peacemaking efforts. Nongovernmental organizations and citizen groups have become increasingly significant actors at the national and international levels in pressing governments toward greater peacemaking efforts and engaging directly in humanitarian and conflict resolution efforts. Nonviolent resistance methods have proven to be "a force more powerful" and have helped to advance political freedom, democracy, and human rights in dozens of countries.

Many other advances have emerged in recent decades in the fields of conflict resolution and peace studies. Well-tested and proven methods exist for mediating disputes and transforming the underlying dynamics that cause violent conflict. Negotiating behavior is more thoroughly understood,

---

[1] Charles Chatfield, *The American Peace Movement: Ideals and Activism* (New York: Twayne Publishers, 1992), 180–2.

and guidelines are available to assist parties in reaching agreement, in "getting to yes," as Roger Fisher and William Ury phrased it.[2] Studies by John Darby and others have examined peace agreements and identified the core elements that are most likely to strengthen or undermine the prospects for lasting settlement.[3] A great deal has been learned about the use of incentives and sanctions and carrots-and-sticks bargaining dynamics. The Carnegie Commission on Preventing Deadly Conflict has produced multiple volumes on the proven methods available to reduce the likelihood of armed conflict. These and other advances in knowledge provide a robust foundation for the principles of peacemaking. The fact that politicians and diplomats so often ignore these principles does not make them less valid.

It is not too bold to suggest that there is an emerging science of peace-building. This new field of knowledge and experience is still incomplete and tentative, but it encompasses a coherent body of theory and practice on ways to prevent war and assure peace. This science of peace-building draws heavily from realist and liberal political theory, but it is intellectually rigorous and distinct in its own right. It is grounded in a wide range of disciplines, from religion and the humanities to the social sciences and practical service, but it has its own unique set of principles and practices. It is multidisciplinary in approach, to account for the diverse factors associated with the causes of war and the conditions for peace, but it is increasingly recognized as a separate field of knowledge and practice. It is embodied in a growing number of peace and conflict studies programs at schools and universities around the world and in an increasingly mature set of scholarly journals and publications. The study of peace is emerging as a legitimate and necessary field of academic inquiry and policy analysis.

ACTION

Peace movements have benefited from the growth of peace-building knowledge and have become more legitimate and persistent. Three of the largest waves of peace mobilization in history have occurred in recent decades – the Vietnam antiwar movement, the nuclear freeze and disarmament campaigns of the 1980s, and the worldwide protest against the US-led invasion

---

[2] Roger Fisher and William Ury, *Getting to Yes: Negotiating Agreement without Giving In* (Boston, MA: Houghton Mifflin, 1991).

[3] Tristan Anne Borer, John Darby, and Siobhán McEvoy-Levy, *Peacebuilding after Peace Accords: The Challenges of Violence, Truth and Youth* (Rirec Project on Post-Accord Peacebuilding) (Notre Dame, IN: University of Notre Dame Press, 2007); John Darby, *The Effects of Violence on Peace Processes* (Washington, DC: United States Institute of Peace Press, 2001).

of Iraq. These upsurges of peace activism were a reaction to the increasing destructiveness and futility of war in the modern era, and to the excesses of US militarization. They also reflected the rise of civil society activism in many nations and the institutionalization of mobilization capacity (greatly multiplied by the power of the Internet). Peace activism not only became more prevalent but also more effective in breaking through the political and cultural barriers that limited effectiveness in the past. The Vietnam antiwar movement was riven by sectarianism, and its public image was damaged by the extreme acts of a few, although public opposition to the war steadily mounted and served as a constraint on US military options. The nuclear freeze movement in the United States projected a moderate, mainstream image, aided immensely by the support of the religious community and by the endorsement of millions of voters during the 1982 nuclear freeze referenda. The freeze campaign and disarmament movements in Europe were able to transcend cold war ideology by appealing to both East and West. The worldwide opposition to war in Iraq was unable to prevent the US invasion, but it helped to block UN Security Council endorsement and denied Washington political legitimacy and military allies. The war was lost politically before it ever began militarily.

Peace activists and scholars operate from the same body of knowledge, but inevitable gaps exist between the world of activism and the realm of research. Partly this reflects the nature of the social mobilization process, which often leaves little room for detached analysis or nuanced interpretation. Some activist campaigns are able to translate opposition to a particular policy into support for a proposed alternative – as the nuclear freeze movement did in turning nuclear fear into the demand for a mutual halt to the arms race – but most activist efforts focus narrowly on stopping immediate dangers. While activists lag behind scholars in some areas, they are ahead in others, particularly in addressing questions of political power. Scholars consider issues of power in the context of the theory of political realism, but they tend to ignore the influence of vested political and military interests when they analyze the causes of war and the requirements for peace. Particularly in the United States, academic journals and scholarly conferences rarely consider the proverbial elephant in the room, the role of state power and the way it which it is often exercised to the detriment of international peace and security. Peace scholars generally avoid these politically controversial issues. Activist groups have no such compunction and by their very nature seek to "speak truth to power." This is another way in which pacifism attempts to become more realistic, by understanding and confronting the power of the vested interests that benefit from militarization and war.

Peace advocates focus attention on the deeply entrenched political and economic interests that feed what Mary Kaldor has termed "the globalized war economy," and that reinforce tendencies toward militarization in Washington, Moscow, and other capitals.[4] Today's activists follow in the tradition of those who condemned the "merchants of death" after World War I, who supported the Nye Committee hearings during the 1930s, and who warned of a military industrial complex during the 1960s. Like the authors of *Speak Truth to Power* in the 1950s they point to the broad tentacles of militarization within society and culture. They highlight the ways in which an overemphasis on military power forecloses peacemaking options and creates a preference for using armed force to resolve political disputes. Restraining militarization is an urgent priority for social progress and an indispensable requirement for peace and justice, part of the ongoing struggle for democracy and human rights.

In the end peacemaking is a moral commitment. Establishing peace, Kant wrote, is the ultimate duty of political action, the highest expression of reason struggling against irrationality.[5] The most fundamental human right, said John XXIII, is the right to life, the right to personal integrity and the development of life.[6] All other rights pale if we are not protected from the predations of armed violence, from the fear of aggression and weapons of mass destruction, from the diversion of vast resources to war preparation. It is our moral duty, Gandhi insisted, to struggle against injustice but to do so through the weapon of nonviolent action. Camus wrote that we must refuse murder with all our force and being. In the endless struggle between violence and persuasion, the only honorable course is to "stake everything on a formidable gamble: that words are more powerful than munitions."[7] Overcoming war involves more than words, though. It demands action. It requires an alternative, a moral equivalent, a means of translating the universal longing for purpose into a strategy for serving the common good. Building peace is that alternative, a commitment guided by ethical principles, chastened by the lessons of history, and embodied in the experience of practical peacemaking.

[4] Mary Kaldor, "The Globalized War Economy," in *New and Old Wars: Organized Violence in a Global Era* (Stanford, CA: Stanford University Press, 2001), 90–111.

[5] Immanuel Kant, "From *The Metaphysical Elements of Right*," in *International Relations in Political Thought: Texts from the Ancient Greeks to the First World War*, ed. Chris Brown, Terry Nardin, and Nicholas Rengger, 450–5 (Cambridge: Cambridge University Press, 2002).

[6] *Pacem in Terris*, Encyclical of Pope John XXIII, promulgated 11 April 1963, para. 11. Available online at Papal Encyclicals, www.papalencyclicals.net/John23/j23pacem.htm (accessed 30 March 2007).

[7] Albert Camus, *Neither Victims nor Executioners* (Philadelphia, PA: New Society Publishers, 1986), 55.

Bibliography

BOOKS

Ackerman, Peter, and Jack DuVall. *A Force More Powerful: A Century of Nonviolent Conflict.* New York: St. Martin's Press, 2000.

Ackerman, Peter, and Christopher Kruegler. *Strategic Nonviolent Conflict: The Dynamics of People Power in the Twentieth Century.* Westport, CT: Praeger, 1994.

Alonzo, Harriet Hyman. *Peace as a Women's Issue: A History of the U.S. Movement for World Peace and Women's Rights.* Syracuse, NY: Syracuse University Press, 1993.

American Friends Service Committee. *Speak Truth to Power: A Quaker Search for an Alternative to Violence.* Philadelphia: American Friends Service Committee, 1955.

Angell, Norman. *The Great Illusion: A Study of the Relation of Military Power to National Advantage.* 4th edn. New York: G. P. Putnam's Sons, 1913.

Ansbro, John J. *Martin Luther King, Jr.: The Making of a Mind.* Maryknoll, NY: Orbis Books, 1994.

Appleby, R. Scott. *The Ambivalence of the Sacred: Religion, Violence, and Reconciliation.* Lanham, MD: Rowman & Littlefield, 2000.

Arendt, Hannah. *On Violence.* New York: Harcourt Brace, 1970.

Aslan, Reza. *No God but God: The Origins, Evolution, and Future of Islam.* New York: Random House, 2005.

Aung San Suu Kyi. *The Voice of Hope: Conversations with Alan Clements.* New York: Seven Stories, 1997.

Axelrod, Robert. *The Evolution of Cooperation.* New York: Basic Books, 1984.

Axworthy, Lloyd. *Navigating a New World: Canada's Global Future.* Toronto: Vintage Canada, 2004.

Bainton, Roland H. *Christian Attitudes Toward War and Peace: A Historical Survey and Critical Re-evaluation.* New York: Abingdon Press, 1960.

Banerjee, Mukulika. *The Pathan Unarmed: Opposition & Memory in the North West Frontier.* Karachi: Oxford University Press, 2000.

Barash, David P. *Introduction to Peace Studies.* Belmont, CA: Wadsworth Publishing, 1991.

Baskir, Lawrence M., and William A. Strauss. *Chance and Circumstance: The Draft, the War and the Vietnam Generation.* New York: Alfred Knopf, 1978.

Beales, A. C. F. *The History of Peace: A Short Account of the Organised Movements for International Peace.* London: G. Bell & Sons Ltd., 1931.

Birn, Donald S. *The League of Nations Union 1918–1945.* Oxford: Clarendon Press, 1981.

Boff, Leonardo, and Clovodis Boff. *Introducing Liberation Theology.* Maryknoll, NY: Orbis Books, 1988.

Bondurant, Joan V. *Conquest of Violence: The Gandhian Philosophy of Conflict.* Rev. edn. Princeton, NJ: Princeton University Press, 1988.

Branch, Taylor. *Parting the Waters: America in the King Years, 1954–63.* New York: Touchstone, 1988.

Brown, Seyom. *The Causes and Prevention of War.* 2nd edn. New York: St. Martin's Press, 1994.

Brock, Peter. *A Brief History of Pacifism from Jesus to Tolstoy.* 2nd edn. Toronto: Distributed by Syracuse University Press, 1992.

Freedom From War: Nonsectarian Pacifism 1814–1914. Toronto: University of Toronto Press, 1991.

Brock, Peter, and Nigel Young. *Pacifism in the Twentieth Century.* Syracuse, NY: Syracuse University Press, 1999.

Brown, Judith M. *Gandhi: Prisoner of Hope.* New Haven: Yale University Press, 1989.

Burrowes, Robert J. *The Strategy of Nonviolent Defense: A Gandhian Approach.* Albany: State University of New York Press, 1996.

Camus, Albert. *Neither Victims Nor Executioners.* Philadelphia: New Society Publishers, 1986.

Ceadel, Martin. *The Origins of War Prevention: The British Peace Movement and International Relations 1730–1854.* Oxford: Oxford University Press, 1996.

Pacifism in Britain 1914–1945: The Defining of a Faith. Oxford: Clarendon Press, 1980.

Thinking About Peace and War. Oxford: Oxford University Press, 1987.

Chatfield, Charles. *The American Peace Movement: Ideals and Activism.* New York: Twayne Publishers, 1992.

Chickering, Roger. *Imperial Germany and a World without War: The Peace Movement and German Society, 1892–1914.* Princeton, NJ: Princeton University Press, 1975.

Clark, Howard. *Civil Resistance in Kosovo.* Sterling, VA: Pluto Press, 2000.

Collier, Paul, *et al. Breaking the Conflict Trap: Civil War and Development Policy.* Washington, DC: World Bank, 2003.

Collins, Canon L. John. *Faith Under Fire.* London: Leslie Frewin, 1966.

Cook, Alice, and Gwyn Kirk. *Greenham Women Everywhere: Dreams, Ideas and Actions from the Women's Peace Movement.* Cambridge, MA: South End Press, 1983.

Cookson, J. E. *The Friends of Peace: Anti-War Liberalism in England, 1793–1815.* New York: Cambridge University Press, 1982.

Cooper, Sandi E. *Patriotic Pacifism: Waging War in Europe, 1815–1914.* New York: Oxford University Press, 1991.

Cortright, David, and Max Watts. *Left Face: Soldier Unions and Resistance Movements in Modern Armies*. Westport, CT: Greenwood Press, 1991.

Cousins, Norman. *Modern Man is Obsolete*. New York: Viking Press, 1946.

The Pathology of Power. New York: W. W. Norton and Company, 1987.

Curti, Merle Eugene. *The American Peace Crusade 1815–1860*. Durham, NC: Duke University Press, 1929.

Darby, John. *The Effects of Violence on Peace Processes*. Washington, DC: United States Institute of Peace Press, 2001.

DeBenedetti, Charles. *Origins of the Modern American Peace Movement, 1915–1929*. Millwood, NY: KTO Press, 1978.

The Peace Reform in American History. Bloomington: Indiana University Press, 1980.

DeBenedetti, Charles, and Charles Chatfield (assisting author). *An American Ordeal: The Antiwar Movement of the Vietnam Era*. Syracuse, NY: Syracuse University Press, 1990.

Divine, Robert. *The Illusion of Neutrality*. Chicago: University of Chicago Press, 1962.

Domke, William K. *War and the Changing Global System*. New Haven: Yale University Press, 1988.

Doyle, Michael. *Ways of War and Peace: Realism, Liberalism, and Socialism*. New York: Norton, 1997.

Easwaran, Eknath. *A Man to Match His Mountains: Badshahkhan, Nonviolent Soldier of Islam*. Petaluma, CA: Nilgiri Press, 1984.

Einstein, Albert. *Einstein on Peace*. New York: Simon and Schuster, 1960.

Elshtain, Jean Bethke. *Women and War*. 2nd edn. Chicago: University of Chicago Press, 1993.

Esquivel, Adolfo Pérez. *Christ in a Poncho: Testimonials of the Nonviolent Struggles in Latin America*. Maryknoll, NY: Orbis Books, 1983.

Evans, Richard J. *Comrades and Sisters: Feminism, Socialism and Pacifism in Europe, 1870–1945*. New York: St. Martin's Press, 1987.

Ferguson, John. *War and Peace in the World's Religions*. New York: Oxford University Press, 1978.

Fischer, Louis. *The Life of Mahatma Gandhi*. New York: Harper & Row, 1950.

Fisher, Roger, and William Ury. *Getting to Yes: Negotiating Agreement Without Giving In*. Boston: Houghton Mifflin, 1991.

Fleischman, Paul R. *The Buddha Taught Nonviolence, Not Pacifism*. Seattle: Pariyatti Press, 2002.

Foley, Michael S. *Confronting the War Machine: Draft Resistance During the Vietnam War*. Chapel Hill, NC: University of North Carolina Press, 2003.

Forest, Jim. *Love Is the Measure: A Biography of Dorothy Day*. New York: Paulist, 1986.

Friesen, Abraham. *Erasmus, the Anabaptists and the Great Commission*. Grand Rapids, MI: William B. Eerdmans, 1998.

Gandhi, Mohandas. *All Men Are Brothers*, ed. Krishna Kripalani. New York: Continuum, 1980.

Gilligan, James. *Preventing Violence*. New York: Thames & Hudson, 2001.

Goodrich, Leland M. *The United Nations*. New York: Thomas Y. Crowell, 1959.

Gopin, Marc. *Between Eden and Armageddon: The Future of World Religions, Violence, and Peacemaking*. New York: Oxford University Press, 2000.

Gorbachev, Mikhail. *Perestroika: New Thinking for Our Country and the World*. New York: Harper and Row, 1987.

Gray, J. Glenn. *The Warriors: Reflections on Men in Battle*. New York: Harper & Row, 1959.

Grey, Viscount of Fallodon, K. G. *Twenty-Five Years 1892–1916*. Vol. I. New York: Frederick A. Stokes Co., 1925.

Gurr, Ted Robert. *Why Men Rebel*. Princeton: Princeton University Press, 1970.

Hallie, Philip P. *Lest Innocent Blood be Shed: The Story of the Village of Le Chambon and How Goodness Happened There*. New York: Harper and Row, 1979.

Hardiman, David. *Gandhi in His Time and Ours*. New Delhi: Pauls Press, 2003.

Harries, Richard. *Reinhold Niebuhr And The Issues Of Our Time*. Grand Rapids, MI: William B. Eerdmans, 1986.

Havel, Václav. *Living in Truth*, ed. Jan Vladislav. London: Faber and Faber, 1986.

Hedges, Chris. *War is a Force That Gives Us Meaning*. New York: PublicAffairs, 2002.

Hershberger, Guy F. *War, Peace, and Nonresistance*. Scottdale, PA: Herald Press, 1946.

Howard, Michael. *The Invention of Peace and the Reinvention of War*. London: Profile Books, 2002.

War and the Liberal Conscience. New Brunswick, NJ: Rutgers University Press, 1978.

Hugo, Victor. *Actes et paroles: pendant l'exil 1852–1870*. Paris: Nelson, Éditeurs, 1912.

Hunt, Andrew E. *The Turning: A History of Vietnam Veterans Against the War*. New York: New York University Press, 1999.

Huxley, Aldous, ed. *An Encyclopædia of Pacifism*. New York: Harper & Brothers, 1937.

Ingram, Norman. *The Politics of Dissent: Pacifism in France 1919–1939*. Oxford: Clarendon Press, 1991.

Iyer, Raghavan, ed. *The Essential Writings of Mahatma Gandhi*. New Delhi: Oxford University Press, 1990.

Jungk, Robert. *Brighter than a Thousand Suns: A Personal History of the Atomic Scientists*. New York: Harcourt Brace & Company, 1958.

Kaldor, Mary. *New and Old Wars: Organized Violence in a Global Era*. Stanford, CA: Stanford University Press, 2001.

Kant, Immanuel. *Perpetual Peace*. New York: Liberal Arts Press, 1957.

Katz, Milton S. *Ban the Bomb: A History of SANE, the Committee for a Sane Nuclear Policy, 1957–1985*. New York: Greenwood Press, 1986.

Keegan, John. *A History of Warfare*. New York: Alfred A. Knopf, 1993.

Kennan, George. *At a Century's Ending: Reflections, 1982–1995*. New York: W. W. Norton, 1996.

Keynes, John Maynard. *The Economic Consequences of the Peace*. London: Macmillan, 1920.

King, Martin Luther, Jr. *Stride Toward Freedom: The Montgomery Story*. New York: Harper & Brothers, 1958.

Where Do We Go from Here: Chaos or Community? New York: Harper & Row, 1967.

King, Sallie B. *Being Benevolence: The Social Ethics of Engaged Buddhism*. Honolulu: University of Hawai'i Press, 2005.

Kisala, Robert. *Prophets of Peace: Pacifism and Cultural Identity in Japan's New Religions*. Honolulu: University of Hawai'i Press, 1999.

Knock, Thomas J. *To End All Wars: Woodrow Wilson and the Quest for a New World Order*. New York: Oxford University Press, 1992.

Kriesberg, Louis. *Constructive Conflicts: From Escalation to Resolution*. 2nd edn. Lanham, MD: Rowman & Littlefield, 2003.

Lederach, John Paul. *Building Peace: Sustainable Reconciliation in Divided Societies*. Washington, DC: United States Institute of Peace Press, 1997.

The Moral Imagination: The Art and Soul of Building Peace. New York: Oxford University Press, 2005.

Preparing for Peace: Conflict Transformation Across Cultures. Syracuse, NY: Syracuse University Press, 1995.

de Ligt, Bart. *The Conquest of Violence: An Essay on War and Revolution*. New York: E. P. Dutton & Company, 1938.

London, Joan, and Henry Anderson. *So Shall Ye Reap*. New York: Thomas Y. Crowell, 1970.

Lorenz, Konrad. *On Aggression*. New York: Harcourt, Brace and World, 1966.

Lynch, Cecelia. *Beyond Appeasement: Interpreting Interwar Peace Movements in World Politics*. Ithaca, NY: Cornell University Press, 1999.

Macgregor, G. H. C. *The New Testament Basis of Pacifism and the Relevance of the Impossible Ideal*. Nyack, NY: Fellowship Publications, 1954.

Mahony, Liam, and Luis Enrique Eguren. *Unarmed Bodyguards: International Accompaniment for the Protection of Human Rights*. West Hartford, CT: Kumarian Press, 1997.

Mansfield, Edward D., and Brian M. Pollins, ed. *Economic Interdependence and International Conflict: New Perspectives on an Enduring Debate*. Ann Arbor: University of Michigan Press, 2003.

McNeal, Patricia. *Harder than War: Catholic Peacemaking in Twentieth-Century America*. New Brunswick, NJ: Rutgers University Press, 1992.

Melman, Seymour. *The Permanent War Economy: American Capitalism in Decline*. New York: Simon & Schuster, 1985.

Mill, John Stuart. *Principles of Political Economy, With Some of Their Applications to Social Philosophy*. Vol. II. Boston: C. C. Little & James Brown, 1848.

Morley, John. *The Life of Richard Cobden*. Vol. II. London, Macmillan and Co., 1908.

Moskos, Charles C., and John Whiteclay Chambers II, ed. *The New Conscientious Objection, From Sacred to Secular Resistance*. New York and Oxford: Oxford University Press, 1993.

Musto, Ronald G. *The Catholic Peace Tradition*. Maryknoll, NY: Orbis Books, 1986.

Nagler, Michael N. *Is There No Better Way? The Search for a Nonviolent Future*. Berkeley, CA: Berkeley Hills Books, 2001.

Nasr, Seyyed Hossein. *The Heart of Islam: Enduring Values for Humanity*. San Francisco: HarperSanFrancisco, 2002.

Nathan, Otto, and Heinz Norden, ed. *Einstein on Peace*. New York: Simon and Schuster, 1960.

Niebuhr, Reinhold. *Christianity and Power Politics*. New York: Charles Scribner's Sons, 1952.

   Moral Man And Immoral Society: A Study In Ethics And Politics. New York: Charles Scribner's Sons, 1932, 1960.

Nkrumah, Kwame. *I Speak of Freedom: A Statement of African Ideology*. New York: Praeger, 1962.

The Nobel Peace Prize Lecture: Desmond M. Tutu. New York: Anson Phelps Stokes Institute for African, Afro-American, and American Indian Affairs, 1986.

Noel-Baker, Philip. *The Private Manufacture of Armaments*. New York: Oxford University Press, 1937.

Nye, Joseph S., Jr. *Understanding International Conflicts: An Introduction to Theory and History*. 4th edn. New York: Longman, 2003.

Nyerere, Julius K. *Freedom and Unity: Uhuru na umoja: A Selection from Writings and Speeches, 1952–65*. London: Oxford University Press, 1967.

Osgood, Charles E. *An Alternative to War or Surrender*. Urbana, IL: University of Illinois Press, 1962.

Page, Kirby. *Must We Go to War?* New York: Farrar & Rinehart, Inc., 1937.

Penn, William. *An Essay Towards the Present and Future Peace of Europe: By the Establishment of an European Diet, Parliament, or Estates*. London: Peace Committee of the Society of Friends, 1936.

Rapaport, Anatol. *Peace: An Idea Whose Time Has Come*. Ann Arbor: The University of Michigan Press, 1992.

Rawls, John. *A Theory of Justice*. Rev. edn. Cambridge, MA: The Belknap Press of Harvard University Press, 1999.

Rochon, Thomas R. *Mobilizing for Peace: The Antinuclear Movements in Western Europe*. Princeton, NJ: Princeton University Press, 1988.

Rosecrance, Richard. *The Rise of the Trading State: Commerce and Conquest in the Modern World*. New York: Basic Books, 1986.

Russell, Bertrand. *Which Way to Peace?* Plymouth, UK: Michael Joseph Ltd., 1937.

Russett, Bruce. *Grasping the Democratic Peace: Principles for a Post-Cold War World*. Princeton, NJ: Princeton University Press, 1993.

Russett, Bruce, and John R. Oneal. *Triangulating Peace: Democracy, Interdependence, and International Organizations*. New York: W. W. Norton & Company, 2001.

Schell, Jonathan. *The Gift of Time: The Case for Abolishing Nuclear Weapons Now*. New York: Metropolitan Books, 1998.

The Unconquerable World: Power, Nonviolence, and the Will of the People. New York: Metropolitan Books, 2003.

Schildgen, Robert. *Toyohiko Kagawa: Apostle of Love and Social Justice.* Berkeley, CA: Centenary Books, 1988.

Schlesinger, Arthur M., Jr. *War and the American Presidency.* New York: W. W. Norton, 2004.

Schock, Kurt. *Unarmed Insurrections: People Power Movements in Nondemocracies.* Minneapolis: University of Minnesota Press, 2005.

Schwartz, Regina M. *The Curse of Cain: The Violent Legacy of Monotheism.* Chicago: University of Chicago Press, 1997.

Sen, Amartya. *Development as Freedom.* New York: Alfred A. Knopf, 1999.

Sen, K. M. *Hinduism.* Baltimore, MD: Penguin, 1961.

Sharp, Gene. *The Politics of Nonviolent Action.* Boston: Porter Sargent, 1973.

Waging Nonviolent Struggle: 20th Century Practice and 21st Century Potential. Boston: Porter Sargent, 2005.

Shutte, Augustine. *Ubuntu: An Ethic for a New South Africa.* Pietermaritzburg: Cluster Publications, 2001.

Singer, Peter. *A Darwinian Left: Politics, Evolution and Cooperation.* New Haven: Yale University Press, 2000.

One World: The Ethics of Globalization. New Haven: Yale University Press, 2002.

Small, Melvin. *Johnson, Nixon, and the Doves.* New Brunswick, NJ: Rutgers University Press, 1988.

Smith, Kenneth L., and Ira G. Zepp, Jr. *Search for the Beloved Community: The Thinking of Martin Luther King Jr.* Valley Forge, PA: Judson, 1998.

Smith, Rupert. *The Utility of Force: The Art of War in the Modern World.* London: Penguin Books, 2006.

Solo, Pam. *From Protest to Policy: Beyond the Freeze to Common Security.* Cambridge, MA: Ballinger, 1988.

Stacewicz, Richard. *Winter Soldiers: An Oral History of the Vietnam Veterans Against the War.* New York: Twayne Publishers, 1997.

Stanton, Shelby L. *The Rise and Fall of an American Army: U.S. Ground Forces in Vietnam, 1965–1973.* Novato, CA: Presidio Press, 1985.

Stoltzfus, Nathan. *Resistance of the Heart: Intermarriage and the Rosenstrasse Protest in Nazi Germany.* New York: W. W. Norton, 1996.

Swanwick, Helena. *The Roots of Peace; A Sequel to Collective Insecurity, Being an Essay on Some of the Uses, Conditions and Limitations of Compulsive Force in the Prevention of War.* London: J. Cape, 1938.

Swartz, Marvin. *The Union of Democratic Control in British Politics During the First World War.* Oxford: Clarendon Press, 1971.

Thapar, Romila. *Aśoka and the Decline of the Mauryas.* 2nd edn. Delhi: Oxford University Press, 1973.

Thomas, Norman. *Is Conscience a Crime?* New York: Vanguard, 1927.

Tolis, Peter. *Elihu Burritt: Crusader for Brotherhood.* Hamden, CT: Archon Books, 1968.

Tolstoy, Leo. *Tolstoy's Writings on Civil Disobedience and Non-Violence*. New York: Bergman Publishers, 1967.

Väyrynen, Raimo, ed. *The Waning of Major War: Theories and Debates*. London: Routledge, 2006.

Wallis, Jim. *God's Politics: Why the Right Gets It Wrong and the Left Doesn't Get It*. San Francisco: HarperCollins, 2005.

The Soul of Politics: A Practical and Prophetic Vision for Change. New York: Orbis Books, 1994.

Walzer, Michael. *Arguing about War*. New Haven: Yale University Press, 2004.

Just and Unjust Wars: A Moral Argument with Historical Illustrations. New York: Basic Books, 1992.

Weisgall, Jonathan M. *Operation Crossroads: The Atomic Tests at Bikini Atoll*. Annapolis, MD: Naval Institute Press, 1994.

Wells, H. G. *The Outline of History; Being a Plain History of Life and Mankind*. New York: Macmillan, 1921.

The Shape of Things to Come. New York: MacMillan Co., 1936.

Wells, Tom. *The War Within: America's Battle over Vietnam*. Berkeley: University of California Press, 1994.

Wink, Walter. *Engaging The Powers: Discernment And Resistance in a World of Domination*. Minneapolis, MN: Fortress Press, 1992.

Wittner, Lawrence S. *One World or None: A History of the World Nuclear Disarmament Movement Through 1953*. Vol. I of *The Struggle Against the Bomb*. Stanford: Stanford University Press, 1993.

Resisting the Bomb: A History of the World Nuclear Disarmament Movement, 1954–1970. Vol. II of *The Struggle Against the Bomb*. Stanford: Stanford University Press, 1997.

Toward Nuclear Abolition: A History of the World Nuclear Disarmament Movement, 1971 to the Present. Vol. III of *The Struggle Against the Bomb*. Stanford: Stanford University Press, 2003.

Wolpert, Stanley. *Gandhi's Passion: The Life and Legacy of Mahatma Gandhi*. New York: Oxford University Press, 2001.

Woolf, Virginia. *Three Guineas*. New York: Harcourt, Brace & World, 1938.

Worcester, Noah, a.k.a. Philo Pacificus. *A Solemn Review of the Custom of War; Showing That War is the Effect of Popular Delusion and Proposing a Remedy*. 5th edn. Cambridge, MA: Hilliard and Metcalf, 1816.

Wright, Robert. *Nonzero: The Logic of Human Destiny*. New York: Pantheon Books, 2000.

Yamamoto, Mari. *Grassroots Pacifism in Post-war Japan: The Rebirth of a Nation*. London: RoutledgeCurzon, 2004.

Yarrow, C. H. Mike. *Quaker Experiences in International Conciliation*. New Haven: Yale University Press, 1978.

Yoder, John Howard. *The Politics of Jesus*. 2nd edn. Grand Rapids, MI: Eerdmans, 1994.

Zinn, Howard. *A People's History of the United States 1492–Present*. New York: HarperCollins Publishers, 2005.

A Power Governments Cannot Suppress. San Francisco: City Lights Books, 2007.

CHAPTERS AND CONFERENCE PAPERS

Atherton, John. "Introduction: Christian Social Ethics in Context." In *Christian Social Ethics: A Reader*. Cleveland, OH: The Pilgrim Press, 1994.

Ballentine, Karen. "Beyond Greed and Grievance: Reconsidering the Economic Dynamics of Armed Conflict." In *The Political Economy of Armed Conflict: Beyond Greed and Grievance*, ed. Karen Ballentine and Jake Sherman, 259–83. Boulder, CO: Lynne Rienner Publishers, 2003.

Ballentine, Karen, and Jake Sherman. "Introduction." In *The Political Economy of Armed Conflict: Beyond Greed and Grievance*, ed. Karen Ballentine and Jake Sherman. Boulder, CO: Lynne Rienner Publishers, 2003.

Bamba, Nobuya. "Kitamura Tōkoku: His Pursuit of Freedom and World Peace." In *Pacifism in Japan: The Christian and Socialist Tradition*, ed. Nobuya Bamba and John F. Howes. Vancouver: University of British Columbia Press, 1978.

Barbé, Domingos. "The Spiritual Basis of Nonviolence." In *Relentless Persistence: Nonviolent Action in Latin America*, ed. Philip McManus and Gerald Schlabach. Philadelphia: New Society Publishers, 1991.

Björkqvist, Kaj. "The Inevitability of Conflict But Not of Violence: Theoretical Considerations on Conflict and Aggression." In *Cultural Variation in Conflict Resolution: Alternatives to Violence*, ed. Douglas P. Fry and Kaj Björkqvist. Mahwah, NJ: Lawrence Erlbaum Publishers, 1997.

Boff, Leonardo. "Active Nonviolence: The Political and Moral Power of the Poor." In *Relentless Persistence: Nonviolent Action in Latin America*, ed. Philip McManus and Gerald Schlabach. Philadelphia: New Society Publishers, 1991.

Brittain, Vera. "Pacifism After Munich." In *Testament of a Generation: The Journalism of Vera Brittain and Winifred Holtby*, ed. Vera Brittain *et al.*, 228–31. London: Virago, 1985.

"Women and Pacifism." [*Peace News*, 15 August 1941]. In *Vera Brittain: Women and Peace*, ed. Yvonne [Aleksandra] Bennett. London: Peace Pledge Union, 1987.

Bull, Hedley. "Disarmament and the International System." In *Theories of Peace and Security: A Reader In Contemporary Strategic Thought*, ed. John Garnett. London: Macmillan, 1970.

Burkholder, J. Lawrence. "The Limits of Perfection: Autobiographical Reflections." In *The Limits of Perfection: A Conversation with J. Lawrence Burkholder*, ed. Rodney J. Sawatsky and Scott Holland. Waterloo, Ontario: Institute of Anabaptist and Mennonite Studies, Conrad Grebel College, 1993.

Carroll, Berenice A. "Feminism and Pacifism: Historical and Theoretical Connections." In *Women and Peace: Theoretical, Historical and Practical Perspectives*, ed. Ruth Roach Pierson. London: Croom Helm, 1987.

Ceadel, Martin. "A Legitimate Peace Movement: The Case of Interwar Britain, 1918–1945." In *Challenge to Mars: Essays on Pacifism from 1918 to 1945*, ed. Peter Brock and Thomas P. Socknat, 134–48. Toronto: University of Toronto Press, 1999.

Cobden, Richard. "From *The Political Writings of Richard Cobden*." In *International Relations in Political Thought: Texts from the Ancient Greeks to the First World War*, ed. Chris Brown, Terry Nardin, and Nicholas Rengger, 538–49. Cambridge: Cambridge University Press, 2002.

Dellinger, Dave. "Gandhi's Heirs." In *Revolutionary Nonviolence: Essays by Dave Dellinger*. Indianapolis, IN: Bobbs-Merrill, 1970.

Deming, Barbara. "On Revolution and Equilibrium." In *Revolution & Equilibrium*. New York: Grossman, 1971.

"To Discover Our Humanity: Adolfo Pérez Esquivel." In *Relentless Persistence: Nonviolent Action in Latin America*, ed. Philip McManus and Gerald Schlabach. Philadelphia: New Society Publishers, 1991.

Dumas, Lloyd J. "Economics and Alternative Security: Toward a Peacekeeping International Economy." In *Alternative Security: Living Without Nuclear Deterrence*, ed. Burns H. Weston, 137–75. Boulder, CO: Westview Press, 1990.

Eglin, Josephine. "Women Pacifists in Interwar Britain." In *Challenge to Mars: Essays on Pacifism from 1918 to 1945*, ed. Peter Brock and Thomas P. Socknat, 149–68. Toronto: University of Toronto Press, 1999.

Ellsberg, Daniel. "Introduction: Call to Mutiny." In *Protest and Survive*, ed. E. P Thompson and Dan Smith. New York: Monthly Review Press, 1981.

Emerson, Ralph Waldo. "War" [1838]. In *The Works of Ralph Waldo Emerson*. Vol. V. New York: Bigelow, Brown and Co., n.d.

Farrugia, Peter. "The Conviction of Things Not Seen: Christian Pacifism in France, 1919–1945." In *Challenge to Mars: Essays on Pacifism from 1918 to 1945*, ed. Peter Brock and Thomas P. Socknat, 101–16. Toronto: University of Toronto Press, 1999.

Franck, James, *et al.* "A Report to the Secretary of War (June 1945)." In *The Atomic Age: Scientists in National and World Affairs*, ed. Morton Grodzins and Eugene Rabinowitch, 19–27. New York: Basic Books, 1963.

Fry, Douglas P. "Conclusion: Learning from Peaceful Societies." In *Keeping the Peace: Conflict Resolution and Peaceful Societies Around the World*, ed. Graham Kemp and Douglas P. Fry. New York: Routledge, 2004.

Gandhi, M. K. "Logical Consequence" [10 August 1938]. In *The Collected Works of Mahatma Gandhi* 74, no. 15. New Delhi: Publications Division, Ministry of Information and Broadcasting, Government of India, 1999. CD-Rom, dynamic collection.

Gandhi, Mahatma. "Satyagraha, Civil Disobedience, Passive Resistance, Non-Co-operation" [*Young India*, 23 March 1921]. In *The Collected Works of Mahatma Gandhi* 22, no. 240 (23 November 1920–5 April 1921). New Delhi: Publications Division, Ministry of Information and Broadcasting, Government of India, 1999. CD-Rom, dynamic collection.

"Working of Non-Violence" [*Harijan*, 6 February 1939]. In *The Collected Works of Mahatma Gandhi* 75, no. 47. New Delhi: Publications Division, Ministry of Information and Broadcasting, Government of India, 1999. CD-Rom, dynamic collection.

Gittelsohn, Roland B. "Pacifist." In *The Challenge of Shalom: The Jewish Tradition of Peace and Justice*, ed. Murray Polner and Naomi Goodman. Philadelphia, PA: New Society Publishers, 1994.

Grünewald, Guido. "War Resisters in Weimar Germany." In *Challenge to Mars: Essays on Pacifism from 1918 to 1945*, ed. Peter Brock and Thomas P. Socknat, 67–88. Toronto: University of Toronto Press, 1999.

Handler, Joshua. "The 1991–1992 PNIs and the Elimination, Storage, and Security of Tactical Nuclear Weapons." In *Tactical Nuclear Weapons: Emergent Threats in an Evolving Security Environment*, ed. Brian Alexander and Alistair Millar, 20–41. Washington, DC: Brassey's, 2003.

Havel, Václav. "Anatomy of a Reticence." In *Open Letters: Selected Writings, 1965–90*, ed. Paul Wilson, 291–322. New York: Vintage Books, 1992.

"The Power of the Powerless." In *Without Force or Lies: Voices from the Revolution of Central Europe in 1989–90*, ed. William M. Brinton and Alan Rinzler. San Francisco: Mercury House, 1990.

Heschel, Susannah. "Theological Affinities in the Writings of Abraham Joshua Heschel and Martin Luther King, Jr." In *Black Zion: African American Religious Encounters with Judaism*, ed. Yvonne Chireau and Nathaniel Deutsch. New York: Oxford University Press, 2000.

Howard, Michael. "Problems of a Disarmed World." In *Studies in War and Peace*. New York: Viking Press, 1971.

Howes, John F. "Uchimura Kanzō: The Bible and War." In *Pacifism in Japan: The Christian and his Socialist Tradition*, ed. Nobuya Bamba and John F. Howes. Vancouver: University of British Columbia Press, 1978.

Ingram, Norman. "Defending the Rights of Man: The Ligue des droits de l'homme and the Problem of Peace." In *Challenge to Mars: Essays on Pacifism from 1918 to 1945*, ed. Peter Brock and Thomas P. Socknat, 117–33. Toronto: University of Toronto Press, 1999.

James, William. "The Moral Equivalent of War." In *William James: The Essential Writings*, ed. Bruce W. Wilshire. New York: Harper Torchbooks, 1971.

Johansen, Robert C. "Enforcement without Military Combat: Toward an International Civilian Police." In *Globalization and Global Governance*, ed. Raimo Väyrynen, 173–98. Lanham, MD: Rowman & Littlefield, 1999.

Kaldor, Mary. "Beyond Militarism, Arms Races and Arms Control." Essay prepared for the Nobel Peace Prize Centennial Symposium, 6–8 December 2001. Social Science Research Council, www.ssrc.org/sept11/essays/kaldor.htm (accessed 22 November 2006).

"The Globalized War Economy." In *New and Old Wars: Organized Violence in a Global Era*. Stanford, CA: Stanford University Press, 2001.

Kant, Immanuel. "From Essay on Theory and Practice." In *International Relations in Political Thought: Texts from the Ancient Greeks to the First World War*, ed. Chris Brown, Terry Nardin and Nicholas Rengger, 428–32. Cambridge: Cambridge University Press, 2002.

"From *The Metaphysical Elements of Right*." In *International Relations in Political Thought: Texts from the Ancient Greeks to the First World War*, ed. Chris

Brown, Terry Nardin and Nicholas Rengger, 450–5. Cambridge: Cambridge University Press, 2002.

Kimelman, Reuven. "Judaism, War, and Weapons of Mass Destruction." In *Ethics and Weapons of Mass Destruction: Religious and Secular Perspectives*, ed. Sohail H. Hashmi and Steven P. Lee. New York: Cambridge University Press, 2004.

King, Martin Luther, Jr. "Letter from Birmingham City Jail." In *A Testament of Hope: The Essential Writings and Speeches of Martin Luther King, Jr.*, ed. James M. Washington. San Francisco: HarperSanFrancisco, 1991.

Luxemburg, Rosa. "Peace Utopias." In *Rosa Luxemburg Speaks*. New York: Pathfinder Press, 1970.

McManus, Philip. "Introduction: In Search of the Shalom Society." In *Relentless Persistence: Nonviolent Action in Latin America*, ed. Philip McManus and Gerald Schlabach. Philadelphia: New Society Publishers, 1991.

Miller, Joseph S. "A History of the Mennonite Conciliation Service, International Conciliation Service, and Christian Peacemaker Teams." In *From the Ground Up: Mennonite Contributions to International Peacebuilding*, ed. Cynthia Sampson and John Paul Lederach. New York: Oxford University Press, 2000.

Morgenthau, Hans J. "Does Disarmament Mean Peace?" In *Arms and Foreign Policy in the Nuclear Age*, ed. Milton L. Rakove, 417–23. New York: Oxford University Press, 1972.

Morison, Samuel Eliot. "Dissent in the War of 1812." In *Dissent in Three American Wars*, ed. Samuel Eliot Morison, Frederick Merk and Frank Freidel. Cambridge, MA: Harvard University Press, 1970.

Niebuhr, Reinhold. "Why the Christian Church is not Pacifist." In *Christianity And Power Politics*. New York: Charles Scribner's Sons, 1940.

Noordegraaf, Herman. "The Anarchopacifism of Bart de Ligt." In *Challenge to Mars: Essays on Pacifism from 1918 to 1945*, ed. Peter Brock and Thomas P. Socknat, 89–100. Toronto: University of Toronto Press, 1999.

Orwell, George. "Notes on Nationalism" [May 1945]. In *The Complete Works of George Orwell. George-Orwell*, www.george-orwell.org/Notes_on_Nationalism/0.html/ (accessed 12 April 2007).

"Reflections on Gandhi." In *A Collection of Essays*. New York: Harcourt Brace Jovanovich, 1946.

Pacem in terris. Encyclical of Pope John XXIII, promulgated 11 April 1963, para. 145. *Papal Encyclicals*, www.papalencyclicals.net/John23/j23pacem.html/ (accessed 12 June 2007).

Pagnucco, Ronald and John D. McCarthy. "Advocating Nonviolent Direct Action in Latin America: The Antecedents and Emergence of SERPAJ." In *Nonviolent Social Movements: A Geographical Perspective*, ed. Stephen Zunes, Lester R. Kurtz and Sarah Beth Asher. Malden, MA: Blackwell Publishers, 1999.

Powles, Cyril H. "Abe Isoo: The Utility Man." In *Pacifism in Japan: The Christian and Socialist Tradition*, ed. Nobuya Bamba and John F. Howes. Vancouver: University of British Columbia Press, 1978.

Richardson, Neil R. "International Trade as a Force for Peace." In *Controversies in International Relations Theory: Realism and the Neoliberal Challenge*, ed. Charles W. Kegley, Jr. New York: St. Martin's Press, 1995.

Russett, Bruce. "Violence and Disease: Trade as a Suppressor of Conflict when Suppressors Matter." In *Economic Interdependence and International Conflict: New Perspectives on an Enduring Debate*, ed. Edward D. Mansfield and Brian M. Pollins. Ann Arbor: University of Michigan Press, 2003.

Said, Abdul Aziz, Nathan C. Funk and Ayse S. Kadayifci. "Introduction: Islamic Approaches to Peace and Conflict Resolution." In *Peace and Conflict Resolution in Islam: Precept and Practice*. Lanham, MD: University Press of America, 2001.

Schwarzschild, Steven S. "Shalom." In *The Challenge of Shalom: The Jewish Tradition of Peace and Justice*, ed. Murray Polner and Naomi Goodman. Philadelphia, PA: New Society Publishers, 1994.

Van Beek en Donk, Jonkheer B. De Jong. "History of the Peace Movement in The Netherlands" [1915]. In Sandi E. Cooper, "Introduction." In *Peace Activities in Belgium and the Netherlands*, ed. Sandi E. Cooper. New York: Garland Publishing, 1972.

Van Den Dungen, Peter. "Critics and Criticisms of the British Peace Movement." In *Campaigns for Peace: British Peace Movements in the Twentieth Century*, ed. Richard Taylor and Nigel Young. Manchester: Manchester University Press, 1987.

Yoder, John Howard. "Peace without Eschatology?" In John Howard Yoder, *The Royal Priesthood: Essays Ecclesiological and Ecumenical*, ed. Michael G. Cartwright. Scottdale, PA: Herald Press, 1998.

JOURNAL ARTICLES

Booth, Ken. "Steps Towards Stable Peace in Europe: A Theory and Practice of Coexistence." *International Affairs* (Royal Institute of International Affairs) 66, 1 (January 1990).

Ceadel, Martin. "The First British Referendum: The Peace Ballot, 1934–5." *English Historical Review* 95, 377 (October 1980).

Chatfield, Charles. "At the Hands of Historians: The Antiwar Movement of the Vietnam Era." *Peace and Change* 29, 3 and 4 (July 2004): 497.

Confortini, Catia C. "Galtung, Violence, and Gender: The Case for a Peace Studies / Feminism Alliance." *Peace & Change* 31, 3 (July 2006): 333.

Cortright, David and George A. Lopez. "Disarming Iraq: Nonmilitary Strategies and Options." *Arms Control Today* 32, 7 (September 2002): 3–7.

d'Escoto, Miguel, M. M. "The Power of the Cross." *Catholic Worker* 45, 2 (February 1979): 6.

D'Souza, Dinesh. "How Reagan Won the Cold War." *National Review* 49, 22 (24 November 1997): 38.

Duram, James C. "In Defense of Conscience: Norman Thomas as an Exponent of Christian Pacifism During World War I." *Journal of Presbyterian History* 52, 1 (Spring 1974): 24.

Eichenberg, Richard C. "Gender Differences in Public Attitudes Toward the Use of Force by the United States, 1990–2003." *International Security* 28, 1 (Summer 2003): 118–20.

Epstein, Barbara. "Notes on the Antiwar Movement." *Monthly Review* 55, 3 (July–August 2003).

Farrugia, Peter. "French Religious Opposition to War, 1919–1939: The Contribution of Henri Roser and Marc Sangnier." *French History* 6, 3 (September 1992): 294–5.

Fogg, Richard Wendell. "Dealing with Conflict: A Repertoire of Creative, Peaceful Approaches." *Journal of Conflict Resolution* 29, 2 (June 1985): 334.

Forsberg, Randall. "A Bilateral Nuclear-Weapon Freeze." *Scientific American* 247, 5 (November 1982): 52–61.

Galtung, Johan. "Violence, Peace, and Peace Research." *Journal of Peace Research* 6, 3 (1969): 167–97.

Hanson, Marianne and Carl Ungerer. "The Canberra Commission: Paths Followed, Paths Ahead." *Australian Journal of International Affairs* 53, 1 (1999): 7.

Harbom, Lotta, Stina Högbladh and Peter Wallensteen. "Armed Conflict and Peace Agreements." *Journal of Peace Research* 43, 5 (2006): 617–31.

Hunter, David G. "A Decade of Research on Early Christians and Military Service." *Religious Studies Review* 18, 2 (April 1992): 87–93.

Huygen, Maarten. "Dateline Holland: NATO's Pyrrhic Victory." *Foreign Affairs* 62 (12 November 1984): 176.

Johansen, Robert C. "Radical Islam and Nonviolence: A Case Study of Religious Empowerment and Constraint among Pashtuns." *Journal of Peace Research* 34, 1 (Feb. 1997): 58.

Lopez, George A., special editor. "Peace Studies: Past and Future." *Annals of the American Academy of Political and Social Science* 504 (July 1989).

Mamdani, Mahmood. "The Politics of Naming: Genocide, Civil War, Insurgency." *London Review of Books* 29, 5 (8 March 2007).

Mead, Margaret. "Warfare Is Only An Invention – Not A Biological Necessity." *Asia* 40 (1940): 402–5.

Mearsheimer, John J. and Stephen M. Walt. "An Unnecessary War." *Foreign Policy* (January–February 2003): 50.

Mueller, John E. "The Search for the 'Breaking Point' in Vietnam: The Statistics of a Deadly Quarrel." *International Studies Quarterly* 24, 4 (December 1980): 497–519.

Niebuhr, Reinhold and Hans Morgenthau. "The Ethics of War and Peace in the Nuclear Age." *War/Peace Report* 7, 2 (February 1967): 7.

Pilisuk, Marc and Thomas Hayden. "Is There a Military Industrial Complex Which Prevents Peace?: Consensus and Countervailing Power in Pluralistic Systems." *Journal of Social Issues* 21, 3 (July 1965): 67–117.

Podhoretz, Norman. "Appeasement by any Other Name." *Commentary* 76, 1 (July 1983): 29.

Polachek, Solomon William. "Conflict and Trade." *Journal of Conflict Resolution* 24, 1 (March 1980): 67.

Rabinowitch, Eugene. "Five Years After." *Bulletin of the Atomic Scientists* 7, 1 (January 1951): 3.

Risse-Kappen, Thomas. "Did 'Peace Through Strength' End the Cold War? Lessons from INF." *International Security* 16, 1 (Summer 1991).

"Ideas Do Not Float Freely: Transnational Coalitions, Domestic Structures, and the End of the Cold War." *International Organization* 48, 2 (Spring 1994).

Sapolsky, Robert M. "A Natural History of Peace." *Foreign Affairs* 85, 1 (January/February 2006): 109.

Schlabach, Gerald. "Just Policing, Not War." *America* 189, 1 (7–14 July 2003): 19–21.

Tucker, Robert W. and David C. Hendrickson. "America and Bosnia." *National Interest* 23 (Fall 1993): 14–27.

van Voorst, L. Bruce. "The Churches and Nuclear Deterrence." *Foreign Affairs* 61, 4 (Spring 1983): 845.

Wallerstein, Immanuel. "U.S. Weakness and the Struggle for Hegemony." *Monthly Review* 55, 3 (July–August 2003): 28.

Yankelovich, Daniel and John Doble. "The Public Mood: Nuclear Weapons and the U.S.S.R." *Foreign Affairs* 63, 1 (Fall 1984): 33–5.

Yoder, John Howard. "Reinhold Niebuhr and Christian Pacifism." *Mennonite Quarterly Review* 29, 2 (April 1955): 101.

Index

Abe Isoo, 199, 236, 263–4
Abe Shinzo, 121
abolition of slavery, 26–7, 31, 32–5, 268
absolute pacifism
  cold war, survival during, 120
  development of concept, 1, 8, 10, 11
  of early Christianity, 18, 185, 193–4
  early peace societies' debate over, 30–1
  internationalism and, 46
  interwar peace movements, 68, 70, 71–5, 89–90
  in Japan, 11–12
  Niebuhr's critique of, 204–5
  nonviolence and, 211
  of nuclear disarmament, 334
  police force, use of, 177
  Tolstoyan, 197–9
Abyssinia (Ethiopia), Italian aggression in, 17, 65, 68, 77, 80–3
Acheson, Dean, 130
Acheson–Lilienthal plan, 131, 133
ACLU (American Civil Liberties Union), 71, 167
activism involved in pacifism, 337–9
Addams, Jane
  concept of pacifism and, 1
  in early peace societies, 25, 43
  on fascism and interwar pacifism, 69–70, 72
  on feminism and women's empowerment, 255, 256
  internationalism of, 59
Afghanistan, 14, 139, 152, 193
Africa, 13–14, 136, 156, 297–8, 299. See also specific countries
African Mission in Sudan (AMIS), 299
African Union (AU), 297, 299
AFSC (American Friends Service Committee), 71, 86, 120, 123, 143
agape, 220–1
ahimsa, 185, 215, 221
Ahmadiyah, 190
Al Qaida, 14, 176, 178, 283, 322
Alabama arbitration decision, 49

Algeria, 156, 280
Allard, Maurice, 96
Allen, Steve, 135
Allen, William, 27, 31
Alliance universelle des femmes pour le désarmement (later Alliance des femmes pour la paix), 95
Alsos, 127–8
alter-globalization movement, 276–8
alternatives to war, peace activists proposing, 3–4
Ambrose of Milan, 194
America First Committee, 90, 318
American Association of University Women, 90, 111, 113
American Civil Liberties Union (ACLU), 71, 167
American Committee for the Outlawry of War, 62
American Friends Service Committee (AFSC), 71, 86, 120, 123, 143
American Nurses Association, 145
American Peace Society (APS)
  early peace societies, development of, 25, 28, 30, 33, 35, 36
  internationalism and, 49, 52
American Revolution, 26, 288
American Society for the Judicial Settlement of International Disputes, 50
American Society of International Law, 50
American Union against Militarism (AUAM), 59, 71, 101
Americans for Democratic Action, 157, 158
Americans United for World Organization, 112
AmeriCorps, 309
AMIS (African Mission in Sudan), 299
Amnesty International, 169
Amory, Cleveland, 135
Anabaptists, 18, 194, 195
Anderson, Martin, 164
Anfal Campaign, Iraq, 285
Angell, Norman, 240, 247
Angola, 174
Annamese, 156
Annan, Kofi, 173, 291, 296

Anpo Tōsō campaign, 120
anthropology and peace, 243–6
Anti-Corn Law League, 237–8
Anti-Preparedness Committee, 71
antislavery movement, 26–7, 31, 32–5, 268
antiwar protests, 1–4, 155–57. *See also specific wars*
APD (*Association de la paix par le droit*), 37, 60, 74, 80, 87, 89, 271
appeasement, 17, 67–9, 79–81, 88–9, 91–2
Appleby, Scott, 183, 200–1
APS *see* American Peace Society
Arbatov, Georgi, 150
arbitration, 42–3, 48–52, 50–1, 239, 313–15
arms control *see* disarmament, pre-nuclear; nuclear disarmament
arms embargoes
    against former Yugoslavia, 96
    in Spanish civil war, 87–8
arms manufacturers
    globalized war economy, 339
    post-WWI backlash against, 94, 98–100, 339
    pre-WWI concern about influence of, 97
Arnaud, Émile, 8–9, 38
Arnoldson, Klas P., 38
Aslan, Reza, 190, 191
Aśoka, 186
Asquith, H. H., 40
Association de la paix par le droit (APD), 37, 60, 74, 80, 87, 89, 271
Association pour la réforme et la codification du droit des gens, 50
Atomic Energy Commission, UN, 130–2
Atomic Veterans Association, 134
atomic weapons *see entries at* nuclear
AU (African Union), 297, 299
AUAM (American Union against Militarism), 59, 71, 101
Augustine of Hippo, 8, 194
Aung San Suu Kyi, 186, 187
Australia, 168, 297, 325–6
Austria, 88
Austrian Peace Society, 39
Austro-Hungary, 36, 39
Axelrod, Robert, 153
"axis of evil," 322
Axworthy, Lloyd, 288, 292
Azzam, Abdullah Yusuf, 192

Baha'ism, 185
Bainton, Roland, 189, 194
Bajer, Fredrik, 38
Bakunin, Mikhail, 262
Baldwin, Roger, 167
Baldwin, Stanley, 80, 81, 83
ban-the-bomb movement *see* nuclear disarmament

Bank, Grameen, 277
Baptists, 144
Barbé, Domingos, 231
Barcelona Report, 316–17
Barnet, Richard, 141
Baruch, Bernard, and Baruch plan for nuclear arms control, 131–3
Bastiat, Frédéric, 96
Beales, A. C. F., 10, 28, 32
Belgian Congo, 156
Benedict XV (pope), 201
Bentham, Jeremy, 235–6, 252
Bernard, John, 87
Bernardin, Joseph, Cardinal, 143
Bernstein, Eduard, 265
Bethe, Hans, 130
Bhagavad Gita,, 127, 185, 213
Bhave, Vinoba, 311
Bible *see* Christianity; Judaism; religion and peace
Bierville Congress (1926), 202
Bikini Atoll, 133, 138
bilateral arbitration agreements, 50–1
bin Laden, Osama, 4, 192, 322
biology and peace, 243–6
blacksmith, learned (Elihu Burritt), 32–3
Blair, Tony, 174, 273, 284
Blix, Hans, and Blix Commission on Weapons of Mass Destruction, 323, 329–31
Bloch, Ivan (Jean de Bloch), 96, 269–70
Boer War, 134
Boff, Leonardo, 7, 13, 224
Bolshevism, 76. *See also* Russia/Soviet Union; socialism and peace
Bondurant, Joan, 215
Borah, William, 55, 62, 101
Bosnia
    antiwar movements, 155
    concept of pacifism and, 14, 15, 96
    disarmament, 96
    human rights, responsibility to protect, 280, 287, 292, 297
    military as security/peacekeeping forces in, 316
    patriotism and peace, 312
Boulding, Kenneth and Elise, 2
Boutros-Ghali, Boutros, 6
Boyer, Mark, 258
Brahimi, Lakhdar, 296–7
Brailsford, H. N., 56
Brazil, 223, 328
Brethren Churches, 168, 172, 312
Bretton Woods, 272
Briand, Aristide, 63–4
Bright, John, 238, 239
Bristol, James E., 123

Britain
  absolute pacifism, interwar, 73, 74–75
  Catholic peace movement in, 201
  CND, 17, 134–6, 137, 147, 152
  conscientious objectors in, 167–8
  Crimean War, 35, 48, 239
  democratic peace theory, 247–8, 251
  disarmament activism and, 102, 104–5
  failure of imperial powers to check fascism,
    79–84
  in "four policemen" scheme of collective
    security, 114
  in India *see* Gandhi, Mahatma; India;
    nonviolence
  international arbitration, 49–50
  Iraq War, opposition to, 173
  isolationism in, 83
  Kellogg–Briand Pact, reaction to, 63
  League of Nations campaign in, 53, 56, 59–60
  Munich settlement, 88–89
  nuclear disarmament, government support for,
    130, 135–7
  Oxford Union peace resolution, 73
  Peace Ballot, 3, 17, 69, 76–9, 80, 91
  peace societies in, 27–8, 31, 35
  Spanish civil war, refusal to intervene in,
    87–8
  Tolstoyan pacifism in, 199
  world federalism in, 117
British Council of Churches, 152
British Peace Crusade, 102
British Peace Society, 29
British Society for the Promotion of Permanent
    and Universal Peace, 27–8
Brittain, Vera, 89, 119, 256
Brown, Judith, 217, 218
Brown, Sam, 160
Buber, Martin, 89
Budapest proposals, 104
Buddhist peace tradition, 183–8, 213–14
Bull, Hedley, 107, 153
Bulletin of Atomic Scientists, 129, 133
Burkholder, J. Lawrence, 196
Burma, 82, 213
Burritt, Elihu, 32–3
Burton, John W., 7
Bush, George H. W., 149, 150–51, 154
Bush, George W.
  concept of pacifism and, 18
  on development and peace, 273
  on Iraq War, 164, 170–1, 174, 177, 280, 284,
    285, 287
  nuclear counterproliferation measures, 322
Butler, George Lee, 321, 326, 329
Byrd, Richard, 86

CAIP (Catholic Association for International
    Peace), 202
Cameroon, 174
Campaign for Nuclear Disarmament (CND), 17,
    134–6, 137, 147, 152
Campaign for Peace and Democracy, 282
Camus, Albert, 109, 125, 220, 339
Canada, 165, 168, 312
Canberra Commission, 323, 325–9
capitalism
  free trade, democracy, and peace, 237–40,
    251–3, 270–1, 276–8
  globalization and global justice movement, 276–8
  socialist critique of, 260–2, 267, 270–1
  Washington consensus on development, 276
Caprioli, Mary, 258
Carnegie, Andrew, 6, 26, 30, 43, 47, 50, 52
Carnegie Commission on Preventing Deadly
    Conflict, 332, 337
Carr, Carrie Chapman, 70
Carson, Rachel, 272
Carver, Michael, 326
Cary, Stephen G., 123
Catholic Association for International Peace
    (CAIP), 202
Catholic Council for International Peace, 201
Catholic Peace Fellowship, 159
Catholic Worker Movement, 202
Catholicism
  appeasement policies and, 91
  Franco, support for, 88
  Gulf War, opposition to, 171
  Iraq War, opposition to, 171–2
  liberation theology, 12–13, 203
  Medellín conference of bishops (Colombia,
    1968), 13, 203, 223
  nuclear disarmament and, 143
  Second Vatican Council
    Catholic peace and social justice
      movement, 202
    Latin American peace tradition, 13
  social justice and peace movement within, 200–3
  Vietnam War, opposition to, 159
CCC (Civilian Conservation Corps), 309
Ceadel, Martin
  on concept of pacifism, 11, 16
  on fascism and interwar pacifism, 67–8,
    78–9, 81
  on internationalism, 60
  on nonviolence, 227
  on peace societies, 27
Cecil, Robert, Lord, 59, 83, 106
Central Conference of American Rabbis, 160
Central Intelligence Agency (CIA), 123, 231
CFE (Conventional Forces in Europe) Treaty, 325

CGT (*Confédération générale du travail*), 264
Chamberlain, Austen, 80
Chamberlain, Neville, 67, 88–9
Charter 77 campaign, 281
Chatfield, Charles, 17, 87
Chavez, Cesar, 215, 225
Chechnya, 312
Chemical Weapons Convention (CWC), 325
Chicago, Democratic National Convention in (1968), 163
Chickering, Roger, 9, 17
Chile, 174, 212, 251
China
  colonialism, protests against, 156
  communism in, 117, 118
  in "four policemen" scheme of collective security, 114
  Korean War, involvement in, 119
  Manchuria, Japanese aggression in, 17, 64–5, 68, 79–80, 91, 106
  market liberalization and rapid development, effects of, 276
  Shanghai, Japanese assault on, 104, 106
  Tiananmen Square, 213
  in Vietnam War, 161
Christian base communities, 223
The Christian Century, 200
Christian Peacemaker Teams (CPT), 312–13
Christian Social Union, 199
Christianity *see also specific denominations*
  absolute pacifism of early Church, 18, 193–94
  Gandhi's study of, 214
  love imperative *see under* love imperative
  Niebuhr's theology of pacifism, 185, 200, 203–6
  nonviolence in, 208–10, 230–1
  peace tradition, 18, 183–5, 193–7
  Sermon on the Mount, 207, 213, 214
  social Christianity, 199–200
  Tolstoyan pacifism, 197–9
  Yoder's theology of pacifism, 185, 206–8
Church Peace Union, 111
Churchill, Randolph, 73
Churchill, Winston, 73, 114, 118
CIA (Central Intelligence Agency), 123, 231
Cicero, 194
civil (intrastate) war
  democratic peace theory limitations and, 250
  rise of, 5
  in Spain *see* Spanish civil war
  US Civil War, 35, 48, 49, 164, 239, 268
Civil Liberties Bureau, 71
civil rights movement, US, 19, 157–8, 204, 209, 222. *See also* King, Martin Luther, Jr.
Civilian Conservation Corps (CCC), 309

Civilian Public Service (CPS) program for nonmilitary alternative service, 168
class analysis of socialism, 268–9, 302
Clausewitz, Carl von, 176
Clemenceau, Georges, 56
Clergy and Laymen (later Laity) Concerned About Vietnam, 159
Clinton, Bill, 96
CND (Campaign for Nuclear Disarmament), 17, 134–6, 137, 147, 152
CNVA (Committee for Nonviolent Action), 281
Coates, Michael, 214
Cobden, Richard, 233, 237–40, 252, 261, 268
Code of Hammurabi, 288
Coffin, William Sloane, Jr., 142–3, 320
Colby, William, 164
cold war, 17, 109–25
  absolute pacifism, survival of, 120
  anticommunist sentiment during, 117–20, 133
  disarmament activists during *see* nuclear disarmament
  end of, 149–51
  freedom, opposition of peace to, 17, 109–25
  human rights, responsibility to protect, 279–83
  Japanese militarization and peace movement, 119, 120–1
  Niebuhr on, 109, 204
  peace associated with communism during, 6, 110, 119–20, 282
  realist and idealist interpretation of, 151–4
  Speak Truth to Power, 110–11, 123–5, 339
  United Nations, creation of, 110, 111–15. *See also* United Nations
  US military interventionist policy and, 122–5, 149–51
  world federalism, 115–18, 119
collective security
  end of British government's support for League of Nations procedures, 83
  "four policemen" scheme of, 114
  internationalism and principle of, 53, 57, 62, 64–5
  isolationism and absolute pacifism, as interwar alternative to, 77, 79
  for nuclear disarmament, 332
  Peace Ballot's support for, 79, 91
Collier, Paul, 274
Collins, Canon L. John, 134, 137
Colombia, 312
colonialism, 56–7, 59, 156
combat refusal in Vietnam War, 165–6
Commission on a Just and Durable Peace, 111
Committee for Concerted Peace Efforts, 89–90
Committee for Nonviolent Action (CNVA), 281
Committee to Study the Organization of Peace, 111

communism. *See also* Russia/Soviet Union;
  socialism and peace
  cold war anticommunist sentiment, 117–20, 133
  Leninism, 264, 266–9, 305
  national liberation movements associated with,
    125, 267
  nuclear disarmament and anticommunist
    sentiment, 132–33
  peace associated with, 6, 110, 119–20, 282
  Trotskyism, 157, 158, 260, 267–8
community-based development, 277
compassion, religious concept of, 184
Comprehensive Test Ban Treaty (CTBT), 325, 330
conciliation and mediation services, 313–15
Confédération générale du travail (CGT), 264
conferences *see* peace conferences
conflict resolution *see* arbitration
Congo, 156
Congregationalists, 30
Congress of Vienna, 28
conscientious objectors, 71, 134, 167–70, 310
conscriptive service, 164–5, 167–70
Constant, Benjamin, 95
Constantine (Roman emperor), 194
Contra War against Sandanistas in Nicaragua, 63,
    231, 251
Conventional Forces in Europe (CFE) Treaty, 325
Cooper, Sandi E., 17, 38, 41
cooperation theory and nuclear disarmament,
    153–4
cooperative view of human nature, 243–6
Correlates of War database, 249
Corrie, Rachel, 313
cosmopolitan principle of Kant, 232–43
Cot, Pierre, 83
Council for a Livable World, 136
Cousins, Norman, 7, 115, 135, 137, 140
CPS (Civilian Public Service) program for
    nonmilitary alternative service, 168
CPT (Christian Peacemaker Teams), 312–13
Cranston, Alan, 116
Cremer, W. Randal, 36, 49
Crimean War, 35, 48, 239
Cromwell, Oliver, 196
Crucé, Émeric, 53, 234
Cruise missiles, 139, 142, 148, 149
Crusade for World Government, 117, 119
CTNT (Comprehensive Test Ban Treaty), 325, 330
Curle, Adam, 2
CWC (Chemical Weapons Convention), 325
Czechoslovakia, 88–9, 280–3

Dalai Lama, 186–7
Dallaire, Roméo, 292
Darby, John, 337

Darfur, 280, 287, 292, 296, 299–301
Darwin, Charles, 36
Day, Dorothy, 202, 256–7
"days of rage" (October, 1969), 163
de Ligt, Bart, 58, 75–6
DeBenedetti, Charles
  on cold war period, 112, 118
  on disarmament, 99, 102
  on internationalism, 50, 51, 52, 54
  on peace societies, 17, 28, 30, 32, 36
  on US antiwar sentiment, 86
  on Vietnam War opposition, 159, 160, 161
Debs, Eugene, 266
defensive war, concept of, 30–1
"definitive articles" of Kant's peace theory, 233–4,
    240–3, 246, 249–55
Delaisi, Francis, 97
Dellinger, David, 76, 158, 220
Deming, Barbara, 76, 158, 212, 213, 219–20,
    225, 230
democracy and peace, 19, 233–59
  bellicosity of democracies towards developing
    nations, 250–1, 302
  Cobden on, 233, 237–40, 252, 261, 268
  early connection between democratic and
    peace movements, 236–7
  Enlightenment thinking on, 233–6
  European Union, 254–5
  evidence for link between, 249–55, 268–9
  feminism and empowerment of women, 255–9
  free trade, 237–40, 251–3, 270–1, 276–8
  human nature, 243–6
  international organization, importance of,
    242, 253
  Kant's philosophy of, 233–4, 240–3, 246,
    249–55, 261, 270–1
  power to wage war, democratic control over,
    237, 246–9
  transitioning states, bellicosity of, 250
Denmark, 38, 228
Desai, Narayan and Mahadev, 311
Descamps, Édouard, 50
d'Escoto, Miguel, 231
d'Estournelles de Constant, Paul-Henri-
    Benjamin, 95
Detzer, Dorothy, 99–100, 101
Deutsch, Karl, 254
Deutsche Friedensgesellschaft (DFG), 39
development and peace, 273–8
  bellicosity of democracies towards developing
    nations, 250–1, 302
  control of development process, 275–6
  globalization and global justice movement,
    276–8
  in Kantian triad, 250–3

development and peace (cont.)
  relationship between war, poverty, and lack of opportunity, 273–5
  United Nations economic development policy, 272–3
  Washington consensus, 276
Dewey, John, 62
DFG (*Deutsche Friedensgesellschaft*), 39
Dhanapala, Jayantha, 329
Dharasana salt works incident (1930), 226
dharma,, 186
Dienstbier, Jiri, 282
disarmament, pre-nuclear, 93–108. *See also* arms manufacturers; nuclear disarmament
  fascism, collapse in face of rise of, 105–6
  initial reluctance of early pacifists to pursue, 95–96
  League of Nations and, 100, 101, 103–4, 106
  logic of argument for, 93–5, 107–8
  nationalist influence on peace movement and, 96
  naval disarmament treaties, interwar, 93, 100–3, 106, 108
  neutrality debate in USA and, 83–4
  post-WWI backlash against arms manufacturers and, 94, 98–100
  pre-WWI rise in pacifist call for, 96–8
  social justice arguments for, 95–6
  Treaty of Versailles on, 100–1, 105
  World Disarmament Conference (1932), 94, 103–5, 106
  WWII preparedness, effect on, 93, 106–8
Divine, Robert, 81
Doble, John, 140
Dodge, David Low, 27, 31
Domke, William, 251
doomsday clock, 129
double-zero proposal regarding INF, 3, 149, 151
draft dodgers and draft resisters during Vietnam War, 164–5
Dulles, John Foster, 111
Dumas, Lloyd J., 251
Dutch Peace Society, 39

East Germany, 280–83
East Timor, 297
Easterly, William, 276
Eastern religious traditions, 183–8, 213–14
ECCO (European Congress of Conscripts Organizations), 169
Economic Community of West African States (ECOWAS), 297
economic theories of peace, 237–40, 251–3
economics of peace
  development *see* development and peace
  free trade principles, 237–40, 251–3, 270–1, 276–8

globalization and global justice movement, 276–8
  socialist critique of capitalism and imperialism, 260–2, 265, 267, 270–1
  United Nations policies, 272–3
ECOWAS (Economic Community of West African States), 297
Edgar, Bob, 176
Edgerton, William B., 123
Egypt, 328
Ehrenreich, Barbara, 245
Eichelberger, Clark, 112
Einstein, Albert
  cold war pacifism and, 110
  concept of pacifism and, 10, 20
  internationalism and, 65
  interwar pacifism and, 72–3, 88, 90–1
  on nuclear weapons, 127, 130, 134, 138
  patriotism and nationalism, dialogue with Freud on, 303–4, 306–7
  on world federalism, 115, 116
  WWII, support for entry into, 90–1
Eisenhower, Dwight D., 121, 122
El Salvador, 312
ElBaradei, Mohamed, 322
Elshtain, Jean Bethke, 256
Emergency Committee of Atomic Scientists, 130, 133
Emergency Peace Campaign, 73, 85–7, 90
Emerson, Ralph Waldo, 32, 245, 305
END (European Nuclear Disarmament), 282
Enlightenment thinking on democracy and peace, 233–6
environmental issues, 140, 271–2, 276
Erasmus, Desiderius, 195
Ethiopia (Abyssinia), Italian aggression in, 17, 65, 68, 77, 80–3
ethnography and peace, 243–6
Europe *see also specific countries*
  colonial interventions of, 156
  conscientious objectors in, 169–70
  EU, 254–5, 316–17
  international arbitration, 49–50
  Iraq War, opposition to, 172–3
  League of Nations, support for, 60
  nuclear activism of, 1970s and 1980s in, 146–9
  peace societies in, 28–9, 31, 36, 38–9
  United States of Europe, early proposals for, 38, 60, 254
European Congress of Conscripts Organizations (ECCO), 169
European Nuclear Disarmament (END), 282
European Union (EU), 254–5, 316–17
Evangelicals for Social Action, 312
Evans, Gareth, 292, 326
"the evil empire," 125

fair trade and global justice movement,
276–78
Fanon, Franz, 224
Farmer's Union, 86
Farrell, Thomas, 126
FAS (Federation of Atomic/American Scientists),
129, 133
fascism *see also* Hitler, Adolf; interwar pacifism
Abyssinia (Ethiopia), Italian aggression in, 17,
65, 68, 77, 80–3
appeasement policies, 17, 67–9, 79–81, 88–9,
91–2
disarmament movement, collapse of, 105–6
imperial powers' failure to confront, 81–4
integral pacifism, breakdown of, 74
Manchuria, Japanese aggression in, 17, 64–5,
68, 79–80, 91, 106
Mussolini, Benito, 76, 81–2, 87, 91
pacifism as concept and rise of, 10
pacifist and internationalist opposition to, 69,
76, 79–81, 88–92
peace advocates and internationalists opposing
rise of, 17
pragmatic pacifism and, 76
Spanish civil war, 17, 65, 76, 84, 87–8, 91
Federal Council of Churches, 85, 101–2, 111, 113,
118, 200
Federal Union, 112
federalism, global (world federalism), 17,
115–18, 119
The Federalist Papers, 237
Federation of Atomic/American Scientists (FAS),
129, 133
Fellowship of Reconciliation (FOR), 70, 80, 86,
120, 143
feminism and peace, 3, 19–20, 70, 255–9
Finland, 169, 170
firmeza permanente, 222
Fischer, Louis, 226
Fisher, Roger, 337
Five Power Naval Limitation Treaty (1922), 102
Foley, Michael, 164
Foot, Michael, 134
FOR (Fellowship of Reconciliation), 70, 80, 86,
120, 143
Ford, Henry, 30
former Yugoslavia *see also specific successor states*
arms embargo against, 96
human rights, responsibility to protect, 280,
287, 289–92, 297
NATO operations in, 15, 155, 289–92, 297
nonviolence in, 213
peacekeeping efforts in, 14, 15, 96, 155
Forsberg, Randall, 141
Fosdick, Harry Emerson, 74, 86, 135

"four policemen" scheme of collective
security, 114
Fourier, Charles, 28
Fournier, François, 96
"Fourteen Points" speech, 55
Fox, Tom, 312
fraggings, 165
France
absolute pacifism in interwar years, 74
Catholic peace movement in, 201–2
colonial interventions of, 156
democratic peace theory, 247, 251
disarmament, pre-nuclear, 96–7
failure of imperial powers to check fascism,
81–4
international arbitration, 49–50
Iraq War, opposition to, 174, 175
Kellogg–Briand Pact, 63
nuclear weapons testing, 136, 326
peace societies in, 28, 36–7, 38–9
Revolution of 1789, 26, 27, 288
socialism and pacifism in, 264
Spanish civil war, refusal to intervene in, 87–8
Francis of Assisi, 194
Franco, Francisco, 87–88
free trade, democracy, and peace, 237–40, 251–3,
270–1, 276–8
freedom, Western emphasis on, 119, 124–5,
283–6
Freivalds, Laila, 329
French Revolution, 26, 27, 288
French Union for Women's Suffrage, 255
Freud, Sigmund, 20, 72, 303–4, 306–7
Fried, Aldred, 269
Fried, Alfred H., 39
Friends *see* Quakers
"friends of peace" movement in eighteenth-
century Britain, 27
Fromm, Erich, 135
Fry, Douglas, 245
Fukuyama, Francis, 171
Fulbright, J. William, 113

Galbraith, John Kenneth, 160
Galtung, Johann, 2, 7
game theory and nuclear disarmament, 153
Gandhi, Mahatma
concept of pacifism and, 7, 19, 20, 21
interwar pacifism influenced by, 73, 74, 75
Khan, Abdul Ghaffar, and, 192, 310–11
on moral imperative for peace, 339
Munich settlement, reaction to, 89
Niebuhr and, 204, 208–10
nonmilitary service (*Shanti Sena*) proposals,
310–11, 313

Gandhi, Mahatma (cont.)
  nonviolent resistance, Gandhian concept of, *see* nonviolence
  patriotism, on harnessing, 304
  religious influences on, 213–15
  Tolstoy's influence on, 197, 198, 214
Gandhi, Rajiv, 193
Garibaldi, Giuseppe, 37
Garrison, William Lloyd, 32, 35
Gaza, 312, 313
Geneva Conventions, 42, 48
genocide *see* human rights, responsibility to protect
Gensuikyo, 121, 138
Georgia, 213
German Union for Women's Suffrage, 255
Germany. *See also* fascism; Hitler, Adolf; Versailles Treaty; World War I; World War II
  Catholic peace movement in, 201–2
  conscientious objectors in, 169–70
  East and West Germany, post-WWII, 280–3
  equal status with other nations, peace activists' call for, 105–6
  Iraq War, opposition to, 174, 175
  League of Nations and, 59, 60, 105, 106
  nuclear disarmament movement in, 140
  nuclear weapons program, WWII era, 127–8, 134
  patriotic pacifism in, 317–18
  peace societies in, 36, 39
  Prussian unification, 303
  socialism and pacifism in, 264–5
Ghana, 136, 212
Ghosananda, Maha, 186, 187
Gilmore, Robert, 123
Girardin, Émile de, 95–6
globalization and global justice movement, 276–8
Goering, Hermann, 1
golden rule, 241
Goldman, Emma, 255
Goodpaster, Andrew, 329
Goodrich, Leland, 54, 65–6
Gopin, Marc, 188
Gorbachev, Mikhail, 149–54, 325
Goss-Mayr, Jean and Hildegard, 223
graduated reciprocation in tension-reduction (GRIT) strategy, 153
Gratry, Alphonse, and Gratry Society, 201
Gray, J. Glenn, 305
Great Britain *see* Britain
Great Depression, 270, 309. *See also* interwar pacifism
Grebel, Conrad, 195
greed theory, 274

Green Party (West Germany), 282
Greenham Common (Britain), women's peace camp at, 147–8
Grey, Sir Edward, 98
GRIT (graduated reciprocation in tension-reduction) strategy, 153
Gromyko, Andrei, 132
Grotius, Hugo, 39, 46–7
Guatemala, 251, 312
Guernica, 104
Guesde, Jules, 264
Guinea, 174
Gulf War, 15, 171, 258, 285
Gumbelton, Thomas, 143
Gurr, Ted Robert, 273, 275
Gutiérrez, Gustavo, 203

Hague Appeal for Peace (1999), 289, 313
Hague Palace of Peace, 43
Hague Peace Conferences (1899 and 1907), 40–3, 50, 198, 289
Hague, Universal Peace Congress at (1913), 97
Haiti, 312
Haldeman, H. R., 161, 166
Hamas, 192
Hamilton, Alexander, 237
Hammond, John Hays, 50
Hammurabi, Code of, 288
Haq, Mahbub ul, 288
Harding, Warren G., 101
Harriman, W. Averell, 160
Hatfield, Mark, 141
Havel, Václav, 228, 279, 281, 282, 300
Hawk, David, 160
Hawken, Paul, 271–2
Hayden, Thomas, 122–3
Hedges, Chris, 305
Hehir, J. Bryan, 143
heiwa shugi, 12
Hélder Câmara, Dom, 223
Helsinki Watch, 288
Henderson, Arthur, 56, 104
Herriot, Édouard, 202
Heschel, Abraham Joshua, 222
Hindu peace tradition, 183–5
Hitler, Adolf. *See also* fascism; World War II
  absolute pacifism affected by rise of, 69, 74
  appeasement of, 67, 88–89, 107
  concept of pacifism and, 1, 17
  disarmament movement, collapse of, 105–6
  Franco, aid provided to, 87
  imperial powers' failure to stop, 82
  Niebuhr on opposition to, 204–6
  nonviolence against, 227
  pacifist opposition to, 69, 76, 88–92

Ho Chi Minh, 57
Hoare, Samuel, 80, 81
Hobson, J. A., 267
Hodgkin, Henry T., 70
Holbrooke, Richard, 291
Hoover, Herbert, 80
Hörup, Ellen, 82
Howard, Michael, 6, 43, 44, 60, 119, 241, 303, 304, 332–3
Hughan, Jessie Wallace, 71
Hugo, Victor, 34–5, 37–8
human nature, views of, 243–6
human rights, responsibility to protect, 279–301
  cold war and Soviet repression, 279–83
  concept of pacifism and, 20
  Darfur, 299–301
  human security concept, 287–9
  Iraq War, 280, 283–7
  Kosovo bombings, 289–92
  R2P commission principles, 292–6
  United Nations on, 113–14, 288, 289, 292–6
  U.S. civil rights movement, 19, 157–8, 204, 209, 222
  Vietnam War, opposition to, 157–8
Human Rights Watch, 284–5, 288
Hurndall, Thomas, 313
Hussein, Saddam, 4, 128, 174, 280, 284–7, 324. *See also* Gulf War; Iraq; Iraq War
Hussites, 194

IMF (International Monetary Fund), 273
imperialism, 122–5, 149–51, 155, 250–1, 265, 267, 270–1
India, 82, 276, 322, 328. *See also* Gandhi, Mahatma; nonviolence
Indochina, 156. *See also* Vietnam War
INF (intermediate-range nuclear forces) and treaty, 3, 139–40, 143, 147–9, 321, 325
Ingram, Norman, 36, 64, 74
Institute for Defense and Disarmament Studies, 141
Institute for Policy Studies, 141
integral pacifism, 74, 89
Interchurch Peace Council, Netherlands, 147
intermediate-range nuclear forces (INF) and treaty, 3, 139–40, 143, 147–9, 321, 325
International Anti-Militarist Bureau, 75
International Arbitration and Peace Association, 50
International Atomic Energy Agency/Authority, 128, 322
International Catholic Peace League, 201
International Commission on Intervention and State Sovereignty (Responsibility to Protect (R2P) commission), 292–6

International Congress of Women in the Hague, 70
International Court of Justice, 51
International Criminal Court, 289
International Federation of League of Nations Societies, 60, 104
International Institute of Intellectual Cooperation, 306
International Law Association, 50
International Monetary Fund (IMF), 273
international nuclear arms control, support for, 130–1
International Peace Bureau, 40, 264
International Peace Campaign (IPC), 83–4
international peace conferences. *See* peace conferences
International Solidarity Movement (ISM), 313
internationalism, 17, 45–66
  arbitration, 48–52
  cold war internationalism and creation of United Nations, 110, 111–15
  collective security, principle of, 53, 57, 62, 64–5
  conservative and progressive approaches to, 47–8, 59
  defined, 9–10, 45–6
  of early peace societies, 39, 45
  fascism, opposition to, 69
  Kantian peace theory on, 115, 242, 253
  League of Nations *see* League of Nations
  origins and development of, 46–9
  outlawing war, concept of, 62–6
  world federalism versus, 115
  WWII, pacifist movement on brink of, 90
Interparliamentary Conference (later Interparliamentary Union), 40, 42, 43
interwar pacifism, 67–92
  absolutist, 68, 70, 71–5, 89–90
  appeasement policies and, 17, 67–9, 79–81, 88–9, 91–2
  disarmament activism *see* disarmament, pre-nuclear
  Emergency Peace Campaign, 73, 85–7, 90
  fascism, pacifist response to *see* fascism
  imperial powers, failures of, 81–4
  naval disarmament treaties, 93, 100–3, 106, 108
  neutrality debate, US, 84–5, 90, 96, 100
  Peace Ballot (1934-5), 3, 17, 69, 76–9, 80, 91
  post-WWI peace movement, 69–71
  revolutionary antimilitarism, 75–6
  social justice and peace, connection between, 270–3
  WWII, response to entry into, 88–92
intrastate war *see* civil (intrastate) war
IPC (International Peace Campaign), 83–4
Iran, nuclear capabilities of, 330

Iraq
  CPT volunteers in, 312–13
  Gulf War, 15, 171, 258, 285
  human rights, responsibility to protect, 280,
    283–7
  nuclear capabilities of, 322–3, 324
Iraq War
  Darfur crisis and, 300
  democratic control over power to wage, 249
  exit strategy, 287
  globalization and global justice
    movement, 277
  human rights, responsibility to protect, 280,
    283–7
  Japanese involvement in, 121
  just war principles, 284–5
  nuclear disarmament argument for, 322–3
  Nuclear disarmament movement affected
    by, 328
  opposition to, 155, 170–6, 337–8
    concepts of pacifism and, 2–4, 14, 18
    development issues, 277
    patriotic pacifism of, 318–19
    terrorism rhetoric used in, 125
  United Nations and, 173–6, 285–6
  US military interventionist policy leading to,
    123, 155
  WMD search compared to search for
    WWII-era German nuclear weapons
    program, 128
Ireland, 328
Islam
  Israeli–Palestinian conflict, 178–9, 312, 313
  jihad, 191–2
  peace tradition of, 183, 184, 190–3
  war on terror and, 178–9
ISM (International Solidarity Movement), 313
isolationism
  in Britain, 83
  collective security as alternative to, 77, 79
  pacifism associated with, 10, 67, 68, 85
  social justice perspective as alternative
    to, 69
  in United States
    cold war internationalism replacing
      isolationism, 112
    Czech invasion, response to, 89–90
    disarmament, pre-nuclear, and, 101
    Emergency Peace Campaign, 85–7, 90
    interwar pacifism and, 68
    League of Nations, opposition to, 61–3, 65
    Ludlow amendment, 86–7, 89–90
    neutrality debate, 84–5, 90, 96, 100
Israel, nuclear capabilities of, 322, 328, 330
Israeli–Palestinian conflict, 178–9, 312, 313

Italy
  Abyssinia (Ethiopia), Italian aggression in, 17,
    65, 68, 77, 80–83
  fascist *see* fascism; World War II
  Iraq War, opposition to, 173
  peace societies in, 39
  socialism and pacifism in, 264

Jack, Homer, 135
Jainism, 184–5, 213–14
James, William, 20, 304, 307–10, 315, 319
Japan
  cold war militarization and peace movement,
    119, 120–1
  colonial interventions of, 156
  democracy and peace in, 236–7
  in Iraq War, 121
  Korean War and, 119, 120
  in Manchuria, 17, 64–5, 68, 79–80, 91, 106
  naval disarmament treaties and, 102, 103, 106
  nuclear disarmament movement in, 120–1,
    138–9, 329
  nuclear strikes on Hiroshima and Nagasaki, 115,
    127, 129, 130, 139
  pacifism in postwar Constitution, 11–12, 120,
    121, 236–7
  peace societies in, 29
  Pearl Harbor, 90
  Russia, war with, 199, 236
  Shanghai, assault on, 104, 106
  socialism and peace in, 263–4
  Tolstoy's influence in, 199
  world federalism in, 117
Japanese National Liaison Committee for
    Nuclear and General Disarmament, 139
Jaurès, Jean, 96, 264, 265, 302
Jay, William, 49
Jefferson, Thomas, 84
Jesus *see* Christianity
Jews *see* Judaism
jihad, 191–2
John XXIII (pope), 202, 339
John Paul II (pope), 203
Johnson, Lyndon B., 18, 156, 159–60
Jones, William, 29
Judaism
  Israeli–Palestinian conflict, 178–9, 312, 313
  King influenced by social theology of, 222
  nuclear disarmament and, 144–5
  peace tradition of, 183, 184, 188–90
Juergensmeyer, Mark, 183
Jungk, Robert, 126, 127
just war principles
  in Christian thought, 8, 184, 194
  in cold war, 125

concept of pacifism and, 8, 14–16
in international law, 48
Iraq War, 284–5
R2P commission on humanitarian
    interventions, 292–6
United Nations peace operations principles,
    298
justice and peace, 7
Justin Martyr, 194

Kagawa Toyohiko, 117, 138
Kaldor, Mary, 5, 149, 282, 283, 303, 316, 339
Kant, Immanuel
    concept of pacifism and, 2–3
    on democracy and peace, 233–4, 240–3, 246,
        249–55, 261, 270–1
    on internationalism, 115, 242, 253
    moral imperative of peace for, 241, 334, 339
    peace societies and, 26, 246
    socialist views of peace and, 261, 268
karma, 187
Kautsky, Karl, 261, 265
Keating, Paul, 325
Keegan, John, 44
Keep America Out of War Congress, 90
Kellogg, Frank, 63–4
Kellogg–Briand Pact, 63–4
Kennan, George, 143, 150
Kennedy, John F., 136–7, 153
Kennedy, Robert, 160
Kent State killings, 163
Kerry, John, 165
Khan, Abdul Ghaffar, 192–3, 304, 310–11
Khudai Khidmatgars, 193, 310–11
Kimelman, Reuven, 189
King, Coretta Scott, 159
King, Martin Luther, Jr.
    in antiwar movement, 158, 320
    concept of pacifism and, 19
    Gandhian nonviolence, influence of, 211, 213,
        215, 217, 219, 220–2, 227, 230, 231
    Latin American nonviolence movement,
        influence on, 223
    love imperative for, 220–2
    on military virtues, 309
    Niebuhr's influence on, 209, 219, 220, 222
    patriotism of, 320
    realistic pacifism of, 219, 334
    on religious belief, 203, 209
    on social justice and peace, 221–2
King, Sallie, 187
King-Hall, Stephen, 134
Kisala, Robert, 12
Kishi Nobusuke, 121
Kissa Khani Bazaar massacre (1930), 311

Kissinger, Henry, 149, 161
Knock, Thomas, 56–7
Koizumi Junichiro, 121
Kōmeitō, 187
Korean protestations of Japanese and European
    intervention, 156
Korean War, 17, 117–19, 120, 152
Kosovo
    antiwar movements and, 155
    bombing campaign, 289–92
    human rights, responsibility to protect, 280,
        289–92, 294, 297, 301
    military as security/peacekeeping forces in, 316
    nonviolent resistance movement in, 213,
        290, 301
Kriesberg, Louis, 153, 249, 252
Kurds, 284, 285
Kuron, Jacek, 282
Kyrgyzstan, 213

Lactantius, 194
Ladd, William, 28
Lafargue, Paul, 264
Lake, Anthony, 300
Latin American peace and nonviolence traditions,
    12–13, 203, 222–4, 230–1. *See also specific
    countries*
Laval, Pierre, 81, 82
League of Nations, 17
    on arms manufacturers, 99
    collective security, principle of, 53, 57, 62, 64–5,
        79, 83
    Covenant, 57–8, 61, 62, 64, 65
    disarmament activism and, 100, 101, 103–4, 106
    early proposals for, 52–4
    Einstein–Freud dialogue and, 306
    failure of, 65–6
    fascism, response to, 79–81
    imperial powers' failure to back, 81–3
    international response to formation of, 58–61
    IPC/RUP and, 83–4
    social justice concerns and, 271
    United Nations compared, 65, 110
    United States and
        opposition to League, 51, 55–6, 61, 112
        support for League, 53–4, 59
    Wilson's vision for, 54–8
    WWII, beginning of, 88, 107
League of Nations (Non-Partisan) Association,
    61, 89, 111, 112
League of Nations Society, 53
League of Nations Union (LNU)
    concept of pacifism and, 3, 10, 17
    disarmament activism of, 104, 106
    early peace societies, development of, 47, 59–60

League of Nations Union (LNU) (cont.)
    Italian fascism, response to, 80, 81
    Peace Ballot, 76–9
    United Nations, creation of, 111
    WWII, entry into, 88–9
League of Universal Brotherhood (LUB), 33
League to Enforce Peace (LEP), 54, 59,
    61, 101
"the learned blacksmith" (Elihu Burritt), 32–3
Lederach, John Paul, 231, 314–15
Lemonnier, Charles, 37, 38
Lenin, Vladimir Illich, and Leninism, 264,
    266–9, 305
Lennon, John, 29
Leo XIII (pope), 200
Leopold (king of Belgium), 156
LEP (League to Enforce Peace), 54, 59, 61, 101
Levinson, Samuel, 62
Libby, Frederick, 85, 100, 101
liberal theories of peace *see* democracy and peace
liberation theology, 12–13, 203
liberation/unification movements, national, 34–5,
    37–8, 125, 267, 302–3. *See also specific*
    movements and countries
Liberia, 297
LICP (*Ligue internationale des combatants de la*
    paix), 74, 80
Liebknecht, Karl, 97
Ligue internationale de la paix et de la liberté, 37,
    38, 262, 302
Ligue internationale des combatants de la paix
    (LICP), 74, 80
Ligue internationale et permanente de la paix,
    36–7, 201
Lilienthal, David, 131, 133
Lincoln Brigade in Spanish civil war, 87
Linder, Ben, 312
Lindh, Anna, 329
Lippman, Walter, 67
Lloyd George, David, 56
LNU *see* League of Nations Union
Locarno Treaties (1925), 105
Locke, John, 263
Lodge, Henry Cabot, 55
London disarmament agreement, 102–3
London Peace Society, 30, 239
Lorenz, Konrad, 245
love imperative
    in Christianity, 193–4, 210
        Catholic social justice and peace
            movement, 200
        King's understanding of, 220–2
        Mennonites and Quakers, 196–7
        Niebuhr's theology, 204–5
        Yoder's theology, 207–8

    in Gandhian nonviolence, 211, 214, 220–2
    in Islam, 190
    in Judaism, 188
Lowenstein, Allard, 159
LUB (League of Universal Brotherhood), 33
Lucky Dragon incident, 138
Ludlow, Louis, and Ludlow amendment, 86–7,
    89–90
Lutherans, 144
Luxemburg, Rosa, 267
Lynch, Cecelia
    on cold war period, 114
    on disarmament, 102, 103
    on interwar pacifism and fascism, 67, 68, 79,
        82, 90
    on social justice and peace, 271
Lytton Commission, 79–80

MacArthur, Douglas, 119
MacDonald, Ramsay, 59, 247, 248
MacGregor, G. H. C., 208
Macmillan, Harold, 136–7
Magna Carta, 288
Magnes, Judah, 89
Malcolm X, 224
Mamdani, Mahmood, 300
Manchuria, Japanese aggression in, 17, 64–5, 68,
    79–80, 91, 106
Manhattan Project scientists, 126–7, 134
Mann, Thomas, 72
Mansfield, Edward, 250, 251–52
Marcellus (Roman martyr), 194
market liberalization, 276–8
Markey, Ed, 146
Marshall, Monty and Donna Ramsey, 258
Martino, Renato, 171
Marx, Karl, and Marxism, 203, 244, 260–2,
    268, 269
Massachusetts Peace Society, 28, 30
Maurin, Peter, 202
Maximilian (Roman martyr), 194
Mayer, Milton, 123
Maziyariyah, 190
Mazzini, Giuseppe, 302–3
McCarthy, Eugene, 159–60
McCarthy, Joseph, 118
McGovern, George, 141
McNamara, Robert, 326
Mead, Margaret, 245
Mearsheimer, John, 4
Medellín conference of bishops (Colombia 1968),
    13, 203, 223
mediation and conciliation services, 313–15
Mélin, Jeanne, 97–98
Melman, Seymour, 94

Mennonites, 15, 168, 172, 195–6, 312, 314
Metallurgical Laboratory, University of Chicago, 128–9
Methodists, 144
Mexico, 32, 156, 174, 328
micro-credit programs, 277
military conscription, 164–5, 167–70
military-industrial complex, US viewed as, 122–3
military interventionist policy of US, 122–5, 149–51, 155, 250–1
military opposition to Vietnam War, 164–7
military serving as security/peacekeeping forces, 315–17
military virtues, "peace corps"-like proposals for harnessing, 307–13
Mill, John Stuart, 238–9, 240, 270
Mills, C. Wright, 122
Milosevic, Slobodan, 213, 229, 290, 291
Mitchell, John, 166
"the Mobe" (New Mobilization Committee to End the War in Vietnam), 158
Montesquieu, Charles-Louis de Secondat, baron de, 235
morality and peace, 227, 240, 241, 334, 339
Moravians, 194
Morel, E. D., 247
Morgenthau, Hans
  on antiwar movements, 159, 160
  on concept of pacifism, 4
  on disarmament, 107, 109, 151, 323, 333
  on religion and peace, 203
Morison, Samuel Eliot, 26
Morse, Wayne, 159
Moscow Human Rights Committee, 288
Mueller, John, 4, 270
Muslims *see* Islam
Mussolini, Benito, 76, 81–2, 87, 91. *See also* fascism; Italy; World War II
Muste, A. J., 123
MX missile program, 151
Mygatt, Tracy, 71

Nagler, Michael, 229–30
Napoleon and Napoleonic wars, 26, 27, 304
National Arbitration League, 50
National Association for the Advancement of Colored People, 113
National Committee for a Sane Nuclear Policy (SANE), 2, 17, 134–6, 157, 158–9
National Council for Prevention of War, 71, 80, 85, 86, 90
National Council for the Prevention of War (formerly National Council on Limitation of Armaments), 102

National Council of Churches, 176, 200
National Council of Jewish Women, 90
National Council on Limitation of Armaments, 101–2
National Grange, 86
National League of Women Voters, 102
National Peace Action Coalition, 158
national unification/liberation movements, 34–5, 37–38, 125, 267, 302–3. *See also specific movements and countries*
nationalism *see* patriotism and peace
NATO *see* North Atlantic Treaty Organization
naval disarmament treaties, interwar, 93, 100–3, 106, 108
Nazi Germany *see* fascism; Hitler, Adolf; World War II
Nehru, nonviolent method of, 211
neo-Confucianism, 29
Netherlands, 39, 75–6, 147
Netherlands Roman Catholic Society for the Promotion of Peace, 201
neutrality debate, interwar, in US, 84–5, 90, 96, 100
New Agenda Coalition, 328
New Deal, 273
New England Non-Resistance Society, 32
New International Economic Order (NIEO), 275–6
New Mobilization Committee to End the War in Vietnam ("the Mobe"), 158
"new religions" movement, Japan, 29
New York Peace Society, 27, 31
New Zealand, 168, 328
Niboyet, Eugénie, 96
Nicaragua, 63, 231, 251, 312
Nicholas II (tsar), 40, 289
Niebuhr, Reinhold
  on cold war, 109, 204
  concept of pacifism and, 18–19
  fascism and WWII, 67, 88, 204–6
  on Gandhian nonviolence, 204, 208–10, 218–19, 224–5, 226
  King influenced by, 209, 219, 220, 222
  theology of, 185, 200, 203–6
  on US civil rights movement, 204, 209
  Vietnam War, opposition to, 206
  Yoder and, 203, 205, 207, 208
NIEO (New International Economic Order), 275–6
Nietzsche, Friedrich, 211, 232
Nixon, Richard M., 18, 156, 160–2, 166
Nkrumah, Kwame, 136, 212
No Conscription Fellowship, 167
No-Foreign War Crusade, 86

Nobel Peace Prize
  Addams, Jane (1931), 70
  Bajer, Fredrik (1908), 38
  Bank, Grameen (2006), 277
  Cremer, W. Randal (1903), 36
  Fried, Alfred (1911), 269
  International Peace Bureau (1910), 40
  Passy, Frédéric (1901), 36
  Pérez Esquivel, Adolfo (1980), 223
  Pugwash movement (1995), 134
  Rotblatt, Joseph (1995), 134, 326
  Sakharov, Andrei (1975), 288
  Tutu, Desmond (1984), 13, 94
  United Nations peacekeeping operations
    (1988), 296
  Yunis, Mohammad (2006), 277
noncooperation *see* nonviolence
noninterference and collective security,
    contradictions in principles of, 64
nonviolence, 211–32
  antiwar protests and, 158, 177
  Christian understanding of, 208–10, 230–1
  concept of pacifism and, 7, 19
  efficacy of, 211–13, 224–9
  in Islam, 192–3
  King's adaptation of, 211, 213, 215, 217, 219,
    220–2, 227, 230, 231
  of Kosovar liberation movement, 213, 290, 301
  in Latin America, 222–4, 230–1
  love imperative in, 211, 214, 220–2
  mechanics of process, 224–7
  moral code of enemies, supposed dependence
    on, 227
  Niebuhr on, 204, 208–10, 218–19, 224–5, 226
  pacifism distinguished, 211–12
  political coercion involved in, 211, 218–20
  religious roots of, 213–15
  satyagraha (social action), 213, 216–18, 232
  suffering and sacrifice involved in, 229–32
  WWII and fascism, in face of, 89
Nonviolent Peaceforce, 313
North Atlantic Treaty Organization (NATO)
  former Yugoslavia, operations in, 15, 155,
    289–92, 297
  human rights, responsibility to protect, 280,
    289–92
  nuclear weapons and disarmament movement,
    3, 139, 147–9
North Korean nuclear capabilities, 322, 323, 330
Norway, 228
NPT (Nuclear Non-Proliferation Treaty), 322
nuclear disarmament, 17–18, 126–54, 321–33
  absolutist nature of pacifism as regards, 334
  anticommunist sentiment and attitudes
    toward, 132–3

Baruch plan, 131–3
Blix Commission, 323, 329–31
Canberra Commission and follow-up reports,
    323, 325–9
CND and SANE, 2, 17, 134–6, 137, 147, 152
cold war, end of, 149–51
  as collective/cooperative security, 332
  concept of pacifism and, 1–4
  cooperation theory and positive reciprocity,
    153–4
  doomsday clock, 129
  END, 282
  end of cold war and, 149–51
  INF, 3, 139–40, 143, 147–9, 321, 325
  international arms control plans, 130–3
  in Japan, 120–1, 138–9, 329
  NPT, 322–5
  nuclear freeze and disarmament movements of
    1970s and 1980s, 139–49, 337–8
    catalysts of, 139–42
    in Europe, 146–9
    mutual disarmament of US and Soviet
      Union as political breakthrough idea,
      141–2
    religious community's involvement in, 142–5
    US nuclear freeze referendum (1982), 145–6
  prohibition rather than abolition, 331–3
  realist and idealist interpretation of, 151–4
  scientists' call for, 126–31, 134, 138
  test ban treaties, 136–7, 153, 325, 330
  unilateral plans, 135–6, 152–4
  women activists, 136, 147–8
  zero option plans, 3, 149, 151, 331–3
Nuclear Non-Proliferation Treaty (NPT), 322
nuclear technology, environmental concerns
    over, 140
nuclear weapons
  access to, 322
  anticommunist sentiment during cold war and,
    117, 118, 120
  atomic scientists' reaction to explosions of,
    126–7
  German WWII-era program, 127–8, 134
  Hiroshima and Nagasaki, strikes on, 115, 127,
    129, 130, 139
  just war principles and, 16
  testing of, 132–4, 136–9, 153, 326
  world federalism and, 115
Nye Committee hearings, 99–100, 339
Nye, Gerald P., 81, 99
Nye, Joseph, 47
Nyerere, Julius, 115, 136

Oakland Stop the Draft Week (1967), 163
One World (Wilkie), 112

Oneal, John R., 250, 252, 253, 254–5
Oppenheimer, J. Robert, 126, 131
Orange revolution in Ukraine, 213
Origen, 194
originating or structural violence, 7
Orwell, George, 216, 217, 303
Osgood, Charles, 153
outlawing war, concept of, 62–6
Oxford Union peace resolution, 73

Pacem in Terris, 202
pacifism *see* peace and pacifism
Pact of Paris (Kellogg–Briand Pact), 63–4
Page, Kirby, 82
Paine, Thomas, 166, 235
Painlevé, Paul, 202
Pakistan, 125, 174, 192–3, 310–11, 322, 328
Palace of Peace, the Hague, 43
Palestinian–Israeli conflict, 178–9, 312, 313
Palme, Olaf, and Palme Commission, 288, 324–5, 329
Panama, US invasion of, 155
papacy *see* Catholicism, and individual popes
Paris Peace Conference (1918), 56–7
passive resistance *see* nonviolence
Passy, Frédéric, 30, 36–7, 41, 49, 95, 156, 263
patriotism and peace, 20, 302–20
   conflict mediation and conciliation services, 313–15
   Einstein–Freud dialogue on, 303–4, 306–7
   influence of nationalism on peace movement, 96
   military serving as security/peacekeeping forces, 315–17
   nonmilitary service proposals, 304, 307–13
   pacifism, patriotic, 317–20
   peacekeeping organizations, nongovernmental, 310–13
   popular bellicose nationalism and xenophobia, 303–6, 319–20
   socialist nationalism, 266
Paul VI (pope), 262
Pauling, Linus, 130, 134, 138
Pax Christi, 143, 172
PBI (Peace Brigades International), 311–12
peace and pacifism, 1–21, 334–9
   absolute *see* absolute pacifism
   activism involved in, 337–9
   African tradition, 13–14
   antiwar protests, 1–4, 155–7. *See also specific wars*
   appeasement distinguished, 17, 67–9, 91–2
   change in nature of war, 4–6
   communism, association with, 6, 110, 119–20, 282

definitions
   pacifism, 8–11
   peace, 6–8
integral pacifism, 74, 89
isolationism, association with, 10, 67, 68, 85
in Japanese postwar Constitution, 1–21
just war principles, 8, 14–16
Latin American tradition, 12–13
morality and peace, 227, 240, 241, 334, 339
nonviolence distinguished, 211–12
practice of, 336–7
pragmatic *see* pragmatic pacifism
realistic pacifism, 219, 334–9
scientific pacifism, 36, 269–70
study of, 2–4
theory of, 335–6
utilitarian pacifism, 72
peace army, Gandhi's concept of, 310–11, 313
Peace Ballot (1934-5), 3, 17, 69, 76–9, 80, 91
Peace Brigades International (PBI), 311–12
peace conferences
   first occurrences of, 34–5
   Geneva conference (1867), 37–8
   Hague Peace Conferences (1899 and 1907), 40–3, 50
   universal peace conferences, 8–9, 40, 43, 97, 201, 246, 263
Peace Corps, 309
"peace corps"-like proposals for nonmilitary service, 304, 307–13
Peace League, 39
Peace Letter campaign, 71
Peace Pledge Union (PPU), 74–5, 76, 88, 89
peace societies, 16–17, 25–44
   absolute versus pragmatic pacifism, debate over, 30–1
   conferences of *see* peace conferences
   expansion throughout Europe, 38–9
   fascism's rise and, 10
   internationalism of, 39, 45
   League of Nations, reaction to, 58–9
   national unification/liberation movements, response to, 34–5, 37–8
   origins of, 3, 26–9
   political agendas of, 30–2
   reinvigoration in late nineteenth century, 35–8
   social background of members, 29–30, 34, 36
   social justice issues, involvement in, 31–3, 36–7
   Tolstoy's disdain for, 198
   women members, 30, 31–2, 69
   WWI and interwar period, 43–4, 69–71
Peace through Justice (*Vrede door Recht*), 39

peacekeeping operations
  military serving as security/peacekeeping
    forces, 315–17
  nongovernmental organizations designed for,
    310–13
  United Nations, 5–6, 253, 296–8
Pearl Harbor, 90
Penn, William, 53, 196–7
People's Coalition for Peace and Justice, 158
perestroika, 149–51, 325
Pérez Esquivel, Adolfo, 223
Permanent Court of Arbitration, 42, 43, 50
Permanent Court of International Justice (World
    Court), 51, 61, 62–3
Perris, G. H., 97
Perry, William, 322
Pershing II missiles, 139, 142, 147–9
Persian Gulf War, 15, 171, 258, 285
Persson, Göran, 291, 329
Philippines, 19, 156, 212, 308, 313
Physiocrats, 235
Pickett, Clarence, 123, 135
Pilisuk, Marc, 122–3
Pinchot, Amos, 59
Pitt, William, the Younger, 27
Pius X (pope), 201
Podhoretz, Norman, 93
Poland, 280, 281, 282, 283
police enforcement against terrorist actions, 176–9
political liberalism *see* democracy and peace
Polk, James, 32
Pollins, Brian, 251–52
Ponsonby, Arthur, 56, 71–2, 74, 247, 248
popes *see* Catholicism, *and individual popes*
positivism, 36
Potonié-Pierre, Edmond, 37
poverty *see* development and peace; economics of
    peace
Powell, Colin, 299
PPU (Peace Pledge Union), 74–5, 76, 88, 89
practice of pacifism, 336–7
pragmatic pacifism, 14–15, 334
  development of concept, 11
  fascism, opposition to, 76
  internationalism and, 46
  peace societies and, 30–1
Pratt, Hodgson, 50
Prendergast, John, 299–300
Pressensé, Francis de, 96
Priestley, J. B., 134
protection, responsibility of *see* human rights,
    responsibility to protect
Protestantism, 143–4, 172, 195, 199–200. *See also*
    specific denominations
Pugwash movement, 134

Quakers, 194, 196–7
  AFSC, 71, 86, 120, 123, 143
  antiwar protests of, 168, 172
  concept of pacifism and, 18
  CPT, 312
  fascism and WWII, 71
  Gandhi and, 214
  mediation and conciliation services, 314
  in peace societies, 27, 30, 31
Quayle, Dan, 150–1
Quesnay, François, 235
Qur'an *see* Islam

R2P (Responsibility to Protect commission or
    International Commission on
    Intervention and State Sovereignty),
    292–6
Rabbinical Assembly of America, 144
Rabinowitch, Eugene, 129
Rapaport, Anatol, 123
Rassemblement universel de la paix pour le droit
    (RUP), 83–4
Rauschenbusch, Walter, 199, 221
Rawls, John, 16
Reagan, Ronald, 4, 125, 139, 145, 148–50, 153
realistic pacifism, 219, 334–9
religion and peace, 18–19, 183–210. *See also specific*
    beliefs, denominations and organizations
  compassion, importance of, 184
  conscientious objection, 167–70
  Gulf War, opposition to, 171
  Iraq War, opposition to, 171–72
  love *see* love imperative
  Meiji-era Japan, neo-Confucianism and "new
    religions" movement in, 29
  nonviolence, Gandhian, roots of, 213–15
  nuclear disarmament movements, 142–5
  nuclear explosions, atomic scientists' reaction
    to, 126–7
  peace societies and revivalism, 26
  Sermon on the Mount, 207, 213, 214
  United Nations, support for, 113
  war on terror and, 176–7
Rerum Novarum, 200
Rescript, Hague Peace Conference (1899), 40–1
responsibility to protect *see* human rights,
    responsibility to protect
Responsibility to Protect (R2P) commission
    (International Commission on
    Intervention and State Sovereignty),
    292–6
revivalist impulse and early peace societies, 26
revolutionary antimilitarism, 75–6
Rice, Susan, 300
Richard, Henry, 49

Ricks, Thomas, 176
Ripon Society, 160
Rocard, Michel, 326–7
Rockefeller, John D., 50
Rolland, Romain, 72–3
Roman Catholicism *see* Catholicism
Rome Airforce Base (NY), women's peace camp
  at, 147–8
Roosevelt, Eleanor, 86, 135
Roosevelt, Franklin Delano
  on CCC, 309
  on disarmament, 98–9
  Einstein's encouragement of nuclear
    development in letter to, 127
  on interwar pacifism, isolationism, and fascism,
    80–1, 85, 86, 88
  on United Nations, 110, 114
Roosevelt, Theodore, 40, 51, 52, 308
Root, Elihu, 51
Rose revolution in Georgia, 213
Rosencrance, Richard, 251
Rostow, Eugene V., 93
Rotblatt, Joseph, 134, 326
Roth, Ken, 284
Rugova, Ibrahim, 290, 301
Rumsfeld, Donald, 67
RUP (*Rassemblement universel de la paix pour le
  droit*), 83–4
Russell, Bertrand, 65, 134, 138
Russett, Bruce, 249–50, 252, 253, 254–5
Russia/Soviet Union
  Afghanistan, invasion of, 139, 152, 193
  cold war anticommunist sentiment and
    attitudes towards, 118, 119
  collapse of Soviet system, 149–51
  Crimean War, 35, 48, 239
  in "four policemen" scheme of collective
    security, 114
  Hague Peace Conference and, 40–1
  human rights, responsibility to protect, 279–83
  Iraq War, opposition to, 174
  Japan, war with, 199, 236
  League of Nations and, 59
  nonviolent resistance to domination of, 229
  nuclear weapons, testing, and disarmament
    see entries at nuclear
  "peace" groups backed by, 119
  perestroika, 149–51, 325
  revolutionary antimilitarism and, 76
  Spanish civil war and, 87
  Tolstoyan pacifism, 197–9
  Vietnam War, 161
Ruyssen, Théodore, 60, 89
Rwanda, 280, 287, 292
Ryan, John, 202

sacrifice and suffering involved in nonviolence,
  229–32
SADC (South African Development
  Community), 297
Sahnoun, Mohamed, 292
sainiks, 311
Saint-Pierre, Abbé de, 53
Saint-Simon, Henri de, 28
Sakharov, Andrei, 288
salaam, 190
SALT (Strategic Arms Limitation Treaties),
  141, 281
Sandanistas, 63, 231, 251
SANE (National Committee for a Sane Nuclear
  Policy), 2, 17, 134–6, 157, 158–9
Sanger, Margaret, 255
Sangnier, Marc, 201–2
Saperstein, David, 144
satyagraha, 213, 215–18, 232
Saudi Arabia, 192
Save Darfur Coalition, 299, 300
Say, Jean-Baptiste, 28
Sayre, Nevin, 100
Scandinavia, 36, 38. *See also specific countries*
Schell, Jonathan
  on cold war, 109
  on concept of pacifism, 7
  on democracy and peace, 233
  on nuclear disarmament, 126, 173, 321, 323, 331–2
  on religion and peace, 228
Schindler, Alexander, 144
Schlabach, Gerald, 177
Schlesinger, Arthur, Jr., 237
Schock, Kurt, 229
Schumpeter, Joseph, 265
Schwarzkopf, H. Norman, 164
Schweitzer, Albert, 138
scientific pacifism, 36, 269–70
scientists' call for nuclear disarmament, 126–31,
  134, 138
Scott, Simon, 14
SDI (Strategic Defense Initiative), 149, 151
SDS (Students for a Democratic Society), 157–8
Second Vatican Council
  Catholic peace and social justice movement, 202
  Latin American peace tradition and, 13, 203
secure community theory, 254
security, collective *see* collective security
security forces, military serving as, 315–17
security, human, 287–9
security, peace-oriented proposals compatible
  with, 4
Seeger, Daniel, 169
selective objection, 169
Sen, Amartya, 258

Serbia, 96, 155, 213, 229, 289–92
Sermon on the Mount, 207, 213, 214
Servicio Paz y Justicia en América Latina (Service
for Peace and Justice in Latin America or
SERP), 223
Shakespeare, William, 1
shalom, 184, 188, 190
Shanghai, Japanese assault on, 104, 106
Shanti Sena, 310–11, 313
Sharp, Gene, 212, 225, 230
Sheppard, Dick, 74–5
Shotwell, James T., 63, 89, 111, 112, 135
Sider, Ronald, 312
Sierra Leone, 297
Simons, Menno, 195
Sklencar, Marge, 160
slavery, abolition of, 26–7, 31, 32–5, 268
Slovenia, 328
Smith, Adam, 238, 240, 260
Smith, Gerard, 141
Smith, Rupert, 4, 5
Snowden, Philip, 247
Snyder, Jack, 250
sociability of human nature, 243–6
social background of peace society members,
29–30, 34, 36
social Christianity, 199–200
Social Gospel, 18, 69, 199–200, 221
social justice and peace, 19, 260–2
development *see* development and peace
disarmament, social justice arguments for, 95–6
early peace societies, 31–3, 36–7
economic theories of, 251–3
globalization and global justice movement,
276–8
human rights *see* human rights, responsibility
to protect
interwar pacifism's development of connection
between, 270–3
isolationism/military internationalism, as
interwar alternative to, 69, 90
King on, 221–2
Latin American tradition, 203, 222–4
liberation theology, 12–13, 203
within Roman Catholicism, 200–3
satyagraha and Gandhian nonviolence, 213,
216–18
US civil rights movement, 19, 157–8, 204,
209, 222
women's empowerment *see* entries at women
social learning theory, 245
socialism and peace, 260–73
capitalism and imperialism, critique of, 260–2,
265, 267, 270–1
class analysis, 268–9, 302

concept of pacifism, 3, 19
differences of early socialism and pacifism,
260–4
disarmament, pre-nuclear, 96
early peace societies, 37
interwar years, 73, 75–6, 90
Japanese cold war peace movement, 121
Leninism, 264, 266–9, 305
liberation theology, 12–13, 203
Marxism, 203, 244, 260–2, 268, 269
scientific pacifism, 269–70
Spanish civil war, 268
Trotskyism, 157, 158, 260, 267–8
Vietnam War, opposition to, 157–9
WWI, cooperation between socialists and
pacifists during and after, 264–6
Socialist Workers Party (SWP), 158
Société de la morale chrétienne, 28
Société de la paix de Génève, 28
Society for the Promotion of Danish Neutrality, 38
Sohyo, 121
Sojourners, 176
Sōka Gakkai, 187–8
Solana, Javier, 316
Solidarity movement, 281
Somalia, 292
SORT (Strategic Offensive Reductions
Treaty), 330
South Africa, 212, 328
South African Development Community
(SADC), 297
South Korea, 125, 330
Soviet Union *see* Russia/Soviet Union
Spanish-American War, 156, 308
Spanish civil war
disarmament and, 91, 103
Guernica, 103
interwar pacifism and, 17, 65, 76, 84, 87–8
socialist involvement in, 268
Spanish opposition to Iraq War, 173
Speak Truth to Power, 110–11, 123–5, 339
Spock, Benjamin, 135, 159
Sri Lanka, 312, 313
SS-20s, 139–40, 142, 147, 149
Stalin, Josef, 227
Stanton, Frederick, 50
Stanton, Shelby, 165
START (Strategic Arms Reduction Treaties),
321, 325
Stead, William T., 41
Stiglitz, Joseph, 276
Stimson doctrine, 80
Stimson, Henry, 87
Strategic Arms Limitation Treaties (SALT),
141, 281

Strategic Arms Reduction Treaties (START), 321, 325
Strategic Defense Initiative (SDI), 149, 151
Strategic Offensive Reductions Treaty (SORT), 330
Stratmann, Franziskus, 201
Streit, Clarence, 111
structural or originating violence, 7
student peace movements
  interwar, 73
  in Japan, 121, 139
  for nuclear disarmament, 139
  Vietnam War, opposition to, 157–8, 163
Student Peace Union, 157
Students for a Democratic Society (SDS), 157–8
Sudan, 280, 287, 292, 296, 299–301
suffering and sacrifice involved in nonviolence, 229–32
suffrage *see* women's rights
Sumner, Charles, 49
Super-GRIT, 153
Suttner, Bertha von *see* von Suttner, Bertha
Swanwick, Helen, 256, 257
Sweden, 38, 165, 328
Sweeney, John, 277
Switzerland, 28, 37, 264
SWP (Socialist Workers Party), 158
Synagogue Council of America, 144–5
Szilard, Leo, 128, 130, 136

Taborites, 194
Taft, William Howard, 51, 53, 59
Tagore, Rabindranath, 72
Taoism, 185
Taylor, A. J. P., 11, 135
Teamsters, 160
technological warfare, 72–3, 74, 103, 104. *See also* nuclear weapons
Teller, Edward, 129
terrorism
  concept of pacifism and, 4, 18
  democratic peace theory limitations, 250
  development–peace nexus, 273
  just war rhetoric and, 14, 125
  nuclear disarmament movement affected by, 328
  nuclear weapons, terrorist access to, 322
  "war on terror," 18, 176–9
Tertullian, 194
Tet offensive, 159
Tharpar, Romila, 186
Thatcher, Margaret, 149
Theorin, Britt, 326
theory of pacifism, 335–6
Thich Nhat Hanh, 186, 187

Thomas, Norman, 70, 88, 135
Thompson, E. P., 282
Thoreau, Henry David, 32
Three Mile Island, 140
Tiananmen Square, 213
Tillich, Paul, 135
Toda Jōsei, 187
Tolstoy, Leo, 197–9, 214
Tonkin China, French in, 156
Treaty of Versailles *see* Versailles Treaty
Treaty of Washington, 49
Treaty on the Renunciation of War (Kellogg–Briand Pact), 63–4
Trevelyan, Charles P., 247
Treves, Claudio, 264
Trotsky, Leon, and Trotskyism, 157, 158, 260, 267–8
Truman, Harry, 130–2
Tulip revolution in Kyrgyzstan, 213
Turkey, 173
Tutu, Desmond, 13, 94
"two percent" solution, 72
Tyler, Patrick, 173

Uchimura Kanzō, 29, 236
UDC (Union of Democratic Control), 53, 247–8
Ukraine, 213
UNCTAD (United Nations Conference on Trade and Development), 273
UNDP (United Nations Development Programme), 252, 273
unification/liberation movements, national, 34–5, 37–8, 125, 267, 302–3. *See also specific movements and countries*
unilateral nuclear disarmament, 135–6, 152–4
Union internationale des associations pour la Société des nations, 60
Union Now (Streit), 111
Union of American Hebrew Congregations, 144
Union of Christian Socialists, 75
Union of Democratic Control (UDC), 53, 247–8
Union of New Religions, 139
Unione lombarda per la pace, 39
Unitarians, 30
United Auto Workers, 113, 160
United Kingdom *see* Britain
United Mine Workers, 86
United Nations
  Catholic peace and social justice movement and, 202
  Charter, 113–14, 261, 272, 285, 289, 297
  cold war internationalism and creation of, 110, 111–15
  economic development policies of, 272–3

United Nations (cont.)
"four policemen" scheme of collective
security, 114
General Assembly, 114
Gulf War and, 171
on human rights, 113–14, 288, 289, 292–6
international arbitration movement and, 51
Iraq, nuclear weapons mission in, 322, 324
on Iraq War, 173–6, 285–6
Korean War, support of, 119
on Kosovo bombings, 290–1
League of Nations compared, 65, 110
on NIEO, 276
on nuclear arms control and disarmament,
130–2, 139, 330, 331
peacekeeping operations, 5–6, 253, 296–8
Security Council, 114
social justice imperative, 261, 272–3
on war on terror, 178
United Nations Association, 112
United Nations Conference on Trade and
Development (UNCTAD), 273
United Nations Convention on the Prevention
and Punishment of the Crime of
Genocide, 289
United Nations Development Programme
(UNDP), 252, 273
United States
Catholic peace movement in, 202
civil rights movement, 19, 157–8, 204, 209, 222
Civil War, 35, 48, 49, 164, 239, 268
conscientious objectors in, 167–8
Czech invasion, response to, 89–90
on Darfur, 300
democratic peace theory, 237, 248–9, 250–1
disarmament, pre-nuclear, 101
Emergency Peace Campaign, 73, 85–7, 90
failure of imperial powers to check fascism, 79–84
in "four policemen" scheme of collective
security, 114
international arbitration, 49–50, 51
Iraq War, opposition to, 171–2, 175
isolationism in see isolationism
Japanese militarization, push for, 120–1
Kellogg–Briand Pact, 63–4
League of Nations
opposition to, 51, 55–6, 61, 112
support for, 53–4, 59
Wilson's vision for, 54–8
as military-industrial complex, 122–3
military interventionist policy of, 122–5, 149–51,
155, 250–1
neutrality debate, interwar, 84–5, 90, 96, 100
nuclear weapons, testing, and disarmament
see entries at nuclear

patriotic pacifism in, 318–20
peace societies in, 27, 31, 35, 36
Pearl Harbor, 90
Revolutionary War, 26, 288
SANE, 2, 17, 134–6, 157, 158–9
socialist party in, 266
Spanish civil war arms embargo, 87–8
Stimson doctrine, 80
Tolstoyan pacifism in, 199
United Nations, support for formation of,
111–14
university peace movement, interwar, 73
in Vietnam see Vietnam War
world federalism in, 116–17
United States of Europe, proposals for, 38, 60, 254
United World Federalists, 116–17, 119
Universal Declaration on Human Rights, 288
universal peace conferences, 8–9, 40, 43, 97, 201,
246, 263
university peace movements see student peace
movements
Upanishads, 185
Ury, William, 337
US Conference of Catholic Bishops, 143, 171–2
US Conference of Mayors, 145
Usborne, Henry, 117, 119
USSR see Russia/Soviet Union
utilitarian pacifism, 72

Vatican see Catholicism, *and individual popes*
Vatican II (Second Vatican Council)
Catholic peace and social justice
movement, 202
Latin American peace tradition and, 13, 203
Väyrynen, Raimo, 4
velvet revolution, 19, 150, 212, 228
Versailles Treaty
on disarmament, 100–1, 105
internationalism and, 56–7, 58, 60, 61
Niebuhr on, 206
socialism versus democracy and, 270
Veterans of Foreign Wars, 101
Vietnam Veterans against the War (VVAW), 166
Vietnam War
arms control not preventing, 152
conscription in, 164–5, 167–70
democratic control over power to wage war
and, 248–9
draft dodgers and draft resisters, 164–5
military force used in, 163
Nixon's peace plan for, 161–2
opposition to, 14, 18, 155–70, 337–8
concept of pacifism and, 1–4
conscientious objectors, 167–70
disruptive actions, 162–3

Heschel's Jewish social theology and, 222
within military, 164–7
new left, old left, and liberal arms of, 157–9
of Niebuhr, 206
patriotic pacifism, 318, 320
Pilisuk/Hayden thesis of US as military-
industrial complex influencing, 122
presidential prerogative, challenges to,
159–62
Tolstoyan pacifism, echoes of, 199
Vietnam moratorium movement, 160–2, 165
Tet offensive, 159
US military interventionist policy leading to,
123, 155
Villard, Oswald Garrison, 58
von Clausewitz, Carl, 176
von Suttner, Bertha
concept of pacifism and, 8
on disarmament, 95, 333
on early peace societies, 30, 39, 41, 43, 44
Fried and, 269
socialist disdain for, 262–3
Vrede door Recht (Peace through Justice), 39
VVAW (Vietnam Veterans against the War), 166

Wald, Lillian, 59
Waldensians, 194
Walk for Peace (San Francisco to Moscow,
1961), 281
Wallerstein, Immanuel, 174
Wallis, Jim, 142–3, 176–7, 216, 221, 286–7
Walt, Stephen, 4
Walzer, Michael, 14, 15, 16, 178, 211, 227, 285, 301
war *see also* just war principles
change in nature of, 4–6
outlawing, 62–6
war of 1812, 26
"war on terror," 18, 176–9. *See also* terrorism
War Powers Act (US, 1973), 249
War Resisters International (WRI), 71, 76
War Resisters League (WRL), 71, 119, 120, 157
Washington consensus, 276
Washington disarmament agreement, 102–3
Washington, George, 84
Washington, Treaty of, 49
Watergate, 166, 248–9
WCC (World Council of Churches), 144,
295–6
Weber, Max, 305
Welby, Lord, 98
Wells, H. G., 56, 72, 115–16, 186
Wells, Tom, 158, 159
Welsh, Elliott, 169
Wemyss, Lord Wester, 98
West Bank, 312

West Germany, 280–3
Wiesniewska, Princess Gabrielle, 95
Wilberforce, William, 27
Wilkie, Wendell, 112
Wilkinson, Ellen, 88
WILPF *see* Women's International League for
Peace and Freedom
Wilson, Dagmar, 136
Wilson (film), 112
Wilson, Woodrow, 17, 25, 54–8, 61, 112, 266
Win Without War, 2, 318–19
Wink, Walter, 207, 213
Witherspoon, Frances, 71
Witness for Peace, 312
Wittner, Lawrence, 137, 318
Wofford, Harris, Jr., 116
Wolpert, Stanley, 218, 229
Woman's Peace Party (WPP), 59, 70, 255
women
as disarmament activists, 98, 101, 102, 103–4
empowerment and peace, 257–9
feminism and peace, 3, 19–20, 70, 255–9
on nuclear disarmament, 136, 147–8
in peace societies, 30, 31–2, 69
United Nations, support for, 113
Women for Life on Earth, 147
Women Strike for Peace, 136
Women's International League for Peace and
Freedom (WILPF)
in cold war, 120
disarmament activism, 99, 102, 104
interwar pacifism and fascism, 70, 80, 86, 88,
89, 90
United Nations, formation of, 113
Women's League for International
Disarmament, 39
women's rights
after WWI, 70
peace, connection to, 255–6
peace societies and issues of social justice,
32, 37
Woolf, Virginia, 255–6, 259
Worcester, Noah, 27
World Bank, 273
World Council of Churches (WCC),
144, 295–6
World Court (Permanent Court of International
Justice), 51, 61, 62–3
World Disarmament Conference (1932), 94,
103–5, 106
world federalism, 17, 115–18, 119
World War I *see also* Versailles Treaty
arms manufacturers, backlash against, 94,
98–100, 339
Bloch's anticipation of, 269–70

World War I (cont.)
  conscientious objectors in, 167
  democratic control over power to wage war
    and, 247
  neutrality debate in US and, 84
  opposition to US entry into, 1, 3
  peace movement and beginning of, 10
  peace societies and, 43–4, 69–71
  postwar peace movement, 69–71
  socialists and pacifists, cooperation between,
    264–6
World War II *see also* fascism
  conscientious objectors in, 168
  disarmament activism and Western
    preparedness for, 93, 106–8
  nonviolent resistance in, 228–9
  pacifist response to Czech invasion and entry
    into, 88–92
  Pearl Harbor, 90
WPP (Woman's Peace Party), 59,
    70, 255
WRI (War Resisters International), 71, 76
Wright, Robert, 244
WRL (War Resisters League), 71, 119,
    120, 157

xenophobia, 303–6, 319–20

Yakovlev, Alexander, 150
Yankelovich, Daniel, 140
Yasumaru Yoshio, 29
Yevtushenko, Yevgenii, 150
Yoder, John Howard
  antiwar protests and, 177
  concept of pacifism and, 15, 16, 18–19
  Mennonite tradition of, 196
  Niebuhr and, 203, 205, 207, 208
  theology of, 185, 206–8
Yoshida Shigeru, 117
Young Socialist Alliance, 158
Young Women's Christian Association,
    111, 145
Yugoslavia, former *see* former Yugoslavia, *and*
    specific successor states
Yunus, Mohammad, 277

Zanuck, Darryl F., 112
Zapatero, José Luis Rodríguez, 173
Zengakuren, 121, 139
zero option plan, 3, 149, 151
Zinn, Howard, 320

CPSIA information can be obtained
at www.ICGtesting.com
Printed in the USA
LVOW04s0418251116
514282LV00015B/199/P